CONTEMPORARY ISSUES IN LAW ENFORCEMENT

CONTEMPORARY ISSUES IN LAW ENFORCEMENT

Jennifer Gossett and Jonathon A. Cooper

Indiana University of Pennsylvania

Bassim Hamadeh, CEO and Publisher
John Remington, Executive Editor
Gem Rabanera, Project Editor
Alia Bales, Production Editor
Jackie Bignotti, Production Artist
Trey Soto, Licensing Coordinator
Natalie Piccotti, Director of Marketing
Kassie Graves, Vice President of Editorial
Jamie Giganti, Director of Academic Publishing

Cover image copyright © 2018 Depositphotos/Fotofabrika.

Printed in the United States of America.

cognella® | ACADEMIC PUBLISHING
3970 Sorrento Valley Blvd., Ste. 500, San Diego, CA 92121

The authors dedicate this book to the following individuals:
David, Addy, and Fielding
—JG
Renz
—JC

CONTENTS

INTRODUCTION   IX

    Reading 0.1 Police Officers as Peace Officers   2

    Michael D. Bush and Kimberly D. Dodson

**PART I ECHOES OF THE PROFESSIONAL
           ERA OF POLICING**   **19**

    Reading 1.1 Toward a New Professionalism in Policing   22

    Christopher Stone and Jeremy Travis

    Reading 1.2 Does Increasing Police Professionalism Make
the Fourth Amendment Unnecessary?   47

    Roger Roots

    Reading 1.3 Democratizing Police Professionalization
and Division of Labor   56

    Jerry Joplin and Sanjay Marwah

PART II YOUTH PERCEPTIONS OF POLICE   **71**

    Reading 2.1 Policing Young People: Can the Notion
of Police Legitimacy Play a Role?   74

    Rick Sarre and Colette Langos

    Reading 2.2 The Effects of Race on Relationships with
the Police   85

    Arthur J. Lurigio, Richard G. Greenleaf, and Jamie L. Flexon

Reading 2.3 Building Connections Between Officers and Baltimore City Youth   106

Elena T. Broaddus, Kerry E. Scott, Liane M. Gonsalves, Canada Parrish, Evelyn L. Rhoades, Samuel E. Donovan, and Peter J. Winch

PART III   THE QUESTION OF POLICE LEGITIMACY   125

Reading 3.1 American Policing at a Crossroads   128

Stephen J. Schulhofer, Tom R. Tyler, and Aziz Z. Huq

Reading 3.2 Don't Trust the Police   161

Peter Hanink

Reading 3.3 Redistributive Policing   178

Nirej S. Sekhon

PART IV   POLICE IN A DIVERSE AND DIVIDED SOCIETY   223

Reading 4.1 Reducing Tensions Between Police and Citizens   226

Scot Haug and Dale Stockton

Reading 4.2 Police, Politics, and Culture in a Deeply Divided Society   234

Badi Hasisi

Reading 4.3 Restoring the Lost Hope   256

Francis D. Boateng

INTRODUCTION

Editors' Introduction

While it may be a bit hyperbolic to suggest that policing is experiencing an identity crisis, it's not too far off the mark. Since the social and political upsets of the 1950s, 60s, and 70s, American policing has tried to be everything to everyone, and with little success. This statement is not to speak poorly of policing; rather, it's to recognize that as public servants, they have many "hats" to wear, and many "bosses" to whom they must answer. In terms of their "hats," the police are administrators of justice, maintainers of order, and social service agents, to name only three. In terms of their "bosses," they have political actors, such as mayors, the civilians whom they both arrest and protect, courts via case law, and a myriad of opinions and perceptions, so many of which are far out of their control, yet plainly impact them. Together, these things place police in what some might describe as an impossible position. But it's a position with which they must contend—and do so all within an environment of intense scrutiny, both from media and from private citizens with smartphones. The nature of policing and the role of the police are incredibly complex.

The articles we have chosen to include in the following collection represent our attempt to bring this complexity to the fore of policing scholarship discussions. We draw specifically from articles that have been published since the turn of the 21st century. The fact that we are able to bring such a collection together speaks to the richness of contemporary policing research, and, we hope, a compliment to and continuation of similar collections from the 1990s (e.g., Alpert & Dunham, 2001; Gaines & Cordner, 1998; Kappeler, first published in 1994, now in its fourth edition). Our goal is therefore to expose students to fresh research and thought on the impact of the 20th century on modern law enforcement; police and the young, a topic that is both current and increasingly sensitive; the role the police play in a democratic society; and the most salient topic of police, politics, minority populations, and the future of the administration of justice through the police.

To this end, our collection is divided into four parts. Part I, "Echoes of the Professional Era of Policing," includes articles that provide a new take on the era of policing widely considered to have dominated the majority of the 20th century. In doing so, the articles also provide alternative approaches to police professionalism. The articles chosen for part II, "Youth Perceptions of Police," focuses narrowly on policing as applied to and experienced by the young of society. A number of topics are considered within this section, such as questions of race and ethnicity and how legitimacy may or may not matter when working with juveniles. The topic of legitimacy is examined explicitly in part III, "The Question of Police Legitimacy." The importance of the legitimacy of the state has been discussed within social science since Max Weber (and within political philosophy at least as far back as Machiavelli, and reasonably even further back to the writings of Augustine and Plato in the West and of Confucius and Sun Tzu in the East), and it remains a salient and timely topic for policing today. These authors question contemporary sources of police legitimacy and provide models to buildingup police legitimacy. Finally, part IV, "Police in a Diverse and Divided Society," presents articles that tackle head on the problems of a divided society as it impacts and is impacted by the police. These are in some respect the most challenging articles, because they question the idea that police are only law enforcement officers and are not, instead, part of the social fabric itself, with all that may imply both for the form and for the function of the police.

Our book ends with some concluding remarks that we hope will provide even more fuel for thoughtful discussion. Indeed, each article selection includes not just a brief introduction (as does each of the four parts), but also provides critical questions after the reading. These questions are designed to stimulate classroom conversation and push students to uncover any hidden assumptions they may have about the nature of crime and justice in society and the very purpose of the police.

Prior to diving in to part I, however, we invite our readers to consider the following article by Bush and Dodson, "Police Officers as Peace Officers: A Philosophical and Theoretical Examination of Policing from a Peacemaking Approach." We begin the work with this particular article because we find its concepts jarring to a typical portrayal of what the police *should* be. But this initial knee-jerk reaction is just that: knee-jerk. Upon reflection, we believe that serious students and scholars of the police will find resonance with what Bush and Dodson are suggesting, even if they are not able to find complete agreement. And that is what this collection of otherwise disparate articles is really about: pushing the conversation forward by challenging accepted norms and paradigms about the police, with the intention of reconsidering not just the role of police in contemporary society, but the role of society in the administration of justice, as well.

We would like to acknowledge the outstanding assistance and support of John Remington and Gem Rabanera and everyone from Cognella, as well as the work from our graduate assistant, Liana Marmolejos.

References

Alpert, G. P., & Dunham, R. G. (2001). *Critical issues in policing: Contemporary readings*. Long Grove, IL: Waveland

Gaines, L. K., & Cordner, G. W. (1999). *Policing perspectives: An anthology*. Los Angeles, CA: Roxbury

Kappeler, V. E. (2019). *The police and society: Touchstone readings* (4th ed). Long Grove, IL: Waveland Press.

Editors' Introduction: Reading 0.1

Arguably, the most compelling questions for policing scholarship, administration, policy making, *and* practice have to do with the relationship between society and police. More specifically, what is the role of the police vis-a-vis society? Even a brief moment of consideration reveals that any single answer to this question is wanting. However, one answers the corollary question, what do police do?, they must stumble through a minefield of ethical and philosophical conundrums. Nowhere is this more apparent than in societies with democratic ideals. How, after all, can a coercive force function within a political system framed by the concept of *liberty*? In this opening article, Bush and Dodson consider these questions and more. While doing so, they also demonstrate how policing has struggled with these questions since its inception. Most importantly, they ask the reader to reconsider just what *is* the role of the police vis-a-vis society: Is their coercive role maintainable in a modern democratic republic? And if not, how can their profession transform to better align it with democratic ideals?

Police Officers as Peace Officers

A Philosophical and Theoretical Examination of Policing from a Peacemaking Approach

Michael D. Bush and Kimberly D. Dodson

Introduction

American policing has experienced significant changes in the past 200 years. More importantly, the changes in American policing have mirrored changes in society as social evolution has required the police institution to respond to political, economic, social, and cultural influences over time. In its early inception, police focused their efforts on maintaining order and providing service to communities. Later their attention shifted to fighting crime and law enforcement, which was accompanied by the advancement of science and technology to create a "professional" police force that was detached from the communities they policed. The current approach attempts to balance law enforcement, order maintenance, and service; however, many of the historical concerns from citizens remain (Gaines & Kappeler, 2011).

Many of our institutions, and our perceptions of these institutions, are so deeply entrenched in our minds and culture that we are often unaware of how our perceptions influence the functioning of social institutions. Citizens, new police recruits, and students of criminal justice often carry preconceived notions about policing that shapes their understanding and expectations for the role of police in society. For example, most believe that much of police work involves fighting crime and battling evil as opposed to the more relatively mundane pursuit of providing civil service. Additionally, citizens expect police to provide safety and security in a way that does not violate their privacy and freedoms. A shift to a peacemaking philosophy and approach for policing could help alter the public expectations and conceptualizations of police in the United States.

The purpose of this paper is to explore how peacemaking can facilitate a better understanding of the role of police for citizens, officers, and students who study criminal justice. We begin with a discussion about the different phases of policing and the shift in focus as policing has moved through these phases. Next, we discuss the peacemaking philosophy and how it can be applied within the policing profession. Then we discuss the major areas in policing that could benefit from a peacemaking approach. Finally, we provide examples of police interactions that exemplify peacemaking and offer suggestions about how peacemaking could be integrated into the policing mission.

The Policing Mission

The evolution of American policing is attributed to the development of civilian policing in England and the rise of the state, in America, as a political organization (Archbold, 2013; Gaines & Kappeler, 2011). American policing has undergone many phases, typically categorized as the Political Entrenchment phase, the Reform Efforts phase, the Professional phase, and the Public and Community Relations phase. Within these various phases, the police mission, and the focus and efforts of individual officers, has shifted overtime to emphasize social service and assistance, law enforcement, police and community relations, and security. These various stages are described below.

During the Political Entrenchment phase, police aimed to provide social service and assistance; however, it was generally offered as an extension of political influence and corruption. Politicians controlled the organization of police departments, the appointment of officers and supervisors, and often decided who was arrested and which laws were enforced (Bartollas & Hahn, 1999; Dunham & Al pert, 2009). Although the police department was responsible for enforcing the city's laws, politicians soon realized they could garner more political support, and favor, by providing social assistance. Consequently, the police became a resource that was easy to exploit for political gain; bribery and corruption became commonplace as officers began to understand their role as an extension of political corruption in this type of system. Predictably, the widespread corruption and political influence during the Political Entrenchment phase encouraged increased efforts to reform the police institution.

Reform efforts typically took one of three forms: investigative commissions, police administrative reform, and general police reform (Archbold, 2013; Walker & Katz, 2008). Investigative commissions were formed and financed by private donations or community groups and focused on suspected incidents of police corruption. In addition, general police reform resulted from citizen pressure to address mismanagement and corruption in local and state government and this pressure was often achieved through investigative commissions. More importantly, police administrative reform was initiated by an increase in the number of conscientious and caring police executives who wanted to improve the quality of law enforcement services to the public and also disliked the control that politicians exerted over the police institution.

The reform efforts pushed the police into the Professional phase where a focus on law enforcement and crime fighting emerged as the primary mission (Dunham & Al pert, 2009; Walker & Katz, 2008). The passage of the 18th Amendment, or the Volstead Act, and the Depression Era of the 1930s were significant social changes that assisted this transformation. Police and community relations became strained as the Volstead Act, or Prohibition, required the police to enforce laws that were opposed by many citizens and officers. The Depression of the 1930s had a similar effect as widespread unemployment, bank failures, property foreclosures, poverty, and homelessness created a desperate time for many Americans and left few alternatives to crime for many to survive. Despite these struggles, police officers were pressured to focus on law enforcement and it was during this era that crime fighting became more important than order maintenance or the provision of services. Police agencies adopted a military organizational model and focused on criminal apprehension and became less concerned with interpersonal relationships with community members. The unintended consequence of this new focus was the evolution of citizens' expectations about the mission of the police institution and the role of police officers.

The increased momentum of the civil rights movement, the riots during the 1960s, the feelings of poverty and helplessness, and general civil discord led many to believe the police institution was ill-equipped to deal with a changing society. As a result of the increasing civil strife, the government created the *Omnibus Crime Control and Safe Streets Act* in 1968, which provided a substantial increase in resources for both local and state police agencies, delivering more equipment, training, and programs. In addition to reducing crime, the new focus would also emphasize the development of programs to improve police and community relations. Over time, this new focus would evolve into community policing. Community policing is an overarching philosophy that combines problem-oriented policing with community-oriented policing and is intended to focus on both problem-solving and community partnerships (Archbold, 2013; Gaines & Kappeler, 2011; Walker & Katz, 2008). This phase of policing evolved throughout the 1980s and 1990s and would acknowledge the importance of police-community relationships in addition to the law enforcement perspective and focus.

Community policing became recognized institutionally with the *Violent Crime and Law Enforcement Act of 1994*, which provided significant funding to community policing programs and initiatives. A variety of programs were implemented under the auspices of community policing as the focus was toward building better relationships with community members, crime prevention, and also law enforcement. Programs included neighborhood meetings, neighborhood newsletters, citizen academies, police athletic leagues, curfew enforcement, code enforcement, enforcement of public intoxication and vagrancy laws, and eviction programs aimed at drug users and traffickers. Despite the continued focus on law enforcement, community policing represented a significant attempt to shift the focus of policing away from the professional model and back to building relationships in communities.

The terrorist events of 9/11 marked the beginning of a new phase of policing, one that would focus on security, or homeland security. Given the underground nature of terrorist activity and the reliance on citizen information to solve crimes and defend against terrorism, the police in-stitution remains dependent on police community relations to function. However, this approach has the capacity to foster a sense of distrust between police and community members as it implies the police mission functions more as a partnership with the federal government than as a partnership with the community. In addition, this approach lends itself to violations of the law in certain instances that are thought to promote safety and security on a larger scale. Perhaps a more viable option is peacemaking policing, or policing from a peacemaking philosophy and approach, where a sense of connectedness, care, and mindfulness can emerge to provide a better relationship between police and community members and a more operative policing mission.

Peacemaking Philosophy

Peacemaking is not a perspective; rather, it is a way of thinking and acting (Dodson, Bush, & Braswell, 2012). The foundation of peacemaking criminology stems from ancient wisdom tradi-tions such as Christianity, Judaism, Buddhism, Hinduism, Islam, and Native American. Peacemaking emphasizes the importance of compassion, forgiveness, restitution, reconciliation, spiritual healing, and restoration (Braswell, Fuller, & Lozoff, 2001). The major concepts, or themes, of peacemaking are connectedness, care, and mindfulness. The theme of connectedness stresses that we are intimately connected and bonded to each other and our environment, rather than isolated and separate from one another (Braswell, McCarthy, & McCarthy, 2012). Connectedness promotes the idea that our actions have consequences for us, individually, and for others, even if we are unable to see the outcomes of those actions. This becomes especially important when considering the various roles and functions that police officers are responsible for within their profession.

Care, or caring, refers to a feminine approach to relationships and concern for others (Noddings, 1986). A feminine ethic of care emphasizes a nurturing concern for others and is grounded in receptivity, relatedness, and responsiveness. In contrast, the masculine approach to relationships and concern for others emphasizes rules, laws, and principles and is more detached than the feminine perspective. Obviously, rules and laws are necessary for a civilized society to function; however, there must also be consideration for others and how these rules and laws impact various societal groups. The theme of caring is specifically concerned with limiting the potential for discrimination, which is especially important given the cultural differences and various belief systems that exist in our society. This is particularly important for policing as officers are often accused of engaging in discrimination.

Mindfulness, or awareness, encourages us to consider the needs of others in addition to our personal desires and sense of self. This theme reminds us to pay attention and consider the impact our decisions have for ourselves and others. Mindfulness can encourage police personnel to examine not only citizens' lawful or unlawful behaviors, but also the behaviors of police agencies and professionals as well.

In addition to the themes of peacemaking, there are four different archetypes that inherently exist within our human nature and can assist with the adoption of a peacemaking model for policing. Arrien (1993) delineates the four archetypes as the Warrior, the Healer, the Visionary, and the Teacher. The Warrior archetype encourages us to "show up, or choose to be present" (Arrien, 1993, p. 7). This archetype suggests that police officers must be present in the moment and active participants when interacting with civilians. Citizens sometimes feel as though police officers are not taking their complaints seriously or feel as though the officer perceives the matter as insignificant. The Warrior archetype invites officers to access their inherent leadership skills and treat every personal issue or call as if it were the most important issue of the day; there are no "garbage calls." Officers also are encouraged to exit the cruiser as often as possible, walk around, and get to know the citizens in the community. Police officers could get to know the business owners, kids, parents, and others in the community in a capacity that is different from enforcing the law or providing service. In doing so, police officers can help to foster connectedness in the community.

The Healer is the second archetype described by Arrien (1993). This archetype extends the Warrior archetype of showing up into paying attention. In the context of the Healer, paying attention refers to police officers listening empathically to citizens to better understand the feelings, concerns, and interests of those they are serving. Many citizens harbor negative attitudes and feelings about police officers and feel as though the police simply do not care about the obstacles and challenges they face. At times, citizens want to feel as though they are being listened to, even if the police cannot resolve a situation. Essentially, there are times when we want to tell our story and feel that others are empathetic.

The third archetype described by Arrien (1993) is the Visionary. This archetype stresses that we tell the truth, without blame or judgment. Although some aspects of policing require deception, such as deceptive interrogation, the police institution could be more honest about the paradoxical nature of truthfulness within the profession. For example, many people have come to understand that when an officer says to be truthful it is to acquire additional information with which to support the decision to arrest. This is necessary, to an extent, but also further damages the police-community relationship considering the current approach to policing that focuses on arresting and punishing offenders. Police officers could also refrain from sitting in judgment, or acting as "judge, jury, and executioner" and police administrators could encourage their officers to impartially investigate criminal matters and to avoid the manipulation of the facts or evidence of a case.

The Teacher is the final archetype described by Arrien (1993) and encourages us to be open to outcomes, but not to be attached to them. Police officers may experience low morale and stress when the outcome of a particular case does not go as expected or desired. For example, officers may feel defeated when they fail to apprehend a suspect, save a victim, win a case in court, or any other type of outcome where the officer perceives an injustice or failure has occurred. The Teacher archetype reminds officers that they are one small part of the justice system and if they have done all they can do, then they can feel good about themselves at the end of the day. In addition, officers must learn that things will not always go the way they hoped or planned and they must have the strength to embrace disappointment because, in the police profession, they will encounter it frequently.

Given the current state of policing and what is required for the police mission to succeed, we argue that policing could benefit from a peacemaking focus, where the primary mission would be to foster a sense of connectedness, care, and mindfulness within and between police officers and citizens. We believe the current approach to policing allows a few major areas of policing to impact the overall effectiveness of the policing mission and these could be alleviated with a different way of thinking about the police mission and the role of the police officer. The overall mission appears to be centered on finding a balance between providing safety and security while also creating and nurturing relationships with citizens. We believe peacemaking can assist in this overall mission. Below we discuss a few of the major areas of policing and also discuss how a peacemaking approach could be beneficial. Then we provide examples of how peacemaking is already at work and how it might be expanded.

Major Areas of Policing

There are a few major areas of policing that impede the overall mission of providing safety and security and fostering relationships within the community. These areas are the conceptualization of police, police and community relations, and job related stress. Furthermore, the interrelated nature of these issues compounds their effects and, ultimately, limits the ability of police to successfully achieve either goal within their mission. A peacemaking philosophy and approach can help address these areas of concern.

Conceptualization of Police

As previously discussed, the conceptualization of the police institution and the mission of police have evolved over time, which has altered the expected roles and functions for police officers. Despite the changes over time, the emphasis on law enforcement that emerged during the professional phase has continued to protrude through whatever mission and approach has come after. The manner in which police are conceptualized is important as it will influence expectations for police from both citizens and officers and will also impact police and community relations and job-related stress.

The law enforcement, or crime-fighting, image dominates the public face of policing. Obviously, law enforcement is an important part of the job and cannot be eliminated. However, police officers are routinely engaged in activities other than enforcing the law. In fact, it is estimated that 80% of a patrol officer's time is devoted to activities other than enforcing the law (Lab, Williams, Holcomb, Burek, King, & Buerger, 2011). Again, this does not mean that law enforcement, or crime-fighting, is not important; although, it may create an inaccurate or limited impression of the police institution and its officers and also create unrealistic expectations for police from both officers and citizens.

It is important to identify the various roles of police to gain a better perspective or understanding of how they function. Roles refer to basic social positions that carry with them certain expectations; they can be very specific or rather vague and are often associated with social institutions, such as the police. In broad terms, police officers have three major roles within police work: law enforcement, order maintenance, and service. In reality, because of the wide range of activities and services provided by police, officers are expected and trained to be generalists, meaning they are trained to respond to a variety of events and incidents in addition to crime.

Although the police are the primary means by which the law is imposed, and only the police have a general mandate to use force for the common good, most incidents are resolved through other means, such as mediation, referral, or the mere threat of arrest (Lab et al., 2011). Furthermore, in some disputes, police officers have no legal authority and serve only as referees or "caseworkers." In fact, those who call for police interventions do not necessarily expect officers to make arrests, as long as order is restored. Contrary to the crime-fighting image, police officers interact with victims of crime as much, or more, as they interact with offenders. Thus, much of what a police officer does is more akin to social work. Consider that social work is defined as a professional and academic discipline that seeks to improve the quality of life and subjective wellbeing of individuals, groups, and communities through research, policy, community organizing, crisis intervention, and teaching. In addition, social workers assist those affected by social disadvantages such as poverty, mental and physical illness or disability, and social injustice, including violations of their civil liberties and constitutional rights. Aside from specific responsibilities for enforcing the law, this sounds very similar to the mission of police. According to Miller and Braswell (2002), a major aspect of police work requires officers to deal with a variety of interpersonal situations as the most frequent request for police services is for crisis intervention calls.

Students and citizens "who expect exciting careers in law enforcement are likely to find that much of their time is devoted to helping people cope with life, occasionally resolving low-level problems, and building interpersonal relationships with community members" (Lab et al., 2011, p. 49). Furthermore, "the police are likely to deal with crimes committed by people who are drunk, depressed, mentally ill, or simply overwhelmed by life stresses" as opposed to evil super-villains or "mastermind" criminals (p. 47). As such, police officers frequently describe their work as "long hours of sheer boredom, punctuated by moments of sheer terror" (p. 48).

Primarily, citizens expect police to keep them safe and secure by reducing and preventing crime, which is very difficult to do given the protections and civil liberties afforded by the U.S. Constitution. This has ultimately led to an expectation that police officers be proactive in fighting crime. Furthermore, some citizens believe that police are incapable of preventing crime, when, ironically, the police are inherently designed to react to crime. This underlying tension ultimately stems from the narrow conceptualization of police officers and the police mission.

Police and Community Relations

Police community relations have always been a concern for the police institution; although, the manner in which those relationships operated was a product of the social environment. Ultimately, building relationships with community members is a vital component of police work as police rely on citizen complaints to become aware of and resolve most situations.

The defining structural characteristic of law enforcement in the United States is decentralization. Decentralization allows each agency to operate with discretion inside the parameters of law and also allows each agency to serve the particular needs of their community. Historically, the emphasis on community control, or decentralization, has persisted for two reasons. First, citizens have been fearful of granting the government too much control over their lives, especially to the police since they have the power to arrest and detain citizens. This fear ultimately stems from governmental abuse of power from the colonial era. Second, American citizens believe that local problems are best solved by people intimately familiar with the issues and their causes.

The need for police-community relations has been reinforced through the various phases of policing. As discussed earlier, the focus of the police mission during the Political Entrenchment phase was social service and assistance, but was inevitably clouded by political corruption. The need for police-community relations was reinforced during the Reform Efforts and the Professional phases of policing as civil disobedience, organized crime, and general distrust with policing eroded any semblance of a relationship between police and community members. The Public and Community Relations phase of American policing, highlighted by Community Policing initiatives, included a concerted effort to rebuild police-community relations; however, the 9/11 terrorist attacks reintroduced tension into the relationship.

The current relationship between police and community is strained at best and, often, antagonistic. The basic structure is set up for police and communities to have a relationship. Similar to a bad romantic relationship, both sides bear some of the responsibility for the current state of affairs and both sides must put in work to make the relationship better. Unlike a bad romantic relationship, there is no exiting the relationship by one party or the other,—both sides are "stuck" in this relationship.

Consider that some citizens believe the police are incapable of performing their professional responsibilities and often lob insults that describe police as lazy, overweight, incompetent, and forever searching for free donuts and coffee. Not to be outdone, the police tend to categorize citizens into three basic categories: the suspicious, the assholes, and the know-nothings (Crank, 2004; Van Maanen, 1978). The suspicious are those who police believe they should pay attention to and are suspected to participate in criminal activities. The assholes are those who question the authority of the police and, in our current climate, are likely those who record police activities in an attempt to portray their lack of professionalism. The know-nothings are individuals who do not fit into either of the other two categories; they are not suspicious and do not question authority. In addition, they are not police officers and as a result, they cannot understand the true nature of policing or the role of police officers. The inherently coercive nature of policing will undoubtedly create hurdles to overcome in the effort to build relationships as will the "Blue Wall of Silence" and the police subculture. However, peacemaking can help police to overcome these barriers. Peacemaking allows for a better relationship between police and community members and can provide avenues for healing this relationship.

Job-related Stress

Job-related stress is another important concern for the police institution. Obviously, stress can impact morale, job satisfaction, and overall job performance. More importantly, the issue of job-related stress is intertwined with the previous issues discussed. In other words, the conceptualization of police officers and police-community relations can impact job related stress and job related stress also impacts police-community relations and the conceptualization of police.

Consider the socialization of police officers through various phases of their career (Braswell, McCarthy, & McCarthy, 2012). The first stage is the choice of the career. Individuals choose police work for various reasons, such as the perceived non-routine or flexibility of the job, the opportunity to work outside and be active, the absence of direct supervision, and the exciting nature of the unknown elements of policing. The profession is also perceived as being socially significant and provides opportunities to help people and their communities. During this stage, new police recruits and those who desire a job in policing view the profession very positively. The second stage is referred to as the introduction. At this stage, the new recruit's optimism and uncritical view begins to fade and the officer's values and attitudes begin to change. The recruit begins to see the agency as an instrument of control, concerned primarily with predictability, stability, and efficiency. Rather than helping people and their communities, the shift in focus is toward a bureaucracy that is considered highly formal, mechanical, and often arbitrary in its approach.

The third stage of socialization is set up by the first two stages. The third stage, referred to as encounter, is where new recruits learn the specifics of policing, or the value system that guides the particular agency they are attempting to join. The primary method for adopting the values of an agency is through the Field Training Officer (FTO). The FTO will evaluate the new recruit's ability to resolve situations in a manner that is acceptable to the FTO. As the individual officer's disposition moves further away from where it was when the choice of occupation was made, the new recruit begins to enter the fourth and final stage of socialization - metamorphosis. During this stage, the officer begins to adopt the social and psychological conceptualization of police officer, or "cop." This conceptualization is marred by the cynicism, sense of abandonment, and disenchantment the new recruit now has for the occupation, which will also impact the officer's ability to enforce a police mission that emphasizes police-community relations.

In addition to the stress officers experience from the socialization process, there is the stress that evolves inherently from the conflicting nature of criminal justice. Herbert Packer (1968) created two models to describe the processes and outcomes of the criminal justice system: the "crime control model" and the "due process model." The crime control model is focused on the quick and efficient apprehension and processing of offenders. This model assumes that suspects are guilty of the charges against them and seeks to process cases as quickly as possible, often referred to as assembly-line justice. In contrast, the due process model emphasizes individual rights and freedoms over the apprehension of offenders and assumes that most suspects are innocent of the charges brought against them.

The reality for police is that these two competing models create an interesting dilemma for police that results in constant criticism from those they have chosen to serve. For example, even if police are doing everything possible to keep communities safe, crime will exist and could increase. When this happens, proponents of the crime control model criticize the police institution's ability to fight crime. However, if the police engage in behavior that questions the violation of a citizen's rights or liberties, then those who favor due process become very critical of the police mission. Although both models are at work to varying degrees within the criminal justice system, the police receive constant criticism for an extremely difficult job. In the end, the police have a very difficult, if not impossible, task of trying to control and prevent crime while maintaining citizens' constitutional rights and civil liberties.

Police Officers as Peace Officers

Most states use the term "peace officer" to describe individuals who have police powers. Peace officers are primarily responsible for order maintenance or keeping the peace, but how peace officers go about keeping the peace is discretionary. The police peacekeeping function does not presuppose that the police operate under a peacemaking philosophy. On the contrary, most police agencies operate under a warmaking model that encourages coercion, intimidation, and, often, violence. The downside of the war model is that it perpetuates distrust, fear, and insecurity among the public and significantly undermines the ability of the police to do their jobs effectively (Pepinsky, 1995). Peacemaking criminologists reject the warmaking philosophy as unjust, violent, and destructive (Fuller, 1998; Pepinsky and Quinney, 1991; Sullivan, 2008).

Contrary to warmaking, peacemaking challenges us to exercise care, connectedness, and mindfulness in our daily lives and in our personal interactions with others. Advocates of peacemaking claim that it may be more appropriate for dealing with, not only criminal behavior, but other societal ills such drug addiction, mental illness, sexism, racism, poverty, and homelessness (Fuller, 1998; Pepinsky, 2000). If police agencies adopted a peacemaking perspective, our criminal justice system would look radically different. We would see a system that is more humane and just, and one that entertains the "possibility of compassion and mercy within the framework of justice" (Braswell & Gold, 2008, p. 27).

There is no denying that news stories are replete with examples of police officers who act unethically and/or violate the public trust. As a result, many have the perception that police officers do more harm than good. The media undoubtedly influences community perceptions because news outlets disproportionately cover negative stories. News cameras seldom capture police officers engaged in good deeds, and cellphone footage almost never portrays police officers in a positive light. It is unfortunate that reporters and citizens are not as zealous about catching police officers doing the right thing. We argue that there are police officers who do act ethically and their actions reflect a peacemaking philosophy.

Throughout the United States, there are stories that give us a glimpse of what policing would look like if police operated under a peacemaking philosophy and these stories showcase police officers who saw someone in need and made an effort to help. New York Police Department Officer Lawrence DePrimo, for example, made headlines when a female tourist photographed him giving boots to a homeless man. When asked why he did it, he stated, "It was freezing out and you could see the blisters on this man's feet. I had two pairs of socks and I was still cold" (Goodman, 2012, p. A22). In a similar incident, Corporal Jeremy Walsh of the Odessa Police Department gave his boots and a bottle of water to a homeless man. Walsh said he knew the homeless man, Anthony, and that the man had a history of frostbite on his feet and he was not wearing shoes. Walsh commented later that giving Anthony the boots was "...the right thing to do. I had something that someone else needed that I didn't need" (Sakoda, 2014, p. 1). Covey (1989) claims that, "To know and not do is really not to know" (p. 12). Both of these police officers knew how the cold temperatures could affect these homeless men and they decided to act.

Officer Charles Ziegler with the Winston-Salem Police Department was working an off-duty job as a church security officer when he spotted a woman and a small child walking in the pouring, freezing rain. He said he had seen the woman and her daughter walking in the neighborhood on many occasions and he did not want them out in the cold. In an interview, Ziegler said later he did not attribute his good deed to being a police officer rather his actions were the result of his roles as a husband and father. He approached the woman and said, "Get in the car, there's no reason for you and your baby to be out here." He added, "You see someone and you just help them" (Jeneault, 2013, p. 1).

A Florida law enforcement officer recently made national headlines when she decided to exercise compassion toward a woman who was caught shoplifting. Jessica Robles stated she was motivated to steal groceries because her three children were hungry and she had no food in her home. Robles lost her job and had no way to pay for the groceries. She walked out of a supermarket with $300 worth of groceries without paying, but was detained by a loss prevention officer. Miami-Dade Officer Vicki Thomas arrived to investigate and she ran a records check on Robles and discovered that the woman had no significant criminal history. As Thomas learned more about Robles's circumstances, Thomas felt that taking her to jail was not going to solve the problem and she felt compelled to help Robles. Thomas made the decision to purchase groceries for Robles and her family. Thomas stated, "I could relate. I was a single mom and, without the help of my family, that could have been me" (CNN Staff, 2013, p. 1).

As a mother, Thomas was mindful of the pain and difficulty of trying to provide for her children, which allowed her to understand Robles's situation in a deeper way. Mindfulness allows us to be more fully aware of the "bigger picture" in terms of the needs of others and helps us to explore a broader range of possibilities when presented with a problem. Because Thomas was mindful, she was able to choose a more compassionate resolution than arresting Robles. Thomas realized that putting Robles in jail would not address the central problem—the need to help three hungry children. Thomas said, "I needed to do my job, but I also needed to help her" (CNN Staff, 2013, p. 1).

In that moment, Thomas felt connected to a woman she had never met because they had a shared human experience. As we become more aware of how we are connected to all of what we are a part of, we will begin to see the importance of acting in more responsible ways. Peacemaking encourages us to recognize our shared experiences as human beings and to avoid behaviors in which we create social barriers or labels that perpetuate isolation. Thomas made the decision to allow her shared experience with Robles to guide her response to the situation instead of judging Robles or her choices.

Thomas's one act of kindness and compassion also created a ripple effect of kindness in the community. After the story aired on local new channels, people all over south Florida called Thomas wanting to help. Thomas collected $700 in donations to be spent on food at Walmart. The store said if there was any leftover money they would give the remainder to Robles to help her family pay bills. Robles even received a job offer for a customer service position from a man who saw her story on the news.

Two police officers in Portland, Oregon, answered a "domestic violence" call that they resolved through kindness and compassion. Officers Rob Jackson and George Weseman heard what they believed to be a screaming woman inside a home. The officers found Margi Seburn inside the house crying. They soon discovered that the woman was crying, not because she was a domestic violence victim, but a distraught mother. It was Christmas time and through tears Seburn explained that she could not afford to purchase food, toys, or a Christmas tree for her three young children. She said that she recently had moved to the Portland area and she had attempted to get help from several charities, but they all turned her away stating that she was too late to sign up for assistance. The officers offered her information about additional organizations that might be able to help her and her children. Jackson and Weseman left and discussed how their words seemed "empty and hollow" and that was when they decided to "do a Christmas mission" (Ashton, 2013, p. 1).

Word of Jackson and Weseman's mission snowballed into many acts of kindness that day. First, the officers explained the situation to their sergeant and he gave them the green light to help Seburn's family. Weseman put out a precinct-wide message on his mobile computer asking if other officers wanted to help. Donation pledges poured in from area officers and a dispatcher suggested that Jackson and Weseman might be able to obtain toys for the children from the Portland Fire Bureau's Toy-n-Joy Makers program. The dispatcher called ahead of their arrival and the volunteers helped the officers select gifts for the children.

Jackson and Weseman picked up food from the Portland Police Bureau Sunshine Division and made arrangements to deliver Christmas dinner to Seburn and her children. The officers also purchased a small tree complete with decorations, Christmas stockings filled with candy, wrapping paper and tape. They even purchased a gift card for Seburn so she would be able to get something for herself.

Jackson and Weseman returned to Seburn's home and made their Christmas delivery. Seburn's said her tears of sorrow and frustration turned to tears of joy when she realized what the officers had done for her family. When the officers were asked what motivated them to help this family, they stated that they "both had a soft spot for kids" and they could identify with Seburn's anguish as a parent (Ashton, 2013, p. 1). The officers stepped in to care for Seburn's children when she could not. Their actions personify the adage, "It takes a village to raise a child." In other words, it takes more than one person to teach our children important life lessons. Through their actions, these two officers taught Seburn's children that kindness and compassion may come from the most unexpected place. Indirectly, the officers also taught her children the value of paying attention to the circumstances of others, and when possible, reaching out to help them.

One of the authors, Kimberly Dodson, served as a law enforcement officer for a little over a decade. Dodson had many interactions with the public and she also had the opportunity to choose peacemaking resolutions. In one such instance, dispatch sent her to back up two emergency medical technicians (EMT) who were attempting to transport a mentally ill man to the hospital for a psychiatric evaluation. When she arrived, the two male EMTs seemed less than impressed that the dispatcher had sent a female deputy. One of the EMTs snidely remarked, "You're the backup they sent?" Dodson quipped back, "Yep, I'm the one with the badge and the gun." It was clear by the looks on their faces that the EMTs did not appreciate her remark.

Although the EMTs were not convinced she could handle the situation, they explained that the man was refusing transport to the hospital. The man was sitting in a recliner and, although he was seated, he appeared to be rather tall and muscular. He had a baby face that seemed to be at odds with his physical size. The young man's mother explained she had an emergency court order to have her son committed to the hospital for a mental evaluation. She confided in Dodson that she was afraid the men would hurt her son. Before she could speak with the man, a male deputy, "Bryant" arrived on the scene. Bryant spoke briefly with the EMTs and handed his Oakley sunglasses to Dodson as he quickly brushed past her and said, "Hold these. I've got this!"

Bryant yelled at the man and warned him that, "You will get in the ambulance one way or another!" The man refused but he looked at Dodson and whispered, "You're not going to let them hurt me are you?" She replied softly, "No, I'm not." Knowing that things were about to escalate, Dodson turned to Bryant and said, "Hey, let me talk to him." She handed him back his sunglasses and walked a little closer to the man. Dodson smiled and calmly stated, "Hi. My name is Kim. What's your name?" He said, "Robert." "Well, Robert it's good to meet you. Your mom called us because she is very worried about you. I'm here today to take you to the hospital, not to jail. Do you understand that?" Dodson replied. Robert smiled and nodded "Yes." She continued, "What can I do so that you'll go to the hospital with us today?" He glanced down at his shoes momentarily then looked up and in a child-like voice asked, "Can you tie my shoes?"

Many may have thought this was a strange and unreasonable request, after all, tying shoes is not taught in the police academy or spelled out in departmental standard operating procedures. Dodson was entertaining the idea when Bryant gave Dodson a disapproving look and in a firm voice he said, "Don't do it." She ignored him. She smiled at Robert and bent down and tied his shoes. From her kneeling position, she looked up at him and said, "Okay, you're all set." He smiled and replied, "Thank you ma'am. You're the only one who's been nice to me today." With that, he got up and calmly walked to the ambulance and the EMTs transported him to the hospital.

Of course, the situation could have gone horribly wrong because she put herself in a vulnerable position. Robert could have kicked her in the face. He could have attempted to physically overpower her or grab her gun. Yet, in that moment, Dodson made a judgment call that Robert was more like a child than his physical size might suggest. She also saw Robert through the lens of a mother and, as a result, she acted with the care and concern that we would expect a mother to exhibit.

According to Nel Noddings (1986), our response to those we interact with should be guided by a feminist ethic of care—similar to the care a mother has for her children. Care-focused feminism encourages receptivity, relatedness, and responsiveness in human interactions. In other words, we must recognize and be attentive to the needs of others if we are to respond in ethical ways (Gilligan, 1982). However, Noddings observes that most of human interactions stem from a masculine approach to ethics. The masculine approach focuses on "justice" and is less concerned with relational ethics. Therefore, from this perspective, human interactions should be directed by analysis and rationalization. Individuals who possess these characteristics tend to categorize human interactions into rigid dichotomies. For example, interactions can be categorized into one of two categories, such as right or wrong, just or unjust, and fair and unfair (Myers & Chiang, 1993).

The masculine approach is clearly the dominant philosophy driving the police mission. Padavic and Prokos (2002), for example, found that in addition to the formal curriculum, which includes the policies, practices, and procedures of being a police officer, police academies taught a "hidden curriculum." The hidden curriculum referred to the implicit lessons instructors taught to students that were outside the explicit curriculum. In the police academy, instructors explicitly stated that policing was a gender-neutral profession; however, the implicit lessons reinforced the notion that masculinity was synonymous with what it means to be a police officer. Padavic and Prokos (2002) found feminine perspectives were not only rejected, but ridiculed by male recruits and instructors. A feminine or maternalistic ethic of care is not exclusive to females. To the contrary, Noddings (1986) points out that maternalistic care is an innate characteristic in all human beings. In other words, feminine, in this context, refers to the psychological traits of masculinity and femininity that reside in each of us. Over time we learn to ignore this characteristic or choose not to cultivate it, which is unfortunate because it could fundamentally change the way we choose to respond to those we encounter.

Bryant and Dodson's interactions with Robert juxtapose the feminine and masculine ethical approaches. Bryant viewed Robert's refusal to comply as "wrong." Thus, Bryant used the threat of physical force to gain Robert's compliance, which is consistent with the coercive nature of the masculine approach. Dodson, on the other hand, defused the situation by showing a maternalistic care and concern for Robert in an effort to gain his compliance and to avoid the need for physical force. If police officers were able to internalize the feminine ethic of care, they might be more inclined to view themselves as peace officers and act accordingly. In the situation discussed above, a peace officer would seek a peaceful resolution first and only resort to physical force if absolutely necessary.

It is clear that police officers undoubtedly touch the lives of those they serve for better or worse. Sometimes one small act of kindness can leave a lasting legacy of love. On August 6, 2011, a video camera captured San Diego Officer Jeremy Henwood's final act of kindness. A thirteen-year-old boy, Daveon Scott was at McDonald's and he was short on cash. He approached Officer Henwood and asked him to borrow ten cents to buy cookies. Instead of giving him the money, Officer Henwood purchased the cookies for Daveon. They engaged in a brief conversation in which Henwood asked the boy what he wanted to be when he grew up. Daveon replied that he wanted to be an NBA star. Henwood told him that it "takes hard work" but to keep working toward his goals (Hood & Young, 2011, p. 1). The entire exchange between the two lasted only a few seconds. Moments after leaving McDonald's, Officer Henwood was shot and killed.

In a recent interview, Daveon admitted that prior to this encounter he did not have a high opinion of police officers. He stated that negative media coverage shaped his perceptions of police officers, but that Henwood's kindness and encouragement helped him to view police officers in a more positive light. Henwood's words also inspired Daveon to work hard and do more to help others. Henwood could have ignored Daveon or declined to help him, and that negative interaction would have reinforced Daveon's unfavorable perceptions of the police. Instead Henwood's final act of kindness turned a brief chance meeting into a powerful transformative moment.

Conclusion

The purpose of this paper was to explore how a peacemaking philosophy and approach could prove beneficial to policing as a profession. A peacemaking approach could help better prepare officers for a job that requires interpersonal skills and critical and dynamic thinking. Peacemaking could also help strengthen police-community relations and help the public better understand the roles and functions of police.

Both the police and the community could benefit from a peacemaking approach. Themes of connectedness, care, and mindfulness could help to broaden the conceptualization of police, improve police-community relations, and decrease job related stress for police officers and general frustration with the criminal justice system for citizens. Police officers are encouraged to show up, pay attention, tell the truth, and not get attached to outcomes.

References

Archbold, C. (2013). *Policing: A text/reader.* Thousand Oaks, CA: Sage.

Arrien, A. (1993). *The four fold way: Walking the paths of the warrior, teacher, healer, and visionary.* San Francisco, CA: Harper.

Ashton, D. F. (2013, December 17). Cops' 'Christmas mission' raises spirits of single mom. *East Portland News*, p. 1.

Bartollas, C., & Hahn, L. D. (1999). *Policing in America*. Boston, MA: Allyn and Bacon.

Braswell, M. C., Fuller, J., and Lozoff, B. (2001). *Corrections, peacemaking, and restorative justice: Transforming individuals and institutions*. Cincinnati, OH: Anderson.

Braswell, M. C., and Gold, J. (2008). "Peacemaking, justice, and ethics." In M. C. Braswell, B. R. McCarthy, and B. McCarthy (eds.), *Justice, crime, and ethics*. Newark, NJ: Matthew Bender & Company, Inc.

Braswell, M. C., McCarthy, B. J., and McCarthy, B. R. (2012). Justice, crime, and ethics. Waltham, MA: Elsevier.

CNN Staff. (2013, October 23). Cop who bought shoplifter groceries" 1 could relate.' Retrieved from http://www.cnn.com/2013/10/23/us/cop-helps-shoplifter/.

Covey, S. R. (1989). *The 7 habits of highly effective people*. New York: Simon & Schuster.

Crank, J. P. (2004). *Understanding police culture*. Cincinnati, OH: Anderson.

Dodson, K. D., Bush, M. D., and Braswell, M. C. (2012). Teaching peacemaking in criminal justice: Experiential applications. *Journal of Criminal Justice Education*, 1–17.

Dunham, R. G., & Alpert, G. P. (2009). *Critical issues in policing: Contemporary readings*. Long Grove, IL: Waveland Press, Inc.

Fuller, J. R. (1998). *Criminal justice: A peacemaking perspective*. Boston, MA: Allyn and Bacon.

Gaines, L. K. & Kappeler, V. E. (2008). *Policing in America* (7th ed.). Newark, NJ: Anderson Publishing Co.

Gilligan, C. (1982). *In a different voice: Psychological theory and women's development*. Cambridge, MA: Harvard University Press.

Goodman, D. (2012, November 28). Photo of officer giving boots to barefoot man warms hearts online. *The New York Times*, p. A22.

Hood, L, and Young, M. D. J. (2011, August 17). Officer Jeremy Henwood's final act of kindness. Retrieved from http://www.nbcsandiego.com/news/local/Officer-Henwoods-Final-Act-of-Kindness127886453.html.

Jeneault, E. (2013, March 4). Cops good deed goes viral. ABC News. Retrieved from http://abcnews.go.com/blogs/headlines/2013/03/cops-good-deed-goes-viral/.

Lab, S. P., Williams, M. R., Holcomb, J. E., Burek, M. W., King, W. R., & Buerger, M. E. (2011). *Criminal justice: The essentials*. (2nd Ed.). New York: Oxford University Press.

Miller, L. & Braswell, M. (2002). *Human relations and police work* (5th Ed.). Prospect Heights, IL: Waveland Press, Inc.

Myers, L. B., and Chiang, C. (1993). Law enforcement officer and peace officer: Reconciliation using the feminine approach. *Journal of Crime and Justice, 16*(2), 31–41.

Noddings, N. (1986). *Caring: A feminine approach to ethics and moral education*. Berkley, CA: University of California Press.

Packer, H. L. (1968). *The limits of criminal sanction*. Stanford, CA: Stanford University Press.

Pepinsky, H. (2000). A criminologist's quest for peace. *Contemporary Justice Review, 3*(2), 175–186.

Pepinsky, H. (1995). Peacemaking primer. *Peace and Conflict Studies, 2*, 32–53.

Pepinsky, H., and Quinney, R. (1991). *Criminology as peacemaking*. Bloomington, IN: Indiana University Press.

Prokos, A., and Padavic, I. (2002). There oughta be a law against bitches': Masculinity lessons in the police academy. *Gender, Work, and Organization, 9*(4), 439–459.

Sakoda, C. (2014, January 21). Police officer's kind gesture caught on camera. *Yahoo News*, p. 1.

Van Maanen, J. (1978). "The asshole." In P. K. Manning and J. Van Maanen (eds.), *Policing: A view from the street*, pp. 231–238. Santa Monica, CA: Goodyear Publishing Company.

Walker, S., & Katz, C. W. (2008). *The police in America: An introduction* (6th ed). Boston, MA: McGraw-Hill.

Critical Thinking Questions

1 What were the four policing phases? What were distinct characteristics of each phase?

2 What are the four archetypes of peacemaking policing? How can these archetypes guide police practice?

3 How can a peacemaking approach to policing help potentially to resolve issues of police and community relations and job-related stress?

4 What were some examples of peacemaking policing in action? How can peacemaking be further implemented in policing?

PART I

ECHOES OF THE PROFESSIONAL ERA OF POLICING

Editors' Introduction

Standard content of any class or textbook on policing is a discussion of the three (or sometimes four) "eras" of American policing history, typically called the political era, the professional (or bureaucratic or legalistic) era, and the community era. While a useful heuristic for the purpose of historical analysis, a hallmark of these three eras is a significant amount of continuity. Indeed, textbooks, while generally agreeing on the shape and characteristics of these eras, tend not to agree on the years each era encompasses. It is also fair to say that there are characteristics of the political era and the professional era that have survived into today's era of contemporary policing, however one may wish to label it. And while the question, "Which era of policing is the most important era for policing?" is radically silly, we are still willing to suggest that, were we pressed, the most correct answer would be the professional era, which spanned from around the turn of the 20th century and into the late 1970s.

Modern American policing is largely a product of events during the professional era of policing. Although policing scholarship has generally labeled policing after this professional era as the "community era," today it is unclear whether this label ("community era") is an apt description of the last thirty years of American policing; and it is even more unclear whether policing in the 1980s can reasonably be said to adequately describe policing in the current decade. Contemporary American policing has been described variously as intelligence-led policing, evidence-based policing, order maintenance policing, scientific policing, etc. However, we want to label policing in the 21st century, it is vital that we view it within a historical and political context, because so much of policing today is a reaction to events in the 1950s, 1960s, and 1970s that involved the police, the public, and politics.

To this end, the readings in this part of our edited collection focus on efforts to both redefine and understand the consequences of this era, an era characterized by its political and social turmoil. While policing during these eras is generally defined as "professional," Stone and Travis qualify this label with the prefix "So-Called" and contrast it to contemporary policing, which they find to be far more professional across several organizational domains. Similarly, Roots also identifies where policing has improved according to the "professionalism" label, but then considers the functional and constitutional ramifications of this increase in professionalism. Finally, Joplin and Marwah redirect the conversation entirely from professionalism to reconsider, but with fresh theoretical eyes, the concept of democratic policing.

Editors' Introduction: Reading 1.1

This reading by Stone and Travis accomplishes more than just outlining just what the professional era was all about—an era that they reasonably label the "So-Called Professionalism of Mid-20th-Century Policing." More so, their intent in discussing the professional era so is to redefine what we mean by "professional policing." As they point out, much of policing during that era was anything but professional. What's more, much of what we see in policing today—in terms of form, function, policy, and procedure—are reactions to such poor professionalism during the 20th century. To this end, Stone and Travis outline what they observe to be a "new professionalism" of policing, defined by its commitment to accountability, legitimacy, innovation, and national coherence. In many respects, Stone and Travis's thesis speaks to the direction we see criminal justice in the United States moving, more generally.

Toward a New Professionalism in Policing

Christopher Stone and Jeremy Travis

Introduction

Across the United States, police organizations are striving for a new professionalism. Their leaders are committing themselves to stricter *accountability* for both their effectiveness and their conduct while they seek to increase their *legitimacy* in the eyes of those they police and to encourage continuous *innovation* in police practices. The traffic in these ideas, policies and practices is now so vigorous across the nation that it suggests a fourth element of this new professionalism: its *national coherence*. These four principles— accountability, legitimacy, innovation and coherence—are not new in themselves, but together they provide an account of developments in policing during the last 20 years that distinguishes the policing of the present era from that of 30, 50 or 100 years ago.

Many U.S. police organizations have realized important aspects of the new professionalism and many more have adopted its underlying values. The ambitions for accountability, legitimacy and innovation unite police organizations in disparate contexts: urban, suburban and rural, municipal, county, state and federal. With approximately 20,000 public police organizations in the United States, national coherence in American policing would be a signal achievement.[1] We do not see this new professionalism fully realized in any single department. We know how difficult it can be to narrow the gap between these ambitions and many deeply ingrained routines and practices. Much policing in the United States remains, in these terms, unprofessional, but professional ambition is itself a powerful force and it is at work almost everywhere.

---

[1] According to the Bureau of Justice Statistics, as of September 2004, 17,876 state and local law enforcement agencies with the equivalent of at least one full-time officer were operating in the United States. Reaves, B. (2007). *Census of Law Enforcement Agencies,* 2004. Washington, D.C.: U.S. Department of Justice, Office of Justice Programs, Bureau of Justice Statistics, 1.

We hear similar ambitions for accountability, legitimacy, innovation and coherence in other countries, from the state police organizations in Brazil and India to the South African Police Service, the French Gendarmerie and the Chilean Carabineros. A global police culture with these same four elements increasingly defines the ambitions of police leaders in most countries. In this paper, however, we focus on the trend in the United States.

To describe and illustrate the elements of this new professionalism, we draw on our own experiences working in and studying police organizations and on the deliberations of two Executive Sessions on Policing, both convened by the National Institute of Justice and Harvard University's Kennedy School of Government: the first from 1985 to 1992 and the second commencing in 2008 and continuing today.

Why a New Professionalism?

We offer the "New Professionalism" as a conceptual framework that can help chiefs, frontline police officers and members of the public alike understand and shape the work of police departments today and in the years ahead. Even as it remains a work in progress, the New Professionalism can help police chiefs and commissioners keep their organizations focused on why they are doing what they do, what doing it better might look like, and how they can prioritize the many competing demands for their time and resources. On the front lines, the New Professionalism can help police officers work together effectively, connect their daily work to the larger project of building a better society, and share their successes and frustrations with the communities they serve. In communities everywhere, the New Professionalism can help citizens understand individual police actions as part of larger strategies, and assess the demands and requests that police make for more public money, more legal authority and more public engagement in keeping communities safe. From all of these vantage points, the New Professionalism helps all of us see what is happening in policing, how we got here and where we are going.

Each of the four elements of the New Professionalism—accountability, legitimacy, innovation and national coherence—has something to offer police and the communities in which they work.

By a commitment to accountability we mean an acceptance of an obligation to account for police actions not only up the chain of command within police departments but also to civilian review boards, city councils and county commissioners, state legislatures, inspectors general, government auditors and courts. The obligation extends beyond these government entities to citizens directly: to journalists and editorial boards, resident associations, chambers of commerce—the whole range of community-based organizations.

By a commitment to legitimacy we mean a determination to police with the consent, cooperation and support of the people and communities being policed. Police receive their authority from the state and the law, but they also earn it from the public in each and every interaction.

Although it is important to derive legitimacy from every part of the public, those citizens and groups most disaffected by past harms or present conditions have the greatest claims to attention on this score because their trust and confidence in the police is often weakest. Fortunately, research we discuss later in this paper suggests that police departments can strengthen their legitimacy among people of color in the United States and among young people of all races and ethnicities without compromising their effectiveness.[2] Indeed, effectiveness and legitimacy can be advanced together.

By a commitment to innovation we mean active investment of personnel and resources both in adapting policies and practices proven effective in other departments and in experimenting with new ideas in cooperation with a department's local partners. Empirical evidence is important here. Departments with a commitment to innovation look for evidence showing that practices developed elsewhere work, just as they embrace evaluation of the yet unproven practices they are testing.

By national coherence we mean that the departments exemplifying the New Professionalism are participating in national conversations about professional policing. They are training their officers, supervisors and leaders in practices and theories applicable in jurisdictions across the country. Not long ago, it was common to hear police officers insist that they could police effectively in their city, county or state only if they had come up through the ranks there: good policing was inherently parochial. Such a belief belies a true professionalism. Inherent in the idea of the New Professionalism in policing is that police officers, supervisors and executives share a set of skills and follow a common set of protocols that have been accepted by the profession because they have been proven to be effective or legally required. That is not to say that local knowledge and understanding are unimportant—they are vital. But they are not everything. There is vital knowledge, understanding and practice common to good policing everywhere, and this common skill set defines police professionalism.

There are many definitions of professionalism and some debate about what it means for policing to be a profession. We take these up at the end of this paper, after putting the New Professionalism in historical context. For now, suffice it to say that for any profession to be worthy of that name, its members must not only develop transportable skills but also commit themselves both to a set of ethical precepts and to a discipline of continuous learning. A look back in history reveals how this meaning of "professional" contrasts with another use of the word employed in the early debates over community policing. The New Professionalism embraces and extends the best of community policing, whereas the "old professionalism" said to characterize policing in the 1960s and 1970s was seen as antithetical to community policing.

---

[2] See the discussion at note 33, *infra,* and the sources referenced therein.

Community Policing and the New Professionalism

Twenty-five years ago, when the elements of the New Professionalism began to emerge in urban American police departments, "community policing" was the organizing framework advanced to describe the new approach and new priorities. To most Americans who heard of the idea, community policing summoned up images of police walking the beat, riding on bicycles, or talking to groups of senior citizens and to young children in classrooms. These images adorn countless posters and brochures produced by individual police departments to explain community policing to local residents. They picture community policing as a specialized program: a few carefully selected officers taking pains to interact with "good" citizens while the rest of the police department does something else.

Inside police departments, however, and at the first Executive Session on Policing, community policing was being described as far more than the next new program. It was promoted as the organizing framework around which police departments were going to change everything they did. Community policing might look like a specialized program when a police department first adopts it, but that is "Phase One," as Lee Brown, who led police departments in Atlanta, Houston and New York City before becoming mayor of Houston, wrote in a 1989 paper for the first Executive Session. Brown explained that "Phase Two":

> ... involves more sweeping and more comprehensive changes .... It is the
> department's *style* that is being revamped ....Although it is an operating style,
> community policing also is a *philosophy* of policing ... (emphasis in original).[3]

Brown went on to explain how, In Phase Two, community policing requires changes to every part of policing, including its supervision and management, training, investigations, performance evaluation, accountability and even its values. True community policing, Brown wrote, requires a focus on results rather than process; it forces decentralization, power sharing with community residents, the redesign of police beats, and giving a lower priority to calls for service. Malcolm Sparrow, a former Detective Chief Inspector in the English police service on the faculty of the Harvard Kennedy School, made the same point in even more dramatic language:

> Implementing community policing is not a simple policy change that can
> be effected by issuing a directive through the normal channels. It is not a
> mere restructuring of the force to provide the same service more efficiently.
> Nor is it a cosmetic decoration designed to impress the public and promote
> greater cooperation.

---

[3] Brown, L. (1989, September). Community Policing: A Practical Guide for Police Officials. *Perspectives on Policing, no. 12.* Washington, D.C.; Cambridge, Mass.: U.S. Department of Justice, Office of Justice Programs, National Institute of Justice; & Harvard University, John F. Kennedy School of Government, Program in Criminal Justice Policy and Management. Hereinafter, publications in this series are identified by their number in the series, Perspectives on Policing. The entire set is available at: www.hks.harvard.edu/criminaljustice/executive_sessions/policing.htm.

> For the police it is an entirely different way of life. It is a new way for police officers to see themselves and to understand their role in society. The task facing the police chief is nothing less than to change the fundamental culture of the organization.[4]

In this grand vision, the advent of community policing marked an epochal shift, replacing an earlier organizing framework: professional crime-fighting. And this, finally, is why the field today needs a "new" professionalism, for the original professionalism was—as an organizing framework at least—discarded in favor of community policing.

In their promotion of community policing and a focus on problem solving, the proponents of reform roundly criticized what they saw as the professional crime-fighting model, or simply the "professional model" of policing.[5] They saw the professional model as hidebound: too hierarchical in its management, too narrow in its response to crime and too much at odds with what police did. Led during the first Executive Session on Policing by the scholarship of three academics—Professors Mark Moore of the Harvard Kennedy School, George Kelling of Northeastern University and Robert Trojanowicz of Michigan State University—the champions of community policing contrasted their principles and methods to this "traditional," "classical," "reform" or, most commonly, "professional" style of policing.[6]

The criticisms made by Moore, Kelling and Trojanowicz of the then-dominant form of policing in U.S. cities were right on the mark, but by labeling this dominant form "professional" crime-fighting, they needlessly tarnished the concept of professionalism itself.[7] Looking back on these debates, it is easy to see that this so-called professional model of policing was at best a quasi-professionalism and at worst an entirely false professionalism. At the time, however, the

---

[4] Sparrow, M. (1988, November). Implementing Community Policing. *Perspectives on Policing, no. 9.* Washington, D.C.; Cambridge, Mass.: U.S. Department of Justice, Office of Justice Programs, National Institute of Justice; & Harvard University, John F. Kennedy School of Government, Program in Criminal Justice Policy and Management, 2.

[5] See, for example, Kelling, G.; &Moore, M. (1988, November). The Evolving Strategy of Policing. *Perspectives on Policing, no. 4.* Washington, D.C.; Cambridge, Mass.: U.S. Department of Justice, Office of Justice Programs, National Institute of Justice; & Harvard University, John F. Kennedy School of Government, Program in Criminal Justice Policy and Management, 6 (where the authors write specifically of "the professional model").

[6] The first Executive Session on Policing convened 31 officials and scholars, but its 16 published papers were authored by only 13 participants. Mark Moore and George Kelling were authors or co-authors on six papers each; Robert Trojanowicz was co-author on three; Malcolm Sparrow, Robert Wasserman and Hubert Williams were authors or co-authors on two each. No one else appeared on more than one. Of the first six papers issued, all were authored or coauthored by Moore, Kelling and Trojanowicz, with no other co-authors; and through the end of 1992, the Executive Session published only three papers that were not authored or co-authored by Moore, Kelling or Trojanowicz. Other scholars played at least as great a role in the formulation of community policing during these years, including Herman Goldstein (who was a member of the first Executive Session) and David Bayley (who is a member of the second Executive Session), but neither wrote for the first Executive Session on Policing.

[7] More recently, the Committee to Review Research on Police Policy and Practices convened by the National Research Council of the National Academies recounted the story in the same way, although choosing in its own analysis to refer to the professional model of policing as the "standard" model. See National Research Council, *Fairness and Effectiveness in Policing: The Evidence,* Committee to Review Research on Police Policy and Practices, Wesley Skogan and Kathleen Frydl, editors, Committee on Law and Justice, Division of Behavioral and Social Sciences and Education (Washington, D.C.: The National Academies Press, 2004), p. 85. (Community policing "is characterized as something that transforms the 'professional' model of policing, dominant since the end of World War II ....")

critique from Moore, Kelling, Trojanowicz and others succeeded in giving professional policing a bad name, so much so that reformers in countries where policing was still entirely a matter of political patronage and a blunt instrument of political power began to ask if they could skip the professional stage of police evolution and proceed directly to community policing.[8]

Community policing was an important improvement on the style of policing it challenged in American cities, but it is time to correct two distortions inherited from that earlier debate. First, what community policing challenged in the 1980s was not a truly professional model of policing, but rather a technocratic, rigid, often cynical model of policing. Moreover, it reinforced pernicious biases deeply entrenched in the wider society. Both good and bad police work was performed in that mode, but it was hardly professional. Second, community policing was only part of the new model of policing emerging in the 1980s, with contemporaneous innovations occurring in technology, investigation and the disruption of organized crime. By reinterpreting the rise of community policing as part of a larger shift to a New Professionalism, we hope simultaneously to rescue the idea of professional policing from its frequently distorted form in the mid-20th century and to show how the elements of this New Professionalism might anchor a safer and more just society in the decades ahead.

The So-Called Professionalism of Mid-20th-Century Policing

Proponents of community policing in the 1980s labeled its mid-century predecessor as "professional crime-fighting," but what sort of policing were they describing? What were the characteristics of the mid-century policing they hoped to replace?

First, in its relationship to citizens, the previous mode of policing was deliberately removed from communities, insisting that police understood better than local residents how their communities should be policed. As George Kelling described it in the first paper in the Perspectives on Policing series, the police had long been seen as "a community's *professional* defense against crime and disorder: Citizens should leave control of crime and maintenance of order to police (emphasis added)."[9] Or, as a separate paper explained, "The proper role of citizens in crime control was to be relatively passive recipients of professional crime control services."[10] In contrast, explained Kelling, under community policing, "the police are to stimulate and buttress a community's ability to produce attractive neighborhoods and protect them against predators."[11]

---

[8] Police officials in Kenya, eager to implement a version of community policing, put this question to one of the authors of this paper in 2000, as did a leader in the military police of Rio de Janeiro in 2001.

[9] Kelling, G. (1988, June). Police and Communities: The Quiet Revolution. *Perspectives on Policing, no. 1.* Washington, D.C.; Cambridge, Mass.: U.S. Department of Justice, Office of Justice Programs, National Institute of Justice; & Harvard University, John F. Kennedy School of Government, Program in Criminal Justice Policy and Management, 2–3.

[10] Kelling, G., & Moore, M. The Evolving Strategy of Policing (note 5). 11

[11] Kelling, G. Police and Communities: The Quiet Revolution (note 9), 2–3.

Second, in terms of tactics, the previous mode of policing relied on a limited set of routine activities. As another 1988 paper in the series explained, "Professional crime-fighting now relies predominantly on three tactics: (1) motorized patrol; (2) rapid response to calls for service; and (3) retrospective investigation of crimes."[12]

Third, the management structure of professional crime-fighting was centralized and top-down. Its management technique was command and control, aiming principally to keep police officers in line and out of trouble. As one paper described it, "the more traditional perspective of professional crime-fighting policing ... emphasizes the maintenance of internal organizational controls."[13] And as another paper explained in more detail:

> In many respects, police organizations have typified the classical command-and-control organization that emphasized top-level decisionmaking: flow of orders from top-level executives down to line personnel, flow of information up from line personnel to executives, layers of dense supervision, unity of command, elaborate rules and regulations, elimination of discretion, and simplification of work tasks.[14]

This mid-century model of policing can be criticized as technocratic and rigid, but it was not all bad. The elevation of technical policing skills, the introduction of hiring standards and the stricter supervision and discipline of police officers improved some police services and helped some police chiefs put distance between themselves and political ward bosses, corrupt mayors and local elites demanding special attention. Prioritizing 911 calls at least allocated police services to anyone with access to a telephone rather than only to those with political connections or in favor with the local police. But these were incremental gains, and policing remained (and remains) closely tied to politics.[15]

Moreover, each of the three elements of so-called professional policing described here—its claim to technical expertise, its tactics and its management strategy—failed to produce adequate

---

[12] Moore, M., Trojanowicz, R., & Kelling, G. (1988, June). Crime and Policing, *Perspectives on Policing, no. 2*. Washington, D.C.; Cambridge, Mass.: U.S. Department of Justice, Office of Justice Programs, National Institute of Justice; & Harvard University, John F. Kennedy School of Government, Program in Criminal Justice Policy and Management.

[13] Wasserman, R. & Moore, M. (1988, November). Values in Policing, *Perspectives on Policing, no. 8*. Washington, D.C.; Cambridge, Mass.: U.S. Department of Justice, Office of Justice Programs, National Institute of Justice; & Harvard University, John F. Kennedy School of Government, Program in Criminal Justice Policy and Management, 5.

[14] Kelling, G.; Wasserman, R.; & Williams, H. (1988, November). Police Accountability and Community Policing, *Perspectives on Policing, no. 7*. Washington, D.C.; Cambridge, Mass.: U.S. Department of Justice, Office of Justice Programs, National Institute of Justice; & Harvard University, John F. Kennedy School of Government, Program in Criminal Justice Policy and Management, 2.

[15] Daryl Gates, then-Police Chief in Los Angeles, explained more fully: "Chiefs today are unfortunately deeply tied to politics and politicians. It's a very sad commentary on local policing. How do chiefs refer to their mayor? 'My mayor.' 'Is your mayor going to win this election?' ... And if they do not, that is the last time we see that commissioner or chief. Gone, because of political whim, not his or her performance as a chief. So, if you do not think politics are tied into policing today, you are being very, very foolish." See Hartmann, F.; ed. (1988, November). Debating the Evolution of American Policing, *Perspectives on Policing, no. 5*. Washington, D.C.; Cambridge, Mass.: U.S. Department of Justice, Office of Justice Programs, National Institute of Justice; & Harvard University, John F. Kennedy School of Government, Program in Criminal Justice Policy and Management, 6.

public safety. Rising crime and disorder in the 1960s and 1970s belied the technical expertise of the police, as did the repressive response to the civil rights and peace movements and the persistence of brutality on the street and during interrogations. A growing body of research evidence demonstrated the ineffectiveness of random patrol, the irrelevance of shortened response times to the vast majority of calls for service, and the inability of retrospective investigation to solve most crimes. As for command-and-control management, the work of frontline police officers, operating outside of line-of-sight supervision, proved ill-suited to this form of supervision.

Ironically, the command-and-control management techniques identified with "professional crime-fighting" were the antithesis of the practices generally used to manage professionals. Instead of depending on continuous training, ethical standards and professional pride to guide behavior, command-and-control structures treated frontline police officers like soldiers or factory workers, yet most of the time the job of policing looked nothing like soldiering or assembly-line production.

Even then, the advocates for community policing recognized that mid-century policing was hardly professional in its treatment of the officers on the street. They minced no words here, explaining that by the 1960s and 1970s, line officers were still

> managed in ways that were antithetical to professionalization ... patrol officers continued to have low status; their work was treated as if it were routinized and standardized; and petty rules governed issues such as hair length and off-duty behavior.... the classical theory [of command-and-control management] ... denies too much of the real nature of police work, promulgates unsustainable myths about the nature and quality of police supervision, and creates too much cynicism in officers attempting to do creative problem solving. Its assumptions about workers are simply wrong.[16]

Of all the problems created by terming mid-century policing "professional," none was more glaring than its dissonance with the experience of African-Americans and other racial and ethnic minorities. Former New York City Police Commissioner Patrick Murphy and former Newark (NJ) Police Director Hubert Williams coauthored a 1990 essay in which they argued that for black Americans, the so-called professional model was infused with the racism that had biased policing since the organization of the police during slavery:

> The fact that the legal order not only countenanced but sustained slavery, segregation, and discrimination for most of our Nation's history—and the fact that the police were bound to uphold that order—set a pattern for police behavior and attitudes toward minority communities that has persisted until the present day. That pattern includes the idea that minorities

---

[16] Kelling, G. & Moore, M. The Evolving Strategy of Policing (note 5), 9, 14.

have fewer civil rights, that the task of the police is to keep them under control, and that the police have little responsibility for protecting them from crime within their communities.[17]

Indeed, as Williams and Murphy pointed out, blacks were largely excluded from urban police departments in the same years that "professional" policing was taking hold, and those African-Americans who were hired as police officers were often given lesser powers than white officers. In New Orleans, the police department included 177 black officers in 1870, but this number fell to 27 by 1880, further fell to five by 1900, and to zero by 1910. New Orleans did not hire another black officer until 1950. Even by 1961, a third of U.S. police departments surveyed still limited the authority of black police officers to make felony arrests. By the end of that decade, anger at racial injustice had fueled riots in more than a dozen cities, and a presidential commission had concluded that many of these riots, as Williams and Murphy underscored, "had been precipitated by police actions, often cases of insensitivity, sometimes incidents of outright brutality."[18]

Today it is clear that the rise of community policing did not mark the end of professional policing, but rather its beginning. Little about policing in the mid-20th century was "professional." Its expertise was flawed, its techniques crude, its management techniques more military than professional, and it reinforced rather than challenged the racism of the wider society. Community policing, with its emphases on quality of service, decentralization of authority and community partnership, was more professional than the style of policing it attempted to displace.

The phrase "community policing" does not, however, adequately describe what replaced mid-century law enforcement and what continues to propel the most promising developments in policing today. What began to emerge in the 1980s was a new, truer, more robust professionalism of which community policing was and remains a part. The proponents of the term "community policing" were, in the 1980s, already aware of this problem with their language. They knew their "community policing" framework was merely a partial replacement for mid-century policing. Yet they resisted the broader labels suggested by their colleagues, clinging to their banner of community policing. Why?

The Attorney General and the Professors

Among the participants in the first Executive Session on Policing was Edwin Meese, then-Attorney General of the United States. Two years into the session, during the discussion of a paper by Professors Moore and Kelling tracing the evolution of policing strategies over the previous

---

[17] Williams, H. & Murphy, P. (1990, January). The Evolving Strategy of Policing: A Minority View, *Perspectives on Policing, no. 13*. Washington, D.C., and Cambridge, Mass.: U.S. Department of Justice, Office of Justice Programs, National Institute of Justice, and Harvard University, John F. Kennedy School of Government, Program in Criminal Justice Policy and Management, 2. The significance of this particular publication is especially great as Murphy had served as president of the Police Foundation from 1973 to 1985, succeeded by Hubert Williams, who continues in that position today.
[18] *Ibid.,* pp. 9, 11.

100 years, an exchange between the Attorney General and Professor Moore captured not only the state of the debate in the policing field, but the reason that Moore and his academic colleagues adopted the phrase "community policing" to describe the broad changes they were both charting and championing.

Emphasizing the historical significance of these changes, Kelling and Moore had argued in their paper that American policing since the 1840s had begun in a "political" era in which policing and local politics had been intimately connected and in which police carried out a wide range of social and political functions, only some of which related to law enforcement. Policing had then passed through a "reform" era, reaching its zenith in the 1950s, in which professional crime-fighting became the dominant organizational strategy. Then, just as the many failures of professional crime-fighting became apparent in the 1960s and 1970s, police departments, according to Kelling and Moore, were achieving new successes with the reintroduction of foot patrol and with experiments in "problem solving." Foot patrol proved both effective at reducing fear of crime and politically popular with residents, merchants and politicians, so much so that voters were willing to increase taxes to pay for it. At the same time, problem solving appeared to capture the imagination and enthusiasm of patrol officers, who liked working more holistically in partnership with residents to resolve neighborhood concerns. This led Kelling and Moore to the principal claim in their historical account: foot patrol, fear reduction, problem solving and partnerships with local residents were "not merely new police tactics." Instead, they constituted "a new organizational approach, properly called a community strategy."[19] Although some departments were introducing foot patrol or problem solving as mere add-ons to professional crime-fighting, their implications were far broader:

> We are arguing that policing is in a period of transition from a reform
> strategy to what we call a community strategy. The change involves more
> than making tactical or organizational adjustments and accommodations.
> Just as policing went through a basic change when it moved from the
> political to the reform strategy, it is going through a similar change now.[20]

Attorney General Meese was sympathetic but skeptical. "I think the paper is good, but perhaps a shade grandiose," he told its authors. "Suggesting that we have 'a whole new era' to be compared with the reform era is too grand an approach." Community policing, the Attorney General insisted, is "only one component of the whole picture."[21] The then-director of the National Institute of Justice, James K. "Chips" Stewart, suggested a different term, "problem-oriented" policing, because police were taking many initiatives, not merely creating community partnerships, to

---

[19] Kelling, G. & Moore, M. The Evolving Strategy of Policing (note 5), 13.
[20] *Ibid.,* p. 14.
[21] Quoted in Hartmann, F. Debating the Evolution of American Policing (note 15), 3.

affirmatively identify and solve problems rather than waiting to respond to reports of crime.[22] Attorney General Meese suggested "strategic policing" because the term embraced not only the work in communities but also the support that community work was going to require (especially the intelligence, surveillance and analysis functions) and the "specialist services that are going to focus on homicide, citywide burglary rings, car theft rings, and organized crime and terrorism." The Attorney General said that his concerns would disappear if the professors talked about community policing as a *part* of a new era of policing, rather than defining the era itself. If they did that, he concluded:

> Everybody would realize that this [community policing] is a very important contribution which, along with other things happening in the police field, marks a new era of strategic policing in which people are thinking about what they are doing.[23]

Not only did the professors continue to insist on using "community policing" to define the new era and its strategy, but they soon persuaded the field to do the same. Community policing became the slogan around which reformers rallied, eventually including President Bill Clinton, who put "community policing" at the heart of his national strategy to deal with crime and to provide unprecedented federal assistance to local police.

In response to Attorney General Meese's suggestion that the professors substitute the term "strategic policing," Professor Moore responded with a four-part argument. First, he agreed that the many elements of strategic policing and problem solving were an important part of the new era. Second, he predicted that most of these new strategies would take hold even without encouragement from leaders in the field or academics. Third, he predicted that police would find most uncomfortable the building of true partnerships with communities. He concluded, therefore, that labeling the entire package of innovations as community policing would give special prominence to the very aspect that would be most difficult for the police to adopt. In short, the name was a dare. As Moore said to the Attorney General:

---

[22] Problem solving was discussed frequently at the Executive Session, often as a component of community policing, but its importance as an independent thrust in police reform has been more widely recognized since then. Herman Goldstein, who coined the term "problemoriented policing," was careful to write at the time of the Executive Session that it "connects with the current move to redefine relationships between the police and community." Goldstein, H. (1990). *Problem-Oriented Policing.* New York: McGraw Hill, 3. Looking back on these discussions in 2003, Goldstein explained that in the years of the Executive Session, "the community policing movement grew rapidly in policing. One element of that movement supported the police becoming less legalistically-oriented: that police should redefine their role in ways that sought to achieve broader outcomes for those, especially victims, who turned to the police for help. Beat-level 'problem solving' was seen as supporting these efforts and therefore often incorporated into the community policing movement. As community policing and problem-oriented policing evolved alongside each other, the two concepts were intermingled. I contributed to some of the resulting confusion." Goldstein, H. (2003). "On Further Developing Problem-Oriented Policing: The Most Critical Need, The Major Impediments, and a Proposal," *Crime Prevention Studies* 15: 13–47, 45, note 2 (citation omitted), available at http://www.popcenter.org/library/crimeprevention/volume_15/01Goldstein.pdf.

[23] Quoted in Hartmann, F. Debating the Evolution of American Policing (note 15), 3.

> Let me say why we keep talking about this phrase "community policing." Let us imagine ... that there are two different fronts on which new investments in policing are likely to be made. One lies in the direction of more thoughtful, more information-guided, more active attacks on particular crime problems. Some are local crime problems like robbery and burglary, and some turn out to be much bigger ... [including] organized crime, terrorism, and sophisticated frauds. That is one frontier. In many respects it is a continuation of an increasingly thoughtful, professionalized, forensic, tactical-minded police department. The other front is ... how to strike up a relationship with the community so that we can enlist their aid, focus on the problems that turn out to be important, and figure out a way to be accountable... . The first strand is captured by notions of strategic and problem-solving policing. The second strand is captured by the concept of community policing. ... My judgment is that the problem solving, strategic thing will take care of itself because it is much more of a natural development in policing. If you are going to make a difference, you ought to describe a strategy that challenges the police in the areas in which they are least likely to make investments in repositioning themselves. That is this far more problematic area of fashioning a relationship with the community.[24]

The dare worked. Not everywhere, and not completely, but many American police departments took up the banner of community policing and found it possible to varying degrees to create partnerships with the communities they policed.[25] The successful marketing of community policing was solidified in the first presidential campaign and then the presidency of Bill Clinton, whose signature policing initiative—federal funding to add 100,000 cops to U.S. police departments—was managed by the newly created Office of Community Oriented Policing Services (COPS Office). With those funds, local police departments pursued hundreds of varieties of community partnerships, and the public came to understand that modern policing was community policing.

But Attorney General Meese was right. Community policing was only one part of the new era in American policing, and police departments did not, indeed could not, transform their entire organizations in service of local community priorities. There were too many things to do that did not fit neatly within that frame. Instead, departments began to change on many fronts at once: incorporating new forensic science technology and new surveillance capabilities, building

---

[24] *Ibid.,* p. 5. In a later paper, Moore suggested, likely in jest, that one could term the new strategy "professional, strategic, community, problem-solving policing." Moore, M. & and Trojanowicz, R. (1988, November). Corporate Strategies for Policing. *Perspectives on Policing, no. 6.* Washington, D.C.; Cambridge, Mass.: U.S. Department of Justice, Office of Justice Programs, National Institute of Justice; & Harvard University, John F. Kennedy School of Government, Program in Criminal Justice Policy and Management, 14.

[25] See, for example, Skogan, W. (2006). *Police and Community in Chicago: A Tale of Three Cities.* New York: Oxford University Press.

new information systems that allowed chiefs to hold local commanders accountable almost in real time for levels of crime in their districts, expanding the use of stop-and-search tactics, responding to criticisms of racial profiling and managing heightened concern about terrorism. And every one of these innovations raised problems, at least in some departments, beyond the guidance that community policing principles provided.

As federal funding for community policing diminished after 2001, police leaders found themselves without a single organizing framework that could allow them to make sense of all of these developments. Soon the labels were proliferating: intelligence-led policing, evidence-based policing, pulling levers, hot-spot policing and predictive policing.[26] Some still argued that community policing, rightly understood, was a vessel capacious enough to contain all of these developments, but others believed that many of these tactics and strategies had become divorced from community engagement and participation. Community policing, in short, lost its power as a comprehensive, organizing concept and again became a single element in the complex and contentious field of policing.

Moreover, even in the Clinton years, community policing succeeded as a political slogan and provided a framework for important changes in police practice, but did not serve as the transformative paradigm that Moore and others thought was needed. Police leaders remain uncertain even to this day what they should ask of their communities. Despite books, trainings, conferences and countless new community policing initiatives, police departments became only marginally better at building broad, trusting, active partnerships with community residents, especially in high-crime neighborhoods. By the time of Barack Obama's election in 2008, community policing had not only lost most of the federal funding and priority it had enjoyed in the 1990s, but the power of the slogan to focus police attention, catalyze public support for police reform and serve as an overarching philosophy was exhausted as well.

The New Professionalism can restore to the field an overarching, organizing framework. It brings together the strategic, problem-oriented, community partnership strands from the 1980s and 1990s and incorporates many additional developments in policing in the new century. Still, the exchange between Attorney General Meese and Professor Moore is worth recalling, for it reminds us that some elements of reform are easier than others for police to integrate into their tradition-bound organizations. As the New Professionalism advances, reformers inside and outside police departments should focus on those aspects that will be most difficult for those departments to embrace.

The New Professionalism in the 21st Century

All four elements of the New Professionalism are already apparent in the values espoused by many police leaders in the United States and in the operations of several of their departments:

---

[26] See, for example, Weisburd, D.; Braga, A.; & eds. (2006). *Police Innovation: Contrasting Perspectives.* New York: Cambridge University Press.

accountability, legitimacy, innovation and national coherence. Indeed, the fourth is why the first three define a true professionalism: a collection of expertise, principles and practices that members of the profession recognize and honor.

Increased Accountability

Police departments used to resist accountability; today, the best of them embrace it. Twenty years ago, the term "police accountability" generally referred to accountability for misconduct. To speak of police accountability was to ask who investigated civilian complaints, how chiefs disciplined officers for using excessive force, and so on—sensitive topics in policing. Police chiefs did not generally feel accountable for levels of crime.[27] The change today is dramatic, with increasing numbers of police chiefs feeling strong political pressure to reduce crime even as they contain costs. The best chiefs speak confidently about "the three C's": crime, cost and conduct. Police departments today are accountable for all three.

Consider accountability for crime. Originating in the New York Police Department (NYPD), the CompStat accountability process, in which chiefs in headquarters hold precinct and other area commanders accountable for continuing reductions in crime and achievement of other goals, is now a staple of police management in most large departments. The CompStat process focuses most intensely on "index crimes": homicide, rape, robbery, aggravated assault, burglary, larceny and motor vehicle theft. At the same time, neighborhood residents in local community meetings question police commanders most commonly about other problems, such as open-air drug markets, disorderly youth, vehicle traffic and noise. In still other forums with more specialized advocates, police executives are expected to account for their responses to domestic violence complaints and hate crimes. In these and other ways, police agencies are now routinely accountable for their ability—or inability—to reduce the volume of crime.

Accountability for cost is hardly new, but the costs of policing are receiving intense scrutiny across the United States as state and local governments cut their budgets. Although some police departments are resorting to familiar cost-cutting strategies—reducing civilian staff, slowing officer recruitment, limiting opportunities for officers to earn overtime and eliminating special programs—others are urging a more fundamental re-examination of how police departments are staffed and what work they do.[28] In Los Angeles, Chief of Police Charles Beck eliminated an entire citywide unit of 130 officers known as Crime Reduction and Enforcement of Warrants (CREW), used for tactical crime suppression. This allowed the department to maintain patrol officer levels in local police districts during a time of budget cuts, even though it deprived his executive team of a flexible resource for responding quickly to new crime hot spots. More than

---

[27] See Kelling, G.; Wasserman, R.; & Williams, H. Police Accountability and Community Policing (note 14), 1. ("Rising crime or fear of crime may be problematic for police administrators, but rarely does either threaten their survival.")

[28] See Gascón, G. & Foglesong, T. (2010, December). Making Policing More Affordable: Managing Costs and Measuring Value in Policing. Washington, D.C.; Cambridge, Mass.: U.S. Department of Justice, Office of Justice Programs, National Institute of Justice; & Harvard University, John F. Kennedy School of Government, Program in Criminal Justice Policy and Management, NCJ 231096.

cost cutting, this is a serious bet on the value of district-level leadership, entailing a public accounting of how the department is managing costs in a tight fiscal environment.[29]

Finally, police leaders are taking responsibility for the conduct of their personnel: not only apologizing promptly for clear cases of misconduct, but also taking the initiative to explain controversial conduct that they consider legal and appropriate. For example, when the Los Angeles Police Department employed excessive force on a large scale at an immigrants-rights rally in MacArthur Park in May 2007, then-Police Chief William Bratton publicly confessed error within days, and followed up with strict discipline and reassignment of the top commander at the scene, who later resigned.[30] Perhaps a less obvious example is the NYPD's annual report on all firearms discharges, in which the department reports the facts and patterns in every discharge of a firearm by any of its officers. In the 2008 report, for example, the NYPD reported on 105 firearm discharges, the fewest in at least a decade. These included 49 discharges in "adversarial conflict" in which 12 subjects were killed and 18 injured. The report takes pains to put these police shootings in context, providing accounts of the incidents, information on the backgrounds of the officers and the subjects shot, and comparisons with earlier years.[31]

The embrace and expansion of accountability is likely to continue as part of the New Professionalism in policing, as it is in most professions. On crime, for example, we expect to see more police agencies conducting their own routine public surveys, as many do now, holding themselves accountable not only for reducing reported crime, but also for reducing fear and the perception that crime is a problem in particular neighborhoods or for especially vulnerable residents. The police department in Nashville has engaged a research firm to conduct surveys of residents and businesses every six months since 2005, tracking victimization as well as the percentage of respondents who consider crime their most serious problem, and sharing the results publicly.[32]

To decrease costs, police departments will likely accelerate the shifting of work to nonsworn, and therefore less expensive, specialist personnel, especially in crime investigation units that are currently staffed mostly with detectives. A range of new specialists, including civilian crime scene technicians, data analysts and victim liaisons, might well replace one-half or more of today's detectives. A wide range of new civilian roles could emerge, boosting the prominence of civilian police careers in much the same way that nurses and technicians have taken on many of the roles traditionally played by doctors within the medical profession. This move is already

---

[29] Beck disbanded the Crime Reduction and Enforcement of Warrants task force (CREW), weathering criticism that this vital unit "comprised quick-strike troops that former Chief William Bratton used to focus on problem gangs and neighborhoods." Beck also reduced the size of other specialized, central units focused on gangs and drugs by 170 officers to maintain patrol levels in the districts. See Romero, D. (2010, February). "LAPD's Beck Shuffles Cops To Deal With Budget Crisis: No New Cars, No Unused Vacation Pay Possible." *LA Weekly,* available at: http://blogs.laweekly.com/ladaily/city-news/lapd-metro-transfers.

[30] See Board of Police Commissioners. (2007, October). Los Angeles Police Department, "An Examination of May Day 2007."

[31] Three police officers were injured by subject gunfire, and none were killed in those incidents. See New York Police Department, "2008 Annual Firearms Discharge Report," 2009.

[32] Personal communication from then-Police Chief Ronald Serpas, November 2009. A copy of the June 2009 survey report is on file with the Program in Criminal Justice Policy and Management at the Harvard Kennedy School.

under way, but it proceeds haltingly and with frequent reversals because of the politics of police budgets in periods of fiscal constraint, when retaining sworn officers becomes an especially high priority for elected officials.

On issues of conduct, the New Professionalism may bring substantial reductions in the use of force—already apparent in several jurisdictions—as police departments become more proficient in analyzing the tactical precursors to use-of-force incidents. Already, some departments are reviewing uses of force not only to determine if the officers were justified in the moment that they pulled their triggers or struck a blow, but also to discern earlier tactical missteps that may have unnecessarily escalated a situation to the point where force was legitimately used. By moving beyond a focus on culpability and discipline to smarter policing that relies less on physical force, more departments can demonstrate their professionalism and better account for the force that they deploy.

Finally, we see a growing appreciation among police executives for their own accountability to frontline officers and other members of the organization. This is the least developed form of accountability, with too many police managers still speaking about doing battle with their unions and too many unions bragging about their control over chiefs. This familiar, bruising fight between labor and management obscures the beginnings of a more professional, constructive engagement between police unions and police executives, where leaders at every level are committed to disciplinary systems that are fair and perceived as fair, the development of rules with robust participation of frontline officers and staff, and codes of ethics and statements of values that speak to the aspirations of men and women throughout policing and are grounded in a participatory process.

Legitimacy

Every public-sector department makes some claim to legitimacy, and policing is no exception. In their account of professional crime-fighting of the mid-20th century, Professors Kelling and Moore identified the sources of legitimacy for policing as "the law" and the "professionalism" of the police. They contrasted these sources of legitimacy with early sources of legitimacy in urban politics. To free themselves from the corruptions of political manipulation, the police of mid-century America, the professors explained, claimed their legitimacy from enforcing the law in ways that were properly entrusted to their professional expertise. By contrast, community policing emphasized the legitimacy that could be derived from community approval and engagement.

The legitimacy of policing under the New Professionalism embraces all of these, recognizing that legitimacy is both conferred by law and democratic politics and earned by adhering to professional standards and winning the trust and confidence of the people policed. The New Professionalism, however, puts a special emphasis on the sources of earned legitimacy: professional integrity and public trust. The last of these—public legitimacy—extends a long-established principle of democratic policing and a tenet of community policing: policing by consent of the governed.

In recent decades, police have had only the weakest means to measure erosion of public legitimacy, mostly derived from the numbers of civilian complaints against the police. As every police officer and police scholar can agree, counting formal civilian complaints produces highly problematic statistics. Relatively few people who feel aggrieved in their encounters with the police make a formal complaint, so the complaints received are unlikely to be representative of wider patterns. Moreover, the police discount complaints from at least two categories of civilians: persistent offenders who use the complaint process to deter police from stopping them, and persistent complainers who file literally dozens of complaints annually. These complainants may be relatively few, but the stories about them circulate so widely among police officers that they undermine the ability of police commanders or outside oversight bodies to use numbers of civilian complaints as a credible measure of public dissatisfaction. Finally, adjudicating civilian complaints is so difficult that most complaints remain formally unsubstantiated, further undermining the process.

The problem is with the use of civilian complaints as the leading measure of public legitimacy, not with the goal of public legitimacy itself. Research conducted by New York University Professor Tom Tyler and others over the last two decades demonstrates that rigorous surveys can reliably measure legitimacy, and that doing so allows police departments to identify practices that can increase their legitimacy among those most disaffected: young people and members of ethnic and racial minority groups. Tyler and others demonstrate that police can employ even forceful tactics such as stop-and-frisk in ways that leave those subject to these tactics feeling that the police acted fairly and appropriately.[33] It is through the pursuit of public legitimacy, guided by repeated surveys that disaggregate results for specific racial, ethnic and age groups, that the New Professionalism can directly address the persistent distrust between ethnic and racial minorities and the police in the United States.

As the New Professionalism develops further, police departments will be able to use better surveys than are common today to measure public legitimacy, allowing them to make more appropriate and modest use of civilian complaints statistics. In 2007, then-Senator Barack Obama underscored the importance of this pillar of the New Professionalism when he promised that, as President, he would work for a criminal justice system that enjoyed the trust and confidence of citizens of every race, ethnicity and age.[34] Public surveys that capture the satisfaction of people in these discrete groups in their encounters with police and in their broader confidence in the police can help measure progress toward that goal.[35]

---

[33] See, for example, Tyler, T. (2004). "Enhancing Police Legitimacy," *Annals of the American Academy of Political and Social Science* 593 (10) (2004): 84–99. See also Tyler, T.; ed. (2007). *Legitimacy and Criminal Justice: International Perspectives.* New York: Russell Sage Foundation.

[34] See Obama, B. (2007, September). *Remarks at Howard University Convocation.* Available at http://www.barackobama.com/2007/09/28/remarks_of_senator_barack_obam_26.php, accessed October 14, 2010.

[35] At a national level, the *Sourcebook of Criminal Justice Statistics* annually reports levels of "confidence" in the police as an institution by age, income, racial and ethnic group, and political affiliation. The results in 2009 showed that 63 percent

Continuous Innovation

One complaint about the old professionalism of mid-century policing is that it stifled innovation at the front lines of policing. Police managers were so concerned about the dangers of corruption and a loss of discipline that they suppressed the creative impulses of frontline officers who wanted to try new ways of solving crime problems and eliminating other conditions that caused people grief. Conversely, a complaint about community policing in the 1990s was that it left problem solving to the variable skills of frontline officers, with only rare examples of senior management investing in departmentwide problem solving or developing responses beyond the "generic" solutions of "patrolling, investigating, arresting, and prosecuting ... without benefit of rigorously derived knowledge about the effectiveness of what they do."[36]

Today, innovation at every level is essential for police agencies charged with preventing crimes and solving problems from terrorism to youth violence, vandalism, mortgage fraud, Internet gambling, drug dealing, extortion, drunk driving, intimate partner violence and so on. The last decade has seen innovation in the strategies, tactics and technologies that police employ against all of these, and in ways that police develop relationships within departments and with the public. Films and television series popularize innovations in forensic sciences, but equally dramatic are innovations in less-lethal weaponry, the use of "verbal judo" to control unruly people without physical force, direct engagement with neighborhood gangs and drug dealers to reduce crime and recruiting techniques that can rapidly diversify the pool of applicants for police jobs. Other innovations boost attention to customer service at police stations, help supervisors identify officers at greater risk of engaging in misconduct, improve the outcomes of confrontations with mentally disturbed individuals and provide more effective service to victims of persistent domestic violence and spousal abuse. It is a dizzying array.

The challenge of the New Professionalism is to encourage innovation within the bounds not only of the law but also of ethical values. The use of value statements to guide police behavior in place of the strict enforcement of detailed regulations continues to gain acceptance in the field, driven first by community policing and problem solving and more recently by reforms to disciplinary processes and closer collaborations between union leadership and police executives. As police departments reward innovators with recognition, resources and promotion, that trend will continue.

As part of the New Professionalism, departments can expand the range of incentives for innovation and build structures that encourage innovation as part of the routine work of police officers and senior management teams. These might include community partnerships that

---

of white adults had "a great deal" or "quite a lot" of confidence in the police, in contrast to 38 percent of black adults. If individual departments track the exact language of these national surveys, they can compare themselves with these national benchmarks. See Pastore, A. & Maguire, K.; eds. (2009). *Sourcebook of Criminal Justice Statistics,* Table 2.12.2009, available at http://www.albany.edu/sourcebook/pdf/t2122009.pdf, accessed August 2, 2010.

[36] Goldstein, H. "On Further Developing Problem-Oriented Policing" (note 22), 21.

go beyond the neighborhood activities of community policing, and joint ventures with other government departments, national and international nonprofit organizations and private-sector companies. Such partnerships encourage police to see crime and crime problems in new forms and new places, well beyond the narrow confines of those reported to the police and recorded in the Uniform Crime Reports.

But innovation alone will not prove valuable without a way to learn from the process. All professions are distinguished from mere trades by their commitment to continuous learning through innovation, whether it is experimentation in medicine, the development of the common law, or the application of engineering breakthroughs in architecture. As Herman Goldstein wrote a few years ago in urging the importance of developing knowledge as part of police reform, "The building of a body of knowledge, on which good practice is based and with which practitioners are expected to be familiar, may be the most important element for acquiring truly professional status."[37]

Knowledge—its creation, dissemination and practical application—is essential to genuine professionalism. Police organizations need not only to encourage innovation but also to measure their outcomes, and reward and sustain innovations that succeed. They should encourage independent evaluations of their policies and tactics. Working with researchers, they should design experiments that rigorously test new ideas. Police organizations must then communicate the reasons for their successes widely and quickly throughout the profession. Formal partnerships with universities and nonprofit think tanks can help, and many departments have already built such partnerships.

All this suggests a new way of learning within policing. The pace of innovation and knowledge development today is simply too fast for police organizations to rely on recruit training and occasional specialized courses. Rather, police departments need to become learning organizations of professionals. For example, analysts in police agencies should not only be studying crime patterns but also analyzing what the police are doing about them and to what effect, informing the development of tailor-made strategies to deal with the underlying problems, and then sharing their analyses widely within the department in forms that busy frontline officers and supervisors can easily digest, retain and apply. Another example: frontline officers and rising managers should be rewarded for the professional habits of reading, learning and actively contributing to the expansion of knowledge in the field.[38]

---

[37] *Ibid.,* p. 46, note 3. Goldstein here describes it as "especially troubling" that the 20th century "professionalization" of policing had not included this element.

[38] The idea of a "learning organization" goes well beyond what we expect of all professional organizations. For more about learning organizations, see Garvin, D. (2000). *Learning in Action: Putting the Learning Organization to Work.* Cambridge, Mass.: Harvard Business School Press.

National Coherence

Achieving accountability for crime, cost and conduct; public legitimacy across social divisions; and continuous innovation and learning at every rank would mark a watershed in policing. These first three elements build on efforts begun with community policing, elevating them to a New Professionalism that infuses all of what police organizations do. To make that New Professionalism worthy of the name, however, requires one more step: achieving national coherence in this radically decentralized business. This element has not yet developed as far as the first three, but it has begun to grow.

Policing in the United States is notoriously parochial, entrusted to something close to 20,000 police departments—the precise number changes so quickly that there is no reliable count. Yet in the last three decades, policing has begun to develop features of a coherent field of professional work. The Police Foundation and Police Executive Research Forum have helped by nurturing national conversations among practitioners and researchers. These conversations took on greater intensity in the first Executive Session on Policing, and they became far more public when Bill Clinton, campaigning for the presidency in 1992, argued for using federal resources to spread community policing to every state. Since then, national discussions and debates about police practices and strategies have become commonplace, thanks in large part to the efforts of the COPS Office, the Office on Violence Against Women and the Office of Justice Programs—all within the Department of Justice—and the conversations hosted by the Major Cities Chiefs Association and other professional associations.[39] Many of the best-known brands in policing practices—"CompStat Meetings," "Fusion Centers" and even older brands like "Weed and Seed" programs—are national in name only, with each manifestation so different from the others that they contribute little to national coherence. Still, even these widely differing practices can create an appetite for more truly coherent practices in an extremely decentralized field.

Most other countries achieve at least some national coherence through a national police agency or a limited number of state police services. England, with only 43 local police services, has recently created the National Police Improvement Agency to assume a variety of shared functions and bring a greater degree of national coherence to policing. Canada uses a mixed model, in which municipalities and provinces contract with the Royal Canadian Mounted Police (RCMP) to provide local or provincial police services according to local specifications aiming to achieve locally negotiated goals. Large jurisdictions, such as the provinces of Ontario and Quebec and the cities of Toronto, Montreal and Vancouver, still choose to field their own police services, but the other provinces and many smaller cities contract with the RCMP.

---

[39] The Major Cities Chiefs Association comprises the chiefs of the 63 largest police departments in the United States and Canada (56 of the departments are in the United States; seven more are in Canada). Members include the chief executive officers of law enforcement agencies in U.S. cities with populations greater than 500,000, the chief executive officer of the largest law enforcement agency in each U.S. Standard Metropolitan Statistical Area with a population greater than 1.5 million, and the chiefs of police in the seven largest Canadian cities. For more information about the association, see the association's website, http://www.majorcitieschiefs.org.

Local control over local policing is deeply ingrained in American political culture, and we do not expect that to change. Some consolidation among the 80 percent of police agencies with fewer than 25 police officers could help residents of those communities receive more professional police services, but such consolidation will not do much for national coherence. Indeed, further progress toward national coherence through the New Professionalism may be necessary for this consolidation to be attractive.

Greater mobility among police departments for officers and professional staff could do more than consolidation to advance national coherence. True professionals are mobile across jurisdictions, even across national boundaries. Engineers, doctors and even lawyers can practice their professions and apply their skills and training almost anywhere. Many professions have local testing and licensing requirements, but reciprocity arrangements recognize that the training and skills of these licensed professionals are portable, and both individuals and organizations take advantage of this portability. Local experience has value in every profession, but local expertise can be balanced with wider knowledge and experience.

Only in the last few decades has it become common for big-city police chiefs to be recruited from outside of their departments and states, though even today most chiefs have spent their entire careers in the departments they lead. That trend needs to deepen, and the profession needs to find ways to encourage greater movement from place to place and across state lines at every stage of police careers. The obstacles are substantial. Police pension rules can create powerful disincentives for officers to move. In some states, such as California, the pension system does not block movement within the state, but creates disincentives for wider moves. In Massachusetts, state laws and contracts make it difficult for veteran officers and supervisors to move even within the state without loss in rank.

If the values of policing are really professional, not local, then departments need not worry that a workforce enjoying geographic mobility will become unskilled or undisciplined. Officers who have worked in the same community for a decade or more and who know the local people and their customs will be invaluable members of any police service, but that is true in many professions. What is needed is a genuine national coherence in the skills, training and accreditation of police professionals.[40]

At stake here is much more than the ability for some police officers to move from one department to another. Citizens should be entitled to professional performance from U.S. police officers wherever they find them. Not only should the definition of professional performance be constantly evolving, but the public—itself mobile across the country—should expect police officers everywhere to keep up with these developments.

---

[40] The issues of national coherence and professionalism can raise questions about minimum standards for police, especially educational standards. Should police officers be required to have a college degree? Should there be educational qualifications for promotion? In light of racial and ethnic differences in formal educational attainment, standards might be more appropriately focused on knowledge rather than years of schooling or formal degrees. Many professions allow apprenticeships to substitute for formal classroom education. The issues also raise questions of pension portability for line officers, which some states are beginning to address with the support of police unions. In general, we have been impressed that many police unions share the ambitions of the New Professionalism.

This kind of coherence implies the development of national norms of how the police respond to situations, particularly to criminal activity, public disorder, political dissent or even a traffic infraction. Consider, for example, a routine traffic stop. This can be a tense moment for a police officer who does not know if the car's occupants were merely speeding or escaping the scene of a crime, just as it is an anxious moment for most drivers. A common protocol for how the police approach the vehicle, what they require of the driver, and how they respond as the encounter proceeds could not only save the lives of officers, but could help motorists as they drive from state to state avoid inadvertently alarming any officers who stop them. Such protocols have already begun to spread, but they could usefully be developed for a much wider range of situations.

The concept of a "protocol," familiar in the medical field, could prove useful in professional policing. Some may become standard because of research findings, others because of judicial decisions, still others because of advances in forensic science. As in medicine, the danger is that protocols will, in the hands of busy police professionals, replace nuanced diagnosis and a plan to address the problems at hand. Careful analysis of local problems and the custom crafting of solutions continue to be necessary. Still, once a tool becomes part of that solution, its use according to standard protocols can save lives, improve effectiveness, reduce costs and let everyone benefit from the accumulation of professional knowledge. Just as systematic evaluation and rigorous research can discipline innovation, they can strengthen national protocols.[41]

Increased mobility and stronger protocols are only two ways in which national coherence can advance. The attraction of the new professionalism is likely to feed a flowering of specialist professional associations, bachelor's and master's degree programs, professional journals and other features of professional infrastructure.

Is the New Professionalism Really New?

We return, finally, to the definitional question: What is professionalism? When an earlier generation of reformers described the police strategy of the mid-20th century as professional crime-fighting, they may have been using the term "professional" merely as the opposite of "amateur." Perhaps they thought of professional police much as people think of professional athletes or professional actors. Through more rigorous selection, better training and tighter command, they had left the ranks of mere amateurs.

It is also likely that this earlier generation wanted to put distance between the police and partisan elected officials. Police departments live with a constant tension between serving the

---

[41] The recently created National Network for Safe Communities, which links more than 50 jurisdictions that are implementing a gang violence reduction strategy piloted in Boston and a drug market reduction strategy piloted in High Point, N.C., represents one such effort to move police practice from experimentation to application and adaptation of common, national protocols. See http://www.nnscommunities.org. A similar national effort, the Policing Research Platform Project, is collecting comprehensive data from new recruits, supervisors and entire police agencies to expand understanding of the career paths of police professionals and of quality policing. See http://www.ojp.usdoj.gov/nij/topics/law-enforcement/administration/policing-platform/welcome.htm.

government leaders of the day, whether mayor, county executive or governor, and remaining independent of partisan politics. In the mid-20th century, reformers deployed the language of professionalism to help manage that tension, hoping to hold the local political machine at arm's length. That aim was laudable, but the claim was false. These departments were not professional.

We describe today's genuine police professionalism as "new" to distinguish it from the earlier rhetoric that mistakenly equated professionalism with an overreliance on technology, central-ization of authority and insulation from the public. These features, found in much policing in the second half of the 20th century, do not define true professionalism.

Consider the parallel with the practice of medicine as a profession. In the 1960s and 1970s, U.S. doctors were often criticized as overly reliant on technology and distant from the patients whom they treated. A wave of reformers in medicine developed new specialties in family prac-tice and championed medical education that trained doctors to communicate with patients respectfully, engaging patients more meaningfully in their own treatment. New roles for nurse practitioners and other health workers made the practice of medicine more humane. Family practice and other reforms aimed to build good relationships between medical practitioners and patients, just as community policing aimed to build good relationships between police and the people they served. But no one seriously suggests that doctors and nurses should abandon their identity as professionals. Instead, professionalism in medicine has come to embrace the respect for patients, accountability and innovations that are improving practice. Medicine has discovered its own new professionalism. So, too, has legal practice, in part through law school clinics that teach the importance of respectful client relationships alongside legal doctrine.

Similarly, in law enforcement, the New Professionalism embraces the respectful engagement of citizens and communities that lies at the core of community policing. Those who continue to champion the aspirations of community policing should understand the New Professionalism as aligned with their ambitions.[42] Moreover, the New Professionalism is clear about its expecta-tions, whereas community policing has become so vague a term that it has lost its operational meaning. As Moore advised two decades ago, the New Professionalism focuses police attention on the very things that are most difficult to achieve: accountability, legitimacy, innovation and national coherence. Community engagement is essential at least to the first two of those and perhaps all four.

Much can be gained from a truer police professionalism. For the public, policing promises to become more effective, more responsive to the opinions of residents and less forceful, less brusque. For members of the police profession themselves, the work promises to become more stimulating with a greater emphasis on learning, innovation, ethics and professional mobility.

---

[42] See, for example, Sklansky, David, *The Persistent Pull of Police Professionalism,* to be published in this series. [National Institute of Justice (NIJ). BiblioGov (August 13, 2012)] Sklansky continues to identify "professionalism" in policing with the desire to centralize police authority, make use of the latest technology, and keep the public at a distance. He decries such professionalism and longs to engage police in questions of genuine partnership with communities. We agree with his ambition but disagree that he needs to strip police of their professional identity to achieve it. We believe the New Professionalism is a more accurate and more attractive banner for this effort than his "advanced community policing."

But the greatest gains are for democratic societies generally and the American experiment in democracy more specifically.

A certain amount of force will always be a part of police work; a degree of coercion is necessary to keep order and enforce the law. What matters is whether policing—when it forcefully asserts its authority—makes democratic progress possible or impedes it. Professional policing enhances democratic progress when it accounts for what it does, achieves public support, learns through innovation and transcends parochialism. That is the promise of the New Professionalism.

Critical Thinking Questions

1 Which of the four elements of the new professionalism is the most difficult to implement? Why?

2 Why did the authors argue that original professionalism was not in fact professional?

3 What aspects of community policing make it a professional style of policing?

4 How does the decentralized nature of policing hinder the implementation of a new professionalism?

Editors' Introduction: Reading 1.2

One of the concerns that grew out of the professional era of policing was civil rights. More specifically, this was the era of Warren's "Due Process Revolution" where police were now being told not just *what to do*, but *how to do it*—or, perhaps more accurately, how *not* to do it. This is the era that gave us the Miranda warnings, for example, as well as numerous extensions of early 20th-century federal court rulings to the states by way of the 14th Amendment, such as the exclusionary rule. Many of these issues were concerned with the Fourth Amendment, which, as Roots points out in the following reading, remains a salient source of discussion in terms of police behavior today. In particular, Roots explores whether increased police professionalism—such as that envisioned in the preceding article by Stone and Travis—in terms of pay, training, and credentialing, has helped alleviate the Fourth Amendment issues we saw throughout the 20th century.

Does Increasing Police Professionalism Make the Fourth Amendment Unnecessary?

Roger Roots

In a 2006 U.S. Supreme Court opinion, *Hudson v. Michigan*, at least four Supreme Court justices indicated a willingness to abolish or severely restrict the Fourth Amendment exclusionary rule. Among their grounds for so fundamentally altering American criminal procedure was the growing body of literature indicating that American police officers have become more professional in recent years. The justices suggested that this professionalization has made the exclusionary rule unnecessary to deter future officers from participating in unreasonable searches and seizures.

The Fourth Amendment states that "[t]he right of the people to be secure in their persons, houses, papers, and effects, against unreasonable searches and seizures, shall not be violated, and no Warrants shall issue, but upon probable cause, supported by Oath or affirmation, and particularly describing the place to be searched, and the persons or things to be seized." This language does not specify what remedy should apply when investigators violate the Amendment, but the Supreme Court has applied the exclusionary rule to most Fourth Amendment violations in federal criminal courts since 1914 (*Weeks v. United States*) and required state courts to follow the exclusionary rule since 1961 (*Mapp v. Ohio*). In general, this means that illegally seized physical evidence—like illegally extracted or coerced confessions—are withheld from the purview of juries in criminal trials.[1]

---

[1] American criminal defendants may opt for judge trials instead of jury trials, in which cases judges must disregard any illegally seized evidence (even though these judges are aware of the existence of the evidence). In general practice, defense attorneys move for suppression of such evidence in pretrial proceedings, and the issue is resolved by the trial court before the start of trial. In some cases, these pretrial hearings occur weeks prior trial, and a determination that crucial evidence must be excluded results in dismissal of criminal charges entirely.

Since the 1961 *Mapp* decision, however, a backlash against the Fourth Amendment exclusionary rule has been unleashed by conservative judges and legal scholars (Roots, 2009). Such judges and scholars argue that only civil remedies are required by the Fourth Amendment, meaning that victims of unreasonable searches and seizures should merely be able to sue in separate civil proceedings. This view denies that the rule of exclusion is constitutionally required, and describes the rule as a mere "prudential [rule]" aimed at stemming the tide of warrantless searches rather than constitutionally mandated" (*Penn. Bd. Of Prob. & Parole v. Scott*, 1998). Accordingly, this view posits that when America's police departments demonstrate appropriate levels of compliance with the Fourth Amendment, the Supreme Court may abolish the exclusionary rule. The Supreme Court's 2006 *Hudson* decision moved the Court's jurisprudence closer to a conservative model that would admit any and all relevant evidence in criminal proceedings regardless of whether police illegally seize the evidence.

Hudson v. Michigan (2006) dealt with the question of whether evidence seized after police forced open an unlocked residential door within seconds upon announcing their presence while executing a warrant should be excluded from evidence. The search violated the traditional "knock and announce" rule requiring that searchers must first knock and announce their presence and then pause for a reasonable time before breaking open the doors of homes to be searched. This requirement, as Justice Scalia conceded, "is an ancient one" in search-and-seizure law. (Justice Breyer in his dissent noted that the knock-and-announce requirement had been traced back to the 13th century.)

The *Hudson* majority held that the rule of exclusion is unnecessary in cases where police fail to properly announce an arrest before breaking open the door of a residence. Justice Antonin Scalia, writing for himself and Justices Roberts, Thomas and Alito, expressed the view that that the rule of exclusion may be unnecessary in a world where police officers have become so competent and well trained that they already recognize and heed the technicalities of Fourth Amendment law. (A fifth vote for the outcome in *Hudson* came from Justice Kennedy, who concurred in the judgment but did not agree with all of Scalia's reasoning; these five votes overcame the dissents of Justices Ginsberg, Sotomayor, Kagan and Breyer.)[2]

Justice Scalia's four-justice plurality suggested that the Court's 1961 decision in *Mapp v. Ohio* (which imposed the exclusionary rule on the court systems of every state) should be reconsidered in light of the growing professionalism and competence of America's police forces. "We cannot assume," wrote Scalia, "that exclusion in this context is necessary deterrence simply because we found that it was necessary deterrence in different contexts and long ago." "That would be forcing the public today," Scalia continued, "to pay for the sins and inadequacies of a legal regime that existed almost half a century ago." Among other changes in legal and police

---

[2] Kennedy's brief concurring opinion is short on discussion, but indicates that Kennedy agreed with the winning plurality, that "[i]n this case the relevant evidence was discovered not because of a failure to knock-and-announce, but because of a subsequent search pursuant to a lawful warrant," while he disagreed regarding the relevance of certain previous Supreme Court rulings ("I am not convinced that *Segura v. United States*, 468 U. S. 796 (1984), and *New York v. Harris*, 495 U. S. 14 (1990), have as much relevance here as Justice Scalia appears to conclude").

practices,[3] wrote Scalia, the professional, well-trained police of today are simply less likely to violate people's Fourth Amendment rights than were the police of yesterday:

> Another development over the past half-century that deters civil-rights violations is the increasing professionalism of police forces, including a new emphasis on internal police discipline. ... [W]e now have increasing evidence that police forces across the United States take the constitutional rights of citizens seriously. There have been "wide-ranging reforms in the education, training, and supervision of police officers." S. Walker, *Taming the System: The Control of Discretion in Criminal Justice 1950–1990*, p 51 (1993). Numerous sources are now available to teach officers and their supervisors what is required of them under this Court's cases, how to respect constitutional guarantees in various situations, and how to craft an effective regime for internal discipline. *See, e.g.*, D. Waksman & D. Goodman, *The Search and Seizure Handbook* (2d ed. 2006); A. Stone & S. DeLuca, *Police Administration: An Introduction* (2d ed. 1994); E. Thibault, L. Lynch, & R. McBride, *Proactive Police Management* (4th ed. 1998). ... Moreover, modem police forces are staffed with professionals; it is not credible to assert that internal discipline, which can limit successful careers, will not have a deterrent effect. *Hudson v. Michigan*, 547 U.S. 586, 598-599 (2006).

Scalia's references to the work of Samuel Walker's book *Taming the System: The Control of Discretion in American Criminal Justice* met with immediate criticism, not the least of which was criticism by Professor Walker himself. On June 25, 2006, Walker authored an opinion piece in the Los Angeles Times stating that his excitement at having been referenced by the Supreme Court "quickly turned to dismay, then horror." According to Walker, Scalia had "twisted [Walker's] main argument to reach a conclusion the exact opposite of what [Walker] spelled out in this and other studies." Walker assured readers that his research on police professionalism by no means suggested that the Fourth Amendment exclusionary rule should be abolished.

The *Hudson* decision represented the high-water mark thus far for judicial efforts to limit the application of the exclusionary rule. The view that the exclusionary rule was required by the Constitution "prevailed, unchallenged, for many years" during the mid-20th century (Clancy, 2013, p. 361). But opponents of the rule have gradually edged out proponents on American court benches, and the rule now teeters on the brink of abolition.

The four-judge plurality opinion can be dismissed as mere dicta, except that it suggests that if even one additional justice were to agree that modern police are sufficiently deterred by other remedies, the Supreme Court may well jettison the application of the exclusionary rule on a

---

[3] Justice Scalia cited the expansion of civil rights lawsuits under 42 U.S.C. § 1983 and the Supreme Court's 1971 recognition in *Bivens v. Six Unknown Narcotics Agents* that the Constitution requires federal agents who violate Fourth Amendment rights to be vulnerable to civil lawsuits even in the absence of a statute so providing.

general scale. Police departments nationwide could expect that any and all evidence they obtain against suspects, no matter how unlawfully obtained, would be admitted in criminal trials.

Of course, no one familiar with police trends would disagree with Justice Scalia's depiction of contemporary policing as being "staffed with professionals" or at least more likely to be staffed with professionals than the police forces of 1961. It is undeniable that police have become higher paid, more educated and more credentialed. But does this increased compensation, education and credentialing translate into greater police respect for the Fourth Amendment such that the exclusionary rule has become superfluous?

Search-And-Seizure Success Rates

Something of an answer can be gained to the questions above by examining "success rates" from police searches and seizures in recent years.

Perhaps nothing in the science of policing is more clear than that officers' assessments of probable cause are less reliable than *the combination* of officers' and judges' assessments of probable cause. Studies of searches by warrant—after judges have agreed with officers that probable cause exists—find very high rates of recovery of contraband and incriminating evidence. For example, Van Duizend's 1985 study of search warrants from seven American jurisdictions found recovery rates of 84% to 97% (Van Duizend, 1985). Benner and Samarkos' 2000 study of narcotics search warrants in San Diego found a success rate of 88%.

These high rates of success are in sharp contrast to outcomes of warrantless searches. Although warrantless searches are more difficult to study because officers do not always leave trails of records to memorialize them (Minzner, 2009), lower rates of success for warrantless searches are significant. Dominitz and Knowles (2006) found "hit rates" (meaning rates of searches yielding contraband of any kind) of 22% for cars driven by white drivers, 15% for cars driven by black drivers and 11% for Hispanic drivers. In Florida, the corresponding rates were 25%, 21% and 12%. In one Minneapolis study, the rates were 13%, 11% and 5%. In Pennsylvania, the rates were 29%, 21% and 17% (Dominitz & Knowles, 2006, p. 369 n.2).

Of these studies, the lowest error rate for warrantless searches, 47% was reported in a study of 2002 Maryland traffic searches (Gross & Bames, 2002). The highest rate of error (98%) was reported in a study of 2007 Illinois traffic consent searches (ACLU, 2008).

Not only do these data indicate that search-and-seizure decisions made unilaterally by police officers are much less likely to yield incriminating evidence than decisions approved by judges. The data also suggest that modern officers—even the professionalized officers described by Justice Scalia in *Hudson v. Michigan*—engage in racially discriminatory searches. "[S]izeable numbers of police officers have been detected" providing false or incomplete data in response to requirements to record racial statistics of motorists stopped for traffic citations (Lundman, 2004, p.312). Data collected by 65 Minnesota police departments during 2002 show that police "searched Blacks, Latinos, and American Indians at greater rates than White drivers, and found contraband as a result of searches of Blacks, Latinos, and American Indians at lower rates than in searches of White drivers" (Institute on Race & Poverty 2003). In Missouri and Florida, according to Dominitz and Knowles, "state-wide hit rates on Hispanic motorists were about half that of white motorists; Minneapolis, where these searches were just over one-third as successful; and Pennsylvania, where searches were less than two-thirds as successful" (Dominitz & Knowles, 2006, p. 368).

Minzner (2009), relying on data culled from the U.S. Department of Justice's (D.O.J.) *Contacts Between and the Police and the Public* survey (2007), documented similarly low rates of recovery of contraband when officers declare that they have probable cause to conduct warrantless searches. Although "a primary purpose of these [D.O.J.] surveys is to determine whether members of racial minorities are treated differently, the surveys also provide data on when law enforcement performs searches and what the results are" (Minzner, 2009, p. 924). And the results have consistently shown that evidence is recovered between 11.6% and 12.6% of the time.

Minzner noted also that police success rates when searching pursuant to a claim of probable cause (but no warrant) are quite similar to success rates garnered from patdowns executed under the less strict "reasonable suspicion" standard (Minzner 2009, p. 924 n.46). Yet the reasonable suspicion standard is supposedly a more relaxed standard justifying lessintrusive searches executed for an officer's safety. Minzner cites the 2006 study by Gelman Fagan, and Kiss of the New York City Police Department stop-and-frisk policies. The study found that when NYPD officers engaged in stops based on what the officer reported as "reasonable suspicion," an arrest resulted about one time in seven, or 14% of the time (Minzner, 2009 (citing Gelman et al., 2006)).

Figure 1.2.1   Success Rates Of Police Searches (Compiled From Various Studies)

STUDY	SUCCESS RATE (CONTRABAND SEIZED)
1985 study of search warrants in seven jurisdictions. (Van Duizend, 1985).	84–97%
2000 narcotics search warrants in San Diego. (Benner and Samarkos 2000).	88%
2002 Maryland warrantless probable-cause traffic searches. (Gross & Barnes, 2002, p. 101).	52.5%
2003 San Antonio car-stop searches. (Lambert, 2003, p. 48, tbl. 8).	35.1%
1999 National Survey, warrantless traffic searches. (Lagan, et al., 2001).	12.6%
2002 National Survey, warrantless traffic searches. (Durose, et al., 2005, p. 13).	11.7%
2005 National Survey, warrantless traffic searches. (Durose, et al., 2007, p. 7).	11.6%
2006 New York City "stops-and-frisks" based on reasonable suspicion." (Gelman, et al., 2007, p. 816).	14%
2007 Illinois traffic consent searches. (ACLU, 2008).	2–9%

The literature of police work is filled with pronouncements of the supposedly great instincts of police for ferreting out crime (Silberman, 1978; Signorelli, 2010). There are accounts by police officers of how court decisions that inhibit officer discretion put officers at risk by thwarting their natural responses to criminal threats on the street. Signorelli (2010), for example, proclaims that court decisions barring the admission of confessions and other evidence taken while officers' guns are drawn can put officers in danger. But the data drawn from warrantless traffic searches based on claims of probable cause tend to refute police claims of such professional instincts.

The low rates of contraband recovery admitted by officers in many jurisdictions seem to be verified by surveys and accounts of motorists who are detained by police. Among those interviewed by the National Crime Victimization Survey in 1999 (80,543), 8.7% reported one or more traffic stops by police while they were driving during the previous year. Of those stopped at least once, 344, or 4.9%, reported that the vehicle they were driving was searched by police. Only 43, or 12.5%, of these searches resulted in a finding of any contraband (Lundman, 2004, p. 319). "The most common illegal evidence police turn up after a leisurely and time consuming rummage through a vehicle is an open container of alcohol" (Lundman, 2004, p. 335). "[According to citizens, police find very little, and what little they do find is not very important" (id.).

Conclusion

Presented here are data that American police officers who stop vehicles on American roadways make incorrect assessments regarding the probability of finding contraband in vehicles from 47% to 98% of the time. When these figures are extrapolated out, they indicate that millions of U.S. motorists are subjected to fruitless (if not baseless) searches annually. Regardless of how well credentialed, trained, or paid modem police officers tend to be, it seems that the "security" of Americans "in their persons, houses, papers, and effects, against unreasonable searches and seizures"—as required by the Fourth Amendment—continues to be in great jeopardy.

References

Benner, L. A., & Samarkos, C. T. (2000). Searching for Narcotics in San Diego: Preliminary Findings from the San Diego Search Warrant Project. *California Western law Review, 36*, 221–266.

Brandon, Alex. (2002). After Katrina, New Orleans Cops Were Told They Could Shoot Looters, *New Orleans Times-Picayune*, July 24. http://www.propublica.org/nola/story/nopd-order-to-shootlooters-hurricane-katrina

Clancy, Thomas K. (2013). The Fourth Amendment's Exclusionary Rule as a Constitutional Right. *Ohio State Journal of Criminal law, Vol. 10*, pp. 357–391.

Dominitz, Jeff, and John Knowles. 2006. Crime Minimisation and Racial Bias: What Can We Learn from Police Search Data?, *The Economic Journal, Vol. 116*, November, pp. F368–F384.

Duróse, Matthew R., et al. (2005). U.S. Dep't of Justice, *Contacts between Police and the Public Findings from the 2002 National Survey.*

Duróse, Matthew R., et al. (2007). U.S. Dep't of Justice, *Contacts between Police and the Public*, 2005.

Gelman, Andrew, Fagan, Jeffrey & Kiss, Alex. (2007). An Analysis of the NYPD's "Stop-and-Frisk" Policy in the Context of Claims of Racial Bias, *Journal of American Statistical Association, 102.* 813–823.

Harki, Gary A. (2009, Nov. 2). South Charleston Police Settle in Roadside Search case, *West Virginia Gazette*, (http://www.wvgazette.com/News/South%20Charleston/200911230665) (accessed March 5, 2010)

Institute on Race & Poverty, University of Minnesota Law School. 2003. *Minnesota Statewide Racial Profiling Report: All Participating Jurisdiction.* Minneapolis: University of Minnesota (report to the Minnesota legislature, Sept. 22, 2003).

Lundman, Richard J. (2004). Driver Race, Ethnicity, and Gender and Citizen Reports of Vehicle Searches by Police and Vehicle Search Hits: Toward a Triangulated Scholarly Understanding, *Journal of Criminal Law & Criminology, 94,* 309–349.

Minzner, Max A. 2009. Putting Probability Back into Probable Cause. *Texas Law Review Vol. 87,* p. 913.

Mulrine, A. (2005). When the Cops Turn into The Bad Guys: The New Orleans Police Department Hits Its nadir. *U.S. News,* October 2, 2005. http://www.usnews.com/usnews/news/articles/051010/10cops.htm

Roots, R. (2009). The Originalist Case For the Fourth Amendment Exclusionary Rule, *Gonzaga Law Review, 45,* 1–66.

Schmalz, Jeffrey. (1989, October 9). 3 Weeks After Storm, St. Croix Still Needs Troops. *New York Times,* page AL.

Signorelli, Walter P. (2010). *The Constable Has Blundered: The Exclusionary Rule, Crime, and Corruption.* Durham, NC: Carolina Academic Press

Silberman, C. E. 1978. *Criminal Violence, Criminal Justice.* New York, NY: Random House.

Walker, Samuel. (2006). "Thanks for nothing, Nino," *L.A. Times,* June 25, 2006. http://articles.latimes.com/2006/jun/25/opinion/oe-walker25 (accessed Sept. 21, 2013).

Walker, Samuel. (1993). *Taming the System: The Control of Discretion in Criminal Justice,* 19501990. Oxford University Press, New York: NY.

Cases

Bivens v. Six Unknown Narcotics Agents, 403 U.S. 388 (1971).

Hudson v. Michigan, 547 U.S. 586 (2006).

Pennsylvania Board of Probation and Parole v. Scott, 524 US 357 (1998).

Mapp v. Ohio, 367 U.S. 643 (1961).

New York v. Harris, 495 U. S. 14 (1990).

Weeks v. United States, 232 U.S. 383 (1914).

Segura v. United States, 468 U. S. 796 (1984),

Critical Thinking Questions

1   What is the exclusionary rule? What led Justice Scalia to argue that the exclusionary rule should be reexamined?

2   How are racial and ethnic minorities inordinately impacted by warrantless traffic searches?

3   What do study findings about warrantless traffic search success rates suggest about the need for constitutional protections?

4   What do you think of Roots's solution to contemporary concerns? Are they feasible? Why? Are there other solutions that you can think of?

Editors' Introduction: Reading 1.3

If the professional model is not *the* answer for the problems of contemporary policing—indeed, if this 20th-century model actually harmed the relationship between police and society, as these articles indicate has been the case—what else can the police do? Joplin and Marwah provide one possible answer. They take up a perennial topic of policing: how to work with police discretion. Rather than suggest new training and accountability mechanisms, per se, Joplin and Marwah suggest that we reconceptualize the very nature of the police vis-a-vis society. This they call a "new professionalism" that involves increasing police officers' opportunities to engage in more than just fighting crime, but also in problem solving. This is nothing new; but what is new is that Joplin and Marwah extend the problem-oriented approach into other social problems, not just crime. This is a radical innovation in policing that builds on democratic concepts.

Democratizing Police Professionalization and Division of Labor

Jerry Joplin and Sanjay Marwah

The history of professionalizing policing is filled with schemes and methods discouraging individual police officer discretion. Usually these methods and schemes focus on a means-oriented bureaucracy (Goldstein, 1990; Kraska & Brent, 2011). A means-focused bureaucracy and means-focused bureaucrats pay exclusive attention to the means to achieve any goal or end of a bureaucracy (identified as instrumental rationality or technical rationality). They place minimal emphasis on the goals or ends. Police bureaucracies operate using instrumental rationality in a circular fashion validating only the determined means (not any ends) deemed appropriate in any decision-making exercise. This dominant instrumental rationality considers rational only those means that are relevant to accomplishing a particular goal. Additionally, instrumental rationality privileges instrumental knowledge, the type of knowledge useful to solve problems only through consideration of means and neglecting ends that are pre-determined by management and authority either within or outside policing organizations (Thacher, 2001). Instrumental knowledge, in turn, highly limits or ignores the selection of appropriate goals or ends, which are critical in any decision. Consequences of this skewed cognitive (thinking and reasoning) orientation may include the establishment of technical bureaucrats, individuals who focus on the technical aspects of achieving goals without considering values, ends, or outcomes.

All of these issues directly relate to professionalization of policing. If professionalizing police requires individual police officers to examine only the means of the police bureaucracy, then discretion is no longer a necessity to professionalizing police. In fact, individual discretion is no longer required as technical bureaucrats are means-oriented. Without any concern about the ends, individual police officers will become robotic, and their own inputs into the ends or goals of their organizations will be devalued.

Police professionalization and individual discretion need not be mutually exclusive, and since discretionary judgments do occur in police bureaucracies, examining how discretion and professionalization benefit one will provide insight into how the individual police officer can contribute not only to the means of effective policing, but also the ends of effective policing. Making a discretionary decision often means making a moral decision in a legal context (Owen, Fradella, Burke, & Joplin, 2012): yet, bureaucratic leaders in the name of police professionalization may create policies and regulations restricting discretion so as to ensure consistency and uniformity (Walker, 1977). While focusing on consistency implies a sense of equality, it does not ensure the best moral decision-making, and while uniformity may please the public and seemingly allow transparency into police decision-making, the best moral decision to be made in a particular situation might be refusing to follow policy and regulations. Training police professionals as experts in following procedures seems counterintuitive toward the professionalization of the individual officer who needs to increase his/her capacities of problem-solving and moral reasoning.

Increasing cognitive capacities of police officers is not an entirely new idea, but this article extends beyond generalized notions of increasing educational standards and training for police. Rather than creating a new set of professional standards, increasing the cognitive capacity of the individual police officer requires revisiting the existing division of labor. Police officers learning police organizational standards from their experience in a command-and-control division of labor may have difficulty conceptualizing another type of division of labor. Yet a democratized society may require a democratized police department of professional police officers who have earned the trust of both their supervisors and the public (Gilmour, 2008). This self-sustaining model is consistent with a more democratic division of labor. Police professionalization has considered professionalization of the individual officer through preparatory education and guided training, setting new standards as opposed to developing new capacities. A constant failure of police professionalization through individual improvement has been the command-and-control division of labor dominant in policing reform efforts. Though today's average individual police officer is better educated and better trained, the dominant command-and-control division of labor has typically used instrumental knowledge (Thacher, 2001) to aid this improved officer with use of problem solving and moral reasoning (examined below). Unfortunately, problem solving and moral reasoning require more flexibility of thought and inclusivity of ideas than instrumental knowledge allows in a given situation. High-quality problem-solving and moral decision-making entails value pluralism—the diversity of ends or goals existing in modern democratic societies (Thacher, 2001). Before reviewing problem-solving capacity and moral-reasoning capacity, this article will reconceptualize the division of labor within the professionalization of policing to yield insights into existing obstacles, i.e., instrumental rationality, technical bureaucrats, means-focusing, etc.

Conceptualizing a New Policing Ethos

This article aims to specify and extend a democratic approach building on the work of seminal scholars like John Dewey (2012) and Robert Merton (1973). This approach requires rethinking professionalization and promoting a new way of thinking drastically different from the increasingly outdated division of labor. In the existing division of labor, police professionals are mostly means-focused, except for the police leadership who engage as political actors with everything outside of police agencies on the ends or values. Even police leadership engages mostly as experts on means (technical bureaucrats) rather than actors engaged in deliberation and decision-making on values, priorities, and ends or goals of police in democratic societies. With a new division of labor, neither police leadership nor those outside of the police bureaucracy exclusively determine both means and ends of effective policing. Because as Dewey claimed (Dewey, 2012) ends are not fixed a priori this new division of labor sees ends as ends-in-view that vary depending upon circumstances. Placing both means and ends in the hands of capable police rank-and-file will more likely ensure democratic validation occurs because of their more frequent interactions with members of society. Increasing the cognitive capacities of the bureaucrats is central to moving policing forward in the 21st century because it alters the role of the bureaucrats in a democratic society and the relationship of the bureaucracy to the public.

The primary alteration of the bureaucracy proposed in this article is the increased cognitive capacities of the service providers within the policing bureaucracy. The cognitive capacities of these lower level bureaucrats can be increased, through education, training, and enhancement of a democratic police ethos as outlined below, ensuring that the ends of the bureaucracy are met in services provided to the public. Currently education and training in professionalization and division of labor are limited. Weapons-training, familiarity with code, and compliance with rules and procedures are important but do not reflect what officers confront in terms of which ends or values are of greater priority in any given incident and situation. As Willis (2013) argued, other values or ends (equity, legitimacy, liberty, and efficiency) come into play for policing professionals besides crime reduction. When police practices allow police officers to determine which values are relevant in any given situation and to determine alternative courses of action to achieve these values, then a democratic policing ethos will establish for police and allow for police to build and apply democratically validated knowledge of all types.

This article contends that the focus must be on increasing cognitive capacities of police to understand, involve, and participate in building and applying all forms of knowledge to address societal problems. Increasing the capacity of the bureaucrat may mean that the bureaucracies become less adversarial in nature because the bureaucrat will not only have the authority to address problem-solving, but as well undertake problem-framing or setting (Thacher, 2001); in other words, police bureaucrats will also have greater ability to both frame and solve problems. Simply freeing lower level police officers to use their personal judgments will not necessarily result in a better police department because the police bureaucracies are not addressing ethos of policing.

The application of Robert Merton's scientific ethos is this article's attempt to advance the police practices and the social science theory of police professionalization (Merton, 1973). While Merton (1973) did not address policing per se, his scientific ethos profoundly applies to professionalizing policing and democratizing the police division of labor. Through the application of this scientific ethos one can begin to see the importance for all levels of police bureaucracies to focus not just on the means of the bureaucracy, but also on the ends of the bureaucracy. Merton's general themes are fourfold. First, universalism applies to professionalized policing (as it does in science) whereby police need to use impersonal criteria for evaluating and validating both ends and means rather than using particularistic standards, which are often predetermined by individuals not at the forefront of democratic policing. These standards are problematic, among other reasons, for ignoring ends and failing to recognize the capacities of individual police officers. Secondly, as Merton would use the term, communism in professionalized policing refers to ownership of collective knowledge produced by police agents. All knowledge is communal, and restricting knowledge may encourage anti-democratic practices. The third theme of this ethos is disinterestedness. In the scientific realm peer controls are important in knowledge-building and application. Similarly, professionalized policing improves by extending greater control to peers. Finally, organized skepticism in science refers to reliance on empirically validated evidence obtained through application of multiple methodologies. Professional policing also needs continual evaluation and assessment to avoid blind adherence to established routines, articles of faith, vested procedures, and promotion of sacrosanct ideologies. Applying this scientific ethos to policing promotes not only individual discretion, but also democracy within bureaucracy and within the society. Further, Merton (1973) stated that in liberal democratic societies greater latitude for self-determination and autonomy assists societies and their institutions and professions by focusing collectively on both means and ends. In contrast, in non-democratic societies, most (if not all) institutions and professions are centrally-controlled and anti-rationalistic (Merton 1973). Thus, professionals of all kinds in democratic societies should be collectively considering, deliberating, and determining means and ends. The application of Merton's scientific ethos to policing should overcome existing anti-democratic tendencies remaining with bureaucracies.

Extending the work of scholars focused on promoting democracy in policing (Marenin, 2007; Sklansky, 2008) while remaining realistic in terms of the implementation of working democratic bureaucracies, this article demonstrates how discretion is possible in the context of professionalized policing. Tamanaha (1997, 2004, 2006) has examined the antidemocratic implications of an instrumental-rationality dominant rule of law in modern democratic societies. Similarly, this article details the undemocratic nature of instrumental rationality, dominant in modem policing: by focusing on cognitive capacities and a new policing ethos, it broadens the application of Tamanaha's perspective. The next section examines the division of labor dominating policing since the 20th century to the present with the two dominant forms of professionalization, command-and-control and discretionary. The following section specifies the conditions of democratic bureaucracies that will enhance police cognitive capacities to exercise discretion democratically. Using and modifying the democratic scientific ethos developed by Merton (1973), police can be professionals with theoretical and practical orientations that will enhance rather than contradict their roles as specialized professionals and contributing members of society.

Rethinking Professionalization: Towards a New Division of Labor

Developing policing as a profession with clear and consistent standards determined independently from a bureaucratic-centered division of labor is difficult because professionalization in police bureaucracies contains pressures to follow a top-down and command-and-control orientation with heavy emphasis on crime control and fighting, creation of a variety of rules to channel and control discretion, and focus on providing impersonal and objective policing for citizens (Walker, 1977). Historically upper-level bureaucrats viewed police professionals as technical experts with a specialized set of skills, organized and distributed within police departments, to contribute to the overall goals of crime fighting and control. The division of labor in police bureaucracies consists of multiple layers from rank-and-file (patrol officers), to specialist officers and detectives, to middle management, to the higher levels of administration and management. Again upper-level bureaucrats saw patrol officers as professionals due to their training mostly on the effective means to achieve the ends of policing. For example, using force in different situations to respond to calls for service and to address crimes, these officers are experts on the appropriate use of force due to their training and experience with weapons and different situations that they confront. Thacher (2001) characterized this specialist knowledge as instrumental knowledge, which ignores the many important value-laden decisions that police end up addressing. Moreover, upper-level bureaucrats do not consult with patrol officers about issues of which values should be prioritized in any given situation even when they end up confronting the inherent ambiguities of values or ends that exist in the real-world situations patrol officers confront daily.

The traditional view of professionalism in policing considers professionalism to be a major source of values or ends as determined by clients they serve, leadership, or a combination of the two. Literature in the field identifies two dominant forms of policing professionalism: command-orientation (or command-and-control) and discretionary (Potts, 1982; White, 1972). The former type of professionalism is crime-reduction focused with leadership-driven goals; the primary one is crime-fighting. In this form of professionalism, police professionals in police bureaucracies at the lowest levels are procedures-oriented and process-oriented. Police officers generally follow rules and procedures provided from the top of the hierarchy of police bureaucracies to ensure objective, impersonal, and efficient crime control. Since the 1950s with the due process revolution, policing professionals have been given greater emphasis on compliance with legal rules to protect suspect and defendant rights (Goldstein, 1990; Walker, 1977). Historically, this type of professionalism emerged in the early 20th century promoted by police leaders and innovators to remove politics, increase educational levels, and centralize and rationalize policing to become more efficient (Goldstein, 1990; Monnkonen, 1992; Uchida, 2009; Walker, 1977). As a consequence of a specialized division of labor to increase efficiencies of all tasks, command-orientation professionalism guards against politicization of the police bureaucracy. This autonomy or independence from politics leads to a focus on instrumental approaches to policing knowledge and its application (Thacher, 2001). In this type of professionalism, discretion is present but narrowly viewed and considered to require control. Willis (2013) argues that this type of professionalism is also consistent with scientific professionalism, including evidence-based approaches being promoted as critical for policing professionals today and for the future. Police professionals would become scientists making decisions and basing any action on evidence-validated knowledge.

While this top-down division of labor has been and is dominant, another form of professionalism has gained importance since the 1960s. In contrast to the emphasis on crime control and process, police officers in discretionary professionalism concern themselves with providing services and achieving a diverse range of outcomes. A great number of sources other than command-oriented professionalism provide values or ends. These can include local demands and pressures, community needs, and police officers' own role perceptions (White, 1972). These types of leaders view discretion positively for allowing flexibility and sensitivity to local conditions. These same leaders value experiential knowledge as a craft increasing the value of policing (Willis, 2013). Practical reasoning is accepted by these same individuals because police provide customized responses to local conditions, specific situations, and for specific populations, communities, groups, and individuals. These same professionals characterize professionalism as more democratic and allowing for police professionals to be human service providers (Willis, 2013).

The potential for politicization of policing at all levels of policing bureaucracies remains the main weakness of discretionary professionalism. Police officers run the risk of falling prey to being controlled by external forces that foster corruption, being captured and controlled from the outside, and undermining of police authority (Gilmour, 2008; Walker, 1977). The result may be that policing loses its autonomy and ability to self-regulate, driving policing to the latest fads or fashions such as ambiguous approaches to community policing. Moreover, leadership levels have not accepted discretionary professionalism with its inconsistencies and because it conflicts with the dominant bureaucratic professionalism on the primary value of crime-fighting and its attempt to control discretion while attempting to ensure uniform, fair, and objective policing. It appears both major types of professionalization co-exist (albeit with tensions and rifts) due to the continued reliance on an outdated division of labor and neglect of the importance of increasing the cognitive capacities of police at all levels of policing bureaucracies. Most of the pertinent literature on police professionalization ignores the problematic nature of the division of labor dominant in policing from its earliest manifestations to the present. The command-and-control division of labor also inhibits increasing the cognitive capacities police officers will need to develop professional policing based on individual improvements. The improvements highlighted here are problem-framing and problem-solving capacities and moral-reasoning capacity.

Problem-Framing and Problem-Solving Capacities

Certainly one can assume that the intellectual capacity of a police officer is comparable to the intellectual capacity of the citizens in the democracy the police officer serves. Individual police officers have more or fewer cognitive capacities, but cognitive capacities are largely ignored in existing policing standards. Many police organizations use entrance exams testing the individual's basic problem-solving skills. The assumption behind these tests is that police should have some minimum capability to solve problems (Goldstein, 1990; Marenin, 2007). Sometimes the test calls for logic and probability, and sometimes for general knowledge, but the focus remains on the individual's problem-solving ability. While the average police recruit demonstrates average problem-solving skills, it is reasonable to assume that the average police officer has better-than-average problem-solving ability. Formal education and experience may assist in the development of these skills. No doubt much of the training a police officer receives throughout his career focuses on problem-solving, and since democratic discretionary decisions may require not only resolution of the problem, but articulation of the resolution to those to whom the police officer is accountable, courses such as logic and/or dispute resolution would assist the officer in articulating his decision-making. These courses, as any other course, cannot guarantee a satisfactory resolution to every problem; however, the purpose of education is to enhance the capacity of the officer functioning in a democratic society. Success cannot be guaranteed, but, again, the goal of building discretionary capacity is to encourage democracy, not necessarily create a perfect state. Certainly, no guidance from a supervisor guarantees a satisfactory performance, and in fact, instrumental knowledge may in some cases actually inhibit the ability to think due to an exaggerated emphasis on means, neglecting ends or goals, and the inherent moral aspects in the exercise of discretion (Owen et al, 2012).

Moral Reasoning Capacity

Of course, the police recruit may be of outstanding moral character and his/her judgment very sound, but the problem is that for the purposes of accountability the police officer must not only make sound moral decisions, he/she must be able to articulate them. Most people are moral most of the time, and, of course, this truism applies to the police as well. While being moral is necessary, it is not sufficient; one must be able to articulate one's moral decision-making. Too often too much is made of the differences of morality between individuals so that one loses focus on the underlying similarities of differently perceived moral orientations. In American society most people are socialized into moral behavior. First-year college students are, for the most part, very moral even though most of them cannot define or describe what it means to be moral. They have an idea about how to treat others and may even have ideas based upon reciprocity or retribution as to why one should be moral, but they have a very difficult time articulating what they believe about morality. Police should have a better understanding of morality than the average first-year college student (Marenin, 2007); in fact, they should have a clear understanding of what it means to be moral and why they have assumed their private ideas of morality. Police officers in the same police department may not agree on the nature of morality, but if they can articulate their respective moral positions, then the public can determine whether each police officer's reasoning justifies the use of discretion. Police officers who can articulate a moral position and avoid prejudice, appeal to emotions, appeals to authority, and rationalizations will find support in a democratic society (Dworkin, 1977).

Police bureaucracies must not insist that there is a moral code that all officers must assume. Effective moral decision-making encourages a diversity of ideas and assumes that police accountability to the public should be based on the values critical to a democracy, i.e., freedom, equality, and fairness. Policing in a democracy places responsibility for fairness and justice not only upon the courts and police administrators, but on the individual police officer as well. Police accountability becomes a community responsibility using the same moral principles the police are expected to use. Increasing the moral capacity of the police officers does not imply that police become the moral arbitrators of a community, but before the police can articulate the reasons for each officer's actions and demonstrate the consistency of their actions and ideas to the public, they will need to increase their capacity for moral reasoning. The expectation is since police officers are capable of thought with an understanding of what morality means they can apply it to problem-framing and problem-solving, thus making legally valid and just decisions without overly depending on policy and precedent.

Increasing the cognitive capacity of the individual police officer will not necessarily produce the professional policing desirable in a democratic society. The restructuring of the division of labor must also accommodate this brand of police professionalization. In the next section, one can see that policing professionalization and democratic policing are not antithetical to each other. Rather, the focus on both process and outcomes is achievable through a new policing ethos that recognizes the cognitive capacities of policing professionals in democratized bureaucracies.

Democratizing Police Bureaucracies and Police Division of Labor

While increasing the capacities of the individual officer is important, the bureaucratic context in which the individual operates is also vital. Without attending to the issues Sklansky (2008) raised concerning the democratic nature of police bureaucracies, increasing the individual's intellectual capacities will only frustrate the individual police officer. A disgruntled police officer can undermine the law and even democracy itself. Merton's perspective on bureaucracies illustrates how increasing the individual's capacities can be related to the ethos of the bureaucracy providing a conducive environment for both the police officer with increased intellectual capacity and for democracy itself.

Policing bureaucracies, like many other types of bureaucracies, face problems with regard to communication across the strata, displacement of ends, and extreme fixation on means over ends (Kraska & Brent, 2011). Despite pressures to not fixate on status and to use impersonal criteria for validation, police organizations and their personnel often devalue the importance of discovering and validating means and ends of their work collectively and experientially to better serve the public. The main reason for this lack of trust and lack of emphasis on developing thinking skills relates to how the police bureaucracy operates with other societal institutions, especially in democratic contexts. This division of labor is idealized when leaders consider police rank-and-file bureaucrats as professionals (experts) on the means and are assumed to interact with the public only in a technical sense (following the law and using their training). In contrast, the public authorizes police management and leadership to deal with both ends and means, represent the bureaucracy, and are involved in broader democratic processes. Both police leadership and rank-and-file have limited interaction with scientific institutions, namely educational ones. Many police professionals regard educators as experts on empirical validation, but their influence is episodic and largely muted by political considerations, namely to determine funding levels for particular programs and to rationalize specific outcomes (or ends). Given that leadership has removed validation of ends from police bureaucrats except for themselves, the resulting state of affairs is problematic. Police officers cannot exercise discretion in relation to alternative ends and means but almost exclusively to pre-determined ends and limited means favored by the leaders of their organizations.

The moral standards of police rank-and-file and police leadership are also considerably different in police bureaucracies as well. While police leaders may not expect police rank-and-file to make moral decisions, they consider themselves to be the formal moral spokespersons and role models. Upper echelons in the police bureaucracy reduce moral standards for the lower level police personnel to procedural (legal) standards, while they are actively involved in reaffirming the morals through legal and other non-legal types of reasoning (Tamanaha, 2007 made the same point for judges and legal leaders). As a result, police often make choices solely on legal considerations without acknowledging the consequences of their choices on offenders, victims, communities, and other relevant parties. Command-and-control leaders excessively claim that discretionary decision-making is formal and any control of such decision-making is strongly protected by police leadership and police bureaucracies (see Marwah, 2012, for a history of discretionary decision-making in criminal justice).

Applying Merton's Scientific Ethos: Universalism and

Other Elements

The division of labor common to democratic policy-making and pragmatic problem-framing and problem-solving can inform policing and democracy relating to both means and ends (Dewey, 2012). Merton's (1973) ethos emphasized democracy and problem-setting and problem-solving as well as understanding the current constraints on the enhancement of policing discretion. While Merton (1973) provided an understanding of the ethos of science and the basic normative structure of science, the discussion on four institutional imperatives (universalism, communism, disinterestedness, organized skepticism) is directly linked with a more democratic policing bureaucracy with emphasis on cognitively capable police officers at all levels in the bureaucracy. Consider universalism, which Merton (1973) explained, refers to the use of pre-established impersonal criteria of validity for scientific knowledge building. One can apply this element of the ethos to knowledge-building in policing contexts, which requires police to exercise discretion without use of particularistic criteria in enforcing laws. In policing contexts and with the exercise of police discretion, universalism means avoiding using both legal and non-legal criteria that unduly impact particular individuals, groups, and organizations in society. The concern with consequences, attention to which moral and legal contexts apply in any given situation, and the need to validate decisions through discretion, assist police practitioners at all levels. Otherwise, particularistic discretionary decision-making is likely to prevail and conflict with democratic principles and practices. For Merton (1973), universalism is linked to democracy as a major guiding principle:

> Democratization is tantamount to the progressive elimination of restraints upon the exercise and development of socially valued capacities. Impersonal criteria of accomplishment and not fixation of status characterize the open democratic society (p. 273).

Merton's reference to universalism in science translates to universalism in policing if one considers knowledge-building in science and legalistic enforcement in policing. Enforcement of laws with only attention to the legal factors in any given incident or case is also part of most conceptualizations of the rule of law, but law enforcement in police is unlike science in that the level and degree of interaction with the public are considerably greater. From a traditional view of democratizing bureaucracies, enhancing engagement of police externally through police leadership or directly working with community members are sufficient. This engagement is accomplished mainly through obtaining inputs from legislators, government executives, and other individuals and groups involved in political decision-making. Using Merton's views, one should not equate democratizing policing solely through obtaining inputs and participation either internally from police personnel or externally from outside of police departments. Rather the emphasis should be on building competency on both means and ends-in-view for all levels of policing. Unlike the application of Merton's ethos to policing, traditional participatory management approaches give prominence to participation rather than competency. For example, Sklansky (2008) saw most police bureaucracies ignoring internal workplace democracy as the true form of democratic policing, but Sklansky (2008) seemed to think the divides between leadership and rank-and-file will be lessened by democratic determination of workplace rules and procedures. Further, legitimacy and public consent emphasizing the acceptance of procedures and rules for the purpose of overcoming the undemocratic influence of the policing subculture in terms of negative consequences to the public remains unaddressed. This emphasis may be due to Sklansky's (2008) neglect of capacity-building for an operating policing bureaucracy.

Communism, Disinterestedness, and Organized Skepticism

The other elements of the scientific ethos also are directly consequential to democratic policing as a democratic bureaucracy. Communism, which refers to common ownership of knowledge for the scientific ethos, may be better translated here as collective capacity to exercise discretion. Collective capacity signifies wider diffusion of wisdom and validated knowledge within police bureaucracies, which like many bureaucracies, are characterized by lack of sharing and communication between personnel at different levels in these organizations. A lack of discussion exists among all members of police bureaucracies about how discretion is exercised, being mindful of the consequences of discretionary choices, and examining morals and consequences underpinning discretionary choices. The cumulative properties of collectively validated discretion allow policing to be internally focused on means and ends as well as externally linked through the experiential exercise of discretion using this collective knowledge.

Similar to universalism, the third element of the scientific ethos, disinterestedness, concerns the establishment of peer controls at the institutional level to avoid having police focus on enhancing their professional status over discovering and testing effective means to achieve goals for policing as a whole. Police leadership and management disproportionately benefit from promotion and use of strategies and policing innovations that recognize their contributions. What is missing is an open and relatively uninterested dialogue on policing ends serving communities and society involving police at all levels. Further, lesser value is placed on the dialogue, discovery, and validation of broader ends if vested parties utilize inappropriate or invalidated means so that personalized and narrow, specific ends dominate. In policing bureaucracies, the divides between leadership and rank-and-file, even with a unified professional stance on being objective and using only legal factors in enforcement of the laws, are key to the lack of effective peer controls. The dominance of the policing subculture over professional norms specifically undermines and decreases formal peer controls as well as results in the predominance of informal norms and control. This dominance is also the area where ends displacement undermines development of a democratic policing bureaucracy. Discretionary capacity, with strong emphasis on legal and moral contexts, addresses the importance of peer controls (interests of police organizations and communities they served are more critical than individual or group-specific status-motivated means and ends) but does not directly address goals displacement and the development of an informal moral system with the policing subculture. However, discretionary capacity-building is more consistent with democratic policing in the potential for building cognitive capacity so as to lessen the negative aspects of a policing subculture.

The final element of the scientific ethos is critical for democratic policing because of the strong orientation to methodological (empirical) validation. Labeled "organized skepticism," this institutional mandate of science exists within data-driven policing innovations such as problem-oriented policing, intelligence-led policing, and focused deterrence and general criminal justice evidence-based approaches that have gained prominence in policing and criminal justice in recent decades (Willis, 2013). In these approaches, and consistent with a democratic policing ethos, testing and validation are ends in themselves, critical to addressing real problems and improving decision-making, more importantly democratizing validation across police and criminal justice organizations. Organized skepticism requires the continual consideration of assessment and evaluation, which are on-going efforts to allow for collective learning, refinement, and improvements, while being data-driven and relying on logic, empirics, and the analysis of consequences of discretionary decisions. These approaches share with democratic discretionary capacity-building the elements of collectively building cognitive capacities of practitioners simultaneously with the use of collectively validated decision-making.

However, on a cautionary note, these problem-solving and evidence-based approaches may be subject to the non-democratic tendencies of the other three elements of the scientific and policing ethos, limiting their effectiveness in terms of garnering democratic policing. The overreliance on the rule of law (external judicial restraints and internal rules and procedures) also bears noting (Tamanaha, 2004). Instead, validation through sharing experiences in decision-making and the exercise of discretionary capacity is consistently more democratic because of the inclusion and examination of the full range of causes and consequences through empirical and experiential validation. In summary, the four elements of the scientific ethos are critical to overcoming the cognitive cultural (meaning commonly held by society) constraints that limit the exercise of democratic discretion by the police. All four elements of Merton's scientific ethos as a whole are to be addressed to enhance a democratic policing ethos. These components of healthy and cognitive-capacity policing include avoiding the application of particularistic criteria in policing (the impersonal criteria towards building capacity in universalism), deemphasizing individualized capacity (knowledge) building (collectivism in the form of common ownership and validation), overcoming the narrowness and vested interests of singular and unique pursuit of recognition and status (use peer controls to reduce tendencies of self-interested police leaders through disinterestedness), and moving away from the use of strategies and practices that are preferred due to ideological, illogical, and unempirical reasons (integrating organized skepticism into the policing ethos).

While these elements address the leadership-personnel divides, the broader division of labor limits building discretionary capacity by extreme fixation on means and self-validation of these means. The dominance of representative democracy and expertise bureaucracy results in the determination of means being placed in the hands of police bureaucrats with the lack of validation of ends and narrow validation of means predominating. However, policing professionalization may be antithetical to validation and problem-solving by stressing an enlightened leadership over a capable rank-and-file. In this sense, the adoption of Merton's four elements for the democratic policing ethos seems less likely because of the lack of institutional support and limited democratic structure. Unlike Sklansky (2008), who views an internal rule of law as essential to workplace democracy, this article asserts that democratic policing flourishes under conditions of peer-centered capacity-building and minimal (only when supported by valid reason and empirical evidence) restraints on cognitive capacity-building. The prospects of such changes remain limited unless trust is placed with the police workforce to exercise its discretion as well as to develop the capacity to do so through democratizing its decision-making.

Conclusions

The value of a new policing ethos centered on cognitive capacities may be a critical missing element in existing literature on democratic policing and other bureaucracies. Most of the extant literature examines professionalization independently of democratization of policing. Sklansky (2008) and Goldstein (1990), for example, failed to recognize the capacities of police officers to discern meaningful ends of police bureaucracies. While police officers would benefit from becoming researchers and problem-solvers in problem-oriented policing, using Goldstein's approach, officers would still use instrumental rationality as technical bureaucrats. Applying Merton's scientific ethos to problem-oriented policing, police will also consider the ends or goals valuable for their work, departments, and society. While Sklansky (2008) in his important work correctly identified the importance of police rank-and-file in having voice and input in their workplaces, he ignored building their cognitive capacities.

This article offers a promising approach to address the exercise of police discretion so as to be consistent with democratic values and a democratic society by explicating the concept of capacity-focused democratic policing and its great promise to build the capacity of rank-and-file to democratize the exercise of their discretion. The benefits of this reorientation are numerous to professionalizing policing together with the democratizing policing. Ultimately, these benefits accrue precisely because they involve sharing of knowledge, and experience, and by using impersonal criteria in decision-making.

Democratic professionalism and discretionary capacity share particular institutional imperatives with the scientific ethos including universalism, communism, disinterestedness, and organized skepticism. In particular, the divide between police leaders and patrol officers may be lessened through institutional support for these four elements. However, the internal and external policing division of labor remains the largest obstacle to widespread adoption of democratic professionalism and discretionary capacity. The potential for police professionalism being used to promote democratic policing may be the best approach to promote a new policing ethos, one that allows for a capable, competent, and democratic policing workforce.

References

Dewey, J. (2012). *How we think.* New York: Renaissance Classics.

Dworkin, R. M. (1977). *The philosophy of law.* New York: Oxford University Press.

Gilmour, S. (2008). Why we trussed the police: Police governance and the problem of trust, *International Journal of Police Science and Management, 10*(1), 51–64.

Goldstein, H. (1990). *Problem-oriented policing.* New York: McGraw-Hill.

Kraska, P. & J.J. Brent (2011). *Theorizing criminal justice: Eight essential orientations.* Long Grove, IL: Waveland Press, Incorporated.

Marenin, O. (2007). Police training for democracy, *Police Practice and Research, 5*(2), 107–123.

Marwah, S. (2012). Discretionary decision-making. In W. Miller (Ed). *The social history of crime and punishment: An encyclopedia* (pp. 469–472). Thousand Oaks, CA: Sage Publications.

Merton, R.K. (1973). *The sociology of science: Theoretical and empirical investigations.* Chicago: The University of Chicago Press.

Monkkonen, E.H. (1992). A history of urban police, *Crime and Justice, 15,* 547–580.

Owen, S.S., H.F. Fradella, T.W. Burke & J.W. Joplin (2012). *Foundations of criminal justice.* New York: Oxford University Press.

Potts, L.W. (1982). *Police professionalism: Elusive or illusory?,* Criminal Justice Review, 7(2), 51–57.

Sklansky, D. (2008). *Democracy and the police.* Stanford, CA: Stanford University Press.

Tamanaha, B.Z. (1997). *Realistic socio-legal theory: Pragmatism and a social theory of law.* Oxford, UK: Oxford University Press.

Tamanaha, B.Z. (2004). *On the rule of law: History, politics, theory.* Cambridge: Cambridge University Press.

Tamanaha, B.Z. (2006). *Law as a means to an end: Threat to the rule of law.* Cambridge: Cambridge University Press.

Thacher, D. (2001). Policing is not a treatment: Alternatives to the medical model of police research, *Journal of Research in Crime and Delinquency, 38*(4), 387–415.

Uchida, C. (2009). The development of the American police: An historical overview. In R. Dunham & G. Alpert (Eds.). *Issues in policing: Contemporary readings* (pp. 17–36). Long Grove, IL; Waveland Press.

Walker, S. (1977). *A critical history of police reform: The emergence of professionalism.* Lexington, MA: Lexington Books.

White, S.O. (1972). A perspective of police professionalization, *Law and Society Review, 7*(1), 61–86.

Willis, J.J. (2013). Improving police: What's craft got to do with it? Retrieved from http://www.policefoundation.org/content/improving-police-whats-craft-got-do-it.

Critical Thinking Questions

1   How do instrumental knowledge and rationality prevent police officers from developing moral reasoning and problem-solving abilities?

2   How do the aspects of traditional policing professionalism conflict with the values of democracy?

3   What are the four elements of the new division of labor? How does the new division of labor resolve issues associated with traditional policing professionalism?

4   What are some challenges to implementing Joplin and Marwah's "new professionalism"? How could these challenges be overcome?

Part I Key Points

- While policing has become more professional, scholars argue that more needs to be done to fully achieve professionalism.
- The bureaucratic nature of policing does not recognize the experience and expertise of police officers.
- The decentralized nature of policing does not encourage the transfer of knowledge that is common to other professions.
- Moral training can help police officers to make ethical decisions while promoting democratic values by recognizing that not all situations can be resolved uniformly.

PART II

YOUTH PERCEPTIONS OF POLICE

Editors' Introduction

Generational differences in the role, status, and experiences with police officers will always exist. Historical accounts show policing as a field of high status and respect (part 1) to current incidents where police officers are questioned and slighted. Experiences with the police, as well as depictions of police officers and police work, shape interactions between them and their community members. A significant factor that impacts police perceptions arises from experiences. Media outlets, early socialization and family values, and peer influences also account for views of police officers. The awareness of police work and officer interactions continues to be a researched area in policing, though it may become more prevalent in the future with the existence of technology (e.g., smart phone and body cameras), social networking/media (e.g., Twitter and Facebook posts), and greater diversity (e.g., diverse police officers).

Today, young people may be more susceptible to media accounts about the police due to their connected lives, which provides a wealth of information at any day or time. Their personal experiences with the police can be intertwined with their digital lives through their YouTube videos and social networking posts. Media outlets function to provide fictional, entertainment, current events, and opinions on everything, including incidents with the police. In a time where the relationships between police and communities are fractured, understanding the views and thoughts of young people may help gauge the future of these interactions, policies, and programs to repair the communication and perceptions for both police officers and young people alike.

The readings for this section provide awareness of perceptions and communication issues as they impact police officer and youth interactions. Although the perceptions of police may not be sought as much from young people in comparison to adults, Sarre and Langos argue that views of police can factor into crime-control measures for not just adults but also juvenile offending. Building trust begins early in the socialization process through family, friends, and media outlets, though numerous other factors are also involved. Lurigio, Greenleaf, and Flexon show this complexity with their survey of high school students in Chicago. Experiences with the police, caring about their teachers, race and ethnicity of students, and other variables were examined, though they noted that numerous factors also influence youth interactions with police beyond their study. The last reading takes existing research and applies Allport's intergroup contact theory to program development in police and young people interactions. Youth and police experiences from a one-day Outward Bound/Baltimore Police Department program were examined and provide insight into future options. Understanding the perceptions of the police and young people will allow for greater awareness of truths for both groups to create a more accurate awareness of each other.

Editors' Introduction: Reading 2.1

The struggle for police agencies to maintain legitimacy for their role in law enforcement and protection of community members is not new. Police legitimacy represents the need and value perceived by the public that impacts their cooperation with policing efforts. This legitimacy can be attained through many facets that include crime-control efforts, mirroring existing legitimate organizations, and community outreach. Sarre and Langos add to police legitimacy efforts by calling for strategies to build trust among young people and the police. Early socialization efforts, in the places where youth are comfortable, may encourage police legitimacy for more positive police perceptions and greater cooperation throughout their lifetime. Innovative efforts by police organizations is imperative in a time where their legitimacy can be questioned and publicized daily through social media outlets.

Policing Young People: Can the Notion of Police Legitimacy Play a Role?

Rick Sarre and Colette Langos

Modern policing is predominantly focused on *responding* to crime. Although some proactive initiatives have been implemented to form part of the current policing framework, reactive strategies (focused on improving efficiency, shortening response times and enhancing 'clear-up' rates) continue to play the primary role in police practises. The defined 'functions' of police typically focus upon responding to emergency situations and preventing crime thereby. A reactive paradigm fits principally with what is understood as an 'instrumentalist' approach to crime reduction. Gary Becker (1974, 9) was a prime figure in instrumentalism. He theorized, for example, that a person will be more likely to commit an offense if the result of the crime (such as riches, or satisfaction arising out of an assault on another person) exceeds the expected result of directing his or her time and resources towards more law-abiding activities. Becker was also of the view that the probability of being caught and convicted has a much greater impact upon this weighing up of options than does the threat or severity of punishment (Becker, 1974, 11), a view that predominates in current discourse as well (see Balko, 2013). There is a corollary in broader policymaking too. Political strategies that see value in promising the implementation of 'tough on crime' policies continue to predominate to this day. They are based essentially on instrumentalist perspectives, and their attendant reactive approaches (Sarre, 2011).

One should not forget, of course, that proactive strategies have a role in policing too. For example, the South Australia Police (SAPOL) 'core functions' include crime prevention objectives (*Police Act 1998* (SA), section 5(c)), which will, presumably, involve the use of situational crime prevention tools such as 'target hardening' and 'designing out crime' (Sarre, 1997; 2003). Those training Victoria Police, too, have been instructed to ensure that proactive approaches to crime prevention are spliced into probationary training (Victorian Parliament, 2012, 126). If one looks internationally, one finds that there is no shortage of evidence that the most effective crime prevention-focused policing requires police to take a proactive approach (ICPC, 2011, 21). However, 'social' crime prevention strategies, such as providing community outreach schemes and pursuing educational and welfare objectives as a prophylactic against anti-social conduct, are not seen as predominant aims, or, indeed, may not be commonly within the bailiwick of police at all.

In other words, proactive crime prevention strategies are rarely in the forefront of the minds of police, nor are they typically, one might assume, in the minds of the public when they are asked to consider the police function. Hence these strategies do not become the focus of police performance measures. It is easy to see why this might be the case. For a start, reactive measures are easier to quantify and measure. It is far more difficult to count what *hasn't* happened. There is often political interference, too; that is, governments keep an eye out for reactive policing responses and highlight them when police feature in them, because politicians know that they need to keep voters happy, and voters are a lot happier, by and large, when policing is immediate and visible.

Thus, in reality, reactive strategies remain the dominant approaches employed by police in the fight against crime. Planning and training continues to be devoted primarily to improvements in police efficiency, response times and clearance rates. Moreover, where there *is* police proactivity in crime prevention, it is far more likely to be of the situational variety than the 'social or structural' variety.

It should not be forgotten, too, that the impact of policing on crime reduction is relatively small. Some twenty years ago David Bayley (1993) made the observation that 90% of the variation in crime rates among population aggregations of substantial size can be predicted by factors *other* than police strength, such as population density, ethnic heterogeneity, unemployment levels, income levels, school leaving rates, and single-parent households. A recent New South Wales Bureau of Crime Statistics and Research (BOCSAR) study reinforces this notion. Its results illustrate the minor roles that police intervention and the likelihood of imprisonment have on rates of crime, certainly when compared with a key demographic variable, namely household income levels (Wan, Moffatt, Jones, & Weatherbum, 2012). The BOCSAR researchers reviewed data from across all Local Council areas in New South Wales from 1996-2008. They examined the effect on violent crime and property crime of changes in the probability of imprisonment and the likelihood of arrest, and then reviewed correlations between the rates of crime and income levels. In relation to violent crime, the researchers determined that a 10% increase in *imprisonment* risk produces a 2% reduction in crime; while a 10% in *arrest* risk produces a 3% reduction in crime. In relation to property crime, the results were slightly different but with the same disparity, namely a 1% and 1.5% reduction in crime respectively. That is, there is evidence that the risk of apprehension is, indeed, a more predictive factor in crime trends (for both violence and property) than the severity of punishment.

However, the study revealed to the researchers that the strongest relationship influencing crime reduction was found not to be as a result of instrumentalist policies (of likelihood of police detection and deterrent punishment) but to household income. A 10% increase in household income correlates with a 15% reduction in violent crime, and a 19% reduction in property crime.

These results should not be surprising. In 2005, Pratt and Cullen reviewed 214 aggregate-level studies published between 1960 and 1999 for their evidence of effectiveness in reducing crime (Pratt & Cullen, 2005). They concluded from their meta-analysis that police expenditure, police numbers, and increases in penalties were among the *weakest* macro-level predictors of crime rates. That is, police have a necessary but not sufficient role in crime prevention and reduction. The outlier, they noted, was the incarceration rate, although they found some difficulty distinguishing between the deterrent effect of the threat (or certainty) of imprisonment and its obvious incapacitation effects (Pratt & Cullen, 2005, p. 417).

There is another thread in this argument, i.e. the growing inventory of compellingly argued work that details the criminality wrought by inequality and social destruction over which police have, arguably, little control. Not only are there strong correlations between lower crime rates and higher household income, as shown by Wan, Moffatt, Jones, and Weatherbum (2012), but there are strong correlations between high crime rates and rates of generational unemployment, mental illness, child neglect, family breakdown, and poverty.

For example, Elliott Currie (2008) has written on the links between child abuse and violent crime, and between school failure and crime (Currie, 2013). Don Weatherbum and Bronwyn Lind (1998) found that juveniles who reside in low socioeconomic neighborhoods are more likely to become involved in crime than those (matched on age, ethnicity, social class and gender) who do not reside in such neighborhoods. Poor child development, too, is a strong predictor of crime (Manning, Homel & Smith, 2010). Drawing on the work of Marmot and Wilkinson (2006), Richard Wilkinson and Kate Pickett (2009) found that economic impediments to citizens feeling valued (impediments such as low wages, low social security benefits and low public spending on housing and education, for example) are strong precursors of crime.

What does this mean for police? Surely one would assume that there is no place for police in driving 'social' crime prevention, given all of the emphasis upon reactive policing and the helplessness that police might feel when confronted with dysfunctional families, poor educational outcomes, Indigenous peoples' disadvantage, poverty and generational unemployment.

On the other hand, a case can be made out that police could and should be involved in fostering societal conditions that make it less likely for people to engage in criminal activity. This is because we now know more about why people *don't* commit crime (rather than why they *do*), and it is linked to police and people's trust in them.

With this premise the next section of this article examines how to use this information to enhance the police role in crime prevention. In this context the discussion focuses on the policing of young people.

Police Legitimacy—The Key to Crime Reduction?

Police legitimacy is one example of institutional legitimacy. Institutional legitimacy is 'the property that a rule or an authority has when others feel obliged to defer voluntarily' (Tyler, 2003, p. 307). It is a social value-based motivation—a normative feeling to obey a particular authority or institution (Sunshine & Tyler, 2003). The driving force behind the legitimacy of institutions is policies which shape an individual's voluntary deference and which builds trust in the institution/system. Police legitimacy relates to the obligation members of a community feel towards complying with the law and the decisions law enforcers (police) make. There is a growing body of research concluding that police legitimacy is correlated with greater public respect for and compliance with the law (Tyler 1990; Sunshine & Tyler, 2003; Tyler 2003). U.S., British, and European studies observe that police legitimacy has an independent influence on compliance, even when controls are placed on estimates of the risk of a person being caught and punished, peer disapproval, the morality of law breaking, performance evaluations of authorities, and demographic characteristics (Tyler & Huo, 2002; Tyler, 2003; Sunshine & Tyler, 2003; Tyler, 2007; Hough, Jackson, & Bradford, 2013a, 2013b; Bradford, Jackson, & Hough, 2013).

Findings from studies examining the association between police legitimacy and compliance suggest that procedural justice (fair and just processes along with respectful treatment of individuals) is fundamental to fostering public perceptions of police legitimacy (Tyler, 2003). These findings are supported by a recent European study examining public trust. The fifth European Social Survey (ESS) was conducted in 28 countries in 2010/2011 (Hough, Jackson, & Bradford, 2013b). The study found that trust in police procedural justice is the strongest and most consistent predictor of a 'felt obligation to obey,' the association being positive and significant in relation to all 26 countries for which a data set became available in 2012 (Hough et al., 2013b). On this view when people view the law and enforcers of the law as acting lawfully and being procedurally fair, they are more likely to defer to rules and to police decisions, and to self-regulate (Sarre, 2012; Tyler, 2003, Tyler & Fagan, 2008; Tankebe, 2013; Hough et al., 2013b). One way to establish positive beliefs regarding the fairness of police practises is to ensure that police are making consistent decisions rather than arbitrary and capricious judgments. According to Tyler, the quality of police decision-making improves when members of the public have the opportunity to be heard by police and when police explain their decisions in a frank and open manner (Tyler, 2003). Where police appear neutral and unbiased and their decisions are perceived as objective, the perceptions of fairness are enhanced (Tyler & Lind, 1992). The experience of being (and perception that one would be) treated with respect and dignity by police assists in building trust between the public and the police. Compliance and co-operation flows therefrom. This fosters police legitimacy, and, in turn, leads to less crime.

What does this mean for our reliance upon instrumentalist policies and reactive policing? Should there be a new emphasis? There is an argument that the answer to this question is 'yes' because the results of surveys show that Australians do not rate police highly in terms of fairness and reliability.

Recent data suggest that only 13.2% of adults (over the age of 18) "strongly agree" that "police can be relied upon" and only 16.8% of adults "strongly agree" that the "police treat people fairly" (Australian Bureau of Statistics, 2013). Whilst around 60% of Australia adults "agree" that police treat people fairly and can be relied upon, 20.2% of adults either "strongly disagree", "disagree" or have "no opinion", and 26.2% of adults either "strongly disagree", "disagree" or have "no opinion" that "police can be relied upon" (Australian Bureau of Statistics, 2013).

Given that perceived trust in police, fair treatment and quality of decision-making are predictors of police legitimacy (Jackson, Bradford, Hough, & Murray, 2012) it may be concluded that this is problematic and priorities may need to be realigned. Tyler posits the view that policy-makers ought to consider redirecting a portion of resources allocated to crime-fighting to developing initiatives focused on building the required trust (Tyler, 1990). He argues that motive-based voluntary compliance based upon perceptions of legitimacy is more economical and more effective over time than compliance based on instrumentalist strategies. That is, crime reduction will be more sustainable in the long term if we make policy choices that favor a broader normative approach over a narrower instrumentalist approach (Tyler 2003, p. 307). This will happen without policy-makers having to increase police numbers (which is an expensive justice option) or to enhance police powers.

The difference between the two approaches is simple: legitimacy functions on normative values supported by policies based on why people *comply* with the law. Instrumentalist strategies, in contrast, are driven by policies based on why people choose to *defy* the law, and seek to punish and deter them from such defiance.

The argument for the former view was well expressed by Antonio Buti (2011) in narrating the tale of the police 'verballing' of the Mickelberg brothers in the so-called 'Perth Mint swindle' in Western Australia in the 1980s:

> Police officers are society's protectors. It is imperative for a civil society, for a just society, that the police do not deny members, all members of the society, their basic human rights and engage in behavior that is corrupt and an abuse of processes. To do so runs the real risk of eroding public confidence in the policing institution necessary for a functioning civil society and for the proper and effective operation of the judiciary and government. ... Police officers, and prosecutors, who contemplate immoral and corrupt shortcuts to get the job done must remember the reason why, in criminal trials, our system of justice demands juries be satisfied beyond all reasonable doubt that the accused is guilty. (Buti, 2011. pp. 228, 229)

Police Legitimacy and Young People

Young people continue to have consistently higher rates of offending than older people (Commonwealth of Australia, 2010). The rate of juvenile offending (youth aged between 10 to 17 years) was consistently higher than that of adult offending for the period 2008–2011 (Australian Institute of Criminology, 2013). Moreover, recent data suggest young Australians aged between 15 to 19 years of age are more likely to be processed by police for the commission of a crime than any other age group (Australian Institute of Criminology, 2013). Given these trends, it is imperative that the policing of young people is accomplished correctly. The current Australian *National Youth Policing Model* aims to promote 'strong and immediate responses to problem behaviors' and advocates 'police participation in prevention and diversion strategies such as education and awareness programs' (Commonwealth of Australia, 2010). A multitude of community engagement projects such as Victoria Police–Assertive Youth Outreach Service; Northern Territory Police–Youth Diversion Scheme; Western Australia Police–Youth at Risk Diversion Programs); Northern Territory Police - School Based Policing; South Australia Police - Crime Prevention Education Program (Commonwealth of Australia, 2010) all have the potential to foster 'trust' and 'respect' in the law and police. One could theorize that this might advance police legitimacy in the eyes of young people.

Will this work to reduce juvenile crime? The argument is that if there are more young people who comply with the law (because they view police as being legitimate agents of the state), there will be less youth offending. Moreover, if young people are receptive to externally-driven values during their developmental years especially at transition points in their lives (France & Homel, 2006) then it is possible to instil legitimacy in the day to day relationships that children of any age have with police officers. Values education has been successfully applied in schools in relation to various social problems (Starratt, 1994). For example, 'acceptable behavior' campaigns (anti-aggression; anti-bullying; cyberbullying campaigns) aim to instil a normative value of respect in school children (by influencing their perceptions as to what is acceptable and unacceptable behavior), which, in turn, may influence a student's voluntary deference to comply with school behavior policies. The argument is that campaigns directed at fostering a positive perception towards police at a young age might instil normative value-based compliance with the law and its agents.

So, what are the most effective strategies for relaying information and communicating messages to young people? One idea emerged from an Australian Human Rights Commission study conducted by the Child Health Promotion Research Centre, Edith Cowan University (Perth, Western Australia). It was designed to identify the most effective strategy to be used to undertake a marketing campaign aimed at encouraging cyberbullying bystanders to take positive action when they witness the conduct (Thomas, Falconer, Cross, Monks and Brown, 2012). Findings from focus groups consisting of over 100 students from Catholic and Independent schools in Western Australia conducted between July 28 and 1 August 2011 identified YouTube (videos and trailers), television advertisements, a combined approach using YouTube and television advertisements, Facebook campaigns, and school-based activities (presentations) as most effective (Thomas et al., 2012). The findings shed new light on which strategies young people generally consider the most effective communication channels. Policies aimed at building trust in police are likely to be most influential when information is presented through these predominantly digital means of communication.

In light of the above discussions, key strategies for building trust in police practises are offered below:

1   Police should be developing online campaigns, including YouTube presentations and Facebook campaigns, aimed at building trust between police and young people by communicating that all people will be treated fairly, that police understand challenges young people face, that young people will be heard and that young people and adults alike will be treated with respect and courtesy.

2   Police should be encouraging further active engagement between themselves and school communities. This may be achieved by increasing the number of police presentations given at schools, including those aimed at encouraging the use of non-violent dispute resolution (Centre for Restorative Justice, 2009). Frequent school/community engagement is likely to assist young people to feel more comfortable with police, which, in turn, may encourage feelings of trust. It may be instructive to involve as presenters young people who have already come into contact with police and the justice system. The process of a young person relaying his or her lived experiences to other young people can be a powerful means of validating police messages. These peer-based intervention strategies can act as pivotal drivers for changing student norms (Willard, 2012).

3   Police should provide further training for all officers to improve their ability to communicate effectively with young people. A recent UK trial study published by the College of Policing reported that police officers who undertook classroom-based learning (focused on developing specific communication techniques broadly linked to procedural fairness) and scenario-based role play exercises improved officer attitudes and behaviors and victim perceptions of treatment by police (Wheller, Quinton, Fildes, & Mills, 2013). Although this study was conducted in relation to adults, employing a like model with the additional focus on teaching communication techniques known to be particularly effective in relation to youths could positively influence interactions police officers have with young people.

4   Long-term solutions should be developed to turn around the lives of vulnerable young people who are 'caught in the system' to minimize the number of youths who are simply 'passed' between police and any number of institutions/care services. Policies should be designed to strengthen relationships between police and professionals who have regular association with vulnerable youths (e.g. social workers; mental

health professionals; child protection officers and children's court lawyers); these should be designed to increase trust and respect for all appropriate government and non-govemment agencies.

Conclusion

They key issue is not whether police have a role to play in reducing crime (which of course they do), but to what extent they can best use their resources for greater crime—reductive effects. Justice policy-makers have traditionally and predominantly favored short-term answers to crime problems such as more police and enhanced police powers. Models of policing built upon costly, populist solutions, however, have been shown to be inadequate in maintaining law and order and reducing the rate of crime. It is perhaps time to seek a new involvement for police in crime prevention (especially around young people) by reference to legitimacy theory. It is argued here that young people are more likely to comply with the law if they view police as being legitimate agents of the state. If that legitimacy can be encouraged, then fewer offenses will be committed and fewer resources will be needed to fight crime in the short-term (youth offending) and in the long-term (adult offending). Fostering a positive perception of police at a young age is particularly important. To that end it would be prudent for policy-makers to adopt modem channels of communication to ensure policy messages enhancing police legitimacy reach as many young people as possible. These approaches and channels warrant further exploration, debate, and consideration.

References

Australian Bureau of Statistics (2013). *Crime Victimisation, Australia 2011–2012* (Catalogue 4530.0). Canberra.

Australian Institute of Criminology (2013). *Australian Crime: Facts and Figures 2012*. Canberra.

Balko, R. (2013). *Rise of the Warrior Cop*, Public Affairs Books, excerpts under title "They throw kids on the ground, put guns to their heads" - The horrors unleashed by police militarization, www.alternet.org/print/civil-liberties/police-brutality viewed July 16, 2013.

Bayley, D. (1993). Back from Wonderland, or Toward the Rational Use of Police Resources, in Dobb, A.N. (Ed.), *Thinking about Police Resources*. Toronto: Centre of Criminology Research Report No. 26, 1–34.

Becker, G. (1974). 'Crime and Punishment: An Economic Approach' in Becker G., and Landes, W. (Eds.), *Essays in the Economics of Crime and Punishment*, Ann Arbor: UMI, 1–54.

Bradford, B., Jackson, J. and Hough, M. (2013). Police Futures and Legitimacy: Redefining 'Good Policing', in Brown, J. (ed.), *The Future of Policing*: London: Routledge.

Buti, A. (2011). *Brothers: Justice, Corruption and the Mickelbergs*. Fremantle, WA: Fremantle Press.

Centre for Restorative Justice (2009). *Effectiveness of Restorative Justice Implementation in South Australian Schools.* Adelaide.

Commonwealth of Australia. (2010). *National Youth Policing Model.* Canberra.

Currie, E. (2008). *The Roots of Danger: Violent Crime in Global Perspective.* Upper Saddle River, NJ: Prentice Hall.

Currie, E. (2013). *Crime and Punishment in America: Why the Solutions to America's Most Stubborn Social Crisis Have Not Worked—and What Will.* (Revised edition). New York: Metropolitan Books.

France, A. and Homel, R. (2006). Pathways and Prevention: Concepts and Controversies. *Australian and New Zealand Journal of Criminology, 39,* 287–294.

Hough, M., Jackson, J. and Bradford, B. (2013a). Legitimacy, Trust and Compliance: An Empirical Test of Procedural Justice Theory Using the European Social Survey, in Tankebe, J. and Liebling, A. (eds.) *Legitimacy and Criminal Justice: An International Exploration,* Oxford: Oxford University Press.

Hough, M., Jackson, J. and Bradford, B. (2013b). Trust Injustice and the Legitimacy of Legal Authorities: Topline Findings from a Comparative European Study, in Gendrot, S., Hough, M., Levy, R., Kerezsi, K., and Snacken, S. (Eds.), *European Handbook of Criminology.* London: Routledge.

ICPC (2011). *Public-Private Partnerships and Community Safety: A Guide to Action.* International Centre for the Prevention of Crime, Montreal, Canada.

Jackson, J., Bradford, B., Hough, M., and Murray, K. H. (2012). Compliance with the Law and Policing by Consent: Notes on Police and Legal Legitimacy, in Crawford, A. and Hucklesby, A. (Eds.), *Legitimacy and Compliance in Criminal Justice.* London: Routledge.

Manning, M., Homel, R., and Smith C. (2010). A Meta-analysis of the Effects of Early developmental Prevention Programs in At-Risk Populations on Non-health Outcomes in Adolescence. *Children and Youth Services Review 32,* 506–19.

Marmot, M. and Wilkinson, R. (Eds.) (2006). *Social Determinants of Health* (2nd ed). Oxford: Oxford University Press.

Pratt, T. and Cullen F. (2005). Assessing Macro-level Predictors and Theories of Crime: A Meta-Analysis. *Crime and Justice 32,* 373–450.

Sarre, R. (1997). Crime Prevention and Police, in P. O'Malley and A. Sutton (eds), *Crime Prevention in Australia: Issues in Policy and Research,* Annandale: Federation Press, 64–83.

Sarre, R. (2003). Some Thoughts on the Relationship Between Crime Prevention and Policing in Contemporary Australia, in S.P. Lab and D. K. Das (eds), *International Perspectives on Community Policing and Crime Prevention,* Upper Saddle River, NJ: Prentice-Hall, 79–92.

Sarre, R. (2011). We get the crime we deserve: Exploring the political disconnect in crime policy, *James Cook University Law Journal, 18,* 144–161.

Sarre, R. (2012). Police, Legitimacy and Crime Prevention: What Are the Intersections? *Australasian Policing: Ajournai of Professional Practice and Research, 4*(2), 13–15.

Starratt, R. J. (1994). Building an Ethical School: A Practical Response to the Moral Crisis in Schools. London: The Falmer Press.

Sunshine, J. and Tyler T. (2003). The Role of Procedural Justice and Legitimacy in Shaping Public Support for Policing. *Law and Society Review 37,* 513–48.

Tankebe, J. (2013). Viewing Things Differently: The Dimensions of Public Perceptions of Police Legitimacy. *Criminology 51,* 103–135.

Thomas, L., Falconer, S., Cross D., Monks H., and Brown, D. (2012). *Cyberbullying and the Bystander: Research Findings and Insights Report.* Sydney: Australian Human Rights Commission.

Tyler, T. (1990). *Why People Obey the Law*. New Haven, CT: Yale University Press.

Tyler, T. (2003). Procedural Justice, Legitimacy, and the Effective Rule of Law. *Crime and Justice 30*, 283–357.

Tyler, T. (2007). *Legitimacy and Criminal Justice: International Perspectives*. New York: Russell Sage Foundation.

Tyler, T. and Fagan, J. (2008). Legitimacy and Cooperation: Why Do People Help the Police Fight Crime in Their Communities. *Ohio State Journal of Criminal Law 6*, 231–275.

Tyler, T. and Huo, Y.J. (2002). *Trust in the Law: Encouraging Public Cooperation with the Police and Courts*. New York: Russell Sage Foundation.

Tyler, T. and Lind, E.A. (1992). A Relational Model of Authority in Groups. *Advances in Experimental Social Psychology 25*, 115–191.

Victorian Parliament (2012) *Inquiry into* Locally Based Approaches to Community Safety and Crime Prevention: Final Report. Drugs and Alcohol Prevention Committee, Parliament of Victoria, Melbourne.

Wan, W-Y., Moffatt, S., Jones, C., and Weatherbum, D. (2012). The Effect of Arrest and Imprisonment on Crime. *Crime and Justice Bulletin* No. 158, 1–20.

Weatherbum, D. and Lind B. (1998). Poverty, Parenting, Peers and Crime-Prone Neighbourhoods. *Trends and Issues in Crime and Criminal Justice, No 85*. Canberra: Australian Institute of Criminology.

Wheller, L., Quinton, P., Fildes, A., and Mills, A. (2013). The Greater Manchester Police Procedural Justice Training Experiment: The Impact of Communication Skills Training on Officers and Victims of Crime. UK: College of Policing.

Wilkinson, R. and Pickett, K. (2009). *The Spirit Level: Why Greater Equality Makes Societies Stronger*. London: Allen Lane.

Willard, N. (2012). *Cyber Savvy: Embracing Digital Safety and Civility*. Thousand Oaks, CA: Corwin Press.

Critical Thinking Questions

1   What is police legitimacy? How does it influence people's compliance with the law?

2   What makes implementing social crime-prevention strategies difficult?

3   Why do police focus on reactive strategies?

4   What are some strategies the authors recommended for improving youth perceptions of policy legitimacy?

Editors' Introduction: Reading 2.2

In the United States, the 1960s marked public and disastrous examples of police brutality and discrimination against African American community members. These same actions were experienced by other racial and ethnic groups, though less noted due to their smaller number and silent voice. These experiences, though similar, might have different perceptions based on the group. Lurigio, Greenleaf, and Flexon explore this with their survey of Chicago youth. Although there were some similarities found among African American and Latino youth in regard to perceptions and relationships with the police, there were also several noted differences in their views. Their discussion provides thoughts on future research as well as the validity of "lumping" minorities into a single research variable.

The Effects of Race on Relationships with the Police

A Survey of African American and Latino Youths in Chicago

Arthur J. Lurigio, Richard G. Greenleaf, and Jamie L. Flexon

R ace is one of the most powerful variables explaining public attitudes toward the police (Skogan 2006). The majority of studies on race and perceptions of the police have explored differences between African Americans and Whites, concluding generally that African Americans are less satisfied with the police than are Whites (Browning, Cullen, Cao, Kopache, and Stevenson 1994; Ho and McKean 2004). The emphasis of previous research on black-white comparisons has left unanswered many questions about differences in minority group attitudes toward the police, especially differences between Latinos and African Americans (Martinez 2007). For example, do Latinos and African Americans have similar views of the police? Do minority groups have different perceptions about whether the police care about their neighborhoods? Are Latino and African American youths similarly stopped and treated disrespectfully by the police? In the current study, we pose these and other questions to a sample of minority students in Chicago's Public School System.

Recent population estimates show that Latinos are now the largest and fastest-growing minority group in the United States (Schaefer 2006). The Latino population in Chicago has been soaring since 2000 (Little 2007). Although considered a heterogeneous population, most Chicago Latinos have their roots in either Mexico or Puerto Rico. According to Schaefer (2006), Latinos differ from one another in their immigration experiences and cultural identities. Although they are brought together by a common language and shared media outlets (e.g., cable TV stations), most Latinos eschew panethnicity or solidarity among ethnic subgroups, preferring instead to be characterized as Mexican American, Cuban, or Puerto Rican. However, the members of these different Latino ethnic groups appear to have quite similar views about the police (Skogan and Steiner 2004).

Evidence suggests that African Americans and Latinos harbor different attitudes and perceptions regarding the police. For example, Skogan and Hartnett (1997) found that awareness of, participation in, and support for Chicago's community policing initiative, Chicago Alternative Policing Strategy (CAPS), were considerably lower among Latinos, as a whole, than among African Americans. Non-English-speaking Latinos in Chicago had particularly unfavorable views of the police and rarely communicated with the police. Skogan and Steiner (2004) also found that although Spanish-speaking residents live in the city's most troublesome communities with high rates of crime and disorder, they are the least likely group to initiate contact with the police. Walker, Spohn, and DeLone (2000) suggested that non-English-speaking Latinos are reluctant to communicate with the police because of the language barrier. Others fear that calling the police will trigger investigations of the immigration status of community residents.

On the one hand, African Americans and Latinos have historically had little in common other than membership in a subordinate class (Schaefer 2006). On the other hand, while African Americans and Latinos in Chicago have competed against each other for jobs and housing, social scientists and political pundits have observed that they have basic mutual interests that include fear of crime, safety in their neighborhoods, and the way they are treated by police officers (Skogan and Hartnett 1997). In the present study, we investigate whether direct contacts with the police affect young minorities' views of officers on key dependent measures.

Peterson and Krivo (2005) highlighted the relative absence of Latinos from criminological and criminal justice research and how this absence limits our understanding of the sources of racial and ethnic disparities in violent crime and criminal justice processing and our knowledge of broader racial and ethnic differences in residents' views of and relationships with police officers (Rosenbaum, Schuck, Costello, Hawkins, and Ring 2005). As Hagen, Shedd, and Payne (2005:384) noted, "While police attention to African American youth is frequent and therefore familiar (Anderson, 1999; Young, 2004), little is known about how Latino youth respond to their experiences with the police—perhaps in part because their experiences with the police are assumed to be less common."

The tremendous growth of the Latino population in the United States has changed the face of communities and has revealed as "obsolete" and simplistic police studies of race that focus on only black-white comparisons (Martinez 2007:57). In response to Martinez's (2007:62) persuasive recommendation to include Latinos in future "research on police treatment," the present investigation compared African American and Latino youths' feelings, attitudes, and behavioral intentions toward the police.

Importance of Studying Race

In terms of citizens' attitudes toward the police, race is perhaps the most studied of all personal characteristics, by itself and in interaction with other variables (e.g., age, gender, previous victimization) (Hurst 2007). Skogan (2006:101) maintained that, "All research on American's [sic] views of the police begins with race." Twenty independent studies, between the late 1960s and the 1970s, showed that African Americans had less favorable attitudes toward the police than did Whites (Peek, Lowe, and Alston 1981). For example, in an early study on the effects of race on perceptions of the police, Smith and Hawkins (1973) reported that African Americans of all ages had unfavorable attitudes toward the police whereas among Whites, older people had more favorable attitudes toward the police than younger people. We cite only a small sample of more recent studies in this vast literature.

African Americans are more likely than members of other racial groups to be victims of crime. They are also more likely to have negative contacts with the police, to be stopped disproportionately by the police, and to report incidents of police harassment and mistreatment (Anderson 1990, 1999; Erez 1984; Schafer, Huebner, and Bynum 2003; Tuch and Weitzer 1997). Skogan (2006) found that 70 percent of young African American males in Chicago reported being stopped by the police, compared to an average of only 20 percent of the total number of residents in the city.

Hagan, Shedd, and Payne (2005) found that African American students in Chicago were more likely than Latino or White students to have encounters with the police, while Latinos were more likely to respond negatively to these encounters than were other youths. Hagan et al. (2005) suggested that adolescent minorities' perceptions of "criminal injustice" and their hostility toward the police are fueled by their lack of attachment to school and their being subjected to frequent and unprovoked police stops. The authors decried the paucity of research on Latinos' responses to police contacts (see also Brown 2004; Martinez 2007).

In New York City, Tyler (2005) investigated two forms of trust in the police: institutional and motive-based. Institutional trust was measured by survey items such as, "I trust the leaders of the NYPD to make decisions that are good for everyone in the city" and "People's basic rights are well protected by the police." Motive-based trust was measured by survey items such as, "The police give honest explanations for their actions to people" and "The police consider the views of the people involved when deciding what to do." Tyler found that African Americans expressed less trust in the police than either Latinos or Whites on both forms of trust. All respondents rated the police slightly lower on institutional trust than on motive-based trust. Tyler concluded that a police officer's display of fairness in the exercise of duty was the most important factor in citizens' trust in the police.

In a national survey of the determinants of satisfaction with the police, Weitzer and Tuch (1999) reported that African American men were significantly less satisfied with the police than were African American women. The perception of personal safety in the neighborhood affected residents' satisfaction with the police. Those who resided in communities in which crime was a minor problem were more satisfied with the police than were those who resided in communities in which crime was a serious problem. Sampson and Bartusch (1998) reported that neighborhood disorder and concentrated poverty account largely for racial differences in satisfaction with the police.

Ho and McKean (2004) studied the relationship between residents and the police in North Carolina, concluding that race was the most important predictor of confidence in the police. African American residents were less likely to report confidence in police officers than were White residents. In addition, the risk of being a past or recent crime victim diminished residents' confidence in the police. Moreover, Hurst, Frank, and Browning (2000) reported that African American teenagers were more negative than White teenagers in their assessments of the police after street encounters even though their respective ratings of police treatment during those encounters were similar. A survey of ninth- and tenth-graders in Chicago found that both Latino and African American students believed that they were more likely than White students to be unfairly stopped and questioned by the police (Consortium on Chicago School Research 2002).

Rosenbaum, Schuck, Costello, Hawkins, and Ring (2005) indicated that vicarious experiences with the police in Chicago were significantly related to attitudes toward the police. Their findings suggested differences in how various racial and ethnic groups process their personal histories or past experiences with the police. The study found that African Americans were more likely to be affected by their indirect or vicarious experiences with the police than were members of other racial groups. Similarly, Weitzer and Tuch (2005) found that vicarious experiences with officers were correlated with lower approval ratings of the police among African Americans and Whites but not among Latinos. The researchers also argued that the mass media affect attitudes toward the police—particularly among African Americans, who are prominently featured in news stories about police officers' abuse of citizens.

Carter (1985) found that Latinos' perceptions of the police and expectations about future encounters with officers become more unfavorable with increasing contact between residents and officers. Hagan et al. (2005) speculated that a similar deterioration in views of the police is less likely to occur among African Americans because police harassment has become an "experience of the expected" (p. 384).

Importance of Studying Youths

Age is another prime predictor of attitudes toward the police (Skogan 2006). Negative, age-related perceptions of the police are associated with different factors. For example, contacts between juveniles and officers typically occur under contentious or adversarial conditions (e.g., being stopped, frisked, or arrested); young males are responsible for committing a significant proportion of crimes and are the most common targets of law enforcement interest (Skogan 2006).

Anti-police sentiments can also be an expression of young people's need for freedom and autonomy. In contrast, older residents are more likely to initiate contacts with the police and to be interested in safety and security issues (Reisig and Correia 1997).

In general, young people have unfavorable attitudes toward the police; they express little confidence in officers and rate them poorly on measures of competency, trust, and overall performance (Adams 1996; Borrero 2001; Decker 1981). Early and more recent studies indicate that negative encounters with the police lead to negative perceptions of officers (Friedman et al. 2004; Wellford 1973). Abusive incidents involving police officers and young people are grossly under-reported (Adams 1996). In interviews with mostly Latino and African American youths living in poor neighborhoods in Hartford, Connecticut, Borrero (2001) recorded hundreds of allegations of police misconduct against juveniles, including physical abuse, verbal harassment, threats, and violent attacks. Not surprisingly, the victims of excessive police force, who are disproportionately young minority males, have the most negative perceptions of the police (e.g., Ben-Ali 1992; Flanagan and Vaughn 1996).

Such encounters lay the foundation for longstanding hostility between the police and neighborhood residents. As adolescents become adults, they remain suspicious and distrustful of the police, decreasing the likelihood that they will report crimes and participate in community anticrime initiatives (Stoutland 2001). Hence, the study of young people's views of the police is critical as criminal justice-related beliefs, such as views of law enforcement officers, emerge and crystallize during middle adolescence and persist into adulthood (Bobo and Johnson 2004; Flanagan and Sherrod 1998; Niemi and Hepburn 1995).

Present Study

The present study explored whether the police-related views of African American and Latino students differ with respect to three major predictive factors. First, based on research showing that commitment to school can affect adolescents' views of the police (Agnew 2005; Levy 2001; Nihart, Lersch, Sellers, and Mieczkowski 2005), we measured youths' attitudes toward school and their teachers. Relying on tenets of social control theory (Hirschi 1969), we hypothesized that students who hold more positive views of school will express more favorable views of the police. Second, based on research showing that the adoption of prosocial values can affect adolescents' proclivities toward delinquent and criminal behaviors and, by extension, their views of the police (Kee, Sim, Teoh, Tian, and Ng 2003), we measured youths' endorsement of conventional beliefs. We hypothesize that juveniles who possess more conventional beliefs would express more favorable views of the police (Hirschi 1969). Third, based on research showing that police treatment of youths during street encounters can affect young people's views of the police (Friedman et al. 2004; Hurst and Frank 2000), we measured youths' experiences after they had been stopped by police officers. We hypothesized that students who had no contact with the police or who were treated respectfully during field contacts would express more favorable views of the police. Thus, demeaning treatment by officers would elicit distrust while fair treatment (or no experience of being stopped) would do the opposite (Tyler 2004).

We used three complementary dependent measures on which we compared African American and Latino youths. We asked them if they thought that the police cared about their neighborhoods. We also asked them whether they respected the police. Finally, we asked them if they would be inclined to help police officers who were in need of assistance. Because of the scarcity of research on racial differences in perceptions of the police among youths, we ventured no specific hypotheses about how Latino and African American adolescents would differ on these measures.

Methodology

Data Collection and Sample

Survey data for this study were obtained from students who were enrolled in 18 Chicago Public Schools in May 2000. Approval for this project was received from the Board of Education's Legal Department, which was highly concerned with maintaining student's confidentiality. Therefore, student surveys were anonymous and information was not collected on the characteristics of the individual schools. All survey data from the schools were aggregated. At each of the 18 high schools, research staff distributed surveys during advising periods that the school had reserved for standardized test administration.

The data were collected during regular school hours in accordance with each high school principal's directions. The questionnaire consisted of 131 items in open- and closed-ended response formats. The survey used several rating scales and explored numerous content domains: demographic characteristics, students' perceptions of the police, personal experiences with the police, and attitudes toward school and other social institutions. (For a more detailed description of the survey, see Friedman et al. 2004.)

A total of 943 students were asked to complete the questionnaire. The average completion time was 25 minutes. The completion rate for the survey was 94 percent ($n = 891$). A total of 47 surveys were incomplete or unusable, and five students refused to participate in the study. Nearly half of the students were freshmen, and 41 percent were juniors. The mean and median age of the students was 16 years. Approximately 55 percent of the respondents were African American, 28 percent were Latino, 7 percent were White, and 3 percent were Asian. Based on 2008 data from the Chicago Public Schools, 8 percent of Chicago's public high school students are white, and 86 percent are African American or Latino—percentages that closely match the racial composition of the current respondents < http://www.catalystchicago.org/guides/index. php?id=17>. The sample consisted of more females (55%) than males (46%). After we excluded all of the students who were neither Latino nor African American, a total of 732 respondents remained in our sample. Two-thirds of the youths in the sample were African American ($n = 490$) and one-third were Latino ($n = 242$).

Variables

Dependent variables

Three items were used to assess students' views of the police; all three were measured on a five-point Likert scale, ranging from "strongly agree" to "strongly disagree." The three measures were combined initially into one dependent variable or scale. However, the reliability coefficient of the scale was low, which suggested that the questions tapped into distinct aspects of students' reactions toward the police: their perceptions, feelings, and behavioral intentions.

The first dependent variable was measured by asking students if they believed that the police cared about what was good for their neighborhood (their perceptions). Higher values on this measure indicated that students believed that the police care about their neighborhoods whereas lower values indicated that students believed that the police did not care. The second dependent variable was measured by asking students whether they respected the police (their feelings). Higher values on this measure indicated that students respected the police whereas lower values indicated that students did not. The third dependent variable was measured by asking respondents whether they would assist a police officer in need of help (their behavioral intentions). Higher values on this measure indicated a willingness to assist officers whereas lower values indicated an unwillingness to help them.

Attitudes toward school and teachers

School is a primary vehicle for transmitting conventional values to students on a considerable breadth of issues, including appropriate deference toward authority figures, such as the police. Teachers are the agents of socialization who communicate those values in and out of the classroom. Hence, we included in the survey two items that measured students' attitudes toward school and teachers. The first item asked students whether they liked school. A five-point Likert scale, ranging from "strongly agree" to "strongly disagree," was used to measure students' responses to this question. Higher values indicated that students liked school whereas lower values indicated that students did not like school.

The second item asked students whether they cared about what their teachers thought of them. This variable was measured using a five-point Likert scale, ranging from "strongly agree" to "strongly disagree." Higher values indicated that students cared about their teachers' opinions of them whereas lower values indicated that students did not care about their teachers' opinions about them. Students who claim to like school and care what teachers think of them should be more attached to conventional values (or socially bonded) than those who claim to not like school or care what their teachers think of them. Hence, the former would have a greater commitment to prosocial activities and better relationships with authority figures than the latter (Hirschi 1969).

Prosocial beliefs

Two questions using a five-point Likert scale, ranging from "strongly agree" to "strongly disagree," measured students' thoughts about delinquent behavior. The first question asked students whether they believed that taking things without permission was acceptable. The second question asked them if they believed that delinquent behavior is harmful. The polarity of these questions was reversed so that higher scores on either of these measures indicated prosocial values whereas lower scores on either of these measures indicated pro-delinquent values.

Experiences with the police

A few studies have found that treatment by the police (respect versus disrespect) was an important predictor of juveniles' attitude toward the police (e.g., Friedman et al. 2004). In the present investigation, students' experiences with the police were measured by using a set of dummy variables. The dummy variables differentiated students not stopped by the police, students stopped and respected by the police, and students stopped and disrespected by the police. Students who were stopped and respected by the police were used as the comparison group for the analyses.

The variables used for not being stopped, being stopped and respected, or being stopped and disrespected by the police were generated from questions that followed a skip pattern in the survey instrument. Students were asked if the police had ever stopped them. Students were then asked whether they were respected or not during the stop. Ignoring the skip pattern in the survey would have introduced incidental selection bias into the model. Incidental selection bias is a methodological artifact that occurs when data are dropped from an analysis in an artificial (incidental to the method) instead of a random (non-artifactual) process.

Students who had not been stopped would have been excluded from the analysis through the incidental selection process. These students might be different from students who had been stopped on characteristics related to the study's outcomes; the not-stopped students would have been missed in the analysis unless they were captured by the survey structure and coding of the data. As mentioned above, dummy variables were created to prevent incidental selection bias and ensure that the entire sample of students (stopped and not stopped by the police) was included in the analyses.

The data were reviewed for inconsistencies in participants' responses and for coding errors that resulted from the survey's skip pattern. For example, some participants responded that they had not been stopped by the police but then indicated that they had been respected or disrespected by the police. Other variations in responses also created inconsistencies. A review of the data identified 37 cases (4%) with inconsistent responses, which were dropped from the analyses.

Control and selection variables

Gender was included in the analyses to control for gender-based differences in students' attitudes toward the police, which were reported in Friedman et al. (2004). Race was used as a

Table 2.2.1   Summary Statistics of Regression Variables

NAME	DESCRIPTION/QUESTION	CATEGORY	MIN	MAX	MEAN	SD	N
Independent Variables Like School	Question: "I like School"	African American[a]	1	5	3.5	1.2	446
		Latino[b]	1	5	3.4	1.1	225
Teachers	Question: "I care what my teacher think of me"	African American[a]	1	5	3.2	1.3	445
		Latino[b]	1	5	3.3	1.2	225
Stealing "not" OK	Question: "It's ok to take things that do not belong to you" [Reversed polarity to measure prosocial values]	African American[a]	1	5	3.7	1.5	445
		Latino[b]	1	5	3.5	1.4	223
Delinquency "not" OK	Question: "Most acts people call delinquent don't reailly hurt anyone" (Reversed polarity to measure prosocial values)	African American[a]	1	5	3.3	1.0	435
		Latino[b]	1	5	3.2	1.0	226
Experience	Dummy Variables;	African American[a]					
	i. Not stopped	i	0	1	.4	.5	453
	ii. Stopped and Respected (comparison group)	ii	0	1	.2	.4	463
	iii Stopped and not respected	iii	0	1	.4	.5	463
		Latino[b] i	0	1	.4	.5	235
		li	0	1	2	.4	237
		iiI	0	1	.3	.5	237
Control Variable Gender	Dichotomous variable measuring respondent sex. Male = 1; female = 0.	African American[a]	0	1	.4	.5	461
		Latino[b]	0	1	.5	.5	237
Dependent Variables Care	Question: "Police really care what is good for my neighborhood"	African American[a]	1	5	2.6	1.0	451
		Latino[b]	1	5	2.7	1.0	230
Respect	Question: "1 respect the police"	African American[a]	1	5	3.5	1.0	449
		Latino[b]	1	5	3.7	1.1	228
Assist	Question: "1 would assist a police officer if he/She needed help"	African American[a]	1	5	2.8	1.2	448
		Latino[b]	1	5	3.1	1.1	228

Note: Figures are rounded.   a. Selected for African Americans   b. Selected for Latinos

selection criterion to determine if the analytic models produced different results for African Americans and Latinos. Table 2.2.1 presents the survey items and summary statistics for each of the study's variables.

Analyses

Ordinary Least Squares (OLS) regression analysis (SPSS 14.0 for Windows) was used to estimate several models that compared African American and Latino students. The variance in each of the dependent measures was sufficient enough to obviate the use of ordinal regression analyses; that is, responses were not heavily concentrated in any one category of any of the dependent measures. OLS regression analysis was also selected for its ease of presentation and interpretation.

The data for African American and Latino students were analyzed in two separate regression models for two reasons: first, to simplify the description of the results on race (the interpretation of interaction terms can be a bit complicated) and second, to diminish the likelihood of multicollinearity. The separate-model approach to test the effects of race could have compromised the robustness of the findings because the number of cases of Latino students was smaller than the number of cases of African American students. Nonetheless, the number of cases available for each analysis was adequate.

Model 1 (African American students) and Model 2 (Latino students) are presented in Table 2.2.3 and examined youths' perceptions about whether the police cared about what is good for their neighborhoods. Model 3 (African American students) and Model 4 (Latino students) are presented in Table 2.2.4 and examined youths' respect for the police. Model 5 (African American students) and Model 6 (Latino students) explored youths' intentions to assist a police officer in need and are presented in Table 2.2.4. All models included the same set of predictor variables.

A cross-coefficient analysis was used to examine differences between the models for African Americans and Latinos. In order to ascertain if any differences in slopes between the models were true differences, a cross-coefficient z-test was computed using the following equation for the analysis (Paternoster, Brame, Mazerolle, and Piquero 1998):

$$Z = \frac{b_1 - b_2}{\sqrt{SBb_1^2 + SBb_2^2}}$$

The equation determines whether observed differences in slopes between sub-samples are statistically significant by generating a z-statistic that tests the null hypothesis that the regression coefficients in the two equations are equal (Paternoster et al. 1998). If the coefficients of the equations are equal, then the variables have similar slopes and predictive power. The significance level used for the cross-coefficient tests was $p = .10$.

Findings

Description of Study Variables

Roughly 50 percent of Latino and African American students agreed or strongly agreed that "they like school." African Americans (23%) were more likely to strongly agree with the statement than were Latinos (14%). Approximately half (48%) of Latinos and 43 percent of African Americans also agreed or strongly agreed that "they care about what their teacher thinks of them." Nearly 25 percent of African Americans and 29 percent of Latinos agreed or strongly agreed with the statement that "it is not wrong to take things that do not belong to you." Roughly 20 percent of

Table 2.2.2   Descriptive Analysis of Study Variables

VARIATILES		STRONGLY AGREE NO. (%)	AGREE NO. (%)	NEUTRAL NO. (%)	DISAGREE NO. (%)	STRONGLY DISAGREE NO. (%)
Independent Variables						
"I care what my teachers think of me"	AA	37 (19.0)	108 (23.6)	128 (18.0)	67 (14.7)	67 (14.7)
	Latino	42 (18.5)	68 (30.0)	67 (29.5)	24 (10.6)	26 (11.5)
"I like school"	AA	104 (22.8)	142 (31.1)	130 (28.4)	40 (8.8)	41 (9.0)
	Latino	32 (14.1)	83 (36.6)	75 (33.0)	20 (8.8)	17 (7.5)
"It is not wrong to take things"	AA	62 (13.4)	53 (11.5)	49 (10.6)	78 (16.9)	220 (47.6)
	Latino	27 (12.1)	37 (165)	32 (14.3)	47 (21.0)	81 (36.2)
"Delinquency does not hurt anyone"	AA	22 (4.8)	62 (13.7)	202 (44.5)	114 (25.1)	54 (11.9)
	Latino	10 (4.4)	37 (16.2)	101 (44.1)	53 (23.1)	28 (12.2)
		YES NO. (%)	NO NO. (%)			
"Have you ever been stopped by the police?"	AA	385 (39.5)	194 (40 5)			
	Latino	151 (54.6)	109 (45.4)			
"Were you treated with respect when you were stopped?"	AA	109 (38.4)	175 (61.6)			
	Latino	131 (51.6)	109 (45.4)			
(see Male- 1)[1]	AA	210 (43.1)	277 (56.9)			
	Latino	124 (51.2)	118 (48.8)			
		SRINGLY AGREE NO. (%)	AGREE NO. (%)	NEUTRAL NO. (%)	DNAGREE NO. (%)	SROETGLY DISTGRCE NO. (%)
Dependent Variables						
"If a police officer needed help ..."	AA	30 (6.6)	99 (21.7)	165 (36.1)	83 (182)	18 (17.5)
	Latino	21 (9.3)	70 (308)	83 (36.6)	29 (128)	24 (10.6)
"I respect the police"	AA	82 (17.9)	141 (30.9)	170 (37.2)	28 (6.1)	36 (7.9)
	Latino	53 (23.3)	92 (40.5)	56 (24.7)	10 (4.4)	16 (7.0)
"Police really care ..."	AA	13 (2.8)	55 (12.0)	201 (44.0)	108 (23.6)	80 (17.5)
	Latino	5 (2.2)	34 (15.0)	118 (52.0)	44 (19.4)	26 (11.5)

*56.9% of ??? American students are females, 48.8% of ??? with the females.

African American and Latino students agreed or strongly agreed that "things they call delinquent do not hurt anyone." In addition, a slightly higher percentage of African American students (60%) than Latino students (55%) reported being stopped by the police. Roughly 62 percent of African Americans and 60 percent of Latinos reported that the police disrespected them during the encounter (See Table 2.2.2). In the Chicago Consortium Study of Chicago Public School students in the ninth and tenth grades, 50 percent each of African Americans and Latinos youths reported that the police had stopped them in the past year (Consortium on Chicago School Research 2002).

Descriptive analyses of the three dependent variables (i.e., "Police care about my neighborhood," "I respect the police," and "I would assist an officer who needed help") showed that respondents had mixed views of the police. Approximately 50 percent of African Americans and 64 percent of Latinos agreed or strongly agreed with the statement, "I respect the police." However, only 15 percent of African Americans and 17 percent of Latinos agreed or strongly agreed with the statement, "The police really care about what is good for my neighborhood." Finally, 40 percent of Latinos but only 28 percent of African Americans responded affirmatively to the statement, "If a police officer needed help, I would be willing to assist him or her." Hence, African Americans' overall views of the police were more negative than Latinos' views.

Police Care about My Neighborhood (Models 1 and 2)

The results of Models 1 (African Americans) and 2 (Latinos) showed that students' experience with the police was significantly related to the study's first outcome variable. Specifically, for both African Americans and Latinos, being stopped and treated disrespectfully by officers negatively affected their perceptions of whether the police care about their neighborhoods ($b = -.59$ for African Americans; $b = -.51$ for Latinos). Being stopped by the police, per se, was not a significant predictor of this outcome for either group; how youths were treated when stopped mattered

Table 2.2.3   Regression Equations Examining Students Perception of Police Caring

PREDICTOR VARIABLES	AFRICAN AMERICAN		LATINOS	
	b	BETA	b	BETA
Like School	.055	.048	.169	.147
Teachers	.099	.099	.236	.230
Stealing not OK	−.065	−.069	−.042	−.048
Delinquency not OK	.094	.092	.104	.111
Not stopped[a]	.044	.020	−.125	−.063
Stooped and disrespected[b]	−.590**	−.249	−.510*	−.245
Stopped and respected[c]	...	...	...	...
Control:				
Gender[c]	.179	.079	.284	.144
Constant	2.19***	...	1.59***	...
F-test	2.93**		4.13***	
R²	.089		.245	
N	218		97	

Note: b Is the unstandardized coefficient: Beta is the standardized coefficient.
Figures are rounded.
a. Coded as 1 = (yes); 0 = (no)
b. Comparison group
c. Coded as 1 = (male); 0 = (female)
*p< 0.5   **p<.01   ***p<.001

more than merely being stopped. Students' perceptions of their teachers and school, and their prosocial beliefs also were statistically non-significant. The results from the cross-coefficient tests supported the regression results and showed no difference in the slopes of the models for African Americans and Latinos.

Respect for the Police (Models 3 and 4)

The model for African American youths (Model 3) demonstrated that respondents who cared what their teachers thought of them had more positive feelings toward police officers than those who cared little or not at all. This finding also applied to Latino respondents (Model 4). Hence, in Model 3 (African Americans) and Model 4 (Latinos), an association was found between respecting the police and students' caring about their teachers' opinions of them. Students who cared about their teachers' opinions were more likely to respect the police than those who did not (b = .32 for African Americans, b = .46 for Latinos).

The results in Model 3 also indicated that African Americans who had been stopped and disrespected expressed more negative feelings toward the police than those who were stopped and respected, showing again the importance of police treatment during street encounters (b = - .77). African American students who were disrespected were significantly

Table 2.2.4   Regression Equation Examining Students Perception of Respect for the Police

PREDICTOR VARIABLES	AFRICAN AMERICAN		LATINOS	
	b	BETA	b	BETA
Like School	.038	.031	.056	.042
Teachers	.324***	.303	.457***	−.384
Stealing not OK	.017	.017	.137	.135
Delinquency not OK	.008	.007	.191*	.176
Not stopped[a]	.105	−.045	.307	.133
Stopped and disrespected[h]	.770***	−.305	−.252	−.105
Stopped and respected[b]	...	...	...	...
Control:				
Gender[c]	−.142	−.059	−.075	−.033
Constant	2.800***	...	1.310**	...
F-test	7.110***		10.590***	
R^2	.192		.454	
N	217		97	

Note: b is the understandized coefficient; Beta is the standardized coefficient.
Figures are rounded.
a. Coded as 1 = (yes); 0 = (no)
b. Comparison group
c. Coded as 1 = (male); 0 = (female)
 *p ≤ 05** p ≤ .01 ***p ≤ .001

less likely to claim that they respected the police than were those who were respected. Being stopped and disrespected by the police was a slightly stronger predictor of African American juveniles' respect for the police than caring about their teachers' opinions of them. However, African Americans also were more likely than Latinos to report that the police had physically mistreated them. Thus, the difference between the two groups might be linked to the intensity of alleged police abuse. Parenthetically, several students claimed that police officers hit and pushed them, pulled a gun on them, and made them lie face down on the ground. Examples of verbal abuse by police officers included being ridiculed, humiliated, called names, and asked inappropriate questions.

Unlike the model for African American youths, Latino students' experiences with the police had no significant effect on their respect for the police. Therefore, in Model 4 (Latinos), no significant relationship was found between police treatment and students' respect for the police. Thus, Latino and African American youths differed on the measure of respect for the police. The model for Latinos (Model 4) also differed from the model for African Americans (Model 3) on another variable. Specifically, Latinos who thought that delinquent acts were harmful were more likely to respect the police (b = .19); African American students were not.

The cross-coefficient analysis supported the differences between Models 3 and 4. The z-test of different slopes in the African American and Latino models for the delinquency variable was statistically significant (p = .06). The z-test that examined the difference between African American and Latino students on being disrespected by the police was also statistically significant (p = .05). These results are consistent with the differences between African American and Latino students that were found in the regression models for experience with the police.

Assisting the Police (Models 5 and 6)

For African American and Latino youths, being pro-school was related to their expressed intentions to aid officers in need of help. The results also suggested that being disrespected by the police negatively affected both African Americans' and Latinos' willingness to assist the police (b = −72 for African Americans; b = − .57 for Latinos). In addition, caring about teachers' opinions of them was related positively to the willingness of students in both groups to assist the police (b = .22 for African Americans, b = .37 for Latinos). The models for African Americans and Latinos differed from each other on the delinquent values variable. Among African Americans, the results showed that believing that delinquency is harmful was negatively related to whether students would assist the police (b = − .18). For Latinos, the belief that stealing was wrong was positively associated with the expressed willingness to assist police officers.

The cross-coefficient z results supported the differences found in the regression analyses for Models 5 and 6. The z-tests of the differences between African American and Latino youths on believing that stealing is wrong and on willingness to assist officers were statistically significant (p = .05). The difference between the models on the belief that delinquency is harmful and

Table 2.2.5 Regression Equations Examining Students Willingness to Assist the Police

PREDICTOR VARIABLES	AFRICAN AMERICAN		LATINOS	
	b	BETA	b	BETA
Like School	.114	.089	.027	.020
Teachers	.219**	.193	.367*	.299
Stealing note OK	.003	.003	,198*	.189
Delinquency not OK	−.181*	−.157	.138	.124
Nol Stopped[a]	−.330	−.132	−.185	−.077
Stopped and disrespected[b]	..719**	−.268	−.574*	−.231
Stopped and respected[b] Control:	...	...	...	...
Gender[c]	−.222	−.086	.206	.087
Constant	2.990***	...	1.127*	...
F-test	4.820***		5.109***	
R^2	.137		.287	
N	220		97	

Note: b is the unstandardized coefficient; Beta is the standardized coefficient.
Figures are rounded.
a. Coded as 1−(yes); 0 = (no)
b. Comparison group
c. Coded as 1 = (male); 0 = (female)
  *$p \le .05$ **$p \le .01$ ***$p \le .001$

its association with a willingness to assist officers was also supported by the cross-coefficient analysis ($p = .01$).

Summary and Conclusions

Several similarities were found between Latino and African American students on the dependent measures. Both African Americans and Latinos who had been stopped and disrespected by the police were less willing to assist them and less likely to believe that the police care about their neighborhoods. Moreover, both Latinos and African Americans who indicated that they cared what their teachers thought of them were more likely to report that they would assist the police and that they respected the police, compared to students who cared less about what their teachers thought of them.

A notable distinction was found between African American and Latino respondents on the delinquent-values variable. Although the beta was not as robust as others in the analyses, Latinos who disapproved of delinquent acts were more likely to respect the police than those who did not. This variable failed to reach statistical significance for African Americans. However, the findings showed that African Americans who believed delinquency was acceptable were more likely to report that they would assist an officer in need of help. This variable did not reach statistical significance for Latinos. Furthermore, being stopped and disrespected was statistically significant only in predicting African American students' respect for the police. No difference was found between Latinos who were stopped and disrespected and those who were stopped and respected on this outcome variable.

Unlike previous studies, contact with the police, by itself, had no negative effects on attitudes, feelings, or behavioral intentions (Sced 2004). However, police treatment during encounters was the most important factor associated with the dependent measures. Among African Americans, police disrespect was strongly related to all three outcome variables, suggesting that adverse contact between police officers and such youths might have an additive rather than a habituating effect on juveniles' reactions to the police (Hagan et al. 2005). This result is germane to the findings of Sunshine and Tyler (2003) who noted that the police can aggressively fight crime and cultivate constructive relationships with community residents only if officers are perceived as legitimate authorities. Community residents will be more inclined to cooperate with the police if they have been treated with fairness and respect. Law enforcement officers' emphasis on process issues or procedural justice can have a positive effect on all racial and ethnic groups.

As a number of other studies have demonstrated, process matters. Residents care as much or more about the nature and tenor of police encounters as they do about the outcomes of those encounters (Tyler 2004). Police officers hold all the power in interactions with juveniles and generally view them with suspicion and disdain (Skogan 2006). Such negative presuppositions promote disrespect toward juveniles, which can have lasting, pernicious effects on police-community relations. In accordance with the principles of asymmetry, negative experiences with the police weigh more heavily in the development of police-related attitudes and perceptions than positive experiences do (Skogan 2006).

Because of the inchoate nature of young people's views of the police, their perceptions are still amenable to change in response to vicarious and direct experiences with police officers (Brunson 2007; Hurst and Frank 2000). Officers should therefore be trained, using realistic scenarios (simulations), in effective techniques for defusing volatile situations with juveniles. Also useful might be open forums for young people and officers that encourage a mutual airing and resolution of grievances (Friedman et al. 2004). The Chicago Alternative Policing Strategy (CAPS) lends itself to such interactions through beat meetings, which are an integral component of Chicago's community policing program. Adolescents of color should have numerous opportunities for favorable interactions with the police to balance the contentious and adversarial experiences that they have with officers during typical street encounters (Dean 1980).

The relationship between caring about teachers and having more favorable perceptions of the police might simply reflect generally positive sentiments toward authority figures. Students who are closer to their teachers might be more likely to view police officers similarly, as helpful and caring adults. Unlike their African American counterparts, Latino students remained respectful of the police even in the face of police disrespectfulness, which might suggest cultural differences between the two groups in terms of deference toward adults in positions of authority. For example, the offering of respect (respeto) toward authority figures is a deeply-rooted value in most Latino households, and it could explain why disrespected Latino juveniles remained respectful toward the police, unlike their African American counterparts (Understanding Bilingual and Monolingual Latino Consumers n.d.).

Among Latino students, prosocial views made youths more favorably inclined toward police officers, whereas among African American students, pro-delinquency views did. By their endorsement of an antisocial statement, African Americans might be recognizing the challenge of policing in high-crime neighborhoods in which antisocial attitudes are more common among younger residents. However, this inconsistency defies ready explanation and might be an artifact of the sample or the measure.

Study Limitations

Contextual or environmental variables can be an important component of research on police-community relations. Nonetheless, the current study was unable to explore the influence of social ecology on juveniles' attitudes toward the police (i.e., neighborhood-level variables), which is an obvious shortcoming of this investigation. As several researchers have observed, neighborhood-level variables can have considerable explanatory power. For example, ecological factors, such as social disorganization or community disorder (e.g, graffiti, vagrancy, drugs, loitering, vandalism, noise, crime), could spawn mistrust and fear of the police (Ross and Joon Jang 2000). Styles of policing in different neighborhoods—another contextual variable—are also critical to research on youth-police relations. Officers' maltreatment of residents or excessive applications of their legal authority have been linked to the order maintenance policing approach, which is applied in varying degrees in Chicago communities (Skogan and Hartnett 1997). "[This] approach privileges the law abider who cares for his home, his lawn, and his children, and the neighborhood merchant. It frowns on the unattached adult and the kids hanging out on corners" (Harcourt 2001:127).

Negative officer perceptions about the communities they patrol can significantly affect the outcome of interactions with young people. For example, in a Canadian study, Schulenberg (2003) found that social disorganization and urban growth affected police behavior toward residents. Regrettably, the current study could not shed light on the impact of the juveniles' neighborhoods on their attitudes toward the police.

The present sample consisted of youths enrolled in public high schools and failed to include dropouts. In addition, juveniles who were enrolled in private or parochial schools were not surveyed. These youngsters might have qualitatively different experiences with and attitudes toward the police, compared to the respondents in the current study. Future researchers should directly observe police-youth interactions in order to assess the validity of the students' reported experiences with officers. Similarly, future researchers should examine police officers' experiences with Chicago's young people from the standpoint of officers who interact frequently with the city's youths.

References

Adams, Kenneth. 1996. "Measuring the Prevalence of Police Abuse of Force." Pp. 52–93 in *Police Violence: Understanding and Controlling Police Abuse of Force*, edited by W. Geller and H. Toch. New Haven, CT: Yale University Press.

Agnew, Robert. 2005. *Juvenile Delinquency: Cause and Control, 2nd ed.* Los Angeles, CA: Roxbury.

Anderson, Elijah. 1990. *Code of the Streets: Decency, Violence and the Moral Life of the Inner City.* New York: Norton.

Anderson, Elijah. 1999. *Streetwise: Race, Class, and Change in an Urban Community.* Chicago, IL: University of Chicago Press.

Ben-Ali, R. 1992. "Deadly Force Wish: An Uneasy L.A. Truce." *Newsday*, May 10, p.7.

Bobo, Lawrence and Devon Johnson. 2004. "A Taste for Punishment: Black and White Americans' Views on the Death Penalty and the War on Drugs." *Du Bois Review* 1:151–80.

Borrero, Michael. 2001. "The Widening Mistrust between Youth and Police." *Families and Society: The Journal of Contemporary Human Services* 82:399–408.

Brown, Ben. 2004. "Community Policing in a Diverse Society." *Law Enforcement Executive Forum* 4:49–56.

Browning, S., F. Cullen, L. Cao, R. Kopache, and T. Stevenson. 1994. "Race and Getting Hassled by the Police." *Police Studies* 17:1–12.

Brunson, Rod. 2007. "Police Don't Like Black People: African American Young Men's Accumulated Police Experience." *Criminology and Public Policy* 6:71–102.

Carter, David. 1985. "Hispanic Perception of Police Performance: An Empirical Assessment." *Journal of Criminal Justice* 13:487–500.

Consortium on Chicago School Research. 2002. *Public Use Data Set: User's Manual.* Retrieved March 5, 2005 (www.consortium-chicago.org).

Dean, D. 1980. "Citizen Ratings of the Police: The Difference Police Contact Makes." *Law and Police Quarterly* 2:445–471.

Decker, Scott. 1981. "Citizen Attitudes toward the Police: A Review of the Past Findings and Suggestions for Future Policy." *Journal of Police Science and Administration* 9:80–87

Erez, Edna. 1984. "Self-Defined Desert and Citizens' Assessment of the Police." *Journal of Criminal Law and Criminology* 75:1275–1299.

Flanagan, Constance and Lonnie Sherrod. 1998. "Youth Political Development." *Journal of Social Issues* 54:447–56.

Flanagan, Timothy and Michael Vaughn. 1996. "Public Opinion about Police Abuse and Force." Pp. 113–128 in *Police Violence*, edited by W. Geller and H. Toch. New Haven, CT: Yale University Press.

Friedman, Warren, Arthur J. Lurigio, Richard G. Greenleaf, and Stephanie Albertson. 2004. "Encounters between Police and Youth: Social Costs of Disrespect." *Journal of Crime and Justice* 27:1–25.

Hagan, John, Carla Shedd, and Monique Payne. 2005. "Race, Ethnicity and Youth Perception of Criminal Injustice." *American Sociological Review* 70:381–407.

Harcourt, Bernard E. 2001. *Illusion of Order: The False Promise of Broken Windows Policing.* Cambridge, MA: Harvard University Press.

Hirschi, Travis. 1969. *Causes of Delinquency.* Berkeley, CA: University of California Press.

Ho, Taiping and Jerome McKean. 2004. "Confidence in the Police and Perceptions of Risk." *Western Criminology Review* 5:108–118.

Hurst, Yolander. 2007. "Juvenile Attitudes toward the Police: An Examination of Rural Youth." *Criminal Justice Review* 32:121–141.

Hurst, Yolander and James Frank. 2000. "How Kids View Cops: The Nature of Juvenile Attitudes toward the Police." *Journal of Criminal Justice* 28:189–202.

Hurst, Yolander, James Frank, and Sandra Browning. 2000. "The Attitudes of Juveniles toward the Police: A Comparison of Black and White Youth." *Policing: An International Journal of Police Strategies and Management* 23:37–53.

Kee, C., K. Sim, J. Teoh, C.S. Tian, and K. Ng. 2003. "Individual and Familial Characteristics of Youths Involved in Street Corner Gangs in Singapore." *Journal of Adolescence* 26:401–412.

Levy, Kenneth. 2001. "The Relationship between Adolescent Attitudes toward Authority, Self-Concept, and Delinquency." *Adolescence* 36:333–346.

Little, Darnell. 2007. "Census Measures Ethnic Shifts." *Chicago Tribune,* August 9.

Martinez, Ramiro, Jr. 2007. "Incorporating Latinos and Immigrants into Policing Research." *Criminology and Public Policy* 6:57–64.

Niemi, Richard and Mary Hepburn. 1995. "The Rebirth of Political Socialization." *Perspectives on Political Science* 24:7–16.

Nihart, Terry, Kim Lersch, Christine Sellers, and Tom Mieczkowski. 2005. "Kids, Cops, Parents and Teachers: Exploring Juvenile Attitudes toward Authority Figures." *Western Criminology Review* 6:79–888.

Paternoster, Raymond, Robert Brame, Paul Mazerolle, and Alex Piquero. 1998. "Using the Correct Statistical Test for the Equality of Regression Coefficients." *Criminology* 36:859–866.

Peek, Charles W., George D. Lowe, and Jon P. Alston. 1981. "Race and Attitudes toward Local Police: Another Look." *Journal of Black Studies* 11:361–374.

Peterson, Ruth D. and Lauren J. Krivo. 2005. "Macrostructural Analyses of Race, Ethnicity and Violent Crime: Recent Lessons and New Directions for Research." *Annual Review of Sociology* 31:331–356.

Reisig, Michael D. and Michael Correia. 1997. "Public Evaluation of Police Performance: An Analysis across Three Levels of Policing." *Policing: An International Journal of Police Strategies and Management* 20:311–325.

Rosenbaum, Dennis P., Amie M. Schuck, Sandra K. Costello, Darnell F. Hawkins, and Marianne K Ring. 2005. "Attitudes toward the Police: The Effects of Direct and Vicarious Experience." *Police Quarterly* 8:343–365.

Ross, Catherine and Sung Joon Jang. 2000. "Neighborhood Disorder, Fear, and Mistrust: The Buffering Role of Social Ties with Neighbors." *American Journal of Community Psychology* 28:401–420.

Sampson, Robert and Dawn Bartush. 1998. "Legal Cynicism and (Subcultural?) Tolerance of Deviance: The Neighborhood Context of Racial Differences." *Law & Society Review* 32:777–804.

Schaefer, Richard T. 2006. *Racial and Ethnic Groups,* 10th ed. Upper Saddle River, NJ: Pearson/Prentice Hall.

Schafer, Joseph, Beth Huebner, and Timothy Bynum. 2003. "Citizens' Perceptions of Police Services: Race, Neighborhood Context and Community Policing." *Police Quarterly* 6:440–468.

Schulenberg, Jennifer L. 2003. "The Social Context of Police Discretion with Young Offenders: An Ecological Analysis." *Canadian Journal of Criminology and Criminal Justice* 45:127–157.

Sampson, Michelle. 2004. *Public Satisfaction with Police Contact. Part I: Police Initiated Contacts.* Adelaide, Australia: Australasian Center for Policing Research.

Skogan, Wesley. 2006. "Asymmetry in the Impact of Encounters with Police." *Policing & Society* 16:99–126.

Skogan, Wesley G. and Susan Hartnett. 1997. *Community Policing: Chicago Style.* New York: Oxford.

Skogan, Wesley G. and Lynn Steiner. 2004. "Crime, Disorder and Decay in Chicago's Latino Community." *Journal of Ethnicity in Criminal Justice* 2:7–26.

Stoutland, Sara. 2001. "The Multiple Dimensions of Trust in Resident/Police Relations." *Journal of Research in Crime and Delinquency* 33:226–256.

Smith, P.E. and R. Hawkins. 1973. "Victimization, Types of Citizen-Police Contacts." *Law & Society Review* 1:135–152.

Sunshine, Jason and Tom Tyler. 2003. "The Role of Procedural Justice and Legitimacy in Shaping Public Support for Policing." *Law and Society Review* 37:513–548.

Tuch, Steven and Ronald Weitzer. 1997. "The Polls: Racial Differences in Attitudes toward the Police." *Public Opinion Quarterly* 61:642–663.

Tyler, Tom. 2004. "Enhancing Police Legitimacy." *The Annals of the American Academy of Political and Social Science* 593:84–99.

Tyler, Tom. 2005. "Policing in Black and White: Ethnic Group Differences in Trust and Confidence in the Police." *Police Quarterly* 8:322–342.

Understanding Bilingual and Monolingual Latino Consumers. nd. retrieved at www.calpoison.org/hcp/Hispanic-findings.pdf.

Walker, Samuel, C. Spohn, and M. DeLone. 2000. *The Color of Justice.* Belmont, CA: Wadsworth.

Weitzer, Ronald and Steven Tuch. 1999. "Race, Class and Perceptions of Discrimination by the Police." *Crime and Delinquency* 45:494–507.

Wellford, C.F. 1973. "Age Composition and the Increase in Record Time." *Criminology* 11:61–70.

Young, Alford. 2004. *The Minds of Marginalized Black Men: Making Sense of Mobility, Opportunity and Future Life Changes.* Princeton, NJ: Princeton University Press.

Critical Thinking Questions

1   How can strained community-police relationships negatively impact goals of policing?

2   What are some of the similarities and differences between Latino and African American students on the three outcome variables?

3   How did Latinos and African Americans differ in their attitudes toward police and willingness to assist police?

4   What are some of the negative consequences of police disrespect on youth's attitudes toward police?

Editors' Introduction: Reading 2.3

Developing tactics for positive police interactions is a challenging one due to the nature of police work, especially for young community members. Using Allport's contact theory as a theoretical framework for this paper, a strategy was used to foster greater understanding and more positive interactions between police officers and youth in the Police Insight Program. Positive interactions can initiate positive attitudes, leading to more prosocial behaviors, though this study found that specific conditions must be met. Even with a limited sample size, the findings suggest that beginning to create positive experiences for both youth and police officers can be beneficial in reducing stereotypes.

Building Connections Between Officers and Baltimore City Youth

Key Components of a Police-Youth Teambuilding Program

Elena T. Broaddus, Kerry E. Scott, Liane M. Gonsalves, Canada Parrish,
Evelyn L. Rhoades, Samuel E. Donovan, and Peter J. Winch

Introduction

Relationships between police and youth in urban America are often strained (Brunson & Weitzer, 2011; Hurst & Frank, 2000; Lurigio, Greenleaf, & Flexon, 2009). Youth living in lower income areas, adolescent males, and African-American and Latino youth are particularly likely to report negative attitudes toward police, that they have been disrespected by police, and that they have experienced unwarranted and harassing stops and searches (Eith & Durose, 2011; Weitzer & Tuch, 2006). In turn, Engel (2003) describes how citizens from historically marginalized social groups, particularly young minority males, may behave in disrespectful and oppositional ways toward police to "symbolize their perceptions of injustice" (p. 477). There is a widespread lack of training programs to prepare officers to deal appropriately and effectively with youth or to address the underlying causes of disproportionate arrests of minority youth (International Association of Chiefs of Police, 2011; Thurau, 2009).

Negative attitudes and interactions between police and youth reduce opportunities for community–police collaboration, which has serious implications for public safety. Police are usually the first—and often the only—representative of the criminal justice system with whom youth interact; these early contacts support the development of stereotypes and inform future interactions between youth and the system (Winfree & Griffiths, 1977). Fagan (2002) describes the law as "the meeting point between citizens and accepted social norms, learned from childhood" (p. 69). When the law is implemented in an unfair manner, which can include uneven application of criminal codes through race-based policing, failure to protect marginalized citizens from crime, and disrespectful treatment by police, disadvantaged groups internalize distrust for authorities and resistance to social regulation and control (Fagan, 2002, 2008).

Positive interactions with police have been found to be predictive of positive attitudes toward the police, while negative interactions have been found to be predictive of negative attitudes (Rusinko, Johnson, & Hornung, 1978). Researchers have noted the tendency of youth to perceive officers as primarily an extension of an oppressive system rather than as individual people (Cooper, 1980; Williams, 1999). Similarly, police officers have been found to make assumptions about young people based on their race, age, dress, and appearance (Fine et al., 2003; Thurau, 2009; Williams, 1999). Researchers have also found evidence that police officers hold unconscious biases against minority youth (Graham & Lowery, 2004) and unconsciously associate African-American male faces with concepts of crime (Eberhardt, Goff, Purdie, & Davies, 2004).

In an effort to improve the quality of officer–youth interactions in a city confronting record-breaking rates of violence and youth incarceration (CDC, 2011), the Baltimore Police Department (BPD) partnered with the Baltimore Chesapeake Bay Outward Bound Center (OB) in 2008 to create the 1-day Police Insight Program (Fenton, 2008). The program runs on a monthly basis and participation in at least one program is required of all BPD officers as part of a mandatory training curriculum. Each Police Insight Program brings together all of the officers who work a given shift from one district (25 to 35 officers) with a roughly equal number of students from a middle school located in that same district. Students participate voluntarily and are invited to take part in the program at the discretion of teachers and school administrators. School staff is encouraged to invite students who span a wide range of academic and behavioral performance levels. The program day consists of small groups of students and officers, usually five of each, working together on a series of games and group challenges led by Outward Bound facilitators at the Baltimore Chesapeake Bay Outward Bound base. Though the base is within city limits, it is located in a large wooded park that contains several miles of hiking trails, several large open fields, and a climbing wall and other ropes-course elements.

The Police Insight Program's emphasis on experiential team-building activities, mandatory participation for officers, and 1-day length differentiate it from other police–youth programs described in the literature. Most of these programs are school-or sports-based, or involve supervised recreation or tutoring programs and are voluntary for all participants (Roth et al., 2000). For example, many police departments throughout the country run Police Explorer programs that provide interested youth with the opportunity to learn about police work (Learning for Life, 2013), School Resource Officer programs place officers in schools to both educate students and enforce rules (Canady, Bernard, & Nease, 2012), and Police Athletic Leagues bring officers and youth together for sports and other recreational activities (National Association of Police Athletic/Activities Leagues Inc., 2013). Other programs involve collaboration on service projects within the communities where youth live, or involve going to a camp or participating in a program where officers teach youth police skills (Anderson, Sabatelli, & Trachtenberg, 2007; Thurman, Giacomazzi, & Bogen, 1993). Studies of school- and sports-based youth–police programs indicate that such interventions have the potential to promote positive youth development (Anderson et al., 2007; Clements, 1975; Roth et al., 2000), as well as to reduce violence and discipline infractions within schools (Johnson, 1999; Yale University Child Studies Center, 2003).

Though few descriptions of police–youth programs specifically address a theoretical framework on which the program is based, many seem to draw on the concept of mentorship, which emphasizes the roles of police as advisers and youth as learners and focus primarily on improving and altering the behavior of the juvenile participants. Such programs emphasize longer-term involvement and repeated interactions, but tend not to focus on the specific conditions under which those interactions take place. In contrast, the Police Insight Program aims to break down hierarchies and stereotypical perceptions held by both youth and officers by bringing them together in a unique setting and atmosphere over the course of 1 day.

Theoretical Framework

Allport's (1954) Intergroup Contact Theory (ICT) provides a theoretical basis for the idea that bringing youth and police officers together under certain optimal conditions may reduce stereotypical ideas that each group holds about the other. Allport specifies that the optimal conditions for improving intergroup relationships are that: (a) the groups share equal status, (b) participants work toward common goals, (c) there is inter-group cooperation, and (d) there is the support of an overarching authority (Allport, 1954). Though it has been critiqued by some as too idealistic (Dixon, Durrheim, & Tredoux, 2005), a meta-analysis of ICT studies supported the concept that intergroup contact under Allport's "optimal conditions" is a practical and effective means of improving intergroup relations (Pettigrew & Tropp, 2006). This meta-analysis also found that the greater the extent to which the contact context incorporates Allport's optimal contact conditions, the greater the reduction in prejudice between groups.

Contact theory has previously been discussed in relation to police–youth programming (Hopkins, 1994; Hopkins, Hewstone, & Hantzi, 1992; Rabois & Haaga, 2002); however, the authors of these studies focused primarily on the issue of "generalization," referring to whether positive views of individuals were generalized to the group as a whole. No studies of police–youth programs have previously examined the extent to which the programs meet Allport's optimal contact conditions, or how the presence or absence of these conditions may contribute to outcomes. Given the focus on "contact conditions" in the theoretical literature on improving intergroup attitudes via contact (Bettencourt, Brewer, Croak, & Miller, 1992; Brewer, 1996; Pettigrew & Tropp, 2006), the conditions created in police–youth programs merit scrutiny.

This paper presents findings from a qualitative study of the Baltimore Outward Bound Police Insight Program. Our primary aims were to identify and describe key program components using Allport's specifications for optimal contact conditions as a framework, and to examine the ways in which key program components relate to participant-described program outcomes. This program description and analysis can help to inform future interventions targeting police–youth relationships in other urban settings.

Methods

The research team, all public health graduate students, developed the study protocol based on input from Outward Bound administrators and instructors, school representatives, police department program coordinators, and other police department officials. Permission for interviewing officers was obtained from the BPD Public Information Office prior to initiating the study; ethical approval for the entire protocol was obtained from the Johns Hopkins Bloomberg School of Public Health Institutional Review Board.

Table 2.3.1   Demographics of Outward Bound Police Insight Program Participants (Sample Demographics from 2 of the 5 Program Days Observed)

	PROGRAM PARTICIPANTS	AGE	GENDER	RACE/ETHNICITY
Program Day Example One	24 Officers	30s and 40s	20 Male 4 Female	13 African-American 7 White 4 Latino
	20 Students	6th, 7th, and 8th grade	7 Male 13 Female	All African-American
	5 Facilitators	20s and 30s	3 Male 2 Female	All White
Program Day Example Two	28 Officers	30s, 40s and 50s	23 Male 5 Female	9 African-American 14 White 4 Latino 1 Asian
	33 Students	8th grade	12 Male 21 Female	19 African-American 10 White 3 Latino 1 Asian
	4 Facilitators	20s and 30s	2 Male 2 Female	All White

Observation of Program Days

The research team conducted semiparticipant observation throughout 5 6-hour program days during the autumn of 2011 and winter of 2012. Each program included 20 to 35 students from grades 6 to 8 and a roughly equal number of officers. Detailed participant numbers and demographics for a sample of 2 program days is presented in Table 2.3.1. Researchers stayed with one group of officers and students throughout the day, observing all activities and discussions.

Researchers used an observation guide and took detailed field notes on topics such as supportive comments or behaviors, signs of boredom or disrespect, and other aspects of group dynamics.

In-Depth Interviews

We conducted 27 in-depth interviews with different members of the five major stakeholder groups: students (10); officers (7); OB facilitators (5); Baltimore City Public School staff (3); and BPD Program Coordinators (2). See Table 2.3.2 for demographic details of respondents. We used a purposive sampling strategy in an attempt to maximize the range of perspectives accessed when recruiting students and officers. We recruited student participants through collaboration with school staff. We asked the school staff for parental contact information for students who would be able to provide us with a variety of perspectives on the program based on their personalities, backgrounds, and enjoyment of the program day. We then contacted parents to seek consent and, if given, sought assent from each student prior to the interview. We were able to reach the parents of 10 students and all provided consent; we were unable to reach the parents of four other students whom we attempted to contact. Due to privacy protection standards, we did not collect any data on the four students whose parents we were unable to reach; therefore, we are unable to comment on potential differences between them and the 10 students we did interview. Those interviewed displayed a range of attitudes toward the police in general and described a wide variety of perceptions of the program. Furthermore, their different descriptions of their experience with the program and their interactions with the officers seemed to accurately reflect our observations of the larger groups of student participants during the program day—in short, these students did not appear to be significantly more positive about the program or better behaved than their peers.

We recruited officers for interviews at the end of each of the 2 winter program days by approaching them individually and asking if they would be willing to leave their contact information with us so we could arrange for an interview. We specifically approached officers who, based on our observations, seemed to have a range of experiences and opinions about the program. We approached 13 officers on program days and all of them indicated willingness to give an interview. When we attempted to contact them later by phone, text, or E-mail we received replies from only eight officers. All eight agreed to be interviewed. However, one officer cancelled his interview at the last minute with no specific reason given, leaving us with seven officer interviews. Despite the low response rate, we still believe that we successfully accomplished our purposive sampling strategy; we retained four officers who had specifically been recruited based on their low enthusiasm levels at certain points of the program day and heard a variety of perspectives on the program. It does not appear that the officers willing to be interviewed were more youth-engaged or enthusiastic than the officers who did not respond to our requests. All of the officer participants we interviewed and observed were from the midnight shift in their given district. We used an exhaustive sampling strategy to recruit OB facilitators, BCPS staff, and BPD program coordinators. This means that we sought interviews with all Outward Bound facilitators within the Baltimore area experienced in working with the Insight Program, as well as all involved BCPS staff and BPD program coordinators. All facilitators and program coordinators responded and were interviewed; however, one of the BCPS staff members declined to be interviewed due to her busy schedule. Student and BCPS staff interviews took place at their school during the day. Interviews with officers, OB facilitators, and BPD program coordinators took place at a location convenient for their participation. Interviews were digitally recorded and then transcribed.

Table 2.3.2   Demographics of the Outward Bound Police Insight Program Stakeholders That Participated in In-Depth Interviews

INTERVIEW PARTICIPANTS	AGE	GENDER	RACE/ETHNICITY
10 Students	12 to 14	3 Male 7 Female	9 African-American 1 White
7 Officers	20s to 50s	6 Male 1 Female	5 African-American 1 White 1 Latino
5 Facilitators	20s to 40s	3 Male 2 Female	2 African-American 3 White
3 School Staff Members	20s to 50s	1 Male 2 Female	All White
2 BPD Program Coordinators	40s to 50s	2 Male	1 African-American 1 White

Data Analysis

After reading all transcripts and observation field notes, the research team discussed key themes and concepts, then used these themes to develop a codebook. To identify and eliminate inconsistencies in different researchers' application of the codebook, all researchers individually applied the codebook to the same two transcripts (one from an officer interview and one from a student interview). After resolving all coding discrepancies that arose, and thus clarifying the appropriate use of each code, the researchers then coded the transcripts of the interviews they had conducted. Field notes from program day observations were not coded but were read carefully and used to inform identification of key concepts in the interview transcripts. Our observation of group discussions of stereotypes and other program day activities enabled us to access comments from and observe the behavior of all participants, not just those with whom we conducted individual interviews. Observations of the changes in officer–student interaction over the course of the day provided critical information when drawing conclusions about the program's outcomes. After coding was complete, we applied Allport's (1954) ICT as a tool for analysis by examining whether our findings fit the theory's contact condition specifications and the outcomes it predicts. This allowed us to develop a deeper theoretical understanding of which program components were most important and how those program components helped produce the outcomes identified. We were also able to generate recommendations for future police–youth programs.

Results

We first present respondent's perceptions of officer–youth interactions outside the program, which illuminate the challenges facing police–youth relations in Baltimore, in order to contextualize the need for the Police Insight Program. We then present key components of the program using ICT as a framework. Finally, we discuss program outcomes, as described by interviewed participants.

Interactions and Perceptions "On the Street"

During interviews we asked students and officers to describe typical interactions with one another in order to better understand the prior experiences and perceptions that shaped their encounter during the program day. Officers spoke at length about the many barriers they faced to building more positive relationships with youth in the city. Many officers described a "culture" of antipathy and distrust toward officers that is passed down to youth from parents and older siblings. The officers overwhelmingly articulated a perception that many adolescents in Baltimore were "not on the right path." One explained that youth are "our predators of the street" (Male Officer 7). Another commented that:

> Just like the kids see negativity from the police... like locking up and things that aren't, aren't positive, you know. They see that and they don't feel like dealing with it. And, it's the same for us. We deal with the kids on a difficult basis and, you just like, ah, I don't feel like dealing with it. (Male Officer 1)

Several officers, youth, and facilitators described a subset of officers who were "jaded" or "angry" and had given up trying to "help"; however, nearly all officers interviewed said they wanted to improve relationships with youth. They expressed frustration that the nature of their work did not allow time or opportunities to socialize positively with young people, as officers are present only in challenging situations.

Only 2 of the 10 student respondents described specific firsthand accounts of interaction with officers, but many had witnessed friends or family members interact negatively with officers, as expressed by this student:

> Like when my siblings or someone in my family get in trouble [with the police]. They just, it, it be crazy. [Gets quieter] Just be crazy
>
> *Interviewer:* Yeah... why do you think that is?
>
> *Student:* I don't know... It probably be because they do somethin' bad. But, it's family over everything. [Gestures to chest.] (Male Student 3)

Students also often described irritation with police officers for bothering young people unfairly, or failing to help in difficult situations. Several students described this failure on the part of officers to respond when needed as evidence of a lack of "caring" on the part of the officers.

Although many students had positive perceptions of a specific officer, frequently one that worked in their school, the vast majority described officers as a group as "mean." Students referred to officers "abusing their authority," threatening and yelling at them, and being "mad," "reckless," and "ignorant."

Interaction Conditions Specified by ICT

We now move on to describe the ways in which the Outward Bound Police Insight Program sought to improve relations between the two groups, arranged into sections by ICT conditions—with components not covered by ICT's specific optimal conditions included in a section at the end of this article. Table 2.2.3 describes how the Police Insight Program satisfies Allport's "optimal" conditions.

Table 2.2.3   Description of How the Outward Bound Police Insight Program Met Each of the Optimal Contact Conditions Specified by Allport's Intergroup Contact Theory

ALLPORT'S CONDITIONS FOR OPTIMAL CONTACT	HOW CONTACT CONDITIONS WERE MET AT THE OUTWARD BOUND POLICE INSIGHT PROGRAM
Equal Group Status	• No police uniforms • Clear expectations for respect, listening, and using first names • Students take on leadership roles during activities • Both groups physically and mentally challenged by climbing activities
Common Goals	• Group members support each other to achieve goals on climbing wall and ropes course • Team-building challenges posed by facilitator
Intergroup Cooperation	• Student–officer pairs required for some activities • Activities tailored to maximize cooperation across groups • Debriefs focused on cooperation • Participants encouraged to talk and get to know each other
Support of Authority	• Students encouraged to participate by school staff members • Officers required to participate as a component of their training • High-ranking police officials present and enthusiastic • Facilitators act as overarching authority figures during the program

ICT Optimal Condition #1: Equal Group Status

According to ICT, establishing the conditions under which stereotypes can be addressed and challenged requires creating a sense of equality between the two interacting groups. While there are certain inherently unequal components of officer and youth identity, such as age difference, education level and (for some) race and social class, which cannot be set aside, the Police Insight Program created interaction conditions that were markedly different from the authority role of police on the street. The Police Insight Program promoted an increased sense of equality between the officers and students in a variety of ways. One key feature of the program was that the officers were all out of uniform—instead wearing sneakers, jeans, and jackets just like the students. Facilitators and program coordinators described this as an essential component of the program, because police uniforms create an immediate barrier between officers and youth. As one officer described, "You know, they see this uniform, it's automatic—they tense up, tense up automatically" (Male Officer 7). Many students described being surprised to find out that all the adults present were officers, and that out of uniform, they appeared "just like regular people" (Female Student 6). When another student was asked during an interview what it would have been like if the officers had worn uniforms, he replied, "I would have automatically knew that they were police officers. And once I knew that, I probably would be less, like, less willing to cooperate with them, because I didn't know their personalities or anything" (Male Student 4).

Facilitators also established clear expectations at the beginning of the program for respecting each other and calling each other by name, with no titles attached. One officer explained:

> When you get to learn a person's name, it means a lot. You're not dealing with a police officer, you're dealing with who I am, and I'm dealing with who that youth is that I'm speaking with... [it] just makes you respect the person more when you refer to them by their name rather than just "some person." (Male Officer 5)

Throughout the day, facilitators encouraged students to take on leadership roles, reversing the usual power dynamics between officers and youth. Many of the activities gave students a chance to take charge and give directions. One example was described by an officer:

> When we were doing the jump rope thing, the girls took over. The two instructors would turn the rope, and you had to get under without the rope touching you...the fun part was because the students, they were like "we got this, we got this." So they would tell us "go now, go now!" (Male Officer 6)

The climbing activities on the rock-climbing wall or ropes-course were particularly important because officers and students had to trust and encourage each other to succeed and officers, as well as students, were often initially frightened by these activities. One officer described the following conversation with a student: "One girl told me, she was like, 'I never knew police officers get scared.' And I said, 'What you mean?' And she said, 'Girl, cause you scared of heights!' I said, 'Well I'm human.'" (Female Officer 2)

ICT Optimal Condition #2: Common Goals

Climbing activities also prompted students and officers to work together toward a common goal. One student's description of her experience climbing the wall provides a good example of this group support:

> So I was real scared. So when I looked down, it looked like a real, real big
> fall. But then, when they was like, "Go ahead you can do it, it's okay, we got
> you," and stuff like that, I was okay and I wasn't all as scared as I was at first.
> (Female Student 6)

Often officers and students would climb the wall together in pairs. One explained, "There was a police officer, she was afraid of heights. And she was the one that I actually climbed with. If she wouldn't have told me she was afraid of heights I wouldn't have gone up. She encouraged me" (Female Student 9).

Though less dramatic than the climbing activities, team-building challenges posed by the facilitator provided groups additional opportunities to strive toward a common goal. For example, one activity required everyone in the group to balance on two planks with one foot on each and hold on to ropes tied to the planks. The group had to use the ropes to raise one board at a time and slide it forward in order to reach a finish line. An officer explained, "That right there, just working with kids we never worked with before, it's just the small things, like, 'Alright everybody, on three, we gonna move the right leg! One, two, three!' So we were coming together and working together." (Male Officer 4)

ICT Optimal Condition #3: Intergroup Cooperation

Facilitators prompted groups to pay attention to the way they were interacting in order to accomplish their shared goals. Activities emphasized cooperation and were frequently followed by "debrief" discussions, in which groups talked about what had worked well and where they could improve when working together. One student explained:

> We had to actually strategize... You have to talk about what you gonna do,
> in order to make something work. So you can't like, just yell at each other.
> You have to like, actually sit and talk about what you're gonna do, and have
> a calm conversation. (Female Student 5)

An officer also noted the way the program activities required a certain level of cooperation and interaction:

> Most of the games, we had to work together to get it done. Well actually all of 'em pretty much, to be honest with you. So, that way, [the students] had to deal with us and we had to deal with them. (Male Officer 6)

While we never observed students or officers being overtly disrespectful of one another, failure to listen to each other or communicate effectively (for example yelling, talking over each other) was occasionally evident. In some cases, students were so excited by the activity that they did not take time to collaborate. At other times, officers seemed intent on completing the activity correctly at the expense of involving students. Debriefs provided an opportunity for facilitators to bring these dynamics to the attention of the group and initiate a discussion about what prompted them and how they could be addressed in the future.

Working together during group games and paired activities helped pave the way to casual conversations between officers and students over lunch, and serious discussions later on about police–youth interactions in their communities. One officer described this as an "opening up" process:

> [The kids] were a little shy at first but, they opened up. It didn't take long. I guess the tasks that they had us participating in as a group kinda opened them up. It opened us up also. Because, whether you can believe, I mean, I was a little shy too. (Male Officer 4)

ICT Optimal Condition #4: Support of Authority

For both students and officers, relevant authority figures were present and involved during the Police Insight Program. Students were accompanied by the teachers or other school staff members, who either selected them or encouraged them to participate in the Police Insight Program. All students arrived knowing that the program was sanctioned and supported by their teachers and school staff. Officers were required to participate in the program as part of a department-wide training program, and high-ranking police officials who helped to coordinate the program were always present, enthusiastic, and, as the only police official in uniform at the base, highly visible. In addition, facilitators acted as overarching authority figures for each group of officers and students, managing any problematic behavior from both adults and youth, selecting and setting rules for group activities, and guiding and moderating group discussions. For example, we observed several instances in which officers who demonstrated outward signs of boredom (joking off to the side with other officers and hanging back from activities) were taken aside by facilitators and encouraged to engage more with the students. During these talks, the officers were reminded that they serve as role models for the youth and that their level of enthusiasm would set the tone for the day. After these one-on-one talks, we noticed that the officers became more engaged.

Important Program Components Not Specified by Intergroup Contact Theory

The following three subsections describe components of the Police Insight Program that did not fit within the particular conditions specified by ICT, yet that our findings indicate are important facilitators of success for a police–youth program. Table 2.3.4 displays Allport's specified conditions, key components of the program not covered by Allport's conditions, and the outcomes that resulted from bringing the two groups of participants together in this program.

Table 2.3.4. Table Displaying Contact Conditions Specified by Intergroup Contact Theory (ICT), Important Components of the Police Insight Program That Are Not Specified by ICT, and Participant-Described Program Outcomes

CONDITIONS SPECIFIED BY ICT	IMPORTANT PROGRAM COMPONENTS NOT SPECIFIED BY ICT	PROGRAM OUTCOMES
Equal Group Status	Neutral Environment	• Reduction in stereotyping
Common Goals	Fun and Engaging Atmosphere	• Positive attitude toward members of the opposite group in the program
Intergroup Cooperation	Open Discussion of Stereotypes	• Positive attitude may not be generalized to opposite group as a whole without follow-up
Support of Authority		• Increased tendency to see each other as people
		• Increased openness to communication
		• Desire for future positive interaction

Non-ICT Condition #1: Neutral Environment

The Police Insight Program's location outdoors in a large wooded park was described as "neutral ground" by several stakeholders. One facilitator said, "It's taking both groups out of their comfort zone, both groups out of the environment that they're used to" (Female OB Facilitator 3). When asked about the police department's decision to partner with Outward Bound at their base in the park, a BPD program coordinator explained:

> There's no brick, there's no row homes, there's no streets. You know, there's no pavement. It's grass, it's woods, it's trees… There are so many places we could take officers and youth to come together. We could take [youth] to the academy, we could have the officers go to the schools, you know. But you need a separate entity. (Male Program Coordinator 2)

Non-ICT Condition #2: Fun and Engaging Atmosphere

Facilitators and program coordinators emphasized how important fun was for getting officers and students to "buy into" the program. Many officers described being skeptical or unenthusiastic about the program prior to participating, and many students said that they initially expected officers to be strict and severe. During observation we noted that at the beginning of each program day few participants spoke or interacted voluntarily with members of the opposite group: students generally clustered tightly in groups whispering to their friends while most officers stood on the opposite side of the program area, some looking bored or making sarcastic comments about the day to come. However, this initial lack of interest and interaction changed quickly during large-group games that involved running around, yelling silly things, laughing, and generally having a lot of fun. One officer said that when she arrived, "I'm gonna be honest. I did not want to go. It was cold. I was sick… but I think the first little bit of warm-ups had us all like, 'Oooh yeah, we're gonna have fun'" (Female Officer 2). Another officer also explained, "You gotta at least fake the fun. You know, you gotta play the game, and, maybe when you're playing the game you start to actually really open up, and be… genuine" (Male Officer 1). Many students said that they initially expected officers to be strict and severe; however, as they saw the officers having fun they seemed less intimidating, and the students started to feel more comfortable interacting with them.

Non-ICT Condition #3: Open Discussion of Stereotypes

An activity described as very memorable by both students and officers was a group discussion about the stereotypes that existed about both officers and youth. Facilitators usually initiated the conversation toward the end of the day, asking participants for examples of how police and youth stereotypically perceived each other. Then facilitators asked participants to comment about what they thought of these stereotypes and whether they applied to the other group members with whom they had spent the day. Often it turned into a question and answer session, with students asking officers why police acted in certain ways, and officers asking students why youth perceived them in certain ways. Members of both groups had the opportunity to explain things from their perspective. One student explained, "[The officers] learned that each and every one of us is different" (Female Student 7). Another student described the conversation in her group, saying:

> They taught us that we should not stereotype. Because like, you think all
> police officers are not cool and are boring or they're mean. But we got
> to know that they are regular people and they're very fun to be around.
> (Female Student 8)

Outcomes

Outcomes for Students

Students interviewed said they enjoyed the program and liked the officers in their group. All students said they would recommend the program to a friend, told their classmates that it was fun, and would like to participate again in the future. Many students said they were happily surprised by how nice the officers were, and how different they were compared to the students' expectations. One student said, "When I looked at them, I thought they was gonna be mean and strict, but they wasn't. They was real laid back and cool and everything, and fun to talk to" (Female Student 2).

Comments varied regarding how the program influenced students' view of officers more generally. Some students said they thought the officers must have volunteered to be there and were the ones who wanted to spend time with kids, indicating they thought most officers did not really like children. However, many students made comments indicating their view of all officers had become more complex due to the program. One student said that during the program, "We learned about police officers. We learned that there's good ones and bad ones. Not just, like, bad and ignorant ones. Also some that can help" (Male Student 4). Many students described seeing officers as more human, and mentioned having a realization that police were actually just "regular people" at some point in the day. Students' comments also indicated they were less likely to make assumptions or automatically believe stereotypes about what police officers were like. One boy explained, "Now I think, some [officers] are cool, and some not. You just gotta talk to them. See how they is. Like, you can't just assume somebody because they police, assume their actions because they police" (Male Student 1).

Outcomes for Officers

Most officers we spoke with said that they liked kids and enjoyed having the opportunity to inter-act with youth in a positive way for a change, rather than being a disciplinarian. Several indicated that the program helped to remind them of the positive "side" of youth. One officer explained:

> You get a perspective, especially working this job for a while, and you get a
> perspective where you say, "there's only a few [youth] that's worth saving."
> And then you look and you say "naw, that ain't right." You go to a program
> like that and you see that. (Male Officer 6)

Officers also echoed comments by students about the important realization that the individuals they were interacting with were people, were human, and were not very different from them:

> The purpose for [police officers] is to let them know the youth are human,
> you know, 'cause I don't think sometimes we look at youth as... individuals. I

think we look at them as a whole different monster... Hopefully the officers really got a good opportunity to see what youth are, you know, what they can possibly be, given the right environment and the right people. (Male Officer 7)

Officers also emphasized the need for program follow-up in order for lasting changes in police–youth relationships and attitudes to occur. They noted the difficulty of trying to build relationships with youth during their normal working hours, saying this would conflict with their law enforcement responsibilities. Many expressed a strong desire for more opportunities for positive interaction. When asked what recommendations he had for improving the program, one officer said:

I'd like to know [the kids'] background a little bit more. And maybe do a follow up or something. Just because then you, you start to build a relationship with them, you know. And, a relationship with them, then it might turn into a relationship with their parents. And then with their parents might help you out on dealing with crime in that neighborhood. Or maybe that parent hated the police, you know, and it changed their outlook on police, or you know, maybe that kid at least changed their outlook. (Male Officer 1)

Discussion

Our study results indicate multiple ways that the Outward Bound Police Insight Program creates optimal contact conditions as specified by Allport in his Intergroup Contact Theory (1954): equal status, common goals, cooperation, and support of an overarching authority. Our results also indicate the importance of certain contact conditions created by the program that are not "captured" by the four conditions Allport describes. Program outcomes for officers and youth include positive feelings toward fellow program participants, a more nuanced and less stereotyped view of the opposite group more generally, and a desire for future positive interactions.

We propose that, in addition to creating Allport's optimal conditions, police–youth programs should also strive to provide (a) a neutral setting distinct from areas where the two groups normally interact, (b) a fun, light-hearted atmosphere, and (c) facilitated communication about stereotypes. Furthermore, a clear theme that emerged from our results regarding post-program outcomes was a need for program follow up. Establishing optimal contact conditions may create the potential for improved longer term intergroup relations, but require follow-up interactions for that potential to be realized. Therefore, we recommend that police–youth programs also incorporate repeated follow-up that involves students and officers working with the same individuals they met during the program, as well as new individuals. Follow-up intergroup contact may not be as dependent on the need for a neutral setting as the initial interaction. Progressive introduction of the more polarizing settings in which the participants normally interact could help consolidate the benefits of the program by encouraging the participants to carry forward their insights into their everyday environment.

Limitations

The short duration of this study did not allow us to assess long-term program outcomes or effects on actual future police–youth interactions. Furthermore, while its qualitative nature allowed us to gain a detailed understanding of the experience of the officers and students that we observed and interviewed, further research in other settings is needed to understand police–youth relationships in other contexts. These research objectives are worthy topics for future studies utilizing mixed-method designs over a longer time frame. Also, as mentioned in the methodology section, we were able to interview only those students whose parents were accessible by phone, and only those officers who indicated they had time available for interviews. These selection criteria may have limited the range of perspectives that we were able to access. Nonetheless, we still interviewed a diverse group of students and officers who presented varying opinions of the program and did not appear to be an especially positive or pro–Outward Bound subpopulation. Our direct program observation also allowed us to overcome this limitation to some extent, as we were able to observe the reactions and comments of all participants, not only those we later interviewed.

Conclusion

Our findings indicate the importance of creating specific conditions when bringing officers and youth together in an effort to reduce stereotypes and improve relationships. The self-reported positive participant outcomes that we documented justify further investment in research to examine program outcomes using rigorous quantitative evaluation methods, as well as longitudinal qualitative follow-up regarding how changes in perspective and stereotyping alter the quality of future encounters between officers and youth. Although we were not able to assess long-term outcomes, our findings suggest that programs following the Police Insight Program model, if paired with further follow-up, could serve as a steppingstone toward improved relationships between officers and youth "on the streets."

About the Authors

Elena T. Broaddus, MSPH, was a student in the Social and Behavioral Interventions Program, Johns Hopkins Bloomberg School of Public Health, Baltimore, Maryland, at the time of this writing.

Kerry E. Scott, MSc, was a student in the Social and Behavioral Interventions Program, Johns Hopkins Bloomberg School of Public Health, Baltimore, Maryland, at the time of this writing. Currently, Ms. Scott is a PhD candidate in international health at the Johns Hopkins Bloomberg School of Public Health.

Lianne M. Gonsalves, MSPH, was a student in the Social and Behavioral Interventions Program, Johns Hopkins Bloomberg School of Public Health, Baltimore, Maryland, at the time of this writing.

Canada Parrish, MSPH, was a student in the Social and Behavioral Interventions Program, Johns Hopkins Bloomberg School of Public Health, Baltimore, Maryland, at the time of this writing. Currently, Ms. Parrish is project coordinator at Afia Clinics International, Tulsa, Oklahoma.

Evelyn L. Rhodes, MSPH, was a student in the Social and Behavioral Interventions Program, Johns Hopkins Bloomberg School of Public Health, Baltimore, Maryland, at the time of this writing.

Samuel E. Donovan, MSPH, was a student in the Social and Behavioral Interventions Program, Johns Hopkins Bloomberg School of Public Health, Baltimore, Maryland, at the time of this writing. Currently, Mr. Donovan is a research assistant at Massachusetts General Hospital, Boston, Massachusetts.

Peter John Winch, MD, MPH, is professor and director, Social and Behavioral Interventions Program, Department of International Health, Johns Hopkins Bloomberg School of Public Health; and Associate Chair, Department of International Health, Johns Hopkins Bloomberg School of Public Health, Baltimore, Maryland.

References

Allport, G. W. (1954). *The nature of prejudice.* Cambridge, MA: Addison-Wesley.

Anderson, S. A., Sabatelli, R. M., & Trachtenberg, J. (2007). Community police and youth programs as a context for positive youth development. *Police Quarterly, 10*(1), 23–40.

Bettencourt, B. A., Brewer, M. B., Croak, M. R., & Miller, N. (1992). Cooperation and the reduction of intergroup bias: The role of reward structure and social orientation. *Journal of Experimental Social Psychology, 28*(4), 301–319.

Brewer, M. B. (1996). When contact is not enough: Social identity and intergroup cooperation. *International Journal of Intercultural Relations, 20*(3–4), 291–303.

Brunson, R. K., & Weitzer, R. (2011). Negotiating unwelcome police encounters: The intergenerational transmission of conduct norms. *Journal of Contemporary Ethnography, 40*(4), 425–456.

Canady, M., Bernard, J., & Nease, J. (2012). *To educate & protect: The school resource officer and the prevention of violence in schools.* Hoover, AL: National Association of School Resource Officers.

Centers for Disease Control and Prevention (CDC). (2011). Violence-related firearm deaths among residents of metropolitan areas and cities—United States, 2006–2007 *Morbidity and Mortality Weekly Report* (Vol. 18, pp. 573–578). Atlanta, GA: Centers for Disease Control and Prevention.

Clements, C. B. (1975). The school relations bureau—A program of police intervention. *Criminal Justice and Behavior, 2*(4), 358–371.

Cooper, J. L. (1980). *The Police and the Ghetto.* Port Washington, New York: Kennikat Press.

Dixon, J., Durrheim, K., & Tredoux, C. (2005). Beyond the optimal contact strategy: A reality check for the contact hypothesis. *American Psychologist, 60*(7), 697–711.

Eberhardt, J. L., Goff, P. A., Purdie, V. J., & Davies, P. G. (2004). Seeing black: Race, crime, and visual processing. *Journal of Personality and Social Psychology, 87*(6), 876.

Eith, C., & Durose, M. (2011). Contacts between police and the public, 2008. Washington, DC: U.S. Department of Justice, Bureau of Justice Statistics.

Engel, R. S. (2003). Explaining suspects' resistance and disrespect toward police. *Journal of Criminal Justice, 31*(5), 475–492.

Fagan, J. (2002). Race, legitimacy, and criminal law. *Souls, 4*(1), 69–72.

Fagan, J. (2008). Legitimacy and criminal justice-introduction. *Ohio State Journal of Criminal Law, 6*, 123.

Fenton, J. (2008, December 18). Getting past the uniform. *The Baltimore Sun.* Retrieved from http://articles.baltimoresun.com/2008-12-18/news/0812170091

Fine, M., et al. (2003). "Anything can happen with police around": Urban youth evaluate strategies of surveillance in public places. *Journal of Social Issues, 59*(1), 141–158.

Graham, S., & Lowery, B. S. (2004). Priming unconscious racial stereotypes about adolescent offenders. *Law and Human Behavior, 28*(5), 483.

Hopkins, N. (1994). Young people arguing and thinking about the police. *Human Relations, 47*(11), 1409–1432.

Hopkins, N., Hewstone, M., & Hantzi, A. (1992). Police-schools liaison and young people's image of the police: An intervention evaluation. *British Journal of Psychology, 83*(2), 203–220.

Hurst, Y. G., & Frank, J. (2000). How kids view cops: The nature of juvenile attitudes toward the police. *Journal of Criminal Justice, 28*, 189–202.

International Association of Chiefs of Police. (2011). *2011 juvenile justice training needs assessment.* U.S. Department of Justice, Office of Juvenile Justice and Delinquency Prevention.

Johnson, I. M. (1999). School violence The effectiveness of a school resource officer program in a southern city. *Journal of Criminal Justice, 27*(2), 173–192.

Learning for Life. (2013). Law enforcement exploring. Retrieved August 1, 2013, from http://exploring.learningforlife.org/services/career-exploring/law-enforcement/

Lurigio, A. J., Greenleaf, R. G., & Flexon, J. L. (2009). The effects of race on relationships with the police: A survey of African American and Latino Youths in Chicago. *Western Criminology Review, 10*, 29.

National Association of Police Athletic/Activities Leagues Inc. (2013). National PAL. Retrieved August 1, 2013, from http://www.nationalpal.org/programs.

Pettigrew, T. F., & Tropp, L. R. (2006). A meta-analytic test of intergroup contact theory. Journal of Personality and Social Psychology, *90*(5), 751–783.

Rabois, D., & Haaga, D. A. F. (2002). Facilitating police–minority youth attitude change. *Journal of Community Psychology, 30*(2), 189–195.

Roth, J. A., et al. (2000). National Evaluation of the COPS Program Title I of the 1994 Crime Act. Series: Research Report. U.S. Department of Justice: Office of Justice Programs, National Institute of Justice.

Rusinko, W. T., Johnson, K. W., & Hornung, C. A. (1978). The importance of police contact in the formulation of youths' attitudes toward police. *Journal of Criminal Justice, 6*(1), 53–67.

Thurau, L. H. (2009). Rethinking how we police youth: Incorporating knowledge of adolescence into policing teens. *Children's Legal Rights Journal, 29*(3).

Thurman, Q. C., Giacomazzi, A., & Bogen, P. (1993). Research Note: Cops, kids, and community policing. *Crime & Delinquency, 39*(4), 554–564.

Weitzer, R., & Tuch, S. A. (2006). *Race and policing in America: Conflict and reform.* New York: Cambridge University Press.

Williams, B. N. (1999). Perceptions of children and teenagers on community policing: Implications for law enforcement leadership, training, and citizen evaluations. *Police Quarterly, 2*(2), 150–173.

Winfree, L. T., & Griffiths, C. T. (1977). Adolescent attitudes toward the police. In T. Ferdinand (Ed.), *Juvenile delinquency: Little brother grows up* (Vol. 2, 79–99). Beverly Hills, CA: Sage Publications.

Yale University Child Studies Center. (2003). Community outreach through police in schools. Washington DC: U.S. Department of Justice, Office for Victims of Crime.

Critical Thinking Questions

1   How are negative perceptions of police reinforced through police-community interactions?

2   What were some preconceived notions youth and police had about each other? How did the Police Insight Program address these biases?

3   What prevents police officers from fostering relationships with youth while on duty? What reasons did officers who participated in the Police Insight Program give?

4   How can police officers incorporate successes of the program while in the field? What would you recommend?

Part II Key Points

- Improving police legitimacy perceptions among youth can serve as a form of crime prevention.

- Open communication between police and youth can reduce negative stereotypes and help to build relationships.

- Outreach initiatives should take into account how race and ethnicity influences youths' perceptions of and experiences with police.

PART III

THE QUESTION OF POLICE LEGITIMACY

Editors' Introduction

Policing is at once guided by operational and nonoperational goals, as is the entire criminal justice system, something that DiIulio pointed out in 1993.[1] What this means is that some police goals can be quantified (such as number of arrests) and measured, and therefore meaningfully compared between two points in time. This, of course, is the basis of the NYPD's famous COMPSTAT system: Precincts are able to compare arrests at time one to arrests at time two and thereby determine whether any given police approach is "successful." But not all of what the police do can be quantified. This is the nonoperational part of policing and includes things such as whether we think the police are "doing a good job" or whether we are "satisfied" with the police. Granted, numerous studies have made efforts to quantify these variables; but at their heart, these are nonoperational, intangible things that quantitative studies can, at best, only abstract. This is borne out in the numerous ways that such variables are specified.

This is not to denigrate such research. Rather, it is to reinforce the point that there are, in fact, nonoperational goals. After all, if they were not abstract, there would not be room for debate in terms of their measurement. But there is room for such debate because of the inherently nonoperational nature of policing. And it is this nonoperational nature of policing that makes the job so difficult: If we only have a vague idea of whether our goals are being accomplished, it's difficult

125

to move toward those goals. This conclusion becomes incredibly salient when we consider the importance of police legitimacy. Police legitimacy is the idea that the body politic believes that the police are important and necessary and is predicated on police not only doing their job, but doing it with *perceived* fairness. What's more, police legitimacy is tied not only to how civilians respond to police intervention, but to lawful obeisance, itself: If the police are perceived to behave unfairly, civilians are less likely to cooperate with the police and are less likely to obey the law.

The readings in this section lay this bare , starting with Schulhofer, Tyler, and Huq. Schulhofer and colleagues, which includes Tom Tyler, arguably the most well-known theorist of police legitimacy, discuss the importance of legitimacy in light of the modern policing emphasis on counter-terrorism. They set the stage to better understand what legitimacy is and why it matters. We see the importance of legitimacy in practice with Hanick's article, which specifically considers COMPSTAT and the stop-and-frisk policing the NYPD employed throughout the 90s and well into the 21st century. Finally, we consider a radical approach to the use of police discretion as it relates to arrest and police legitimacy in a legal article written by Sekhon. In many respects, these readings are tough and controversial but provide a necessary conversation regarding the role police play in society.

References

Dilulio, J. J. (1993). Measuring performance when there is no bottom line. In J. J. Dilulio (Ed.), *Performance Measures for the Criminal Justice System* (pp. 147–160). Washington, DC: U.S. Government Printing Office.

Editors' Introduction: Reading 3.1

A running theme through almost all of the readings of this volume is the legitimacy of the police: their socially accepted mandate to do what they do. When that legitimacy is called into question, not only is the police mandate jeopardized, but so too is the entire social contract. Few have discussed the implications of this more cogently than Schulhofer, Tyler, and Huq, who, in the following article, argue that the time is long due to reassess how policing is done, with an eye explicitly turned not to crime control but to police legitimacy. Their "due process model" is grounded in robust theory and decades of empirical research and forces us to reconsider the relationship between police and society in terms not of what police *do*, but in terms of *how* they do it.

American Policing at a Crossroads

Unsustainable Policies and the Procedural Justice Alternative

Stephen J. Schulhofer, Tom R. Tyler, and Aziz Z. Huq

Introduction

As victimization rates have fallen, public preoccupation with policing and its crime control impact has receded. Terrorism has become the new focal point of public concern. But the apparent satisfaction with ordinary police practices hides deep problems.

Public order successes have been achieved at great cost to politically powerless communities. As the controversy surrounding the recent arrest of Harvard Professor Henry Louis Gates illustrated,[1] our laws and the way they are enforced have resulted in public attitudes sharply polarized along racial lines,[2] a division that is scarcely sur-

---

[1] Gates was arrested at his Cambridge home by a police officer who suspected him of a house break-in. Though circumstances were disputed, many whites assumed the officer would not have acted without good reason, while others (especially blacks) found it unlikely that a middle-aged professor, standing on the porch of his own home, would have been viewed with suspicion and then arrested if he had been white. *See* Cambridge Review Comm., Missed Opportunities, Shared Responsibilities: Final Report of the Cambridge Review Committee 16–21 (June 2010) [hereinafter Cambridge Review Committee], *available at* http://www.cambridgema.gov/CityOfCambridge_Content/documents/Cambridge Review_FINAL.pdf; Cambridge Police Dep't, Incident Report #9005127, July 16, 2009, *available at* http://www.samefacts.com/archives/Police report on Gates arrest.PDF (detailing the officer's account); Dayo Olopade, *Skip Gates Speaks*, Root (July 21, 2009), http://www.theroot.com/views/skip-gates-speaks?page=0,l (for Gates's view).

[2] In one careful survey, less than twenty percent of African Americans considered the American legal system fair. Richard R.W. Brooks, *Fear and Fairness in the City: Criminal Enforcement and Perceptions of Fairness in Minority Communities*, 73 S. Calif. L. Rev. 1219, 1247 (2000). After President Obama criticized the officer's actions, a poll found that twice as many whites as blacks disapproved of the President's comments. *See* Pew Research Ctr., Obama's Ratings Slide Across the Board 15–17 (2009), *available at* http://people-press.org/report/532/obamas-ratings-slide. Similar findings recur throughout the literature.

prising in a nation marked by conspicuous racial disparities in its prison populations.[3] And the costs of current strategic choices are no longer confined to minorities and the poor. Through its criminogenic impact, imprisonment has cross-cutting effects for the wider population, promising safety through deterrence at the same time as it increases victimization at the hands of former inmates.[4] These costs are compounded by fiscal consequences that are now impossible to ignore. In California, reliance on long-term imprisonment as a crime-control strategy has choked off funds for education and pushed the state to the brink of insolvency.[5] Budget imperatives are forcing the state to reduce its prison population by 6,500 inmates, even in the face of recidivism rates of nearly 40%, among the highest in the nation.[6] One prisoner brought home the dilemma and triggered widespread alarm when he was released early but then promptly re-arrested for attempted rape.[7] In other places, incarceration policies generate fiscal burdens that, if less dire, are nonetheless patently unsustainable.[8] Highly stretched police forces from New York City to Tulsa, Oakland, Los Angeles, and elsewhere are facing cuts in personnel, even in their high priority units.[9]

The pressures have become especially acute because we can no longer subordinate conventional law enforcement to the newer preoccupation with terrorism. That domain was long seen as far removed from everyday policing. But government measures in this once-distant arena

---

[3] *See generally* MICHELLE ALEXANDER, THE NEW JIM CROW: MASS INCARCERATION IN AN AGE OF COLORBLINDNESS (2010); MARC MAUER, RACE TO INCARCERATE (rev. ed. 2006).

[4] *See, e.g.,* Coleman v. Schwarzenegger, No. CIV S-90-0520, 2009 WL 2430820, at *84 (E.D. Cal. Aug. 4, 2009) ("[T]he state's continued failure to address the severe crowding in California's prisons would perpetuate a criminogenic prison system that itself threatens public safety."), *appeal docketed sub nom* Schwarzenegger v. Plata, 130 S. Ct. 3413 (2010); Jeffrey Fagan, Valerie West & Jan Holland, *Reciprocal Effects of Crime and Incarceration in New York City Neighborhoods,* 30 FORDHAM URB. L. J. 1551, 1554 (2003).

[5] *See, e.g.,* Wyatt Buchanan, *Has the Golden State Gone Bankrupt?,* S.F. CHRON., Feb. 22, 2010, at A1, *available at* http://articles. sfgate.eom/2010-02-22/news/17950763_l_bankruptcy-treasurer-bill-lockyer-golden-state; Larry Gordon, Gale Holland & Mitchell Landsberg, *Lowered Expectations for Model of Higher Education,* L.A. TIMES, July 31, 2009, at A1, *available at* http://articles.latimes.com/2009/jul/31/local/me-college-cuts31.

[6] Randal C. Archibold, *Driven to a Fiscal Brink, A State Throws Open The Doors to Its Prisons,* N.Y. TIMES, Mar. 24, 2010, at A14. In a 2005 analysis, the three-year recidivism rate for California offenders released from incarceration and returned to prison or jail after conviction for new crimes was 37%. An additional 32% of released offenders were returned to custody for technical parole violations. *See* Ryan G. Fischer, *Are California's Recidivism Rates Really the Highest in the Nation? It Depends on What Measure of Recidivism You Use,* THE BULLETIN, UC Irvine Center for Evidence-Based Corrections, Sept. 2005, at 2, *available at* http://ucicorrections.seweb.uci.edu/pdf/bulletin_2005_vol-L_is-L.pdf.

[7] Archibold, *supra* note 6, at A14.

[8] *See, e.g.,* Nicholas Riccardi, *Laws Loosen to Free Inmates,* L.A. TIMES, Sept. 5, 2009, at A20 (discussing states where cost constraints have forced prison releases; Kentucky granted early release to 3,000 inmates).

[9] *See, e.g.,* Joel Rubin, *LAPD Cuts Killed Terrorism Unit,* L.A. TIMES, May 6, 2010, at AA3; Maya Rao, *NJ. Layoffs Grow in Public Sector,* PHILA. INQUIRER, Apr. 13, 2010, at B04 (describing police force cuts in New Jersey); Nicole Marshall, *TPD Making Fewer Arrests,* TULSA WORLD, Mar. 28, 2010, at A1 (describing layoffs of 124 Tulsa police officers); Bobby White, *Cuts to Police Force Test a Safer Oakland,* WALL ST. J., July 11, 2009, at A4 (describing decision to lay off nearly 20% of Oakland police force and similar cuts throughout California and other states); *cf.* David W. Chen & Javier C. Hernandez, *Putting Blame on Albany, Mayor Unveils Budget With Heavy Cuts,* N.Y. TIMES, May 7, 2009, at A22 (describing a budget-driven plan to cut 892 police officers, later reversed—at the expense of teachers and other city employees—after the failed Times Square bombing plot); David Seifman & Dan Mangan, *A Cop Priority Thanks to Thug—NYPD Spared Slashes After Terrorist Bust,* N.Y. POST, May 6, 2010, at 4 (same).

increasingly intersect with local efforts to control ordinary crime.[10] And, as we discuss below, the local policing practices currently favored in much of America not only have hidden costs for effective crime prevention but also can directly undermine sound responses to the threat of terrorism.

The time is ripe, therefore, for rethinking the assumptions that have guided American police for most of the past two decades. Zero-tolerance policies and the order-maintenance model, as well as their various cousins, for all of their apparent success must be reoriented to make room for different priorities. We see no need for a radical restructuring of the police function, but what we propose is nonetheless a significant shift in emphasis, a shift to what we call a *procedural justice model* of policing.

The procedural justice approach is grounded in empirical research demonstrating that compliance with the law and willingness to cooperate with enforcement efforts are primarily shaped not by the threat of force or the fear of consequences, but rather by the strength of citizens' beliefs that law enforcement agencies are *legitimate*. And that belief in turn is shaped by the extent to which police behavior displays the attributes of *procedural justice*—practices, described in more detail below, which generate confidence that policies are formulated and applied fairly so that, regardless of material outcomes, people believe they are treated respectfully and without discrimination. When policing approaches the procedural justice model, law enforcement can be even more effective at lower cost and without the negative side effects that currently hamper our responses to international terrorism. Indeed, the procedural justice model has direct relevance for the development of successful strategies within that domain itself.

In Part II of this Article, we situate the procedural justice approach by reviewing the principles that inform the police function and the ways they have changed over recent decades. Part III describes the procedural justice model and explains its theoretical and empirical foundations. Part IV focuses on concrete policy implications for ordinary policing and for efforts to combat international terrorism. Part V offers concluding thoughts.

Changing Conceptions of the Police Function

Goals and Principles

From their beginnings in the early 1800s and for more than a century thereafter, urban police in America were a politically attuned branch of municipal government, charged not only with preserving order but also with relaying citizen requests for city services and delivering benefits

---

[10] *See* TO PROTECT AND TO SERVE: POLICING IN AN AGE OF TERRORISM (David Weisburd et al. eds., 2009); Matthew C. Waxman, *Police and National Security: American Local Law Enforcement and Counter-terrorism After 9/11,* 3 J. NAT'L SECURITY L. & POL'Y 377, 385–91 (2009).

to constituents at the precinct and ward levels.[11] As American cities mushroomed in size and density and as local political machines flourished, the police, deeply engaged in collecting and distributing patronage, occasionally brutal and often corrupt, became an indispensable arm of the ruling establishment.[12] The title of one scholarly study summed it up: *Police: Streetcorner Politicians*.[13] The dilemma of "law enforcement in a democratic society"[14]—the need not only to endow officials with authority to deploy deadly force but also to preserve democratic control—precipitated a "preoccupation with legitimacy."[15]

The solution that began to emerge in the 1950s, prominently endorsed in 1967 by the President's Commission on Law Enforcement and the Administration of Justice, was *professionalization*).[16] Henceforth, police were to be organized and managed as a highly-trained civil service devoted to crime control, and were designed to be "insular, homogeneous, and largely autonomous," with guarantees of independence from politics, and "purposely distanced" from the communities they were assigned to protect.[17] The importance of gaining and holding the community's trust was widely acknowledged, and police leaders typically assumed that trust would flow from legitimacy. But legitimacy came to be identified with professional norms, a military style of leadership, and a detached, reactive mode in which officers responded when called for help but deliberately kept their distance from individuals in the local community.[18]

The professional model bolstered one sort of democratic legitimacy—political independence—but undermined another—the authority grounded in the needs and preferences of the polity itself. Just at a time when broad grassroots authenticity was becoming the hallmark of democracy,[19] police were reaching for an elite mantle of detached expertise.[20] Once again, their legitimacy suffered.

Two adjustments were brought to bear. One was substantive: the due process model through which the Warren and Burger Courts reaffirmed constraints on law enforcement power and insisted that they be enforced not only by the police bureaucracy but also by an independent judiciary.[21]

---

[11] *See* Eric Monkkonen, *History of Urban Police,* 15 Crime & Just. 547, 549–52 (1992). In Britain, where modem policing originated in 1829 at the behest of Sir Robert Peel, the emphasis was different, and the police function was not embedded in municipal politics. *See generally* Wilbur R. Miller, Cops and Bobbies: Police Authority in New York and London (1999).

[12] *See generally* Jonathan Rubinstein, City Police (1973); M. Craig Brown & Barbara D. Warner, *Immigrants, Urban Politics, and Policing in 1900,* 57 Am. Soc. Rev. 293 (1992).

[13] William Ker Muir, Jr., Police: Streetcorner Politicians 271 (1977) (describing this phenomenon but by no means endorsing it).

[14] Jerome H. Skolnick, Justice Without Trial: Law Enforcement in Democratic Society (1966).

[15] *See* David Alan Sklansky, Democracy and the Police 93 (2008) (discussing "[t]he [p]reoccupation with [l]egitimacy").

[16] *See* President's Comm'n on Law Enforcement & Admin. of Justice, The Challenge of Crime in a Free Society (1967).

[17] Sklansky, *supra* note 15, at 6.

[18] *Id.* at 93–94.

[19] *See* David Alan Sklansky, *Police and Democracy,* 103 Mich. L. Rev. 1699, 1756–62 (2005) [hereinafter Sklansky, *Police and Democracy*] (describing the movement in favor of participatory democracy in the 1960s and 1970s).

[20] *See* Mark Harrison Moore, *Problem-solving and Community Policing, in* Modern Policing 99, 117 (Michael Tonry & Norval Morris eds., 1992) (noting that police "became cut off from the aspirations, desires, and concerns of citizens").

[21] *See* Lucas A. Powe, Jr., The Warren Court and American Politics 379–411 (2000) (summarizing case law); *cf.* Sklansky, *Police and Democracy, supra* note 19, at 1749 (noting criticism of Warren Court precedents).

The other adjustment was strategic. Emphasizing concepts like "community policing" or "problem-oriented policing," law enforcement priorities were recalibrated.[22] Police effort henceforth would be guided (or would claim to be guided) by the expressed preferences of "the community," as revealed in listening sessions at the grassroots and meetings with acknowledged or self-proclaimed community leaders.[23]

A related model with a significantly different emphasis, "order-maintenance policing" made it a priority for police to address local problems, even those that did not rise to the level of grave crimes.[24] Its widely accepted watchword was that "'[b]roken windows' do need to be repaired quickly."[25] Unlike many versions of community-oriented policing, however, some versions of the order-maintenance approach assigned to the police themselves the responsibility for identifying disorder. Another conception of reform went a step further, from maintaining order to eliminating all forms of disorder. Its message was zero tolerance: even minor misconduct was to be systematically suppressed. Legitimacy would come not from participatory democracy but from effectiveness; police authority would be accepted and respected because it would achieve results.

Thus, for more than half a century, achieving and maintaining "legitimacy" has been a central preoccupation both for those who support law enforcement and for those who want to constrain it. But legitimacy has been understood in sharply different terms: alternatively constitutional (compliance with the rule of law), political (governance in conformity with community preferences), or instrumental (success in reducing crime). The politically-charged disagreements have produced profound transformations, but one thing largely missing from the debates has been any effort to define precisely what "legitimacy" means or how to measure it empirically. Instead, an apparent consensus about the importance of police legitimacy has masked radically different assumptions about what that is and how it can be achieved.

Conceptual ambiguity and a failure to study empirical data bearing on issues of broad policing strategy are mirrored in conclusory debates about appropriate tactics for individual officers on the street. The debates, roughly speaking, center on competing preferences for being tough or being fair.

---

[22] *See generally* JEROME H. SKOLNICK & DAVID H. BAYLEY, THE NEW BLUE LINE (1986) (describing police innovation in six American cities); *id.* at 10–11 (noting "the beginnings of a social reconstruction of American policing" and "a strong inclination to recognize the significance of community trust and cooperation"); *id.* at 211 (characterizing the new approach as "community-oriented policing").

[23] *See generally* Moore, *supra* note 20; Jerome Skolnick & David Bayley, *Theme and Variation in Community Policing*, 10 CRIME & JUST. 1 (1988). Despite its many purely cosmetic features, the community policing movement also wrought many real and important changes. *See* David Alan Sklansky, The Persistent Pull of Police Professionalism (July 2010) (unpublished manuscript) (on file with authors).

[24] GEORGE L. KELLING & CATHERINE M. COLES, FIXING BROKEN WINDOWS: RESTORING ORDER AND REDUCING CRIME IN OUR COMMUNITIES 160 (1996).

[25] WESLEY G. SKOGAN, DISORDER AND DECLINE: CRIME AND THE SPIRAL OF DECAY IN AMERICAN NEIGHBORHOODS 75 (1990).

Tactical Choices: Toughness versus Fairness

Tough cops are not automatically unfair, and civil libertarians are not automatically soft, but being tough and being fair are often assumed to be in tension. A perception that police must choose between them arises almost everywhere in policing and in criminal law generally: street stops, surveillance, *Miranda* rights, and so on. In each instance, some people feel sure that social protection requires police powers that are unconstrained by procedural niceties, and others are equally convinced that harsh measures, if insensitive to individual rights, will prove counterproductive.

A similar argument arises in areas far outside of criminal justice. During the Vietnam War, the issue was framed as a debate about whether we should burn down villages sympathetic to the Viet Cong or focus instead on winning hearts and minds.[26] The same dilemma is now one of our military's biggest preoccupations in Iraq and Afghanistan.[27] A commentator who admires former President George W. Bush recently stated that we must "project global power and military might [or else our] hegemony will be challenged."[28] A recent op-ed in the *New York Times* derided our focus on hearts and minds in Afghanistan, arguing that it was more important to kill members of the Taliban than to worry about civilian casualties.[29] General Charles Krulak, a former commandant of the Marine Corps, takes exactly the opposite view. He claims that the United States military must use power sparingly because "the fundamental precept of counterinsurgency" is to "[u]ndermine the enemy's legitimacy while building our own."[30]

Many Americans have little doubt that in each of these areas the tough approach, whatever its moral drawbacks, at least will make them safer.[31] Another group feels equally sure that being tough can be counterproductive. The impact of toughness on effectiveness may be the most fundamental question in the whole field of social conflict and social control. Though the question is undeniably empirical, it is rarely treated as such; across the political spectrum, nearly everyone assumes that it can be answered on the basis of confident intuitions about the essence of human nature.

For police officers, toughness has not always been preferred. In the early days of modern urban policing, British Prime Minister Sir Robert Peel stressed that "[t]he police must secure the willing cooperation of the public" and that "[p]olice should use physical force ... only when the

---

[26] The debate is vividly presented in the 1974 documentary film *Hearts and Minds,* directed by Peter Davis. HEARTS AND MINDS (BBS Productions & Rainbow Releasing 1974); *see also* Elizabeth Dickinson, *A Bright Shining Slogan,* FOREIGN POL'Y, Sept./Oct. 2009, at 29.

[27] *See, e.g.,* Lara M. Dadkhah, *Empty Skies over Afghanistan,* N.Y. TIMES, Feb. 18, 2010, at A27.

[28] Nile Gardiner, *Bush Demonstrates That Hard Power Matters,* DAILY TELEGRAPH, Dec. 27, 2008, at 33.

[29] Dadkhah, *supra* note 27, at A27.

[30] Charles C. Krulack & Joseph P. Hoar, *Fear Was No Excuse To Condone Torture,* MIAMI HERALD, Sept. 11, 2009, at 25A.

[31] *See* Herring v. United States, 129 S. Ct. 695, 700–01 (2009) (quoting Illinois v. Krull, 480 U.S. 340, 352–53 (1987)) (internal quotation marks omitted); City of Chicago v. Morales, 527 U.S. 41 (1999) (plurality opinion) (discussing Chicago crackdown on "gang-loitering"); Dadkhah, *supra* note 27, at A27 (arguing for aggressive use of airpower in Afghanistan); John F. Harris, Mike Allen & Jim VandeHei, *Cheney Warns of New Attacks,* POLITICO (Feb. 4, 2009, 6:12 AM), http://www.politico.com/news/stories/0209/18390.html.

exercise of persuasion, advice, and warning is found to be insufficient."[32] Yet in more recent times, a preference for toughness has long held sway. Indeed, toughness has often been defended as beneficial for everyone. Police scholar William Muir described the mindset of police who believed that "[t]he nastier one's reputation, the less nasty one has to be."[33] Skolnick and Fyfe observe the prevalence of the same way of thought, adding that "[c]ops and everyone else understand the reality of this paradox. And whether or not they actually articulate it, cops develop styles of policing in response to it."[34]

The instinctive preference of the cop on the beat using the tough approach to policing style was potentially in tension with the notion that police agencies should be "problem-oriented" or "community based."[35] But that tension dissolved in certain versions of the "order-maintenance" approach, which emphasized aggressive street stops, along with "proactive enforcement of misdemeanor laws and zero tolerance for minor offenses."[36] In their seminal "Broken Windows" essay, Wilson and Kelling described the perspective of departments that made it a priority to prevent low-level disorder on the streets: "In the words of one officer, 'We kick ass.'"[37] A Chicago police officer who was "not prepared to stand by and watch gangs terrorize his family, friends, and neighbors" described "how he dealt with gang members who would not follow his orders: 'I say please once, I say please twice, and then I knock them on their ass.'"[38]

Even where police advocates of "community policing" were not committed to zero-tolerance or aggressive tactics, meetings with neighborhood groups evolved from the orientation required in community-based models—a reciprocal problem-solving conversation—into "a bland, one-sided, impersonal opportunity for city bureaucrats to manufacture consent" for measures they had already decided to implement.[39]

Although early assessments suggested that various order-maintenance approaches were "working" (i.e., reducing crime), more careful analysis revealed that aggressive street-level enforcement focused on quality-of-life offenses did not make cities safer.[40] Where genuine crime-control successes have been achieved, they seem attributable, at best, only to discrete, narrowly targeted programs that are unrelated (or antithetical) to order-maintenance enforcement

---

[32] John S. Dempsey & Linda S. Forst, An Introduction to Policing 8 (5th ed. 2010).

[33] Muir, *supra* note 13, at 41, 44, 101.

[34] Jerome H. Skolnick & James J. Fyfe, Above the Law: Police and the Excessive Use of Force 95 (1993). Skolnick and Fyfe are quick to note, however, that the tough style is not always successful. *Id.*

[35] See Sklansky, *supra* note 15, at 4, 123.

[36] Bernard E. Harcourt, Illusion of Order: The False Promise of Broken Windows Policing 2 (2001).

[37] James Q. Wilson & George L. Kelling, *Broken Windows: The Police and Neighborhood Safety,* Atlantic Monthly, March 1982, at 29.

[38] Kelling & Coles, *supra* note 24, at 166.

[39] *See* William Lyons, *Partnerships, Information and Public Safety,* 25 Policing Int'l J. Police Strat. & Mgmt 530, 534 (2002) (describing Seattle experience); *cf.* Wesley G. Skogan & Susan M. Hartnett, Community Policing, Chicago Style 113–14 (1997) (describing the interactive nature of Chicago's community policing program "beat meetings").

[40] *See* Harcourt, *supra* note 36, at 6–11, 59–121; *see also* Hubert Williams & Antony M. Pate, *Returning to First Principles: Reducing the Fear of Crime in Newark,* 33 Crime & Delinq. 53, 67 (1986) (noting that order-maintenance policies in Newark failed to achieve their goals); Frank Zimring, *The City that Became Safe: New York and the Future of Crime Control,* Sci. Am. (forthcoming August 2011) (manuscript on file with authors).

of low-level crimes.[41] Similarly, research does not support the widely held belief that police are always wise to seek to dominate situations by force; when police react to perceived threats by displaying force, their actions often escalate the conflict.[42]

How could it be that energetic policing, with a high volume of street stops, searches, and arrests, was *not* helping to reduce crime or protect officer safety? One place to look for a possible answer is the tradition that sees the legitimacy of official authority not through the lens of constitutional law, politics, or economic efficiency, but rather from the perspective of empirical social psychology.

Legitimacy as a Psychological Attribute

The psychological model of legitimacy posits that people obey the law, irrespective of expected rewards and penalties, when they view the government as worthy of trust and respect. This model's theoretical foundation is found in the work of Max Weber, who argued that legitimacy in this psychological sense was the key to *the effectiveness of the* state.[43] People must believe "that some decision... is entitled to be obeyed by virtue of who made the decision or how it was made."[44]

In the context of criminal justice, a large body of research confirms the links between perceived legitimacy and willingness to obey the law. To be sure, potential criminals are sometimes influenced by straightforward material incentives. People who steal cars or rob banks often take into account the chances of getting caught. There is much evidence that criminals can be influenced to commit their crimes at different times or places. And sometimes potential sanctions induce them to commit the offenses less frequently or not at all.[45]

But research also finds strong support for the psychological legitimacy model. In many situations, people obey the law not because of fear of getting caught but simply because they view the legal authorities as legitimate and believe that legitimate authorities should be obeyed.[46] Perceived legitimacy is assessed by asking people to express their degree of faith in various public institutions, as measured by their belief that officials are trustworthy, concerned about the welfare of those with whom they deal, able to protect citizens against crime, and otherwise

---

[41] *See* Zimring, *supra* note 40, at 30 (arguing that crime-control successes in New York City cannot be attributed to aggressive quality-of-life law enforcement, that in fact the NYPD, its rhetoric notwithstanding, de-emphasized this tactic, and that at most only one aspect of New York's aggressive street-stops approach (the targeting of certain "hot-spots") *may* be responsible for New York's crime-control gains).

[42] JOHN D. MCCLUSKEY, POLICE REQUESTS FOR COMPLIANCE: COERCIVE AND PROCEDURALLY JUST TACTICS 171 (2003).

[43] MAX WEBER, ON LAW IN ECONOMY AND SOCIETY 336 (Max Rheinstein ed., Edward Shils & Max Rheinstein trans., 1954) (noting that "every domination... always has the strongest need of self-justification through appealing to the principles of legitimation"); *id.* at 341 (describing legitimacy as prestige resting on beliefs of members of a political community).

[44] Tom R. Tyler, *Psychological Perspectives on Legitimacy and Legitimation,* 57 ANN. REV. PSYCHOL. 375, 377 (2006).

[45] Daniel Nagin, *Criminal Deterrence Research at the Outset of the Twenty-First Century,* 23 CRIME & JUST. 1, 12–15 (1998) (summarizing studies on the effect of sanctions on criminal deterrence).

[46] *See* TOM R. TYLER, WHY PEOPLE OBEY THE LAW 59 (rev. ed. 2006) [hereinafter TYLER, WHY PEOPLE OBEY]; *cf.* Clemens Kroneberg, Isolde Heintze & Guido Mehlkop, *The Interplay of Moral Norms and Instrumental Incentives in Crime Causation,* 48 CRIMINOLOGY 259, 283 (2010) (suggesting that although normative mechanisms are more important, some people only respond to incentives).

do their jobs well.[47] People who express a high degree of confidence in public authorities comply with the law either because of social influence (they want to avoid the disapproval of their social group) or because of internalized moral norms (they want to see themselves as decent people who do the right thing).[48] Legitimacy thus enables authorities to maintain social order almost automatically, without incurring the heavy costs required by instrumental strategies relying on arrest, adjudication, and incarceration.[49]

How can the police build this valuable attribute of legitimacy? Empirical research indicates that this sort of legitimacy is sustained not by an aggressive style that subordinates individual rights but rather by something closer to its opposite—practices that can be grouped under the heading of *procedural justice.*

The Procedural Justice Model

The procedural justice concept captures the fairness of the process used to make and apply rules and the quality of the personal treatment people receive from authorities.[50] Perceived fairness in decision-making has been found to be determined by such matters as whether police are viewed as unbiased and consistent and whether they give people opportunities to be heard before they take action. Perceived fairness of treatment, the research shows, is determined by such matters as whether police are courteous and respectful of people and their rights.

Conventional wisdom posits that the primary issue for people dealing with legal authorities is the outcome of the interaction. It is assumed, for example, that when a driver receives a traffic ticket, he is likely to be upset, but that if the encounter ends without issuance of a ticket, the driver is more likely to be happy. But empirical research tells a different story. An extensive body of data demonstrates that while people are happier when they do not receive an unfavorable result such as a traffic ticket, the principal factor shaping their reactions is whether law enforcement officials exercise authority in ways that are perceived to be fair.[51] This is true for

---

[47] *See* Tom R. Tyler & Jeffrey Fagan, *Legitimacy and Cooperation: Why Do People Help the Police Fight Crime in Their Communities?*, 6 Ohio St. J. Crim. L. 231, 270–71 (2008).

[48] *See* Kroneberg, Heintze & Mehlkop, *supra* note 46, at 259 (using survey data to determine the influence of different factors upon compliance); Paul H. Robinson & John M. Darley, *The Utility of Desert,* 91 Nw. U. L. Rev. 453, 468 (1997) (summarizing research that indicates an alternative explanation for obedience of the law because "fear of arrest and incarceration in prison is not effective in causing people to obey the law").

[49] *See* Tom R. Tyler, *Legitimacy and Criminal Justice: The Benefits of Self-Regulation,* 7 Ohio St. J. Crim. L. 307, 309 (2009) [hereinafter Tyler, *Legitimacy*] (reviewing literature to this effect).

[50] *See* Tom R. Tyler, Psychology and the Design of Legal Institutions 36–43 (2007); Jason A. Colquitt et al., *Justice at the Millennium: A Meta-Analytic Review of 25 Years of Organizational Justice,* 86 J. Applied Psychol. 425, 426 (2001).

[51] *See* Tom R. Tyler & Yuen J. Huo, Trust in the Law: Encouraging Cooperation With the Police and the Law (2002); Kimberly Belvedere, John L. Worrall & Stephen G. Tibbetts, *Explaining Suspect Resistance in Police-Citizen Encounters,* 30 Crim. Just. Rev. 30 (2005); Ben Bradford, Jonathan Jackson & Elizabeth A. Stanko, *Contact and Confidence: Revisiting the Impact of Public Encounters with the Police,* 19 Policing and Soc'y 20 (2009); Jacinta M. Gau & Rod K. Brunson, *Procedural Justice and Order Maintenance Policing: A Study of Inner-City Young Men's Perceptions of Police Legitimacy,* 27 Just. Q. 255 (2010); Lyn Hinds, *Youth, Police Legitimacy and Informal Contact,* 24 J. Police & Crim. Psychol. 10 (2009); Stephen D. Mastrofski,

both those who do and those who do not receive the unfavorable result. These findings have been replicated using a wide array of methodologies such as field research, panel studies, and experimental studies in "dozens of social, legal, and organizational contexts."[52]

The implications of this research for policing tactics are obvious but seldom appreciated. When police ramp up their arrest rates for low-level offenses like vandalism and vagrancy, the broken windows hypothesis suggests that neighborhood residents should be pleased by these efforts to combat disorder.[53] But opinion surveys often confound that expectation, finding that where arrest rates for these offenses rise or where other "crackdown" tactics are implemented, approval of the police has declined.[54] In light of the research we have canvassed, these results are not mysterious: tough measures, if implemented without fairness, are likely to arouse resentment rather than appreciation.

By contrast, toughness *with* fairness can be productive. In a study that interviewed New Yorkers both prior to and following a personal experience with the police, people who received a traffic citation from an officer who treated them fairly tended to view the police as *more* legitimate and were significantly *more* willing to cooperate with the police than they had been before that encounter.[55] As a result, the police can take actions to control crime and build legitimacy at the same time.

The assumption that there is a zero-sum trade-off between individual rights and public safety is therefore far too simple. When perceptions of procedural justice and legitimacy decline, people's willingness to obey also declines, but when authorities build their legitimacy, people are more willing to comply with the law.[56] And importantly, procedural fairness matters in similar ways for white, African-American, and Hispanic respondents, with only minor variations reflecting differences in the issues that are most salient to different ethnic groups.[57]

Jeffrey B. Snipes & Anne F. Supina, *Compliance on Demand: The Public's Response to Specific Police Requests,* 33 J. Res. Crime & Delinq. 269 (1996); Michael D. Reisig & Meghan Stroshine Chandek, *The Effects of Expectancy Disconfirmation on Outcome Satisfaction in Police-Citizen Encounters,* 24 Policing: Int'l J. Police Strategies & Mgmt. 88 (2001); Tom R. Tyler, *Procedural Justice, Legitimacy, and the Effective Rule of Law,* 30 Crime & Just. 431 (2003).

[52] Robert MacCoun, *Voice, Control, and Belonging: The Double-Edged Sword of Procedural Fairness,* 1 Ann. Rev. L. & Soc. Sci. 171, 173 (2005).

[53] *See, e.g.,* Randall Kennedy, Race, Crime, and the Law 301–10 (1996) (emphasizing "the sector of the black law-abiding population that desires more rather than less prosecution and punishment for all types of criminals"); Dan M. Kahan & Tracey L. Meares, *The Coming Crisis of Criminal Procedure,* 86 Geo. L.J. 1153, 1169–70 (1998) (same).

[54] Wesley G. Skogan, Disorder and Decline 15, 118 (1990); Brooks, *supra* note 2, at 1225.

[55] Tyler & Fagan, *supra* note 45, at 261.

[56] *See* Jason Sunshine & Tom R. Tyler, *The Role of Procedural Justice and Legitimacy in Shaping Public Support for Policing,* 37 Law & Soc'y Rev. 555 (2003). Some suggest that this line of argument glosses over a causal ambiguity: Citizens' perceptions of procedural fairness may be "colored by [their] views about the legitimacy of the police or courts." David J. Smith, *The Foundations of Legitimacy, in* Legitimacy and Criminal Justice: International Perspectives 29, 32–33 (T. Tyler et al. eds. 2007). If so, perceived legitimacy may shape perceptions of procedural fairness, rather than the other way around. The legitimacy research has used a variety of strategies to exclude this possibility. *See, e.g.,* Tyler & Fagan, *supra* note 47, at 251 (using panel data to measure judgments of legitimacy and procedural justice before and after encounters with the police).

[57] *See* Tom R. Tyler, *Policing in Black and White: Ethnic Group Differences in Trust and Confidence in the Police,* 8 Police Q. 322, 336 (2005).

Few would argue that compliance can never be achieved in the absence of procedural justice. Obedience can still be obtained, but only through intensive enforcement and harsh punishment. And that route—the one America has largely followed since the 1960s—is not only expensive from the start, but it can also trigger a downward spiral. Harsh repression enhances material incentives for compliance, but it weakens perceptions of fairness and thus the willingness to comply *voluntarily.* And that effect requires yet another increase in the use of aggressive enforcement measures, a step which in turn weakens voluntary compliance even more.

Most of the research testing the legitimacy model has focused on willingness to *violate* the law. But recent research also examines the links between procedural justice, legitimacy, and police capacity to secure *cooperation* from the general public.[58]

When police are combating crime and disorder, they need the help of the community.[59] People who discover a criminal in hiding have to decide whether to report him. When a crime is occurring, they have to make a similar decision. They may also be asked to attend community meetings to discuss policing strategies or to participate in activities such as neighborhood watch. In all these cases, police success in fighting crime depends upon public cooperation. And cooperation is a more fragile commodity than compliance, because it is easy for people not to cooperate. Even when material incentives have only limited impact on behavior, they are far more likely to influence *compliance* than *cooperation*. When does a mere bystander face penalties for *not* reporting a crime or for *not* attending a community meeting? People must *want* to cooperate with the police.

Yet in many low-income African-American and Hispanic neighborhoods, anti-snitching campaigns and other signs of mistrust make clear that, even where citizens are law-abiding and desperate to have safe neighborhoods, their cooperation with the police cannot be taken for granted.[60]

The research on cooperation finds that willingness to assist the police—for example, by reporting suspicious behavior or by participating in crime prevention programs—is strongly linked to a person's belief that police authority is legitimate. And that belief is strong only when officials exercise their authority fairly. Conversely, when perceptions of procedural justice and legitimacy decline, willingness to cooperate also declines.[61] In one study, procedural fairness was

---

[58] *See, e.g.,* Lyons, *supra* note 39; Tyler & Fagan, *supra* note 47; Tom R. Tyler, Stephen J. Schulhofer & Aziz Z. Huq, *Legitimacy and Deterrence Effects in Counter-Terrorism Policing: A Study of Muslim Americans,* 44 Law & Soc'y Rev. 365 (2010).

[59] *See* Robert J. Sampson, S. W. Raudenbush & F. Earls, *Neighborhoods and Violent Crime: A Multilevel Study of Collective Efficacy,* 277 Science 918 (1997).

[60] *See* Richard Delgado, *Law Enforcement in Subordinated Communities: Innovation and Response,* 106 Mich. L. Rev. 1193 (2008).

[61] *See* Lyons, *supra* note 39, at 536, 538 (profiling and other tactics resented in minority communities "make it more difficult for citizens in those communities with the information we seek to communicate [it] effectively .... Effective partnerships ... only produce the desired forms of cooperation when they operate as a mechanism to increase understanding, trust and respect among the parties ....").

more than twice as important for securing cooperation as judgments about police competence or the fairness of outcomes.[62]

In short, an emphasis on fairness appears to be central to police success in maintaining social order. Even though tough enforcement measures seem to increase an offender's probability of apprehension and conviction, the net effect of tough measures can be the opposite, and not only because toughness tends to chill voluntary compliance. Toughness also chills cooperation from the law-abiding community. That reduced cooperation in turn decreases the probabilities of apprehension and conviction, and those effects in turn decrease even the involuntary compliance achieved through the threat of sanctions.

Policy Implications of the Procedural Justice Model

In this Part, we discuss the implications of the procedural justice research for concrete policy measures in two areas of conventional policing—control of ordinary crime and control of misconduct by the police themselves. We then turn to its implications for domestic counterterrorism policing.

Controlling Ordinary Crime

Many zero-tolerance and order-maintenance models of policing, along with other instrumental approaches, emphasize efforts to control crime by increasing the density of police on the street and the frequency of street stops. For example, over a three-year period, a Chicago initiative aimed at containing misbehavior by unruly youth and gang members led police to order over 89,000 individuals to disperse and resulted in the arrest of over 42,000 people on charges of "gang loitering."[63] From 2003 to 2007, the number of street stops in New York City rose 500%, even though the crime rate was stable.[64] And these stops were disproportionally concentrated among minority group members.[65] Data from other jurisdictions show similar patterns.[66]

The procedural justice research described above suggests, however, that these efforts are likely to produce mixed or even counterproductive results. If carefully targeted crackdown measures do indeed have some crime-control payoff, as may have been the case recently in New York City,[66][67] and if such measures are therefore to be replicated and extended, it becomes

---

[62] See Tyler, *Legitimacy, supra* note 49, at 379–80 (comparing influence of perceived legitimacy and police effectiveness on willingness to cooperate).

[63] City of Chicago v. Morales, 527 U.S. 41, 49–50 (1999) (plurality opinion).

[64] Jeffrey Fagan, Amanda Geller, Garth Davies & Valerie West, *Street Stops and Broken Windows Revisited: The Demography and Logic of Proactive Policing in a Safe and Changing City, in* RACE, ETHNICITY, AND POLICING 309 (Stephen K. Rice & Michael D. White eds., 2010).

[65] See Andrew Gelman, Jeffrey Fagan & Alex Kiss, *An Analysis of the New York City Police Department's "Stop-and-Frisk" Policy in the Context of Claims of Racial Bias,* 102 J. AM. STAT. ASS'N 813, 813–14 (2007) (finding that African-American and Hispanic pedestrians in New York City were stopped more frequently than whites, even after controlling for race-specific estimates of criminal offending).

[66] In Los Angeles, for example, in 2003–2004 there were 4,569 stops per 10,000 African-American residents, but only 1,750 stops per 10,000 white residents. See IAN AYRES & JONATHAN BOROWSKY, A STUDY OF RACIALLY DISPARATE OUTCOMES IN THE LOS ANGELES POLICE DEPARTMENT 5–7 (2008), *available at* http://www.aclu-sc.org/documents/view/47.

[67] See Zimring, *supra* note 40.

particularly important to ensure that they are implemented wisely; the police departments that resort to them must exercise special care not to arouse resentment that offsets most of the expected benefits. Even worse, to the extent that stop-and-search practices and frequent arrests for low-level public-order offenses are seen as severe or racially selective, as they apparently are in many urban communities,[68] these practices may actually *impede* compliance and voluntary co-operation with law enforcement. "[Intensive frisks and needless arrests can often be a source of friction," thereby "undermining the very sense of legal legitimacy they were designed to foster."[69]

The damage can be especially great when street sweeps and arrests for "loitering" bear down on youth who are perceived as threats to a well-ordered community. The views of children and adolescents about law and the courts are shaped by many factors, including parents, teachers, gangs, the media, and interactions with the police.[70] Because adult orientations toward the law are often formed during adolescence, these precursors of adult attitudes are crucial. A considerable literature inspired by the broken windows hypothesis has posited that norms of law-abiding behavior can be nurtured by a strong law enforcement presence that exerts control over public spaces, stigmatizes gang membership, and drives disorderly youth off the streets.[71] Yet the empirical research canvassed here suggests the opposite—that intensive law enforcement and a readiness to arrest for low-level offenses is far more likely to arouse resentment, weaken police legitimacy, and undermine voluntary compliance with the law.[72]

Tactics that emphasize procedural justice can be equally effective with fewer negative side effects. In the procedural justice model, officers are not oriented toward addressing situations primarily with the threat of force. Instead, officers are trained to view every citizen contact as an opportunity to build legitimacy through the tone and quality of the interaction, with force a last resort.

Although police leaders have long paid lip service to the importance of gaining community trust, concrete steps to further this goal were either nonexistent or (as in the community policing movement) centered on discussion forums largely divorced from the daily activity of the cop on the beat. More recently, police departments across the country have begun to make more tangible efforts, but only in discrete programs of limited scope. An innovative Boston initiative engaged inner-city ministers and other community leaders in an effort to convince

---

[68] *See supra* text at notes 65–66.

[69] Reed Collins, *Strolling While Poor: How Broken-Windows Policing Created a New Crime in Baltimore,* 14 GEO. J. ON POVERTY L. & POL'Y 419, 426 (2007); *see also* Delgado, *supra* note 60, at 1202; K. Babe Howell, *Broken Lives from Broken Windows: The Hidden Costs of Aggressive Order-Maintenance Policing,* 33 N.Y.U. REV. L. & SOC. CHANGE 271, 313 (2009).

[70] Jeffrey Fagan & Alex R. Piquero, *Rational Choice and Developmental Influences on Recidivism Among Adolescent Felony Offenders,* 4 J. EMPIRICAL LEGAL STUD. 715, 718–19 (2007).

[71] *See, e.g.,* MARTIN S. JANKOWSKI, ISLANDS IN THE STREET: GANGS AND AMERICAN URBAN SOCIETY 193–202 (1991); Debra Livingston, *Police Discretion and the Quality of Life in Public Spaces,* 97 COLUM. L. REV. 551, 640–42 (1997).

[72] *See supra* text at notes 54, 56; Jeffrey Fagan & Tom R. Tyler, *Legal Socialization of Children and Adolescents,* 18 SOC. JUST. RES. 217 (2005); *see also* Tracey Meares, *The Legitimacy of Police Among Young African-American Men,* 92 MARQ. L. REV. 651 (2009). To be sure, further research is needed to clarify the links between adolescent experience and adult attitudes toward authority.

at-risk youth to steer clear of firearms.[73] In High Point, North Carolina, police managed to shut down open-air drug markets by offering dealers a dignified opportunity to avoid arrest in return for a commitment to abandon the drug trade.[74] A Chicago program has reportedly succeeded in reducing violence and recidivism by organizing discussion forums in which gun offenders on probation or parole meet with police officers, neighborhood residents, and social workers for discussions in which their concerns are treated with respect and their needs are addressed with support instead of only threats of punishment.[75] Reportedly, as many as seventy-five cities are now implementing legitimacy-inspired initiatives of this kind.[76]

Although the value of such programs is now widely recognized, police departments have yet to fully appreciate their psychological basis and their relevance to the full range of policing activity. Perhaps more worrisome is the fact that in many departments, officers have learned to acknowledge verbally the need to build community trust even when their behavior on the beat brazenly contradicts that commitment. In a 2004 study, Gould and Mastrofski observed officers subjecting black suspects stopped on the street without justification to humiliating strip searches and rectal examination in public settings; back at the stationhouse, the same officers "expressed a desire to establish strong bonds with neighborhood residents and to treat all citizens, including suspects, with a respectful demeanor."[77] Clearly, much more must be done to communicate convincingly to police officers the substance of that objective. And equally important, officers must fully appreciate its rationale and empirical foundations, if they are to internalize the message.

Forcible street contacts will inevitably cause anxiety and discomfort for pedestrians and motorists who are stopped, and police departments must therefore remain sensitive to the need to control their frequency, especially when declining rates of success in the resulting searches and declining arrest rates (as a percentage of all stops) signal diminishing returns. But forcible stops obviously should not be withdrawn from the law enforcement arsenal. Stops based on objective indications of a serious offense are almost always warranted, and they need not trigger community mistrust if police pay attention to what happens during such stops. Indeed, the available data suggest that although African Americans resent high levels of arrest for public-order offenses, their approval of the police is "positively correlated with arrest rates for more serious offenses."[78]

Thus, if stops are carefully initiated, police would not have to reduce their frequency. But even then, the procedural justice approach emphasizes a need for change: police departments must

---

[73] See Anthony A. Braga, David M. Kennedy, Elin J. Waring & Anne Morrison Piehl, *Problem-Oriented Policing, Deterrence, and Youth Violence: An Evaluation of Boston's Operation Ceasefire*, 38 J. Res. Crime & Delinq. 195, 198, 220 (2000).

[74] See Mark Schoofs, *New Intervention: Novel Police Tactic Puts Drug Markets out of Business*, Wall St. J., Sept. 27, 2006, at A1.

[75] See Andrew V. Papachristos, Tracey L. Meares & Jeffrey Fagan, *Attention Felons: Evaluating Project Safe Neighborhoods in Chicago*, 4 J. Empirical Legal Stud. 223, 254 (2007).

[76] See Meares, *supra* note 72, at 665 & n.95; *see also* Mark A.R. Kleiman, When Brute Force Fails: How to Have Less Crime and Less Punishment (2009) (discussing strategies to reduce crime with less reliance on arrest and incarceration).

[77] Jon B. Gould & Stephen D. Mastrofski, *Suspect Searches: Assessing Police Behavior Under the U.S. Constitution*, 3 Criminology & Pub. Pol'y 315, 345 (2004).

[78] Brooks, *supra* note 2, at 1225–26.

focus on altering the dynamics of police-citizen interaction. Instead of seeking to instill fear or project power, officers would aim to treat citizens courteously, briefly explain the reason for a stop, and, absent exigent circumstances, give the citizen an opportunity to explain herself before significant decisions are made. Moreover, they must be trained to maintain this orientation from the beginning of an encounter. An officer who initiates a stop in an aggressive manner, assuming the worst, cannot easily pivot to a polite, diffident stance if his suspicions prove unfounded. And even if he can do so, his explanations and apologies are unlikely to go far with an innocent citizen subjected to peremptory language and rough treatment at the outset.

These elements of procedurally-fair interaction go well beyond constitutional minimums, which typically focus on limiting *what* the government can do. But many requirements of constitutional law and criminal procedure do limit *the way* that government power is exercised. Even when officers have probable cause and a search warrant, the Fourth Amendment normally requires them to knock, announce their presence, state the basis of their authority, and give the homeowner an opportunity to admit them peaceably.[79] Officers normally must give the homeowner a copy of the warrant, to provide official confirmation of their authority and the limits on the permitted scope of the search.[80] After the search, they must deliver an inventory of items seized to establish a record of their actions and a readily understood basis for challenging unauthorized conduct.[81] These requirements, so often celebrated in Fourth Amendment tradition,[82] are not about limiting the tangible burdens government may impose; indeed the traditional abhorrence of clandestine searches[83] is hard to understand from a purely material perspective. The point of these requirements is essentially the same as that which the procedural justice findings stress—the importance of government's perceived legitimacy, sustained by actions that build trust and treat citizens with respect. The *Miranda* warnings were designed to serve the identical purpose, communicating to the suspect that officers will treat him with dignity and acknowledge his rights.[84]

---

[79] *See, e.g.,* Banks v. United States, 540 U.S. 31, 41 (2003) (discussing requirement of "reasonable wait time"); Richards v. Wisconsin, 520 U.S. 385, 394 (1997) (finding failure to knock and announce permissible only when officers have reasonable suspicion that doing so would be dangerous or futile); Wilson v. Arkansas, 514 U.S. 927, 929 (1995) (holding that common law "knock and announce" requirement forms part of the Fourth Amendment reasonableness inquiry).

[80] The obligation to provide a copy of the warrant is typically grounded in statutes or court rules but generally has not been treated as a Fourth Amendment requirement. *See* Wayne R. LaFave, Jerold H. Israel & Nancy J. King, Criminal Procedure § 3.4, at 177–78 (3d ed. 2000).

[81] City of West Covina v. Perkins, 525 U.S. 234 (1999) (basing this requirement on Fourteenth Amendment due process rather than the Fourth Amendment).

[82] *See, e.g., Wilson,* 514 U.S. at 931–33 (tracing lineage of the knock-and-announce rule back to the thirteenth century and finding that it "was woven quickly into the fabric of early American law").

[83] *See, e.g.,* United States v. Villegas, 899 F.2d 1324, 1336 (2d Cir. 1990) (finding clandestine search permissible only when secrecy is "essential"); United States v. Freitas, 800 F.2d 1451, 1456 (9th Cir. 1986) (holding that when circumstances justify clandestine search, notice to homeowner must nonetheless be given within seven days; extensions of this period permissible only on a "strong showing of necessity").

[84] Miranda v. Arizona, 384 U.S. 436, 457–60 (1966) (stating that in the absence of warnings, custodial interrogation "trades on the weaknesses of individuals" and is "destructive of human dignity"; "the constitutional foundation underlying the privilege [against self-incrimination] is the respect a government—state or federal—must accord to the dignity and integrity of its citizens.").

There is no reason, however, for police conceptions of fair treatment to stop with the constitutional minimum. In connection with street stops, operational guidelines within each department could formalize appropriate steps, such as the need for courteous treatment, the obligation to give the citizen a reason for the stop, and a chance to explain the circumstances. In this spirit, the review committee established to examine the Gates incident in Cambridge cautioned that "actions that police take to protect their safety and the safety of others can seem cold, insensitive, or overly authoritarian.... Whatever police can reasonably do to explain the reasons for the interaction and deescalate a situation is vital to the peaceful resolution of the encounter."[85] Such steps could be made a routine part of every officer's behavior on the beat. With their low cost and potential for high crime-control payoff, changes like these are a smart use of limited police resources.

As a simple way to put such priorities into practice, officers could easily carry and give to those they stop a card containing a short statement of the rules that govern police stops. The card would enumerate the rights that must be respected (including the right to have the reasons for the stop explained and the right to tell their side of the story before decisions are made) and the procedures for complaining about unfair treatment. Such efforts help communicate to the public that procedural justice principles are taken seriously.

Because trust in the police varies dramatically across racial lines,[86] policing methods must be especially attuned to racial sensibilities. Of course, that point in itself is not new. But we can illustrate the need for a new emphasis by considering the issue of "profiling" and the Gates incident in particular. Traditionally the study of racial profiling has focused upon whether reliance on racial markers actually occurs. We might ask, for example, if Officer Crowley took into account Professor Gates's African-American appearance or whether the police generally profile minorities. To do so we would collect statistics on street stops, adjust them for actual rates of offending in the target population, and analyze the data to determine if the police stop African Americans more often than is justified by objectively based concerns about crime.

Following the argument of this Article, however, the Gates case (and other minority experiences with the police) would be approached *from* a different perspective. People generally view racial profiling as unfair, and when police action leads people to feel they have been profiled, it prompts hostility.[87] This response was evident when Professor Gates reacted to his perception that his treatment was explained simply by the fact that he was a "Black man in America."[88] The *belief* that the police are using unfair procedures delegitimates their authority and leads people to resist it.

This finding has two important implications. First, a person can be strongly affected by police contact even if nothing legally significant happens. Even when people are not arrested, they

---

[85] *See* Cambridge Review Committee, *supra* note 1, at 27.

[86] *See supra* text at note 2.

[87] Tom R. Tyler & Cheryl Wakslak, *Profiling and the Legitimacy of the Police: Procedural Justice, Attributions of Motive, and the Acceptance of Social Authority,* 42 Criminology 13, 13–42 (2004).

[88] *See* Cambridge Review Committee, *supra* note 1, at 56.

can still feel disrespected, and this will change their views about the police. As a consequence, experiences need to be evaluated in terms of their influence upon the person's views about the police, not just in terms of whether people were arrested and searched, or why (from the officer's perspective) he decided to act. Even trivial incivilities contribute to a climate of illegitimacy. The Supreme Court, along with countless other observers, has repeatedly missed this point.[89]

Second, people can have a *positive* experience even when the police take some potentially unwelcome enforcement action. Police can therefore act to control crime and build legitimacy at the same time. As shown in the research we have canvassed above, people who received a negative decision (such as a traffic ticket) from an officer who treated them fairly viewed the police as *more* legitimate than they did before the encounter.[90] In short, police who treat people even-handedly and with respect can reinforce their legitimacy even when they are compelled by the situation to act firmly and aggressively—force is more acceptable when it is viewed as reasonable and justified and when it is delivered through just procedures. These implications are relevant to much more than just race relations. The research on legitimacy establishes that America's policing model for dealing with people in all communities and of all ethnicities needs to change.

Of course, there is a danger here. Police who successfully cultivate a courteous, self-effacing demeanor could use that façade to mask discriminatory and unnecessarily intrusive practices. We should perhaps be careful what we wish for. But police are as yet light years away from acquiring the attitudes and behavior on patrol that could make this danger a reality. The prospect of that unintended consequence simply underscores that a new emphasis on the neglected qualitative dimension of police-citizen interaction must complement but not displace the equally import- ant quantitative dimensions. The frequency of stops, the success rates of associated searches, and the distribution of these outcomes across racial and ethnic groups are already important tools for gauging police performance. We claim that these metrics have too often monopolized attention, but an appreciation for the significance of perceived legitimacy would not by any means render these measures irrelevant or obsolete.

Police Misconduct

Attention to legitimacy is important for another sort of compliance—compliance by police officers themselves.

Nearly all existing models of policing posit that an officer seeking to prevent crime and disorder *wants* to exert force (conducting stops, searches, and arrests) and that this desire is held in check by an unwelcome, externally imposed constraint—the obligation to remain within

---

[89] *See, e.g.,* Whren v. United States, 517 U.S. 806 (1996) (upholding authority of vicesquad officers to make arrest for failure to signal a turn, whether or not their action was pretextual). *Compare* United States v. Martinez-Fuerte, 428 U.S. 543, 560, 563 (1976) (holding "objective intrusion" was "minimal" because of stops' "public and relatively routine nature," even though stops were made "on the basis of apparent Mexican ancestry"), *with id.* at 573 (Brennan, J., dissenting) (positing that the "experience [would be] particularly vexing for the motorist of Mexican ancestry who is selectively referred, knowing that the officers' target is the Mexican alien").

[90] *See supra* text at note 50.

constitutional boundaries. Professor Herbert Packer captured this notion and etched it into several generations of criminal procedure scholarship with his influential paradigm contrasting a "crime control model" (one that emphasizes the goal of reducing crime as efficiently as possible) with a "due process model" (one that gives priority to maintaining respect for individual rights).[91]

In this view, police who disregard search and seizure rules may face penalties (suppression of evidence, civil damages, or administrative sanctions), and such penalties are assumed to encourage compliance through the instrumental logic of deterrence. The officer considers every stop and every search as potentially beneficial, but she must weigh those benefits against potential sanctions. When the officer can foresee that an exclusionary rule applies, the expected costs will outweigh benefits, misconduct will be deterred, and compliance with constitutional norms will be achieved. Conversely, if an officer cannot foresee the prospect of an exclusionary sanction, her behavior supposedly cannot be affected. For the current Supreme Court, this logic has become an analytic obsession, as a majority of the Justices now approach nearly every issue concerning the exclusionary rule by examining the details of presumed deterrence effects under particular circumstances.[92]

From a legitimacy perspective, inquiries of this sort (whatever then-conclusions) are profoundly misguided. The empirical research makes clear that fear of sanctions by itself generates only weak, poorly motivating incentives, which in turn produce at best a sullen, resentful, imperfect form of compliance. And this is exactly what we often observe in the case of police officers asked to comply with the rules of search and seizure. Indeed, the payoff from instrumental deterrence in that context is especially poor, just as we would expect, because those rules and their accompanying sanctions enjoy little legitimacy in the eyes of the police to whom they are addressed. Like the exclusionary rule and for similar reasons, damage suits and institutional reform litigation have had only mixed success in changing the culture of police organizations.[93]

The legitimacy perspective makes clear that seeking to compel change through suppression remedies, lawsuits, and consent decrees can have only limited effectiveness because the police then seek ways to avoid detection and accountability. Just as with achieving compliance by the public, so with the police: we need to change what they want to do.

The difference between Fourth and Fifth Amendment requirements is telling here. Police compliance with the rules of search and seizure is always in doubt; evasion and even outright perjury are sometimes the officer's preferred course.[94] In contrast, police interrogators for the

---

[91] HERBERT L. PACKER, THE LIMITS OF THE CRIMINAL SANCTION (1968).

[92] *See, e.g.,* Herring v. United States, 129 S. Ct. 695, 702 (2009) (exclusionary rule applies only when exclusion can "meaningfully deter" police misconduct); Hudson v. Michigan, 547 U.S. 586, 596–97 *(2006)* (same); United States v. Leon, 468 U.S. 897, 907 (1984) (same). *But see* Rakas v. Illinois, 439 U.S. 128 (1978) (exclusionary rule may not be invoked to suppress fruits of an illegal search that did not violate the defendant's personal rights).

[93] *See* Barbara Armacost, *Organizational Culture and Police Misconduct,* 72 GEO. WASH. L. REV. 453, 464–78 (2004) (cataloguing reasons why individual remedies are ineffective at changing police institutions); David Rudovsky, *Police Abuse: Can the Violence be Contained?,* 27 HARV. C.R.-C.L. L. REV. 465, 480–88 (1992) (discussing lack of success in judicial efforts to change police culture).

[94] *See, e.g.,* Myron W. Orfield, *Deterrence, Perjury, and the Heater Factor: An Exclusionary Rule in the Chicago Criminal Courts,* 63 U. COLO. L. REV. 75, 82–83 (1992) (documenting pervasive police perjury used to avoid exclusionary rule in

most part follow *Miranda* and give the warnings routinely. The reason is simple: police have learned that they *benefit* from compliance, because the *Miranda* warnings tend to put suspects at ease by creating a (false) sense of security and thereby help officers to get confessions.[95]

The procedural justice model is promising from this perspective both for the reasons outlined above and because the changes in police practices it calls for[96] are simple to implement and relatively inexpensive. More important, they benefit the police themselves, not just outside citizens and "bad guys." By projecting sensitivity to procedural justice, officers build their legitimacy and nurture public support. They thereby gain community respect, enhance the safety of their working environment, and create conditions likely to elicit greater cooperation in fighting crime. The police are gradually transformed from an occupying force into genuine partners with all components of the community, minorities and the poor included. And, of course, such changes also benefit the community, in particular minorities and the poor, who are policed in a more professional and respectful manner.

We do not doubt the importance of penalties such as the exclusionary rule and will have more to say about them in a moment. But reform of police organizations must start from within. Articles that make a seemingly similar point—for example, urging reliance on internal police guidelines, civilian review boards, and administrative sanctions—are too numerous to count, but nearly all proposals of this sort lack an essential feature: positive motivation. The empirical findings make clear that police must *want* to follow such guidelines, because (as in the case of citizens who might contemplate other sorts of wrongdoing) the probability that a violation will be detected and punished often is too low to provide in itself a sufficiently strong reason for obedience.

Creating positive motivations for compliance is essential not only to ensure respect for citizens' rights but also to achieve adherence to a broad range of internal operational standards and norms. A working environment conducive to those motivations involves several elements. The management literature develops them in detail,[97] and we do not propose to discuss them in depth here. But the key ingredient is worth emphasizing, though it is obvious from what we have already said, because the criminal procedure and organizational-reform literature almost always assumes that ingredient to be missing and unattainable. The ingredient, of course, is the *legitimacy* of the rules in question. And by legitimacy here, we do not mean a legal or constitutional legitimacy grounded in a duly enacted text. Rather, as we have stressed throughout, the key concept is social and psychological legitimacy, from the perspective of the target audience whose compliance is sought. Officers must come to understand that observing the tenets of procedural justice will serve their own interest, apart from the constitutional pedigree of these

---

important cases).

[95] *See* Stephen J. Schulhofer, Miranda's *Practical Effect: Substantial Benefits and Vanishingly Small Social Costs,* 90 Nw. U. L. Rev. 500, 516–38 (1996) (reviewing evidence to this effect).

[96] *See supra* text at notes 73–90.

[97] *See, e.g.,* V. Lee Hamilton & Joseph Sanders, *Responsibility and Risk in Organizational Crimes of Obedience,* 14 Res. Organizational Behav. 49 (1992).

norms, even when (as with many of the fair-treatment dimensions of procedural justice) the norms are by no means constitutionally mandated.

Tone from the Top

Attaining this sort of legitimacy begins with the "tone from the top." Police leaders must empha-size the value of building public support, helping citizens to feel comfortable and safe rather than threatened by the police presence. Leaders must communicate that while force will always have a role in policing, that role should be as a last resort, one that should seldom need to be used.

Recognition and Reward

Police reward structures also need to be reshaped so that building legitimacy in the community is viewed as a goal of equal importance to issuing traffic tickets and making arrests. If officers believe that then-advancement, compensation, and respect in the eyes of their leadership are linked to their ability to create legitimacy and motivate cooperation, they are more likely to follow the principles of procedural fairness in their behavior on the street.

When considering incentive structures, it is important to think beyond material rewards. Studies of work organizations suggest that the impact of material rewards generally flows through their role in signaling management respect for employees and their contributions. Employees want to know that their efforts are valued by their superiors.[98] Studies of police orga-nizations indicate that one of the best ways to communicate respect is to follow the principles of procedural justice (fair decision-making and fair interpersonal treatment) in dealing with officers themselves. Officers in the ranks should be afforded a voice in the formulation of the rules that govern their performance (a step to which police departments have recently become more receptive), and they must feel fairly treated in connection with internal discipline and civil-ian review board procedures. Officers who feel respected are more likely to accept departmental policies as legitimate and to comply with them voluntarily."[99]

Correspondingly, officers need to believe that their adherence to these policies will be recog-nized by their superiors. Being able to reward the police in this way requires new sorts of data. Routine efforts to follow up on police-citizen contact can verify compliance with procedural justice principles and reinforce a procedural justice culture within the police department. Police statisticians must move beyond their preoccupation with clearance rates to measure trends in public confidence in the police and in public evaluations of the fairness of police practices, both among those who have had personal experiences with the police and in the community generally. In London, for example, the Metropolitan Police now routinely surveys the public to

---

[98] *See* Tom R. Tyler & Steven L. Blader, *Can Businesses Effectively Regulate Employee Conduct? The Antecedents of Rule Following in Work Settings,* 48 Acad. Mgmt. J. 1143, 1153 (2005).

[99] Tom R. Tyler, Patrick E. Callahan & Jeffrey Frost, *Armed, and Dangerous (?): Motivating Rule Adherence Among Agents of Social Control,* 41 Law & Soc'y Rev. 457, 481, 483 (2007).

ascertain levels of public confidence in law enforcement and willingness to cooperate.[100] Such data collection efforts nurture the legitimacy of procedural justice norms in the eyes of the cop on the beat while also signaling to the public that support for these norms is genuine within the police department itself.

A similar linkage between public perceptions and police attitudes in matters of procedural justice could profitably be examined in connection with civilian review boards or purely internal disciplinary processes. We need to pay more attention to the ways in which these review mechanisms are seen in the eyes of both citizens and the cops who are potentially subject to them. And in line with the theme of nurturing legitimacy by rewards as well as sanctions, civilian review boards could well make it part of their mission to look for successes as well as the most egregious failures, and to ensure that successes are appropriately recognized.

The Exclusionary Rule

If the perceived legitimacy of the rules governing police behavior is the key to compliance, and if instrumental incentives have little bite, can we dispense with sanctions like the Fourth Amendment exclusionary rule? The question is by no means merely academic. A chorus of voices has argued that changes in urban politics and in the demography and professionalism of the police have made obsolete the judicially enforced criminal procedure restraints developed by the Warren and Burger Courts in response to police oppression of minorities.[101] And the Supreme Court itself seems increasingly ready to gut the exclusionary rule or abandon it completely.[102] There is much to be said on the other side of this debate,[103] but here we focus solely on the research findings concerning procedural justice and legitimacy.

---

[100] For details on the methodology and results of the most recent survey, see Metropolitan Police Service (London), *Public Confidence in Policing London,* http://www.met.police.uk/about/performance/confidence.htm (last visited Jan. 17, 2011).

[101] *See, e.g.,* Hudson v. Michigan, 547 U.S. 586, 598 (2006) (stating that "[a]nother development over the past half-century that deters civil-rights violations [thus making the exclusionary rule less necessary] is the increasing professionalism of police forces, including a new emphasis on internal police discipline"); Kahan & Meares, *supra* note 53, at 1169–70 (stating that in "today's inner city... the citizens who support giving more discretion to the police are the same ones who are exposed to the risk that discretion will be abused").

[102] *See, e.g.,* Herring v. United States, 129 S. Ct. 695, 702 (2009) (rejecting the rule that suppression is presumptively mandated for all illegally seized evidence and holding that "police conduct must be sufficiently deliberate that exclusion can meaningfully deter it, and sufficiently culpable that such deterrence is worth the price paid by the justice system"); *Hudson,* 547 U.S. at 591, 597, 599 (stating that the exclusionary rule should be applied only where deterrence benefits outweigh its "massive" social costs, and, because "much has changed" since 1961, exclusion is not necessarily justified today simply because that remedy was held necessary "in different contexts and long ago").

[103] The Fourth Amendment at its inception had nothing whatever to do with preventing racial oppression, and to the extent that this concern has greater salience today, it is not plausible to suggest that American policing tactics have rendered it obsolete. In any event, there is no evidence to support (and much evidence to contradict) the Court's assumption in *Hudson,* 547 U.S. at 597–98, that civil damage liability provides all the deterrence needed *See id.,* at 609–11 (Breyer, J., dissenting) (arguing that any damages awarded are likely to be nominal); *Herring,* 129 S. Ct. at 709 n.6 (Ginsburg, J., dissenting) ("[P]rofessionalism is a sign of the exclusionary rule's efficacy—not of its superfluity"); David Alan Sklansky, *Is the Exclusionary Rule Obsolete?,* 5 OHIO ST. J. CRIM. L. 567, 579–82 (2008) ("Despite the genuinely

From its inception, the exclusionary rule has reflected two distinct, though complementary concerns. One is the desire "to deter—to compel respect for the constitutional guaranty in the only effectively available way—by removing the incentive to disregard it."[104] But in adopting the exclusionary rule in *Mapp v. Ohio,* the Court also stressed that "there is another consideration—the imperative of judicial integrity."[105]

For both Justice Holmes and Justice Brandeis, "judicial integrity" was the decisive point. As Justice Brandeis put it, exclusion of tainted evidence is essential "to maintain respect for law... [and] to preserve the judicial process from contamination."[106] The objective, he said in one of his best known opinions, is not to tip the balance of an individual officer's incentives but to protect the foundations of government itself: "Our Government is the potent, the omnipresent teacher. For good or ill, it teaches the whole people by its example.... If the Government becomes a law-breaker, it breeds contempt for law;... it invites anarchy."[107] Justice Brennan urged the same view, emphasizing that suppression of tainted evidence "assur[es] the people... that the government would not profit from its lawless behavior, thus minimizing the risk of seriously undermining popular trust in government."[108]

In its latest opinions, the Court acknowledged that this perspective dominated at the outset, but declared that "we have long since rejected that approach."[109] Instead, the Court now insists that exclusion is justified solely by potential deterrence of police misconduct, and it gives that rationale a newly constrained form. Two conditions must be met: there must be "appreciable" deterrence and, in addition, "[t]o the extent that application of the exclusionary rule could provide some incremental deterrent, that possible benefit must be weighed against [its] substantial social costs."[110] As a result, exclusion now is "our last resort, not our first impulse."[111] And raising even further this barrier to a suppression remedy, the Court seems to have set aside the long-standing rule of exclusion for the fruits of objectively unreasonable police searches and arrests. Instead, "[t]o trigger the exclusionary rule, police conduct must be sufficiently deliberate that exclusion can meaningfully deter it, and sufficiently culpable that such deterrence is worth the price paid by the justice system."[112] This new approach gives the police, and is expressly designed to give the police, much greater freedom to secure convictions by using illegally seized evidence.

---

vast changes in law enforcement over the past forty years, the exclusionary rule probably still does a lot of work that no other remedy stands ready to duplicate.").

[104] Mapp v. Ohio, 367 U.S. 643, 656 (1961) (quoting Elkins v. United States, 364 U.S. 206, 217 (1960)) (internal quotation marks omitted).

[105] *Id.* at 659 (quoting *Elkins,* 364 U.S. at 222) (internal quotation marks omitted).

[106] Olmstead v. United States, 277 U.S. 438, 484 (1928) (Brandeis, J., dissenting); *see also id.* at 470 (Holmes, J., dissenting) ("[I]t [is] a less evil that some criminals should escape than that the Government should play an ignoble part.").

[107] *Id.* at 485 (Brandeis, J., dissenting).

[108] United States v. Calandra, 414 U.S. 338, 357 (1974) (Brennan, J., dissenting).

[109] *Hudson,* 547 U.S. 586, 591 (2006) (acknowledging that "[e]xpansive dicta in *Mapp* ... suggested wide scope for the exclusionary rule").

[110] Herring v. United States, 129 S. Ct. 695, 700–01 (2009) (quoting Illinois v. Krull, 480 U.S. 340, 352–53 (1987)) (internal quotation marks omitted).

[111] *Hudson,* 547 U.S. at 591.

[112] *Herring,* 129 S. Ct at 702.

The present Court's assumption that suppression inflicts substantial costs, by weakening our ability to impose criminal punishment, is of course the polar opposite of the Brandeis view that it is the *failure* to suppress that will breed lawlessness. As an *a priori* matter, neither view is intrinsically implausible. But the empirical research canvassed here has direct relevance for this debate. And those studies provide compelling support for the Brandeis insight on which the exclusionary rule originally rested. Indeed, Justice Brandeis's reasoning presciently expresses the best current understanding of the connections between legitimacy, procedural justice, and the control of crime.

As we have developed in detail throughout this Article, the research regularly finds that people comply with the law not primarily because of fear of sanctions but rather because they believe that authorities that have legitimacy should be obeyed. And such legitimacy flows from people's confidence that officials are trustworthy, that they abide by the law, and that they treat citizens with respect.[113] Official disregard for the law—made evident when misconduct can be openly exploited to prosecutorial advantage in court—is the kind of behavior that, the research establishes, tends to weaken perceived legitimacy and willingness to cooperate with law enforcement.

Opponents of the exclusionary rule sometimes suggest that the notion of "judicial integrity" argues *against* suppression of illegally seized evidence. Contrary to Justice Brandeis, they insist that because suppression can allow obviously guilty defendants to go free, it *undermines* public confidence in the criminal justice system.[114] The legitimacy research has not tested this sort of claim in the specific context of the exclusionary rule. But the general question this argument poses—whether legitimacy is shaped more strongly by police effectiveness than by procedural justice—has been studied in depth across a wide variety of law enforcement situations.[115] And the findings are consistent: in virtually every context studied to date, law enforcement effectiveness has displayed at best only a weak influence on perceived legitimacy, while procedural justice concerns are strongly linked to legitimacy, voluntary compliance, and willingness to cooperate.[116]

Against this background, relaxation of the exclusionary rule represents a direct assault on the capacity of our law enforcement system to succeed in its mission of maintaining social order. To be sure, a prosecutor's ability to use illegally seized evidence increases her capacity to secure a conviction and a long sentence, an unequivocal crime control benefit if viewed strictly in the short term. But the strong and consistent finding of the relevant research is that the net effect of law enforcement disregard for the law is likely to be the opposite, because judicial tolerance for Fourth Amendment violations will generate disrespect for authority, chill voluntary compliance,

---

[113] *See supra* text at notes 50–55.

[114] *See, e.g.,* Carol S. Steiker, *Counter-Revolution in Constitutional Criminal Procedure? Two Audiences, Two Answers,* 94 Mich. L. Rev. 2466, 2513 (1996) (describing this argument and its role in the development of the good faith exception to the exclusionary rule).

[115] *See, e.g.,* Tyler, Why People Obey, *supra* note 46; Tyler & Fagan, *supra* note 47; Tyler, Schulhofer & Huq, *supra* note 58.

[116] *See, e.g.,* Tyler, Why People Obey, *supra* note 46, at 59 (linking procedural justice concerns to compliance); Tyler & Fagan, *supra* note 47, at 251 tbl.3 (linking procedural justice concerns to cooperation); Tyler, Schulhofer & Huq, *supra* note 58, at 380 (linking procedural justice concerns to cooperation).

and discourage law-abiding citizens from offering the cooperation that makes it possible to apprehend and convict other offenders in future cases.[117]

Controlling ordinary crime and controlling police misconduct thus are closely connected. And if we are to succeed at both, procedural justice concerns must be placed at the center of attention.

Domestic Counterterrorism

Terrorism is generally considered a problem to be distinguished from ordinary wrongdoing. Like efforts to combat drug trafficking and some forms of organized crime, preventing terrorist attacks requires close attention to international linkages, and federal enforcement agencies take the lead. Yet terrorism differs significantly from other sorts of transnational criminality. Its motivations are usually political rather than financial, its potential for social harm is vastly greater, and its connections to foreign policy and armed conflict are more prominent. Partly for those reasons, the structure of law enforcement is distinctive. Local policing is sometimes relegated to an afterthought; the federal government is expected to play, and does play, an overwhelmingly dominant role.[118]

In light of these contrasts, the applicability of the procedural justice approach to counterterrorism can hardly be taken for granted. Yet criminal justice theory and the dynamics of terrorism both suggest that this model has powerful relevance. And as we discuss below, the empirical research specific to this context, though less comprehensive than that in the area of ordinary crime, confirms its importance at all levels, from grand strategy in the federal agencies to the daily behavior of the cop on the beat.

Start at the place that usually gets the least attention—local policing. Despite the widespread assumption of federal primacy, law enforcement officials increasingly recognize that local police must play a significant role. Collaboration has even been channeled through formal institutions such as Joint Terrorism Task Forces and "fusion centers."[119]

In part, the growing involvement of local police flows from perceived changes to the nature of the terrorist challenge. In the aftermath of the September 2001 attacks, the threat was perceived as a largely foreign-source affair. The July 2007 National Intelligence Estimate played down terrorist threats of domestic origin and identified the growing strength of al Qaeda in western

---

[117] *See, e.g.,* Lyons, *supra* note 39, at 538 (finding that desired cooperation occurs only when police build community "understanding, trust and respect"); Tyler, *Legitimacy, supra* note 49, at 379–80 (police effectiveness is much less important than perceived legitimacy in predicting willingness to cooperate); Tyler, Schulhofer & Huq, *supra* note 58, at 380 tbl. 1 (finding perceived effectiveness of police has no significant correlation with willingness to cooperate, but that procedural justice concerns are strongly correlated with willingness to cooperate).

[118] *See, e.g.,* David Thacher, *The Local Role in Homeland Security,* 39 Law & Soc'y Rev. 635, 669 (2005) (describing factors that prompt federal institutions to take lead); Dafna Linzer, *In New York, a Turf War in the Battle Against Terrorism,* Wash. Post, Mar. 24, 2008, at A1 (describing FBI reluctance to cede responsibilities to New York City Police Department). *But see* Samuel J. Rascoff, *The Law of Homegrown (Counter) Terrorism,* 88 Tex. L. Rev. 1715 (2010) (arguing that local police must play significant role).

[119] *See* John Rollins, Congressional Res. Serv., No. RL34070, Fusion Centers: Issues and Options for Congress 1–2 (updated Jan. 18, 2008), *available at* http://fas.org/sgp/crs/intel/RL34070.pdf.

Pakistan as the principal danger to the United States.[120] In late 2009, this perception began to change with a series of allegations concerning terrorism conspiracies developed within the United States.[121] The 2010 National Security Strategy warned that "recent incidences of violent extremists in the United States" demonstrate "the threat to the United States and our interests posed by individuals radicalized at home."[122] Of 202 people charged with serious terrorist crimes since September 11, 2001, more than half have been U.S. citizens, and over one-third of those have been American-born.[123]

These new threats give local law enforcement increased prominence, but its importance is now acknowledged even in connection with dangers emanating abroad. A recent RAND Corporation report, drawing from global counterterrorism experiences, notes that terrorism is largely a policing problem, not a military matter, because local police are best able to build relationships with the communities in which terrorists try to hide and recruit members. The report urges police to "actively encourage and cultivate cooperation by building stronger ties with community leaders...."[124] Another RAND report observes that "state and local law enforcement agencies ... may be uniquely positioned to augment federal intelligence capabilities by virtue of their presence in nearly every American community [and] their knowledge of local individuals and groups ...."[125] These conclusions are consonant with a broader stream of thought that understands global terrorism as a form of "insurgency" most easily defeated by winning the loyalty of the communities in which terrorists may be found.[126] Even in foreign theaters of military operation, heavy firepower, though still favored by some,[127] is increasingly de-emphasized in favor of at least partial reliance upon measures akin to domestic policing.[128]

---

[120] Nat'l Intelligence Council, National Intelligence Estimate: The Terrorist Threat to the US Homeland 5 (2007). The National Intelligence Estimate summarizes "the Intelligence Community's (IC) most authoritative written judgments on national security issues ...." *Id.* at 2.

[121] These conspiracies included the decision of a Somali-American to travel to Somalia and become the first American suicide bomber, the July 2009 arrest of seven North Carolina Muslims on allegations they intended to commit suicide attacks, the September 2009 arrest of Afghan-born Najibullah Zazi based on allegations that he intended to attack the New York subway system, the October 2009 arrest of Pakistani-American David Headley in connection with the 2008 Mumbai attacks, and the May 2010 attempt by Pakistani-born American citizen Faisal Shahzad to explode a car bomb in New York's Times Square. *See* Jerome P. Bjelopera & Mark A. Randol, Congressional Res. Serv., American Jihadist Terrorism: Combating a Complex Threat 74–76, 79, 81–82, 86–91 (2010), *available at* http://www.fas.org/sgp/crs/terror/R41416.pdf; Karen J. Greenberg, *Homegrown: The Rise of American Jihad,* New Republic, June 10, 2010, at 6, 7.

[122] President of the U.S., National Security Strategy 19 (May 2010).

[123] Greenberg, *supra note* 121, at 6–7.

[124] Seth G. Jones & Martin C. Libicki, How Terrorist Groups End: Lessons for Countering al Qa'ida 27 (2008).

[125] K. Jack Riley et al., State and Local Intelligence in the War on Terrorism ix (2005); *accord* Gary LaFree & James Hendrickson, *Build a Criminal Justice Policy for Terrorism,* 6 Criminology & Pub. Pol'y 781, 783 (2007) ("In many ways the community-oriented approach favored by successful police departments is the same kind of approach that is most likely to uncover terrorist operations.").

[126] *See, e.g.,* David Kilcullen, Counterinsurgency 3–5 (2010).

[127] *See supra* text at notes 28–29 (discussing commentators who urge the U.S. to make greater use of air power against the Taliban, even at the risk of extensive civilian casualties).

[128] *See, e.g.,* U.S. Dep't of the Army, U.S. Army Field Manual No. 3-24, Marine Corps Warfighting Publication No. 3-33.5, Counterinsurgency Field Manual xxv (2007) (noting that "the civilian population [is]... the deciding factor in the struggle," with the key issue being the ability to secure their support).

Local police thus play a crucial role by virtue of their familiarity with neighborhoods and their ability to elicit information held within domestic communities. And with counterterrorism as with policing against conventional crime, community cooperation is essential if the police are to perform this role successfully. Moreover, as with traditional policing, cooperation cannot be taken for granted. Indeed, cooperation may be even more fragile in the context of counterterrorism than in ordinary law enforcement: Law-abiding members of the relevant community, though unswervingly loyal to the United States, know that cooperation could mean exposing people with whom they share close ethnic and religious ties to unusually harsh procedures and sanctions. Shaping sound policy to navigate these sensibilities is thus vitally important but exceptionally delicate.

Law enforcement agencies, however, do not follow a unified approach. The decision to opt for policing rather than a military model leaves open important choices. One is whether to focus on intrusive enforcement and intelligence-gathering methods that promise instrumental gains (at possible cost to perceived legitimacy), or whether instead to emphasize long-term efforts to build community trust. Second, where priority is given to the objectives of trust and cooperation, should those goals be pursued primarily by a "top down" approach (building ties to community leaders, as recommended in the RAND report[129]), or should officials emphasize a "bottom up" policy stressing the quality of interaction with individuals in ordinary street-level encounters?

In Dearborn, Michigan, which has an Arab-American community of 200,000, law enforcement has made the maintenance of good police-community relations a "major concern."[130] In other cities, relations between Muslim-American communities and local police departments are strained.[131] At the federal level, community outreach has not been ignored,[132] but policy has been dominated by measures that relax procedural restraints on investigation and detention while expanding substantive criminal offenses to reach behavior with only tenuous connections to acts of violence.[133] From the general public to many of our highest officials, it is often considered self-evident that tougher measures will pay greater dividends.[134] In Britain, in contrast, those who lead the counterterrorism effort often stress that success depends on building community

---

[129] *See* JONES & LIBICKI, *supra* note 124, at 27.

[130] Thacher, *supra* note 118, at 649.

[131] *See, e.g.,* Richard Winton & Teresa Watanabe, *LAPD's Muslim Mapping Plan Killed,* L.A. TIMES, Nov. 15, 2007, at A1 (describing controversy over a police department effort to address "radicalization" with aid of a "community mapping" plan to identify geographic locations of Muslim populations).

[132] *See* Andrea Elliott, *White House Quietly Courts Muslims in the U.S.,* N.Y. TIMES, Apr. 18, 2010, at A1.

[133] Prominent examples include expansion of search and surveillance powers, military detention of alleged "enemy combatants," aggressive use of immigration detention and deportation, and enactment of broader definitions of prohibited "material support" for terrorism. *See, e.g.,* Holder v. Humanitarian Law Project, 130 S. Ct. 2705 (2010) (upholding the constitutionality of a prohibition on giving "material support" by acts intended to support humanitarian and political activities). *See generally* STEPHEN J. SCHULHOFER, THE ENEMY WITHIN (2002) (cataloguing post-9/11 measures that expand intelligence gathering and law enforcement powers).

[134] *See, e.g.,* Harris, Allen & VandeHei, *supra* note 31 (quoting former Vice President Dick Cheney, stating that counterterrorism is "a tough, mean, dirty, nasty business …. [W]e're not going to win this fight by turning the other cheek …. The United States needs to be not so much loved as it needs to be respected. Sometimes, that requires us to take actions that generate controversy").

trust by adhering to traditional conceptions of due process.[135] In short, no unified approach to counterterrorism policing has emerged. Instead, officials commonly emphasize intrusive or coercive tactics without examining their collateral costs, or focus on generating cooperative relationships with Muslim community leaders while neglecting the character of daily interactions at the grassroots. A central concern is the need to determine which approaches yield the best results in terms of security.

The available empirical evidence offers stark warnings about the potentially counterproductive effects of harsh measures. A study of British counterterrorism policies in Northern Ireland found that of six high-visibility crackdown initiatives, only one had an observable deterrent effect.[136] Two others had no statistically significant impact, while two intrusive policies were associated with significant *increases* in violence.[137] The researchers hypothesized that erroneous arrests and the adoption of internment without trial contributed to this backlash by undermining the legitimacy of anti-terrorism efforts.[138] Similarly, studies have found that perceived injustice on the part of U.S. forces in Iraq is a strong predictor of support for resistance there.[139]

Turning to counterterrorism tactics in the American domestic context, many thoughtful scholars have suggested that the heightened threat environment post-9/11 may justify wider use of ethnic profiling[140] and other enhanced police powers, such as greater ability to establish

---

[135] *See, e.g.,* Peter Clarke, The Courts and Terrorism: Transatlantic Observations, Lecture at NYU Law School 2–3 (Apr. 15, 2009) (on file with the authors) (stating, as former chief of counterterrorism in London's Metropolitan Police, that "[for] deeply pragmatic reasons,… it is absolutely essential to adhere to due process …. People … must have confidence and trust in the authorities …. They must believe … that information … will not be used … to stigmatize their communities or to justify extrajudicial action"). For an assessment suggesting mixed results from British efforts to build community trust through its "Prevent" program, see HOUSE OF COMMONS, CMTYS. & LOCAL GOVERNMENT COMMITTEE, PREVENTING VIOLENT EXTREMISM 3–4 (Mar. 30, 2010), *available at* http://www.publications.parliament.uk/pa/cm200910/ cmselect/cmcomloc/65/65.pdf; Vikram Dodd, *Communities Fear Project Is Not What It Seems,* GUARDIAN (U.K.), Oct 17, 2010, *available at* http://www.guardian.co.uk/society/2009/oct/16/prevent-counter-islamic-extremism-intelligence.

Responding to such concerns (among others), the British government has proposed to roll back many powers granted since September 11, 2001; the authority to detain terrorism suspects for up to twenty-eight days prior to charge would be reduced to fourteen days. Protection of Freedoms Bill, 2011, H.C. Bill [146] cl. 57, *available at* http://www.publications. parliament.uk/pa/bills/cbill/2010–2011/0146/2011146.pdf. The proposal regarding pre-charge detention reflects concerns that the extended power is unnecessary and "has a negative impact on Muslim communities." HM GOVERNMENT, REVIEW OF COUNTER-TERRORISM AND SECURITY POWERS: REVIEW FINDINGS AND RECOMMENDATIONS 7 (2011), *available at* http://www.homeoffice. gov.uk/publications/counter-terrorism/review-of-ct-security-powers/review-findings-and-rec?view=Binary.

[136] Gary LaFree, Laura Dugan & Raven Korte, *The Impact of British Counterterrorist Strategies on Political Violence in Northern Ireland: Comparing Deterrence and Backlash Models,* 47 CRIMINOLOGY 17, 25–27, 34 (2009).

[137] *Id.* at 32–34. The sixth intervention studied by LaFree, et al. involved a shift from military methods to locally administered criminal justice procedures, treating captured terrorists as ordinary criminal suspects in an effort to delegitimate their cause. The detainees responded with a hunger strike to obtain a return to "prisoner-of-war" status. Further anti-British animosity resulted, and violence subsequently increased. *Id.* at 36. That finding underscores the point that both deterrence and backlash effects can be highly sensitive to context.

[138] *Id.* at 33–34.

[139] *See, e.g.,* Ronald Fischer, et al., *Support for Resistance Among Iraqi Students,* 30 BASIC & APPLIED SOC. PSYCHOL. 167, 173 (2008).

[140] *See, e.g.,* Samuel R. Gross & Debra Livingston, *Racial Profiling Under Attack,* 102 COLUM. L. REV. 1413, 1436–38 (2002) (approving such measures in some circumstances, though urging cautious implementation).

roadblocks and checkpoints.[141] Yet we have already noted the potential negative impact of such policing activities; in the context of ordinary law enforcement, zero-tolerance measures have often backfired, encouraging crime and discouraging cooperation by creating resentment in minority communities.[142] A similar problem could well defeat efforts to augment counterterrorism powers. Indeed, because terrorism is a relatively dispersed and infrequent phenomenon, posing a threat to a near-infinite range of symbolic targets and typically using operatives with no prior record of terrorist activity, accurate and timely information to separate genuine threats from background noise has enormous value. Community cooperation therefore assumes even greater than usual importance. To the extent that terrorist groups seek either to recruit or hide within co-religionist communities, cooperation can provide information at lower cost and with fewer negative side effects than coercive or intrusive forms of intelligence gathering.

That said, we cannot assume that findings from ordinary law enforcement will apply in a straightforward way to counterterrorism policing. Because terrorism is motivated by ideology rather than desire for material gain, co-religionists or members of the same ethnic community may share some ideological perspectives with those who plan acts of terror. As a result, law-abiding individuals may be reluctant to put politically radical members of their communities at risk, even when they themselves oppose violence. In addition, because al Qaeda invokes religious justifications for its goals and methods, the religiosity of law-abiding Muslims could conceivably alter the importance of procedural justice for securing their cooperation. Finally, because links between procedural justice and willingness to comply or cooperate have not been found in all societies,[143] recent Muslim immigrants who have lived under repressive governments could conceivably have different notions of legitimacy or its importance for cooperation.

To test the links between legitimacy, procedural fairness, and cooperation in communities impacted by counterterrorism enforcement, we conducted extensive interviews and random polling of Muslim-American residents of New York City.[144] We found little evidence that religiosity, cultural differences, or political background play a significant role in determining willingness to cooperate. The same is true for strength of identification with the Muslim community; disagreement with American government policies on Iraq, Afghanistan, and Israel; and instrumental concerns such as a belief that the police are effective.[145] In contrast, as in the case of conventional law enforcement, we found a strong association between willingness to cooperate with anti-terrorism policing and perceptions of procedural justice.[146]

---

[141] *See, e.g.,* William J. Stuntz, *Local Policing After the Terror,* 111 Yale LJ. 2137, 2141–42 (2002).

[142] *See supra* text at notes 54, 61–62.

[143] *See, e.g.,* Joel Brockner et al., *Culture and Procedural Justice: The Influence of Power Distance on Reactions to Voice,* 37 J. Experimental Soc. Psychol. 300, 314 (2001) (finding that, in China, people do not react as strongly as in other cultures to procedural unfairness).

[144] *See* Tyler, Schulhofer & Huq, *supra* note 58.

[145] *Id.*

[146] *Id*

Table 3.1.1   Relationships Within Prior-Attitude Subgroups: Police Behavior and Perceived Procedural Justice as Correlated to Muslim-American Willingness to Cooperate

PRIOR ATTITUDES	PUBLIC/CLANDESTINE POLICE ACTION	POLICE TARGETING OF MINORITIES	PROCEDURAL JUSTICE OF THE POLICE
Terror Is Serious			
No	–.26*	–.21*	.37***
Yes	–.08	–.23*	.40***
Police Are Effective			
No	–.18*	–.12	.41***
Yes	–.02	–.11	.26**
Police Help You Feel Safe			
No	–.19*	–.13*	.36***
Yes	–.07	–.10	.49***
Preference for Law Enforcement Authority			
No	–.20*	–.20*	.41***
Yes	–.09	–.10	.29***
Respect for Hierarchy			
Low	–27***	–20*	.40***
High	–.13	–.11	.32***

*=p<.05; **=p<.01; *** =p <.001.

(Entries are subgroup correlations with a combined measure of legitimacy and cooperation.)

One way to test the force of these relationships is to look separately at groups that have particular views about law enforcement or terrorism. For example, people who consider the terror threat very serious presumably will be much more willing to cooperate and their willingness might not be affected so much by whether they think police actions are intrusive or procedurally irregular. Likewise, people who consider the police effective and people who are inclined to defer to authority presumably will be willing to cooperate and again their willingness might not be affected so much by whether they think police practices are fair.

To look at those possibilities, we divided our sample into people who think that the terror threat is serious (or not), people who think the police are effective (or not), and likewise for the other pairs of attitudes. Table 3.1.1, drawn from the New York City data, shows these relationships.

Part of what Table 3.1.1 shows is not surprising. Among people who think the terror threat is not serious, willingness to cooperate is reduced substantially by perceptions that the police use intrusive tactics, target minorities, or act unfairly. We see roughly the same effect for the negative alternative in the case of each of the other prior attitudes as well. In other words, among people who can be considered law enforcement skeptics (people who prefer liberty to order, reject hierarchies, and think the police are not effective), cooperation drops substantially when police are perceived as intrusive or unfair. These are largely the results we would expect, but they underscore the importance of fairness for cooperation among a substantial segment of the population.

When we look at the lower row of each pair, those who think terrorism *is* a serious problem and generally favor law enforcement authority, we see in column 1 that cooperation *is not* affected by the use of intrusive tactics. These people seem more focused on instrumental payoffs than on legitimacy. They are generally willing to accept intrusive tactics when they accept hierarchical authority and consider the police effective.

But two relationships are less predictable. First, even when these respondents consider the terror threat very serious, cooperation drops substantially if they believe the police are targeting people in their community. And second, in the lower row of *all* of these pairs (i.e., among those who broadly support law enforcement), column 3 shows that cooperation drops substantially, with very high statistical significance, when police use unfair procedures, such as stopping people without explanation, denying them any opportunity to be heard, and failing to treat them with courtesy. In other words, for all of these subgroups, regardless of prior attitudes about the police, civil liberties, and so on, perceptions of procedural justice have a major impact on willingness to cooperate.

We can illustrate the concrete impact of these relationships by separating the respondents into quartiles based on the extent to which they saw the police as respecting (or not respecting) the requirements of procedural justice. We can then focus on willingness to cooperate within each group. By highlighting the differences between the groups, Tables 2 and 3 illustrate the consequences of failing to nurture perceptions of procedural fairness.

These tables show in more tangible terms the impact of procedural justice on cooperation. Table 3.1.2 focuses on perceived fairness in establishing counterterrorism policies. When people believe that overall policies are established fairly, willingness to work with the police rises by 11%, and even more strikingly, willingness to report suspicious activity rises by 61%. That 61% figure is an increase of enormous significance for successful intelligence gathering: Fairness in establishing policies makes it 61% more likely that people in this community will be willing to report suspicious behavior.

Table 3.1.2   Willingness to Cooperate Among Muslim-Americans

BELIEF THAT POLICY IS CREATED FAIRLY	N	PERCENT OF EACH QUARTILE WILLING TO: WORK WITH POLICE	ALERT POLICE
Very Low	71	82%	49%
Medium Low	69	78%	66%
Medium High	83	88%	67%
Very High	68	91%	79%
Difference		+9 pts (+11%)	+30 pts (+61%)
(Respondents grouped by perceptions of fairness in policy creation.)			

Table 3.1.3 shifts the focus to perceived fairness in enforcement. When people believe that policies are fairly implemented, willingness to report suspicious activity increases by 41% and willingness to work with the police increases by 62%.

Table 3.1.3   Willingness to Cooperate Among Muslim-Americans

BELIEF THAT POLICY IS ENFORCED FAIRLY	N	PERCENT OF EACH WORK WITH POLICE	QUARTILE WILLING TO: ALERT POLICE
Very Low	71	39%	41%
Medium Low	69	43%	43%
Medium High	83	51%	57%
Very High	68	63%	58%
Difference		+24 pts (+ 62%)	+17 pts (+41%)
(Respondents grouped by perceptions of fairness in enforcement.)			

One somewhat unexpected finding is that willingness to *work with* police in anti-terror initiatives is only modestly affected by fairness in the formation of policy but is extremely sensitive to fairness in enforcement. In contrast, willingness to *alert the police* decreases in response to both sorts of unfairness, but in the reverse order: it is much more sensitive to whether overall policies are established fairly. We suspect that because working with the police is local and personal, willingness to do so is more strongly driven by the trustworthiness of officials nearby than by large questions of policy, such as the decision whether to maintain a detention camp at Guantanamo Bay. Conversely, willingness to report suspicious activity seems more likely to be affected by respondents' perceptions of overall systemic fairness: how such information will be processed by higher officials and how fairly suspects will be treated once they come to law enforcement attention. If so, it makes sense that willingness to report would be very sensitive to perceived fairness of the system as a whole but less affected by respondents' trust in officials with whom they and then-neighbors interact in the neighborhood.

Dynamics of this sort can of course be explored in considerably greater detail. But the existing research is already ample to establish our two central points. First, apart from any civil liberties considerations, tough measures that skirt traditional conceptions of due process take a substantial toll on law enforcement effectiveness. And second, procedural justice concerns accordingly should be allotted a central place in all efforts to design and implement counterterrorism policy. As in other contexts, sensitivity to procedural justice serves to promote rather than impair the security effort.

Conclusion

This is an ideal moment to reconsider the principles that guide American policing. If we can adopt policing styles that communicate respect and nurture public trust, we can address the central concerns of both minority and majority populations.

Research consistently shows that whites and minorities want the same thing from the police: fair treatment. Minorities are, however, more apt to say that historically they have been treated unfairly and that they do not receive fair treatment even now. This perceived unfairness leads to lower legitimacy ratings, less deference to the law among minorities, and lower levels of cooperation with the police.

Addressing these concerns involves reframing the way we think about the goals of policing, in the context of both counterterrorism and ordinary law enforcement. At all levels, government agencies must pay attention to public judgments about how they exercise their authority because such judgments shape the behaviors that are of primary importance to the police, in particular the willingness of individuals to obey the law and their willingness to cooperate in efforts to enforce the law against others.

Critical Thinking Questions

1   How do the order maintenance and procedural justice models differ in their approaches to achieving legitimacy?

2   What are the four pillars of procedural justice? How does procedural justice help shape legitimacy and prevent crime?

3   How would eliminating the exclusionary rule impact legitimacy?

4   How do current policing strategies contradict the community policing message?

Editors' Introduction: Reading 3.2

In the following article, we see the importance of how police go about their job in terms of their perceived legitimacy among the body politic. Specifically, Hanink considers one of the most popular 20th- and 21st-century policing strategies: CompStat and its tactical counterpart, the stop and frisk. By examining the behavior and subsequent results of the New York Police Department's aggressive use of stop and frisk, as guided by their monthly CompStat meetings, Hanink demonstrates the danger to legitimacy that these quantitative and crime-control methods can pose for the legitimacy of the police insofar as such an approach tends to be disproportionately focused on minority and structurally disadvantaged communities.

Don't Trust the Police

Stop Question Frisk, CompStat, and the High Cost of Statistical Over-Reliance in the NYPD

Peter Hanink

O nce the poster child for rampant crime and urban decay, New York City is now the "safest big city in America" with the same rate of violent crime as Sunnyvale, California.[1] While the precise cause of this dramatic decline in violent crime remains a topic of scholarly debate, within popular media and among police departments, much of the credit has gone to reforms carried out by former Boston, New York City, and Los Angeles Chief of Police William Bratton (Fagan & MacDonald, 2012, p. 14; Kelling & Sousa, 2001; Eck & Maguire, 2000). Bratton's major contributions to the NYPD were the wide-scale adoption of the practice of "stop question frisk" ("SQF") guided by the "Broken Windows" philosophy of crime prevention (Kelling & Bratton, 1998; Wilson & Kelling, 1982) and the implementation of CompStat, short for "COMPuter STATistics," a management system that uses statistics to inform police decision-making (Bratton & Knobler, 1998; Skolnick & Caplovitz, 2001).

This article shall examine how the practice of SQF was implemented in New York City along with CompStat, discuss the impact of these implementations, and measure how a practice that is, on its face, race-neutral may have become race-based in practice.

---

[1] Press Release, Mayor Bloomberg And Police Commissioner Kelly Announce New York City Remains The Safest Big City In America According To FBI Uniform Crime Report (September 13, 2010) *available at* http://www.nyc.gov/html/nypd/html/pr/pr_2010_nyc_safest_big_city.shtml.

What Is CompStat?

CompStat is the New York City Police Department's (NYPD) "strategic control system," designed "to gather and disseminate" crime statistics, and provide managers with the ability to oversee longitudinal efforts to deal with crime (Weisburd, Mastrofski, Greenspan, & Willis, 2003, p. 426). However, CompStat has also become "shorthand" for a broader range of police reform efforts within the NYPD, including, most notably, the high profile "pop quizzes"[2] called "Crime-Control Strategy Meetings." During these meetings, "crime statistics and other information about a pre-cinct and its problems are projected onto overhead screens" (Weisburd, Mastrofski, Greenspan, & Willis, 2004, p. 3), and precinct commanders are "quizzed" on "details of individual crime problems, including where and when crime occurred, and the age, race, and sex of any suspects" rather than the how or why they chose particular crime control strategies (Willis, Mastrofski, & Weisburd, 2007, p. 165). This focus on facts and figures has led organizational theorists to conclude that the architecture of CompStat's oversight system "prioritizes generalists who specialize in territory rather than function," resulting in "more police operations being geographically based" (Willis et al., 2007, p. 154).

Implementing CompStat in New York

In the 1990s, the NYPD implemented CompStat along with community policing strategies inspired by Broken Windows Theory (Fagan & Davies, 2000). Traditionally, community policing was characterized by literally putting police back in a community (Genelin, 1998) and fostering daily relationships between the police and community members (Skolnik, 1999). Two of the chief goals of community policing are restoring trust between police and community and gathering place-specific information such as which types of crimes are being committed most often in each community and who is committing them (Gramckow, 1997).

However, critics argue that when implemented in New York City along with CompStat, com-munity policing was transformed into something else. Instead of taking advantage of the newly opened lines of communication between the police and the community, the NYPD relied upon CompStat to determine what the community needed (Fagan & Davies, 2000, p. 472). This shift from bottom up information gathering to top down number crunching may have had a more significant effect: the implementation of *de facto* racial profiling.

Theoretical Foundations

If indeed CompStat has transformed, from a race neutral, statistically-driven, crime control strategy to a race-based, profiling strategy, how did this transformation take place? Setting aside

---

[2] *See e.g. The Wire*: "Time After Time" (HBO television broadcast Sept. 19, 2004) (dramatizing a CompStat style meeting in the Baltimore Police Department).

the possibility of race motivated precinct commanders intentionally manipulating the statistics to justify prejudice driven policing, CompStat should be race blind. Looking to the intellectual foundation of Bratton's transformation of the NYPD, Broken Windows Policing, and juxtaposing it against Social Disorganization Theory and Conflict Theory may explain this transformation.

Broken Windows

Based upon Wilson and Kelling's (1982) seminal article in *The Atlantic Monthly*, Broken Windows Theory holds that the key to reducing crime is shifting the focus of policing from "law en-forcement" to "order maintenance." Broken Windows theory holds that to remedy crime, police must begin by dealing with relatively low-level offenses, some of which, such as vandalism and prostitution, are more common in poor minority communities than in wealthy White ones (Skogan, 1990).

In implementing Broken Windows Theory, the NYPD principally relied upon "an aggressive form of stop and frisk policing," which was "disproportionately concentrated in minority neigh-borhoods and conflated with poverty and other signs of socio-economic disadvantage" (Fagan & Davies, 2000, p. 462). Furthermore, following the dictates of Broken Windows Theory, police engaged in searches incident to arrest for low-level offenses such as "riding a bicycle on the sidewalk or drinking beer in public," and did so predominantly against non-White racial minori-ties (Skolnick & Caplovitz, 2001, p.415). As Fagan and Davies (2000, p. 471) have articulated, the NYPD implemented Broken Windows policing "out of context" –instead of focusing on signs of *physical disorder*, SQF was used to address signs of *social disorder*. Instead of focusing on quality of life offenses, SQF increasingly was viewed as a way to reduce serious crimes, specifically gun violence (Fagan & Davies, 2000, p. 471).

From the outset, proponents recognized that any approach that relied heavily upon SQFs informed by outward signs of disorder would inevitably have a racial dimension. One of the architects of Broken Windows Theory, James Q. Wilson (1994) argued that while it was possible, and even probable that racial minorities would be disproportionately stopped and frisked under a Broken Windows–based policing strategy, such an outcome was necessary in order to reduce crime.

Social Disorganization Theory

Social Disorganization Theory holds that "patterns of residential inequality" create socially iso-lation and community disadvantage that ultimately reduce control of crime (Sampson & Wilson, 1995, p. 178). According to this view, while social disorganization is often manifested along racial lines, the characteristics of the place matter far more than the characteristics of an individual, such as race. Shaw and McKay noted that race often influenced the social disorganization of a neighborhood by means of the neighborhood's racial or ethnic composition, specifically, through its ethnic heterogeneity (1942).

Social disorganization theory analyzes race according to its relationship with disorder; a relationship shaped by implicit societal beliefs that associate African Americans and members of other minority groups to undesirable characteristics such as "crime, violence, disorder, welfare, and undesirability as neighbors" (Sampson & Raudenbush, 2004, p. 320). As with many stereotypes, these beliefs are grounded in the observable association of many such communities with poverty, blight, and disorder (Sampson & Raudenbush, 2004, p. 320). As Sampson and Raudenbush put it, the fact "on *average*, levels of observable disorder are higher in Black neighborhoods than in White" leads many to conclude that "a specific all-Black neighborhood has a disorder problem" (2004, pp. 320–1) Thus, Sampson and Raudenbush suggest that when observers identify disorder, they may in fact really just be seeing race and poverty.

Moreover, given that poor, majority-minority communities are linked, both statistically and in the popular imagination, with crime and disorder, such communities may be more likely to be subjected to heightened policing (Massey & Denton, 1993; Thompson, 1999; Loury, 2002; Fagan, 2008; Sampson & Raudenbush, 1999, 2004; Alpert, Macdonald, & Dunham, 2005; Ferguson, 2007; Massey, 2007). This conclusion is supported by an analysis of pedestrian stops in New York City conducted by Fagan and Davies in which they argue, "policing is not about disorderly places, nor about improving quality of life, but about policing poor people in poor places" (2000, p. 457).

Conflict Theory

Conflict Theory holds that the criminal law is used by the powerful to define as criminal behaviors that threaten their interests (Turk, 1969) and that these definitions are used "for the purposes of establishing domestic order" (Quinney, 1977, p. 16). According to Conflict Theory, the economically powerful exert their influence over lawmakers to control groups they consider threats in order to preserve economic stratification (Takagi, 1974). The powerful often consider culturally dissimilar groups to threaten social order (Turk, 1969). Thus, the process of "law making, law breaking and law enforcement," (Vold, 1958, p. 339), according to conflict theory, entails the powerful identifying those behaviors and groups that threaten their interests, defining those so-identified as criminal, and wielding the power of the state apparatuses against them.

In assessing Conflict Theory, theorists have hypothesized that there should be a measurable relationship between the presence of groups conceived of as threats and the behavior of police. That is, the greater the racial or economic threat, the greater the expected police response. Economic inequality has been found to be correlated with the strength of the police force (Jacobs, 1979), the rate of arrests for property and personal crimes (Liska & Chamlin, 1984), and the number of civil rights complaints against the police (Holmes, 2000).

In their study of the Richmond, Virginia police, Petrocelli, Piquero, & Smith (2003, p. 7) found that while the crime rate was the only statistically significant predictor of the stop rate, the percentage of the population that is Black statistically predicted the rate of stops that result in searches and arrests. Similarly, in their analysis of stop rates in Kansas City, Novak and Chamlin (2008) found no statistically significant relationship between measures of economic inequality, the percentage of the population that was Black, and neighborhood stop rates.

Within New York City, evidence for the racial threat hypothesis of Conflict Theory can be found as far back as 1999 within a comprehensive report prepared by the New York Attorney General's Office on the New York Police Department's "Stop & Frisk" practices (Spitzer, 1999). For example, African Americans make up little more than 25% of the population, but represent fully one-half of the persons subject to a *Terry* search (Spitzer, 1999, p. 94). Similarly, Hispanics, who make up 23.7% of the population, were a full one-third of all persons "stopped" (Spitzer, 1999, p. 94). For perspective, Whites make up 43.4% of the population, yet only 12.9% of all persons stopped (Spitzer, 1999, p. 94).

While overall, the ratio of stops to arrest was 9:1, this ratio varied by race: The ratio for African Americans was 9.5 *Terry* searches for every 1 arrest of an African American; for Hispanics, 8.8:1; for Whites, 7.9:1 (Spitzer, 1999, p. 111). These statistics imply that either police are less efficient at pursuing crime subjects who are racial minorities than they are at pursuing those who are White, or, in the alternative, that they are engaging in racially discriminatory profiling (Rudovsky, 2001). Indeed, the OAG report shows the statistical disparity is most stark in majority White areas (Spitzer, 1999, p. 106). In such areas, African Americans and Hispanics each make up less than one-tenth of the population and yet together represent more than half of the *Terry* searches.

Of course, the ready response is that as the majority of crimes are committed in majority minority areas, it is appropriate that racial minorities should be disproportionately represented in the data. In order to evaluate this possibility, the OAG conducted various regression analyses, the results of which suggest that disparate crime rates alone could not account for disparate SQF rates (Spitzer, 1999, p. 119–24, 130). After controlling for the effect of differing crime rates of African Americans, Hispanics, and Whites, the regressions showed that African Americans were stopped 23% more often than Whites and Hispanics were stopped 39% more often than Whites (Spitzer, 1999, p. 123).

Current Focus

This study focuses on how neighborhood characteristics influence the rate of SQF in New York City. In their analysis of NYPD SQF data, Gelman, Fagan, and Kiss (2007) found Blacks and Hispanics were more likely to be stopped than Whites, but that such stops had lower "hit rates" –that is, were less likely to result in arrests. Gelman *et al.* suggest that the lower "hit rates" for non-Whites may either be driven by an *intentional* targeting of non-Whites, consistent with pretextual stops, or be influenced by an *implicit* association of non-Whites with suspicion, consistent with racial stereotyping (2007, p. 822).

In their study of stops in six high crime neighborhoods in New York between 1998–2006, Fagan, Geller, Davies, West, *et al.* (2009) found that stops disproportionately occurred in predominantly Black neighborhoods. Fagan *et al.* (2009) further found that, as measured by subsequent arrest rates, such stops had diminishing returns; over time fewer and fewer stops ultimately resulted in arrests.

Population

This study shall examine the rates of SQF for the New York Police Department ("NYPD") during 2010. The term SQF refers to a practice by which police officers temporarily detain, question, and frisk a citizen ostensibly upon a reasonable suspicion of criminal activity.

Hypotheses

Based upon conflict theory and social disorganization theory, the following hypotheses are tested:

- **H1: Racial Threat.** The percentage of the precinct that is Black will influence the stop rate. Precincts with a greater percentage of Black residents will have higher stop rates.

- **H2: *Seeing* Disorder.** Traditional characteristics of social disorganization will influence stop rates. Precincts with greater proportions of their populations below the poverty line and more ethnic heterogeneity will have higher stop rates.

- **H3: Racial Disorder.** Precincts with high rates of poverty, ethnic heterogeneity, and a greater percentage of Black residents will have higher stop rates. The inclusion of the percent Black variable should decrease the impact of ethnic heterogeneity.

- **H4: Racial & Economic Threat.** The presence of poor Blacks influences the stop rate. Precincts with higher proportions of poor Blacks will have higher stop rates.

Variables

The dependent variable, the SQF rate, will be obtained by dividing the number of stops in a given police precinct by the population of that precinct. The stop and frisk data are reported by the NYPD at the precinct level. For purposes of this study, the Central Park precinct (22) will be excluded as it has no permanent population.

The first set of independent variables, poverty rate, and ethnic heterogeneity rates, are associated with Social Disorganization Theory. The poverty rate is the percent of the population living below the poverty line and will be obtained from the American Community Survey taken from the 2010 U.S. Census at tract-level. The ethnic heterogeneity rate will be calculated at the U.S. Census tract-level. The ethnic heterogeneity rate will be calculated by taking the product of the percent of the tract that is Black and the percent of the tract that is non-Black (Miethe & Meier, 1994, p. 85). The independent variable, percent Black, is a measure of racial threat associated with Conflict Theory. This variable will be obtained from the U.S. Census. All U.S. Census tract-level measures will be aggregated to the precinct-level for analysis.

The independent variable, the crime rate, is included to measure the alternate hypothesis, that crime rate alone should predict the stop rate. This will be taken at the NYPD police precinct level.[3] The crime rate will based on the total number of arrests for murder, rape, robbery, burglary,

---

[3] The precinct-level is the smallest unit at which the NYPD reports crime rates. This introduces measurement error as it assumes a uniformity of crime rates within a precinct.

felony assault, grand larceny, and grand larceny auto in a precinct in 2010 divided by the population and will be obtained from the NYPD.

A final independent variable, Black poverty, is an interaction variable between percent Black and the poverty rate. This variable is obtained by multiplying the values of percent Black and poverty rate.

Results

Spatial Analyses

Figures 3.2.1 through 3.2.4 present the result of spatial analyses of the relationships between the "stops rate" and the crime rate, poverty rate, percent Black, and the "Black poverty" interaction variable, respectively. The spatial analyses were conducted by the author using ArcGIS mapping software.

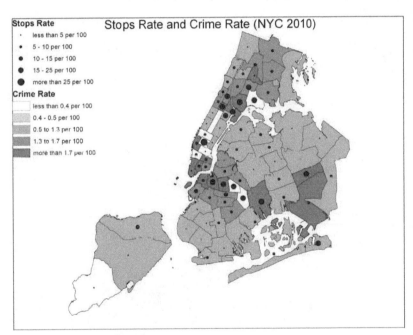

**Figure 3.2.1: Stops Rate and Crime Rate. Data Source: NYPD.
Map Source: Author Generated.**

As seen in Figure 3.2.1, while there is generally a clustering of higher SQF rates in precincts with higher crime rates, there are also precincts with higher stop rates and lower crime rates.

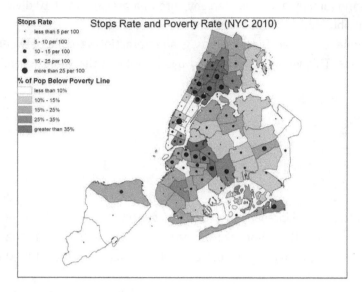

Figure 3.2.2: Stops Rate and Poverty Rate. Data Source: NYPD & U.S. Census. Map Source: Author Generated.

As seen in Figure 3.2.2, there is generally a clustering of higher SQF rates in precincts with higher rates of poverty.

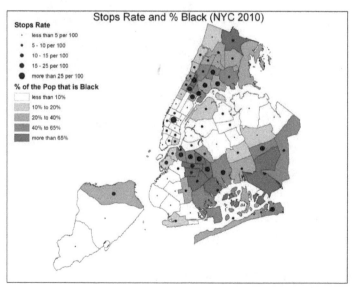

Figure 3.2.3: Stops Rate and Percent Black. Data Source: NYPD & U.S. Census. Map Source: Author Generated.

As seen in Figure 3.2.3, there is a discernable clustering of higher SQF rates within those precincts with the highest Black population as a percentage of the total population.

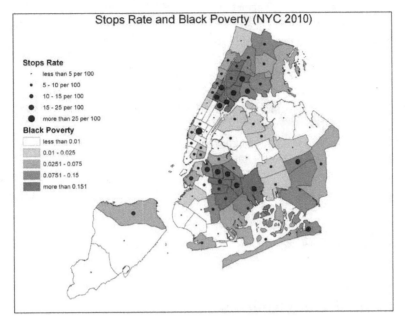

Figure 3.2.4: Stops Rate and Black Poverty. Data Source: NYPD & U.S. Census. Map Source: Author Generated.

As seen in Figure 3.2.4, there is a discernable clustering of higher stops rates within those precincts with the greatest rates of Black poverty.

OLS Regression Analysis

Table 3.2.1 presents the results of OLS multiple regression analysis of the various models. In all four models, the crime rate is a statistically and practically significant predictor of the stop rate. This supports the finding that the underlying crime rate in a precinct is clearly the highest predictor of the stop rate. In Models I and III, which test H1 and H3, respectively, the percent Black in a precinct is both statistically and practically significant.

As predicted, the inclusion of *Percent Black* in Model III renders ethnic heterogeneity no longer significant. Furthermore, the coefficient on the interaction variable, *Black Poverty*, in Model IV, demonstrates that the interaction between poverty and *Percent Black* in a precinct is both statistically and practically significant when predicting the stop rate.

Table 3.2.1   Stop Rate regressed against predictor variables

VARIABLE	DESCRIPTION	(I)	(II)	(III)	(IV)
Total Crime Rate	Total Crime in Precinct per population	3.706 *** (0.290)	3.689 *** (0.2668)	3.68 *** (0.261)	3.627 *** (0.251)
Ethnic Heterogeneity Rate	% Black times %Non-Black		0.223 ** (0.069)	0.126 (0.080)	
Poverty Rate	% of Precinct Pop below Poverty Line		0.152 ** (0.055)	0.149 ** (0.053)	0.023 (0.072)
Percent Black	% of the Precinct Pop that is Black	0.099 *** (0.019)		0.049 * (0.022)	-0.034 (0.039)
Black Poverty	Interaction Variable between % Black & Poverty Rate				0.548 ** (0.186)
Constant		0.003 (0.009)	-0.029 ** (0.011)	-0.029 ** (0.011)	0.001 (0.013)
R^2		0.73	0.77	0.78	0.79

$* = p<0.05, ** = p<0.01, *** = p<0.001$
$n = 75$ (excludes Central Park Precinct 22)

Discussion and Conclusions

This study set out to explore the relationship between race, measures of disorder and disorganization, and the use of SQF as a police practice. Previous analyses had established that there was a clear link between the rate of SQF and the racial makeup of precincts. This study confirms this finding and adds to the research by demonstrating that this effect can be observed at the precinct level throughout New York City. Perhaps most significantly, the finding on the interaction between percent Black and poverty suggests that some combination of racial and economic threat is at play in policing. While clearly driven in largest part by the crime rate, that the rate of SQF is also influenced by the rate of Black poverty suggests that Conflict Theory may account for how SQF have actually been implemented in practice and how a race neutral program such as CompStat may have transformed into a race-influenced strategy of social control.

Consequences for Police Legitimacy

Critiques of racial profiling have ranged from criticisms of its soundness[4] (Glasser, 2000) to indictments of its morality (Harris, 1997).[5] The most significant problem with racial profiling

---

[4] As Ira Glasser (2000, p. 712) has suggested "Most players in the NBA are black. But if you were trying to get a team together, you wouldn't go out in the street and round up random African Americans."

[5] "When officers stop disproportionate numbers of African-Americans because this is 'just good police work,' they are using race as a proxy for the criminality or 'general criminal propensity' of an entire racial group. Simply put, police are

however, might just be that, at least when it arises, as it has in New York City, from a vigorous community policing effort, it undermines the very thing that it sought to foster: better relations between the community and the police in order to reduce crime.

The consequences for the community credibility of the NYPD may be severe. As seen in Table 3.2.2, Whites, Hispanics, and Blacks express differing approval rates for the police. So what accounts for the greater disapproval expressed by Blacks? As seen in Table 3.2.3, one possible factor may be the use of SQF. Indeed, the correlation between disapproval of the NYPD and disapproval of SQF is 0.946, a finding that suggests a strong relationship between the two. For context, a nationwide Gallup poll conducted at the same time reveals that 68% of Whites express "a great deal" or "quite a lot" of confidence in the police, compared to 55% for Hispanics and 38% for Blacks.[6]

Table 3.2.2   2013: "Do you approve or disapprove of the way the New York City police are doing their job?"[7]

	APPROVE	DISAPPROVE	NOT SURE
Total	61%	31%	8%
Whites	75%	19%	5%
Hispanics	61%	31%	9%
Blacks	41%	47%	12%

Table 3.2.3   2013: "Do you think stop and frisk is excessive and innocent people are being harassed, or do you think stop and frisk is an acceptable way to make New York City safer?"[8]

	APPROVE	DISAPPROVE	NOT SURE
Total	46%	49%	5%
Whites	60%	35%	5%
Hispanics	38%	58%	4%
Blacks	28%	67%	4%

---

targeting all African-Americans because some are criminals. In essence, this thinking predicts that all blacks, as a group, share a general propensity to commit crimes. Therefore, having black skin becomes enough—perhaps along with a minimal number of other factors, perhaps alone--for law enforcement to stop and detain someone" (Harris, 1997, p. 572).

[6] Gallup Polling (June 20, 2013) http://www.gallup.com/poll/163175/minorities-less-confident-policesmall-business.aspx

[7] Quinnipiac University Polling Institute (May 23, 2013) http://www.quinnipiac.edu/institutes-andcenters/polling-institute/new-york-city/release-detail?ReleaseID=1897

[8] Quinnipiac University Polling Institute (May 23, 2013) http://www.quinnipiac.edu/institutes-and centers/polling-institute/new-york-city/release-detail?ReleaseID=1897

Procedural Justice

This correlation between police approval and opinion of SQF may be explained by *procedural justice*, which holds that perceptions of fairness and the legitimacy of state institutions are inextricably linked. According to procedural justice, the very legitimacy of state institutions is a function of how fair the public perceive authorities to be when carrying out the law and using discretion (Sunshine & Tyler, 2003, 515).

Procedural justice makes four assumptions: That legitimacy is important for 1) law compliance, 2) civilian cooperation with law enforcement efforts, 3) empowering police to use discretion, and that 4) police approval depends more upon their perceived fairness, or procedural fairness, than efficacy (Sunshine & Tyler, 2003, p. 523–4). These may roughly be categorized as the *consequences* of legitimacy (compliance, cooperation, empowerment) and the *cause* of legitimacy (perceived fairness).

But are these assumptions borne out?

In their study of African American, White, and Hispanic New Yorkers, Sunshine and Tyler (2003) found general support for these assumptions. Their study showed that "perceptions of police legitimacy" predicted compliance, cooperation, and empowerment (what Sunshine and Tyler call the "consequences of legitimacy")[9] (2003, p. 529–30). Further, Sunshine and Tyler found that procedural justice,[10] more than distributive justice or police performance evaluations, predicted police legitimacy (2003, p. 530). Thus, an inquiry into racial groups' divergent perceptions of the police must occur not at the highest level (at which legitimacy shapes compliance, cooperation, and empowerment), nor at the intermediate level where perceptions of procedural justice influence legitimacy, but at the lowest level, where encounters between the police and citizens influence perceptions of procedural fairness.

At this level, the differences among racial groups in attitudes towards the police are obvious and dramatic. New York is not alone in its disparity between police approval rates among different racial groups. On the contrary, nationwide, race has been found to be one of the most effective predictors of approval of the police (Webb & Marshall, 1995). The Bureau of Justice Statistics has found that African Americans and Hispanics are twice as likely as Whites to state that they felt a traffic stop was unjustified and African Americans were half as likely to approve of the police as Whites (2002).

Bobo and Thompson found that African Americans and Whites had radically diverging expectations and beliefs about the criminal justice system (2006, p. 463). Whites were twice as likely as African Americans to believe their calls to the police would be taken seriously and that African Americans were 75% more likely than Whites to engage in jury nullification (for a non-violent drug arrest) when there were allegations of racial police bias (Bobo & Thompson, 2006, p. 463). These findings underscore the impact of procedural justice upon the "consequences" of legitimacy.

---

[9] *compliance* (beta = 0.14, $p < 0.001$), *cooperation* (beta = 0.14, $p < 0.001$), *empowerment* (beta = 0.35, $p < 0.001$).

[10] procedural justice (beta < 0.35, $p < 0.001$).

A psychological theory called "attribution" helps to explain how this occurs. According to attribution theory, persons distinguish between "causes that are 'achieved,' that is, that are due to [their own] actions, and causes that are linked to 'ascribed characteristics' of the person--their race, age, or gender" (Tyler, 2003). In the context of race and perceived fairness of police interactions, attribution theory holds that as individuals "do not feel responsible and accountable for ascribed characteristics," such as their race, they would be more likely to evaluate any treatment they receive that they perceive as racially motivated as unfair, that is, procedurally unjust (Tyler, 2003, p. 325).

The impact of racial profiling may ultimately prove to be withdrawal of public support for the police and the refusal to cooperate with police efforts (Sunshine & Tyler, 2003). This conclusion is supported by the fact that as the public, especially racial minorities, are already aware of the practice of racial profiling, (Knowles, Persico, & Todd, 2001), citizens "enter into the interaction [a police stop] with identity concerns highly salient" (Tyler, 2003). Thus, given the current climate surrounding racial profiling, attribution theory suggests that, "the simple fact that a police officer has stopped a member of a minority group may in itself be a cue that a negative stereotype about the person stopped may be relevant to the situation" (Tyler, 2003).

Thus procedural justice provides an additional level of analysis that provides more details on how the negative emotional states produced by the racially charged perceived unfairness that characterizes interactions between racial minorities and the police manifest themselves as reduced police legitimacy with its incumbent consequences.

Limitations and Areas for Future Research

This study is an incomplete analysis of the complex relationship between race, class, and policing. More sophisticated analysis techniques such as factor analysis may help disentangle the obviously highly correlated characteristics of race and class. Further, an extension of the sample to include years before and after 2010 may establish whether this effect persists across time. Inclusion of measures of residential mobility will allow for a more thorough testing of the impact of social disorganization upon policing. Inclusion of other neighborhood level characteristics such as age and unemployment may further aid in the development of these models. Finally, a measure of subsequent arrest statistics would aid in determining whether stops are indeed merely pretextual or based upon articulable suspicions.

Conclusion

The impact of racial profiling upon police legitimacy is well established and troubling. If Fagan et al. (2009) are correct and the NYPD is continuing to pursue the practice of SQF long after the point of diminishing returns in a quest to further drive down the crime rate, then the consequences may be severe. Conflict theory suggests that this process is likely to continue as long as the powerful feel threatened, be it racial or economic. While the continued use of SQF as a police practice in New York City is in doubt in light of recent court rulings and the stated opposition to the practice by Mayor de Blasio, the recent appointment of William Bratton as the NYPD police chief once again raises questions about whether the practice may be resurrected in a different form. Should such practices continue to be influenced by factors such as race and class, then the NYPD may well lose what remaining legitimacy it has in the eyes of racial and ethnic minorities and in the process continue to lose their cooperation and compliance.

References

Alpert, G., Macdonald, J.H. & Dunham, R.G. (2005), Police suspicion and discretionary decision making during citizen stops. *Criminology, 43* (2): 407–434.

Bobo, L. D., & Thompson, V. (2006). Unfair by design: The war on drugs, race, and the legitimacy of the criminal justice system. *Social Research: An International Quarterly, 73*(2), 445–472.

Bratton, W. (1998). *The turnaround: How America's top cop reversed the crime epidemic.* Random House Digital, Inc.

Eck, J. E., and Maguire, E. (2000). Have changes in policing reduced violent crime? An assessment of the evidence. In *The crime drop in America,* edited by Alfred Blumstein and Joel Wallman. New York: Cambridge University Press.

Fagan, J. (2008). Legitimacy and criminal justice. *Ohio State Journal of Criminal Law, 6,* 123–140.

Fagan, J., & Davies, G. (2000). Street stops and broken windows: Terry, race and disorder in New York City. *Fordham Urban Law Journal, 28,* 457–504.

Fagan, J., Geller, A., Davies, G., & West, V. (2009). Street stops and broken windows revisited: The demography and logic of proactive policing in a safe and changing city. *Race, Ethnicity, And Policing: New And Essential Readings,* Stephen K. Rice and Michael D. White, eds., New York, NY: New York University Press, 09–203.

Fagan, J., & MacDonald, J. (2012). Policing, crime and legitimacy in New York and Los Angeles: The social and political contexts of two historic crime declines. *Columbia Public Law Research Paper,* (12–315).

Ferguson, A. G. (2007). High crime area question: Requiring verifiable and quantifiable evidence for Fourth Amendment reasonable suspicion analysis. *American University Law Review, 57,* 1587–1644.

Gelman, A., Fagan, J., & Kiss, A. (2007). An analysis of the New York City police department's "stop-and-frisk" policy in the context of claims of racial bias. *Journal of the American Statistical Association, 102*(479), 813–823.

Genelin, Michael (1998). Community prosecution: A difference. 10 *Prosecutor's Brief* 13.

Glasser, I. (1999). American Drug Laws: The New Jim Crow. *Albany Law Review, 63,* 703–724.

Gramckow, H. (1997). Community prosecution in the United States. *European Journal on Criminal Policy and Research, 5*(4), 9–26.

Harris, D. A. (1996). Driving while black and all other traffic offenses: The Supreme Court and pretextual traffic stops. *Journal of Criminal Law & Criminology, 87,* 544–582.

Holmes, M. D. (2000). Minority threat and police brutality: Determinants of civil rights criminal complaints in U.S. municipalities. *Criminology, 38*(2), 343–368.

Jacobs, D., & Britt, D. (1979). Inequality and police use of deadly force: An empirical assessment of a conflict hypothesis. *Social Problems, 26,* 403–412.

Kelling, G. L., & Bratton, W. J. (1998). Declining crime rates: Insiders' views of the New York City story. *Journal of Criminal Law and Criminology, 88*(4), 1217–1232.

Knowles, J., Persico, N., & Todd, P. (1999). *Racial bias in motor vehicle searches: Theory and evidence* (No. w7449). National Bureau of Economic Research. Liska, A., & M. Chamlin, (1984). "Social structure And Crime control Among Macrosocial units." *American Journal of Sociology, 90,* 383–395.

Loury, G. C., & Loury, G. C. (2009). *The anatomy of racial inequality.* Cambridge, MA: Harvard University Press.

Massey, D. S. (1993). *American apartheid: Segregation and the making of the underclass.* Cambridge, MA: Harvard University Press.

Massey, D. S. (2007). *Categorically unequal: The American stratification system.* New York, NY: Russell Sage Foundation.

Miethe, T. D., & Meier, R. F. (1994). *Crime and its social context: Toward an integrated theory of offenders, victims, and situations.* Albany, NY: SUNY Press.

Novak, K. J., & Chamlin, M. B. (2012). Racial threat, suspicion, and police behavior the impact of race and place in traffic enforcement. *Crime & Delinquency, 58*(2), 275–300.

Petrocelli, M., Piquero, A. R., & Smith, M. R. (2003). Conflict theory and racial profiling: An empirical analysis of police traffic stop data. *Journal of Criminal Justice, 31*(1), 1–11.

Rudovsky, D. (2001). Law enforcement by stereotypes and serendipity: Racial profiling and stops and searches without cause. *University of Pennsylvania Journal of Constitutional Law, 3,* 296–366.

Sampson, R. J., & Raudenbush, S. W. (2004). Seeing disorder: Neighborhood stigma and the social construction of "broken windows". *Social psychology quarterly, 67*(4), 319–342.

Sampson, R. J., & Wilson, W. J. (1995). 'Toward a theory of race, crime, and urban inequality. *Race, crime, and justice: A reader,* 177–190. New York, NY: Routledge.

Shaw, C. R., & McKay, H. D. (1942). Juvenile delinquency and urban areas. Chicago, IL: University of Chicago Press.

Skogan, W. G. (1990). *Disorder and decline: Crime and the spiral of decay in American neighbourhoods.* Los Angeles, CA: University of California Press.

Skolnik, S. (1999). DOJ puts big bucks behind community prosecution. *Legal Times,* (Feb. 8, 1999).

Skolnick, J. H., & Caplovitz, A. (2001). Guns, Drugs, and Profiling: Ways to Target Guns and Minimize Racial Profiling. *Arizona Law Review, 43,* 413–437.

Spitzer, E. (1999). *The New York City Police Department's stop and frisk practices: A report to the people of the state of New York from the Office of the Attorney General.* Darby, PA: Diane Publishing,

Sunshine, J., & Tyler, T. R. (2003). The role of procedural justice and legitimacy in shaping public support for policing. *Law & Society Review, 37*(3), 513–548.

Takagi, P. (1974). A garrison State in "Democratic" society. *Crime and Social Justice, 1,* 27–33.

Thompson, A. C. (1999). Stopping the usual suspects: Race and the fourth amendment. *New York University Law Review, 74,* 956–1013.

Turk, A. T. (1969). *Criminality and legal order.* Chicago, IL: Rand McNally.

Tyler, T. R. (2003). Procedural justice, legitimacy, and the effective rule of law. *Crime and justice, 30,* 283–357.

Vold, G. (1958). *Theoretical Criminology.* New York: Oxford University Press.

Weisburd, D., Mastrofski, S. D., Greenspan, R., & Willis, J. J. (2004). *The growth of Compstat in American policing.* Washington, DC: Police Foundation.

Weisburd, D., Mastrofski, S. D., McNally, A., Greenspan, R., & Willis, J. J. (2003). Reforming to preserve: Compstat and strategic problem solving in American policing. *Criminology & Public Policy, 2*(3), 421–456.

Webb, V. J., & Marshall, C. E. (1995). The relative importance of race and ethnicity on citizen attitudes toward the police. *American Journal of Police, 14*(2), 45–66.

Willis, J. J., Mastrofski, S. D., & Weisburd, D. (2007). Making sense of COMPSTAT: A theory based analysis of organizational change in three police departments. *Law & Society Review, 41*(1), 147–188.

Wilson, J. Q. (1994, March 20). Just take away their Guns. *New York Times Magazine*, § 6 at 1.

Wilson, J. Q., & Kelling, G. (1982). The police and neighborhood safety: Broken Windows. *Atlantic Monthly, 249*(3), 29–38.

Critical Thinking Questions

1   Which four theories did the authors examine as possible explanations for how CompStat created racial disparities in pedestrian stops? How does theory explain racial disparities in policing?

2   How did the NYPD's implementation of broken windows differ from the original theory?

3   Which variables did the author predict would influence the stop rate in a precinct? Did the results support the author's hypotheses?

4   Which variable had the greatest influence on the stop rate in a precinct? Why was this the case?

Editors' Introduction: Reading 3.3

The evidentiary threshold within the due process model is generally *probable cause* (typically with a warrant, and with plenty of warrantless exceptions that lower this threshold to reasonable suspicion). Legitimacy can therefore be understood to be garnered by police acting within a framework of probable cause: If an officer has probable cause to effect an arrest, he or she may do so. Legitimacy is threatened when probable cause is unduly ignored. Sekhon turns this idea on its head and suggests that probable cause is *not* enough to fairly effect an arrest; rather, police departments and officers must in addition take into consideration the *distribution* of their arrests across a host of variables, including geography, race, and class. Sekhon's article poses a radical challenge not just to how police do their work, but to those who believe that as long as police just "do their job" their legitimacy is assured.

Redistributive Policing

Nirej S. Sekhon

Introduction

Courts imagine police discretion in terms of the decisionmaking latitude that individual officers enjoy.[1] Officers make choices about whom to stop, search, and arrest. Constitutional criminal procedure attempts to regulate how officers make those choices by prescribing the quantum of information they must possess regarding a suspect's likely guilt before they may intrude upon her privacy or liberty.[2] In other words, the judicial approach to police discretion assumes that individual officers are the principal discretion-wielding actors in policing and that the central problem they confront is distinguishing the guilty from the innocent. From this perspective, it follows that any arrest supported by probable cause is a legitimate one.[3]

This Article critiques the narrowly individualistic conception of police discretion that predominates in law, scholarship, and public discourse.[4] Casting the individual officer as the central discretion-wielding agent in policing obfuscates the arrest's role as a policymaking device with broad distributive consequences. If law is to ensure an egalitarian arrest distribution it should treat police departments, not officers,

---

[1] *See infra* notes 11–29 and accompanying text.

[2] *See infra* notes 37–40 and accompanying text.

[3] The Supreme Court has held exactly that. Whren v. United States, 517 U.S. 806, 813 (1996).

[4] Popular culture is preoccupied with police behavior at the individual officer level: high-speed chases, excessive use of force, and the like are staples for the evening news. And many people experience "the police" in terms of an individual encounter with an officer; typically, that encounter is in the traffic context. *See* MATTHEW R. DUROSE ET AL., BUREAU OF JUSTICE STATISTICS, U.S. DEP'T OF JUSTICE, CONTACTS BETWEEN POLICE AND THE PUBLIC, 2005, at 1 (Apr. 2007) (finding that more than half of all civilian-police contacts occur in the traffic context).

as the primary discretion-wielding actors. Modern police departments exert high degrees of control over individual officers and rely heavily on arrest as an enforcement strategy. The central problem confronting police departments is not distinguishing the guilty from the innocent, but rather distinguishing *among* the guilty. Police departments—i.e., administrators and policymakers—regularly choose to target some offenders and to let others engage in comparable criminal activity without consequence. This is most true in the "proactive policing" context, where the police themselves (as opposed to a victim or some other witness) identify criminal misconduct. Because criminal procedure is hushed about departmental discretion and because retributive, expressivist, and utilitarian theories dominate scholarly discussion of the criminal sanction, departmental discretion is under-theorized in legal scholarship. This Article describes departmental discretion's mechanics and anti-egalitarian consequences. It then sketches a normative vision for regulating departmental discretion relying on distributive justice theory.

I argue that three dimensions of departmental discretion bear on how proactive policing arrests are distributed across a jurisdiction: geographic deployment, enforcement priority, and enforcement tactics. How different groups bear the costs and benefits of arrests within a jurisdiction raises serious questions of democratic fairness. For example, narcotics enforcement has swelled America's prison populations with poor men of color.[5] The pool of prospective narcotics offenders in a given city will typically be larger than could ever be arrested with complete enforcement. Offenders' demographic profile will depend on where in a city police target—e.g., the race and class profile of narcotics offenders at an elite, liberal arts college on the urban periphery might be different from that of narcotics offenders in working class neighborhoods closer to the urban core. Departmental choices about geographic deployment, enforcement priority, and enforcement tactics determine whether and how these areas are targeted.[6] I argue that police departments tend to make such choices in a manner that generates unjustified inequality.

Normatively, I argue that courts and scholars should conceptualize arrests, and proactive policing more generally, as a distributive good. Criminal enforcement's moral legitimacy is typically grounded in retributive, expressivist, or utilitarian theories. These theories offer little guidance on how to accommodate egalitarianism in proactive policing. On the other hand, distributive justice's central preoccupation is with how political institutions in a liberal democracy should achieve an egalitarian distribution of the benefits and burdens that collective political existence generates.[7] Distributive justice animates discussions in various policy contexts and I argue that the same should be true for police department discretion. That discretion is most pronounced in the proactive policing context where there are few legal or political checks on departmental discretion. Distributive justice suggests that the mere fact of a criminal law violation is insufficient to legitimate proactive policing arrests. The costs and benefits of arrest distribution, just as with

---

[5] *See* MICHAEL TONRY, MALIGN NEGLECT: RACE, CRIME, AND PUNISHMENT IN AMERICA 67, 104, 112–13 (1995); *infra* Part III.B.1 (discussing a case study focusing on narcotics enforcement in Seattle).

[6] Individual officer bias would have no bearing on the arrestees' demographic profile. *See* JOHN C. LAMBERTH, LAMBERTH CONSULTING, DATA COLLECTION AND BENCHMARKING OF THE BIAS POLICING PROJECT: FINAL REPORT FOR THE METROPOLITAN POLICE DEPARTMENT IN THE DISTRICT OF COLUMBIA 57 (2006) (finding no evidence of profiling apparent in minority neighborhoods).

[7] *See infra* notes 271–272 and accompanying text.

other policy choices, should be shared equally amongst all communities within a jurisdiction. Distributive justice principles also dovetail with a representation-reinforcing theory of judicial review. In tandem, the two suggest a much more active role for courts in constraining police departments' discretion to ration arrests.

The Article proceeds in three parts. Part II demonstrates how scholars and courts have addressed the police "discretion problem." Legal scholars have not systematically accounted for how departmental discretion operates. This is unsurprising given that constitutional criminal procedure has narrowly conceptualized police discretion in terms of individual officers' assessments of individual suspects' likely guilt. Part III argues that departmental policies regarding geographic deployment, enforcement priority, and enforcement tactics drive proactive policing's anti-egalitarian consequences. Case studies on narcotics enforcement and quality-of-life policing demonstrate departmental choices' salience in producing inequality. Part IV evaluates departmental discretion through the lens of distributive justice and concludes that where popular politics is unable to prevent the unequal distribution of proactive policing arrests, courts should do so.

The "Discretion Problem"

Scholars and courts tend to localize the "discretion problem" to the moments leading up to and during contact between individual officers and civilians. This conceptualization decouples police discretion from distributive justice—most significantly, it avoids the question of whether arrest policies' benefits and burdens are fairly distributed across a jurisdiction.[8] This Section accounts for the decoupling. It begins with scholars rather than courts. It was scholars, beginning in the late 1950s, who identified a "discretion problem." They suggested that police departments delegated excess policymaking discretion to individual officers and those officers, in turn, used that discretion inconsistently if not abusively. Courts and more recent scholarship have continued to echo that conceptualization.

The "Discovery" of Police Discretion

Scholars "discovered" the discretion problem in the 1950s.[9] In 1956, the American Bar Foundation (ABF) issued a report concluding that considerable discretion existed in policing.[10] "Discovery" is a curious metaphor for describing an endemic feature of policing. But, prior to the ABF report, scholars and lawyers tended to embrace the mythology of "complete enforcement"—i.e., the notion that police attempt to apprehend each and every violator of the criminal code.[11] For early

---

[8] *See infra* Part IV.A.

[9] SAMUEL WALKER, TAMING THE SYSTEM: THE CONTROL OF DISCRETION IN CRIMINAL JUSTICE, 1950–1990, at 6–7 (1993) (summarizing early research).

[10] *See* Michael Tonry, *Foreword* to DISCRETION IN CRIMINAL JUSTICE, at xiii–xiv (Lloyd E. Ohlin & Frank J. Remington eds., 1993) (discussing the origins and influence of the ABF report).

[11] KENNETH CULP DAVIS, POLICE DISCRETION, at iv (1975).

law and society scholars, the discretion problem brought the disjuncture between law and social practice into stark relief. Early discretion scholars problematized the disjuncture at its most primary level: the individual officer.

Early discretion scholars cast the discretion problem in terms of an inverted pyramid. Ordinarily, one would expect the most senior members of a governmental institution to enjoy the greatest discretion. In police departments, early police scholars contended, discretionary latitude appeared to increase *down* the line of command.[12] Kenneth Culp Davis argued that this, in effect, rendered individual patrol officers "policy makers" for their beats.[13] Davis noted that many police departments did not have policy manuals at all and, for those that did, the manuals said nothing about enforcement priorities.[14] Taking cover under the rhetorical blanket of "full enforcement," police department administrators deferred almost completely to patrolmen to decide when and against whom to enforce criminal laws.[15] The absence of departmental intelligence as to crime's distribution or the nature of officers' practices compounded the discretion problem.[16] In the absence of departmental directives, patrol officers were free to devise enforcement protocol based on hunch, habit, and bias.[17] The early scholars were particularly troubled by officers' decisions *not to* enforce criminal laws because these decisions were entirely invisible to supervisors.[18]

Early discretion scholarship reflects the mid-twentieth century's scholarly zeitgeist. Intellectuals were preoccupied with identifying the "authoritarian personality" in its various guises.[19] The vivid memories of fascism's horrors impelled scholars to scrutinize the psychological predilections of individuals who might be particularly susceptible to populist totalitarianism. Police officers figured prominently as examples of the authoritarian personality.[20] True to the times, intellectuals were not particularly moved by popular democracy's capacity for restraining the authoritarian personality. The ground between popular democracy and populist totalitarianism seemed precariously slippery.[21] It is no wonder that intellectuals—the early police discretion scholars among them—were quick to posit political insulation, technocratic rationalization,

---

[12] DAVIS, *supra* note 11, at v, 47, 99, 139; Tonry, *supra* note 10, at xiv–xv (summarizing ABF survey); JAMES Q. WILSON, VARIETIES OF POLICE BEHAVIOR 7 (1968).

[13] DAVIS, *supra* note 11, at 99, 139.

[14] *Id.* at 32–38.

[15] *Id.* at 52–53 ("The police assume full enforcement is required by [statute and ordinance], and when insufficient resources or good sense requires nonenforcement they also assume that they must do what they can to conceal the nonenforcement. So the only open enforcement policy is one of full enforcement .... Because of the false pretense of full enforcement, no studies are ever made to guide the formulation of enforcement policy.").

[16] *Id.* at 41, 44.

[17] *See id.* at 46–47. "Hunches" and "habits" may be a more polite way of talking about biases to the extent that officers' expectations of criminality are racialized. *See* L. Song Richardson, *Arrest Efficiency and the Fourth Amendment*, 95 MINN. L. REV. 2035, 2042–52 (2011) (reviewing the science of implicit bias).

[18] Wayne R. LaFave, *Police Rule Making and the Fourth Amendment: The Role of Courts, in* DISCRETION IN CRIMINAL JUSTICE, *supra* note 10, at 214–15 (characterizing early scholars' concerns).

[19] T.W. ADORNO ET AL., THE AUTHORITARIAN PERSONALITY 1–11 (1950); *see also* DAVID ALAN SKLANSKY, DEMOCRACY AND THE POLICE 29–30 (2008).

[20] SKLANSKY, *supra* note 19, at 30, 39–43.

[21] *Id.* at 18–21 (discussing pluralist scholars' anxieties about mass politics).

and professionalization as the best approaches to containing and directing the authoritarian personality towards benevolent ends.[22]

According to the early scholars, the locus of the discretion problem was the individual patrolman and the locus of the solution was departmental control. Early scholars posited departmental authority as the best mechanism for restraining and guiding individual officers. Kenneth Culp Davis, for example, argued that police departments should promulgate regulations following public comment, much like administrative agencies do.[23] Other early scholars concurred, arguing for various combinations of external and internal rules regulating police officer discretion.[24] The analogy between an administrative agency and a municipal police department is far from perfect.[25] The differences between the two may explain why police departments have, by and large, not heeded the early scholars' recommendations.[26] More significant for my purposes, however, is that early scholars embraced an officer–department dualism. That dualism defined the field and continues to inform how contemporary scholars theorize the discretion problem.

Although early scholars noted that non-white communities might bear the brunt of the discretion problem's harmful consequences,[27] their concern about discretion was not expressed in terms of racial disparity so much as fear of general arbitrariness.[28] Even though contemporary legal scholarship on policing squarely addresses race, it echoes the early scholars' officer–department dualism, positing increased departmental regulation as the answer to the discretion problem.[29] Moments of poorly calibrated officer discretion saturate popular discourse: police shootings, high-speed chases, and the like make for good news. Even scholars who insist on

---

[22] *Id.* at 36–37.

[23] *See* DAVIS, *supra* note 11, at 100, 106, 113–20. Davis argued that individual officers should have discretion to make decisions in individual situations, but should not have discretion to make "policy." *Id.* at 99, 139. He didn't, however, precisely articulate the difference between these two things.

[24] *See, e.g.,* GEORGE E. BERKLEY, THE DEMOCRATIC POLICEMAN 29, 135–36 (1969) (arguing for internal rules with public comment); WALKER, *supra* note 9, at 154 (arguing for better departmental control over individual officers); Wayne R. LaFave, *Controlling Discretion by Administrative Regulations*, 89 MICH. L. REV. 442, 504–08 (1990) (arguing constitutional rules should encourage departments to create regulations).

[25] *See* Ronald J. Allen, *The Police And Substantive Rulemaking: Reconciling Principle and Expediency*, 125 U. PA. L. REV. 62, 96–97 (1976).

[26] Although most large metropolitan police departments now have policy manuals, those manuals tend to focus on narrow personnel issues and not on enforcement priority or protocol as the early scholars had hoped. *See* GEORGE L. KELLING & CATHERINE M. COLES, FIXING BROKEN WINDOWS 180–83 (1996); *see also* Elizabeth Joh, *Breaking the Law to Enforce It: Undercover Police Participation in Crime*, 62 STAN. L. REV. 159 (2009) (discussing internal police regulation of undercover operations).

[27] *See, e.g.,* DAVIS, *supra* note 11, at iii, 113–20.

[28] *See id.* at 15. The early scholars' work addressed race in passing. *See id.* at 161–62; JEROME H. SKOLNICK, JUSTICE WITHOUT TRIAL 77–80 (3d ed. 1994) (describing research based on fieldwork conducted in 1962). The absence seems jarring particularly given the salience of racial unrest at the time and the police's role in fomenting it. *See* THE NAT'L ADVISORY COMM'N ON CIVIL DISORDERS, REPORT OF THE NATIONAL ADVISORY COMMISSION ON CIVIL DISORDERS 301–07 (1968).

[29] *See* Barbara E. Armacost, *Organizational Culture and Police Misconduct*, 72 GEO. WASH. L. REV. 453, 506–15 (2003) (noting that organizational culture accounts for officer behavior and arguing that it accounts for use of excessive force); Erik Luna, *Transparent Policing*, 85 IOWA L. REV. 1107, 1140–41, 1156, 1167–69 (2000) (noting that excessive officer discretion leads to racial disparity and excessive force and suggesting department regulations as one possible solution); Tracey Maclin, *Race and the Fourth Amendment*, 51 VAND. L. REV. 331, 373–74 (1998) (suggesting that officers are inclined to think that black motorists are more likely to have contraband).

race's centrality in structuring law enforcement priority and protocol tend to reproduce the officer–department dichotomy. Despite being considerably more sophisticated around race than early discretion scholarship,[30] much contemporary criminal procedure scholarship still takes the individual officer as the most relevant unit of analysis.[31] Similarly, contemporary race scholars tend to characterize departmental responsibility in terms of "omission"—e.g., failing to regulate rogue officers or eradicate "cultures" of racism.[32]

Some scholars have recognized that police departments are significant discretion-wielding actors.[33] That recognition is implicit in work addressing the relationship between arrest disparity and narcotics enforcement[34] as well as in work addressing "overenforcement" in minority communities.[35] Scholars, however, have not systematically analyzed the incidents of departmental discretion or how those incidents specifically relate to egalitarianism. This may be because scholars take their cues from courts and constitutional criminal procedure is not especially concerned with departmental discretion.

---

[30] *See, e.g.*, Richardson, *supra* note 17, at 2052–53 (arguing that recent psychological theories regarding "implicit bias" explain why police offers may inordinately target minorities); Anthony C. Thompson, *Stopping the Usual Suspects: Race and the Fourth Amendment*, 74 N.Y.U. L. Rev. 956, 987–88 (1999) (using psychological theories of cognition to account for how officers perceive race).

[31] *See* Hadar Aviram & Daniel L. Portman, *Inequitable Enforcement: Introducing the Concept of Equity into Constitutional Review of Law Enforcement*, 61 Hastings L.J. 413, 424 (2009) (noting factors that bear on an officer's decision to arrest or pursue investigation); Bennett Capers, *Policing, Race, and Place*, 44 Harv. C.R.-C.L. L. Rev. 43, 75 (2009) (noting that "motivating officers to set aside inappropriate biases" is among the key solutions to racially disproportionate targeting); Elizabeth E. Joh, *Discretionless Policing: Technology and the Fourth Amendment*, 95 Calif. L. Rev. 199, 233 (arguing that technological innovation might be a solution to "the potential dangers associated with the discretion afforded to police officers in their day-to-day activities"); Kevin R. Johnson, *How Racial Profiling in America Became the Law of the Land: United States v. Brignoni-Ponce and Wren v. United States and the Need for Truly Rebellious Lawyering*, 98 Geo. L.J. 1005, 1007 (2009) (criticizing Supreme Court cases for allowing "profiling by law enforcement officers to go largely unchecked"); Maclin, *supra* note 29, at 378 (criticizing the probable cause requirement because it "fails to diminish the discretion possessed by officers, but may actually facilitate arbitrary seizures"); Richardson, *supra* note 17, at 2092–97 (proposing changes in training and hiring that will reduce officer bias); Thompson, *supra* note 30, at 1002 ("Officers must offer race-neutral reasons for their conduct to survive constitutional scrutiny.").

[32] *See, e.g.*, Armacost, *supra* note 29, at 523; Capers, *supra* note 31, at 75; Brandon Garrett, *Remedying Racial Profiling*, 33 Colum. Hum. Rts. L. Rev. 41, 54 (arguing that improper training and supervision lead to racial profiling).

[33] *See* Sklansky, *supra* note 19, at 176–77 (noting that massive individual and departmental discretion is unavoidable); William J. Stuntz, *Unequal Justice*, 121 Harv. L. Rev. 1969, 2038 (2008).

[34] Gabriel J. Chin, *Race, the War on Drugs, and the Collateral Consequences of Criminal Conviction*, 6 J. Gender Race & Just. 253, 265–67 (2002) (noting disparity in narcotics arrests); William J. Stuntz, *Race, Class, and Drugs*, 98 Colum. L. Rev. 1795, 1820 (1998) (stating that aggressive narcotics policing in poor, minority neighborhoods tends to be an inexpensive way to generate arrests).

[35] *See* Tracey L. Meares, *Place and Crime*, 73 Chi.-Kent L. Rev. 669, 695 (1998) (arguing that overenforcement and underenforcement in minority communities undermine social cohesion and norms); Eric J. Miller, *Role-Based Policing: Restraining Police Conduct "Outside The Legitimate Investigative Sphere,"* 94 Calif. L. Rev. 617, 665 (2006) (proposing a solution to overenforcement that uses non-deputized municipal actors to police minor offenses); Alexandra Natapoff, *Underenforcement*, 75 Fordham L. Rev. 1715, 1720, 1772 (2006) (criticizing policy choices that lead to the related phenomenon of underenforcement and overenforcement of criminal laws in minority communities).

Courts

Constitutional criminal procedure's modern origin is rooted in federal courts' efforts to contain racist, mob justice in the pre-civil rights South.[36] In other words, promoting egalitarianism was among the Court's chief purposes in creating modern criminal procedure. Over time, criminal procedure has increasingly focused on how individual police officers differentiate guilty from innocent individuals. Ironically, that preoccupation has led criminal procedure away from questions of egalitarianism.

Fourth Amendment

The Fourth Amendment regulates officer discretion with a view to limiting searches and seizures that might unduly burden the "innocent."[37] The Court has organized Fourth Amendment jurisprudence around how officers distinguish the prospectively innocent from the prospectively guilty. The Court has done so to the exclusion of how individual officers, let alone departments, distinguish between categories of offenders. And the Court has altogether written race out of Fourth Amendment jurisprudence.

The Fourth Amendment's requirement of "individualized suspicion" highlights why courts conceptualize the discretion problem around individualized citizen–officer interactions. The Fourth Amendment requires that an officer have either "probable cause," or at least "reasonable suspicion based on articulable facts," that a crime has occurred (or will occur) before the officer can legally detain and search an individual or her property.[38] In theory, individualized suspicion ensures a quantum of certainty regarding criminal activity that protects innocent citizens from the inconvenience and indignity of a police search or seizure.[39] Whether individualized suspicion exists is a judgment to be made by a particular officer.[40]

Under the Fourth Amendment, courts are agnostic on whether the police target one group of offenders as opposed to another. The Court has interpreted the Fourth Amendment to be "transubstantive"—i.e., it does not require that intrusions upon liberty or privacy be calibrated

---

[36] *See* Robert M. Cover, *The Origins of Judicial Activism in the Protection of Minorities*, 91 YALE L.J. 1287, 1306 (1982); Michael J. Klarman, *The Racial Origins of Modern Criminal Procedure*, 99 MICH. L. REV. 48, 56–57 (2000). In the early cases, the Supreme Court used the Fourteenth Amendment to reverse convictions of poor black defendants who were very likely innocent of criminal wrongdoing. *See* Klarman, *supra*, at 53, 57, 61.

[37] *See* William J. Stuntz, *Waiving Rights in Criminal Procedure*, 77 VA. L. REV. 761, 765 (1989) (arguing that the Fourth Amendment is interpreted to protect innocent third parties).

[38] *Compare* Katz v. United States, 389 U.S. 347, 357 (1967) (holding a search conducted without a warrant based on probable cause is per se unreasonable), *with* Terry v. Ohio, 392 U.S. 1, 21 (1968) (holding that individualized suspicion based on articulable facts justifies police intrusion as an exception to the warrant requirement). Because it is a less stringent standard, "individualized suspicion" permits a less intrusive police invasion than does "probable cause." *Terry*, 392 U.S. at 27 (holding that police intrusion on the grounds of "individualized suspicion" must be limited to a search for weapons only).

[39] *See Katz*, 389 U.S. at 357.

[40] *See, e.g., Terry*, 392 U.S. at 21 ("[T]he *police officer* must be able to point to specific and articulable facts which ... reasonably warrant [an] intrusion." (emphasis added)).

to the suspected offense's severity.[41] Once an officer has probable cause to believe that an individual is committing a crime, however minor, the officer may detain and search the suspected offender. The Court has made it clear that it will not use the Fourth Amendment to restrain even outrageous exercises of police authority if there is any basis in the criminal code to think that a crime is occurring.[42] The sheer number of criminal laws means that police have considerable discretion in choosing among different kinds of offenders. As discussed in detail in Part III below, that discretion is not best conceptualized at the individual officer level.

If there is individualized suspicion to believe that any crime has occurred, the Fourth Amendment is agnostic as to whether race animated the police's enforcement decisions.[43] In *Whren v. United States,* the Court held that an officer's subjective motivation for detaining an individual is irrelevant to whether there was a Fourth Amendment violation.[44] In *Whren,* undercover narcotics officers had probable cause to believe that Whren had committed a minor traffic violation. But the facts surrounding the detention suggested that the real reason the officers pulled Whren over was not for the relatively minor traffic violation, but because the officers thought Whren, an African-American male, had narcotics in his vehicle.[45] Departmental regulations prohibited undercover narcotics officers from enforcing minor traffic violations.[46] Whren argued that, absent the officers' stereotype-driven assumption that black motorists are likely to have narcotics, they would not have stopped him at all. The Court rejected Whren's argument that the "pretextual" stop violated the Fourth Amendment.[47]

Whren emblematizes the Court's refusal to use the Fourth Amendment to regulate race-based stops or promote adherence to departmental regulations.[48] In *Whren,* the Court made clear that there would be no Fourth Amendment consequence if individual officers violate

---

[41] *See, e.g.,* William J. Stuntz, *OJ. Simpson, Bill Clinton, and the Transsubstantive Fourth Amendment,* 114 Harv. L. Rev. 842, 869–70 (2001) (arguing that the Fourth Amendment search standard should account for the substantive seriousness of the offense being investigated); *accord* Akhil Reed Amar, The Constitution and Criminal Procedure 32–35 (1997) (arguing that the Fourth Amendment standard should be linked to the importance of the government's purpose in searching).

[42] Atwater v. City of Lago Vista, 532 U.S. 318, 325–26 (2001) (holding that the Fourth Amendment permits an officer to arrest for violating a seatbelt law).

[43] *See* Whren v. United States, 517 U.S. 806, 813 (1996).

[44] *Id.* The Court has, in a limited subset of search cases, distinguished between an officer's subjective motivation and a department's "programmatic purpose." *See* City of Indianapolis v. Edmond, 531 U.S. 32, 44–45 (2000) (distinguishing *Whren*). Police may conduct searches without individualized suspicion when the search advances a public welfare function that, in the first instance, is not simply "crime control." *Id.; see also* Illinois v. Lidster, 540 U.S. 419, 424–25 (2004) (finding a suspicionless checkpoint stop permissible where the purpose was to obtain information regarding a hit and run that had already occurred); Mich. Dep't of State v. Sitz, 496 U.S. 444, 455 (1990) (finding a suspicionless stop at a drunk driving checkpoint permissible because of the state's interest in preventing unsafe driving); Camara v. Mun. Court, 387 U.S. 523, 539 (1967) (finding a municipal health and safety inspection permissible without individualized suspicion because the purpose was not punitive). No published opinion, however, suggests that a court has ever scrutinized a police department's reasons for arresting one group of offenders versus another under the guise of ascertaining the department's primary purpose.

[45] *Whren,* 517 U.S. at 809.

[46] *Id.* at 815.

[47] *Id.* at 813.

[48] *See* LaFave, *supra* note 24, at 504–08.

departmental regulations.[49] This, in tandem with the Court's transubstantive application of the Fourth Amendment, means that the Fourth Amendment has no role in regulating enforcement choices that have racial disparity. In *Whren*, the Court noted that the Fourteenth Amendment is the only constitutional check on such discretion.[50]

Fourteenth Amendment

Nominally, courts are willing to address the racial consequences of police discretion under the Fourteenth Amendment, but practically, courts have limited its application by localizing the inquiry to the moment of contact between individual police officers and citizens. Much like in the Fourth Amendment context, the "discretion problem" is cognizable as a Fourteenth Amendment problem when realized at the individual level.[51]

Equal protection claims have been most successfully advanced in the context of traffic stops where police use minor traffic infractions as a device for searching otherwise innocent minority motorists for narcotics.[52] Advocates for the campaign against racial profiling on the nation's highways organized their legal and political message around the indignity and inconvenience of profiling on "innocent" minority motorists.[53] Race is a bad proxy for guilt.[54] And the "driving while black" (DWB) campaign was successful only to the extent that it helped cement the pithy, popular wisdom that profiling is "wrong." The DWB campaign, however, may very well have consolidated popular and legal disinterest in how the police parse the guilty from the guilty.[55]

---

[49] *Whren*, 517 U.S. at 815; *see also* Bertine v. Colorado, 479 U.S. 367, 374 (1987) (approving a police regulation that allowed officers discretion on whether to conduct suspicionless inventory searches).

[50] *Whren*, 517 U.S. at 813 ("[T]he constitutional basis for objecting to intentionally discriminatory application of laws is the Equal Protection Clause, not the Fourth Amendment.").

[51] The Court has increasingly individualized equality rights in general. *See* Adarand Constructors, Inc. v. Pena, 515 U.S. 200, 227 (1995) (reasoning that the Equal Protection Clause "protect[s] *persons*, not *groups*"). This is true even in a context like voting rights where no individual could conceivably have "the right" to select the winning candidate. *See* Miller v. Johnson, 515 U.S. 900, 911–12 (1995).

[52] *See, e.g.*, Chavez v. Ill. State Police, 251 F.3d 612, 623–25 (7th Cir. 2001) (describing plaintiffs); ACLU OF N. CAL., THE CALIFORNIA DWB REPORT: A REPORT FROM THE HIGHWAYS, TRENCHES AND HALLS OF POWER IN CALIFORNIA 15–40 (2002), *available at* http://www.aclunc.org/library/publications/asset_upload_file305_3517.pdf (detailing individual profiling narratives); David A. Harris, *"Driving While Black" and All Other Traffic Offenses: The Supreme Court and Pretextual Traffic Stops*, 87 J. CRIM. L. & CRIMINOLOGY 544, 564–65 (1997) (describing the allegations in Complaint, Wilkins v. Md. State Police, Civil No. MJG-93-468 (D. Md. 1993)); David A. Harris, *The Stories, the Statistics, and the Law: Why "Driving While Black" Matters*, 84 MINN. L. REV. 265, 270–75 (1999) (detailing the evidence of innocent, middle-class African-American victims of profiling). By "successful," I mean that such litigation has generated several settlement agreements. *See* Press Release, ACLU of N. Cal., In Landmark Racial Profiling Settlement, Arizona Law Enforcement Agents Agree to Major Reforms (Feb. 2, 2005), *available at* http://www.aclu.org/racial-justice/landmark-racial-profiling-settlement-arizona-law-en-forcement-agents-agree-major-refor; Press Release, ACLU of N. Cal., In Landmark Racial Profiling Settlement, California Highway Patrol Agrees to Major Reforms (Feb. 27, 2003), http://www.aclunc.org/news/press_releases/in_landmark_ra-cial_profiling_settlement,_california_highway_patrol_agrees_to_major_reforms.shtml.

[53] *See* Devon Carbado, *(E)racing the Fourth Amendment*, 100 MICH. L. REV. 946, 1034–35 (2002).

[54] *See* BERNARD E. HARCOURT, AGAINST PREDICTION 119 (2007) (noting a study of traffic stops that indicates a higher "hit rate" for white drivers than minority drivers).

[55] *See* R. Richard Banks, *Beyond Profiling: Race, Policing, and the Drug War*, 56 STAN. L. REV. 571, 593–94 (2003). Even where there is documented racial disparity in stop and search rates, it does not necessarily follow that there is racial disparity in arrest rates. *Compare* Bernard Harcourt, *Henry Louis Gates and Racial Profiling: What's the Problem?* 2–3 (John M. Olin

To challenge how the police parse the guilty from the guilty, a defendant must demonstrate that the police enforced a criminal law against him because of his membership in a protected class, e.g., race.[56] In order to prevail on a "selective enforcement claim," one must prove disparate impact and intentional discrimination.[57] "Disparate impact" means that there is a universe of "similarly situated" offenders, i.e., offenders who are not members of the protected group *and* against whom the police did not enforce the criminal law at issue. For example, a minority motorist who alleges selective enforcement of the speed limit would have to demonstrate that law enforcement permitted white individuals to speed with impunity while enforcing the speed limit against minority motorists. To succeed, the minority challenger would also have to prove that the police intentionally targeted minority motorists on account of their race. Proving racial animus or "intent" is difficult.[58] It is more difficult to establish a case of selective enforcement than other kinds of discrimination because the Court has made it difficult to even obtain discovery.[59]

The Supreme Court has held that, to obtain discovery for a selective enforcement claim in a criminal case, a defendant must demonstrate that "similarly situated defendants of other races could have been prosecuted, but were not."[60] To satisfy the "similarly situated" requirement, courts have required defendants to produce evidence of offenders who are virtually identical to the defendant in every regard save for race.[61] In *United States v. Barlow*, for instance, the Seventh Circuit elided the requirement for individualized suspicion with that for similarly situated offenders.[62] Barlow argued that federal agents targeted black passengers for investigation at Chicago's main train station. Rejecting his selective enforcement claim, the Seventh Circuit stated that, to be similarly situated, white offenders would have had to engage in the same microbehaviors ("i.e., looking nervously over their shoulders") that the arresting officers claimed drew their attention to Barlow.[63] Such a narrow interpretation of the similarly situated requirement makes it virtually impossible to obtain discovery regarding, let alone to challenge, how police officers weigh various factors In distinguishing different categories of offenders. For example, a criminal defendant might charge that the police more intensively enforce narcotics laws in a particular neighborhood on account of race. There will, however, always be a host of racial and

---

Law & Econ., Working Paper No. 482, 2009), *available at* http://ssrn.com/abstract-1474809 (summarizing profiling studies), *with* Jeffrey Fagan et al., *An Analysis of the NYPD's Stop-and-Frisk Policy in the Context of Claims of Racial Bias*, 102 J. Am. Statistical Ass'n 813, 815–16 (2007) (summarizing New York's stop and frisk study).

[56] *See* United States v. Armstrong, 517 U.S. 456, 465 (1996).

[57] *See id.* (noting that selective enforcement claims are governed by "ordinary equal protection standards").

[58] *Id.* at 463–64 (noting the standard for proving a claim is "demanding").

[59] In *United States v. Armstrong*, the Court held that defendants must show disparate impact just to obtain discovery relating to their claim of selective enforcement. *Id.* at 465. The Court made it clear that its purpose in so requiring was to make selective enforcement claims more difficult. *Id.* at 464–66; *see also* United States v. Bass, 536 U.S. 862, 863–64 (2002) (per curiam) (noting that statistics showing blacks are charged with death-eligible offenses more frequently than whites does not constitute evidence of disparate impact).

[60] *Armstrong*, 517 U.S. at 468.

[61] *See* United States v. Barlow, 310 F.3d 1007, 1012 (7th Cir. 2002); United States v. Turner, 104 F.3d 1180, 1185 (9th Cir. 1997).

[62] *Barlow*, 310 F.3d at 1012.

[63] *Id.*

non-racial differences that characterize offender populations across geographic boundaries. The Ninth Circuit foreclosed just such an inquiry in *United States v. Turner*.[64] A selective enforcement claim is viable only in the unlikely event that there is a white offender virtually identical to the defendant who the arresting officer chose not to target.[65] As a practical matter, individual officers are rarely in such a position.

Challenging police discretion under the Fourteenth Amendment is most plausible under the Due Process Clause. So-called vagueness challenges are rare, and the Court's opinions further demonstrate the extent to which it has organized criminal procedure around the individual officer–citizen encounter.

The Court will declare a criminal statute void for vagueness if it is insufficiently specific to apprise an ordinary person of the conduct that the legislature has criminalized.[66] That is to say that the vague statute does not adequately distinguish guilty from innocent conduct and "entrusts lawmaking to the moment-to-moment judgment of the policeman on his beat."[67] The Court has been particularly skeptical of anti-loitering-type statutes because of fear that police enforce such laws against minorities and political dissenters.[68] The Court has used vagueness doctrine as a kind of surrogate for equal protection: vagueness doctrine allows the Court to control for prospective racial harms that excessive officer discretion may engender without having to address race squarely.[69]

In its most recent opinion voiding for vagueness, the Court invalidated a Chicago gang-loitering ordinance.[70] The ordinance permitted law enforcement to arrest suspected gang members for failing to disperse on command.[71] The Court rejected Chicago's argument that departmental regulations restricting enforcement sufficed to control individual officer discretion.[72] Instead, choices about where and how to enforce accounted for the high number of minority arrests pursuant to the ordinance.[73] Nonetheless, the opinion casts the "discretion problem" as one of individual officers haphazardly enforcing an ordinance that fails to adequately distinguish the innocent from the guilty. However, as noted by Debra Livingston in detail,[74] even narrowly drafted criminal laws permit considerable officer discretion, particularly when considered as an entire

---

[64] *See Turner*, 104 F.3d at 1185 (noting that similarly situated white offenders would have to be "gang members who sold large quantities of crack"); *see also* United States v. Alcaraz-Arellano, 302 F. Supp. 2d 1217, 1232 (D. Kan. 2004) (explaining that, to be similarly situated, white offenders had to display the same indicators of drug trafficking that minority defendants did).

[65] *See* United States v. Dixon, 486 F. Supp. 2d 40, 46 (D.D.C. 2007) (noting that to qualify as similarly situated offenders must have been overlooked by the same officers that arrested defendant).

[66] *See* Papachristou v. Jacksonville, 405 U.S. 156, 162 (1972).

[67] City of Chicago v. Morales, 527 U.S. 41, 60 (1999) (quoting Kolender v. Lawson, 461 U.S. 352, 360 (1983)).

[68] *See Papachristou*, 405 U.S. at 163.

[69] Debra Livingston, *Police Discretion and the Quality of Life in Public Places: Courts, Communities, and the New Policing*, 97 Colum. L. Rev. 551, 647 (1997).

[70] *Morales*, 527 U.S. at 51.

[71] *Id.* at 47.

[72] *Id.* at 62–64.

[73] *See infra* Part III.B.2.ii.

[74] Livingston, *supra* note 69, at 616–17, 629, 650.

body of law.[75] *Morales* is deeply flawed because it assumes both the primacy of individual officer discretion in generating racial harm and that statutory language has the unmediated capacity to constrain police discretion. Neither is true.

Departmental Discretion

Scholars have documented that minorities and the poor are more likely to be arrested and incarcerated than non-minorities and the middle class.[76] This Section demonstrates that such disparities are not the simple consequence of law-breaking patterns or individual officers' biases.[77] How arrests are distributed across a jurisdiction is not the aggregate effect of individual officers' discretionary decisions. Rather, it is departmental choices—choices made by policymakers and administrators—that determine how arrests are distributed. This picture of departmental discretion suggests that many categories of arrests should be conceived as distributive phenomena. Departmental choices create benefits and burdens for individuals and communities. Accordingly, police departments should calibrate those choices to achieve egalitarian results. That discussion is taken up in Part IV.

Subsection A below shows how, in the proactive policing context, departmental policies regarding geographic deployment, enforcement priority, and enforcement tactics determine how the benefits and burdens of policing are distributed. Modern policing relies heavily on arrests as a crime-control strategy. That strategy, coupled with the dramatic expansion of *mala prohibita* offenses, has conferred enormous discretion upon police departments to decide when, where, and by what means (if at all) to enforce criminal laws. Subsection B illustrates how departmental discretion drives inequality in the narcotics and quality-of-life contexts.

---

[75] *See infra* notes 142–159 and accompanying text. Ironically, Professor Livingston argues that the answer to excessive discretion in the order-maintenance context is to pass more criminal laws authorizing order maintenance. *See* Livingston, *supra* note 69, at 560, 626, 635–36.

[76] *See, e.g.*, TONRY, *supra* note 5, at 67, 104, 112–13.

[77] Criminology tends to suggest that "attitudinal factors," such as racial animus, do not play a significant role in explaining how patrol officers exercise their arrest authority. *See* Geoffrey P. Alpert et al., *Police Suspicion and Discretionary Decision Making During Citizen Stops*, 43 CRIMINOLOGY 407, 426 (2005) (concluding that race predicts how officers form suspicions, but not how they make arrest decisions); Allison T. Chappell et al., *The Organizational Determinants of Police Arrest Decisions*, 52 CRIME & DELINQ. 287, 302 (2006) (concluding that situational determinants are more important than structural ones); Robert E. Worden, *Situational and Attitudinal Explanations of Police Behavior: A Theoretical Reappraisal and Empirical Assessment*, 23 LAW & SOC'Y REV. 667, 702 (1989) (noting empirical studies that suggest officers' attitudes do not inform their arrest decisionmaking). Rather, "situational factors" go much farther in explaining officer choices. *See* Douglas A. Smith et al., *Equity and Discretionary Justice: The Influence of Race on Police Arrest Decisions*, 75 J. CRIM. L. & CRIMINOLOGY 234, 246–47 (1984) (discussing how class issues and the tendency of police to attach pejorative traits to minority suspects may contribute to racial disparities in arrests); *see also* Scott W. Phillips & Sean P. Varano, *Police Criminal Charging Decisions: An Examination of Post-Arrest Decision Making*, 36 J. CRIM. JUST. 307, 308 (2008) (summarizing previous research on situational factors and arrest decisions).

Departmental Discretion and Proactive Policing

The proactive policing model relies on departmental decisionmakers' discretion—i.e., the discretion of policymakers and administrators above the individual officer level—to determine how arrests are distributed across a jurisdiction and, by extension, arrestees' demographic profile. In proactive policing, the police themselves must generate knowledge and enforcement priorities regarding crime. This model is in contrast to "reactive" policing, where the police respond to specific reports of criminal misconduct, typically made by victims or witnesses.

"Vice," public nuisance, and traffic crimes are examples of proactive policing. These crimes do not typically involve a particularized victim. Some related crimes, such as drunk driving, are distinct from vice and minor crimes because they create inordinate risk of generating a particularized victim. In stark contrast, the victims of vice crimes are often complicit in or responsible for the criminalized activity, as in the hapless drug addict who might be cast as a "victim" of narcotics trafficking. Victims of vice crimes may also be members of a community who are exposed to illicit activity's secondary consequences, such as increased property crimes associated with narcotics or the aesthetic harms associated with graffiti.[78] But, such "victims" are not particularized in the same way as is typically true in reactive policing.[79] This distinction matters because arrest disparity for victim-initiated crimes has remained relatively stable since the 1970s.[80] Proactive policing, particularly narcotics enforcement, accounts for the massive increases in minority incarceration rates since the 1970s.[81] In the proactive policing context, departmental discretion shapes arrest outcomes.[82]

Departmental discretion operates in three related dimensions: geographic deployment, enforcement priority, and enforcement tactics. Geographic deployment refers to where in a jurisdiction officers are deployed. Urban police departments are typically segmented into precincts.[83]

---

[78] Some would suggest that "community policing" is the best way to address the needs of such victims. In theory, community policing "seeks to address the causes of crime and reduce the fear of crime and social disorder through problem-solving strategies and police-community partnerships." *See* Matthew J. Hickman & Brian A. Reaves, Bureau of Justice Statistics, Community Policing in Local Police Departments, 1997 and 1999, at 1 (rev. 2003). In practice, however, there is considerable variation and debate as to what community policing means. *See* Edward R. Maguire & Charles M. Katz, *Community Policing, Loose Coupling, and Sensemaking in American Police Agencies*, 19 Just. Q. 503, 510–11 (2002). While many departments report that they are engaged in "community policing," this claim may only be loosely related to what the department is actually doing. *See id.* at 530. Federal grant-reporting requirements may also have created incentives for departments to report that they are doing community policing when they are not. *See id.*

[79] "Victim" as a social category is, in part, constituted through state action. "Harm" and "victims" seem to be ever widening social categories. *See* Bernard E. Harcourt, Illusion Of Order 212 (2001); *see also* Jonathan Simon, Governing Through Crime 75–110 (2007).

[80] Tonry, *supra* note 5, at 112–13 (explaining that the war on drugs, not violent crime rates, accounts for dramatic increases in the black incarceration rate).

[81] *Id.* at 4, 6 (arguing that federal policymakers in the Reagan and Bush administrations knew racial disparity would result from the federal "war on drugs"); David Garland, The Culture of Control 132 (2001).

[82] *Cf.* Wilson, *supra* note 12, at 86, 100 (arguing that departmental discretion has a marked impact on policing vice and minor crimes).

[83] For example, the New York Police Department (NYPD) is divided into numerous precincts. *See Precincts*, NYPD, http://www.nyc.gov/html/nypd/html/home/precincts.shtml (last visited Aug. 25, 2011).

Patrol officers are typically assigned not only to a particular precinct, but to details that have specified geographic boundaries.[84] Specialized units may also be assigned to particular precincts. This, for example, would likely be true for undercover units focusing on small-scale narcotics transactions or other minor crimes.[85] Given the entrenched patterns of economic and racial segregation in most American cities,[86] different precincts will often encompass populations with different demographic profiles.[87] How police departments distribute police officers among and within precincts will play a significant role in determining the demographic profile of arrestees. This does not simply mean that arrestees will be "whiter" in whiter precincts (or more minority in minority precincts).[88] Officers may be deployed inordinately in a white precinct because its residents have political clout and believe that minorities are largely responsible for crime in the precinct.[89] But the mere presence of police officers in a particular place does not, by itself, mean that there will be arrests at all, let alone minority arrests.[90]

Departmental decisions regarding enforcement priority will determine what kinds of crimes (if any) officers in a particular location will concentrate on. The range of criminalized conduct is vast.[91] It is, therefore, common for police to systematically overlook an entire range of crimes, particularly minor, *malum in se* ones.[92] It may well be that a particular community's mores permit certain forms of criminalized misconduct.[93] If such conduct is also viewed as unimportant by the police department, officers will have little incentive to enforce against it.[94] A departmental decision to begin enforcing against erstwhile unenforced, minor crimes will have a significant effect on individual officers' behavior.[95] This has proven particularly true where a department's choices are part of a wider policy program to interdict "disorderly" behavior under the rubric of "quality-of-life" policing.[96] Another common example is in the narcotics context: departments may elect to focus on particular narcotics over others for a host of reasons, or none at all.[97]

---

[84] EDWARD CONLON, BLUE BLOOD 4 (2004).

[85] *Id.* at 149 (noting that anti-crime teams that focus on street-level narcotics operate at the precinct level in the NYPD); Tal Klement & Elizabeth Siggins, *A Window of Opportunity: Addressing The Complexities of the Relationship Between Drug Enforcement and Racial Disparity in Seattle*, 1 SEATTLE J. SOC. JUST. 165, 193 (2003) (noting the same for Seattle).

[86] *See* LAMBERTH, *supra* note 6, at 57; Capers, *supra* note 31, at 47.

[87] *See, e.g.*, Klement & Siggins, *supra* note 85, at 195–98, 249 nn.39, 42, 45 & 48 (describing demographic profiles of the Seattle Police Department's four precincts).

[88] *See id.* at 197–98, 249 n.48 (noting that 60% of those arrested in Seattle's West Precinct for a drug violation were non-white even though the vast majority of residents in the precinct are white).

[89] *Id.* at 205.

[90] *See, e.g.*, Kimberly D. Hassell, *Variations in Police Patrol Practices*, 30 POLICING 257, 268 (2007) (noting that policing tactics may vary considerably among precincts in one police department).

[91] *See infra* Part III.A.2 (discussing "overcriminalization").

[92] While rarely memorialized in official policy, selective non-enforcement of the criminal code is a long-recognized fact of policing. *See supra* notes 12–18 and accompanying text.

[93] *See* SUDHIR ALLADI VENKATESH, OFF THE BOOKS 79, 359–60 (2006) (noting that residents of some inner city communities accept "backroom negotiation" between police and gang leaders that would not be tolerated in middle-class communities).

[94] *See id.* at 359.

[95] *See* WILSON, *supra* note 12, at 100.

[96] *See infra* Part III.B.2.i (discussing a quality-of-life policing case study).

[97] *See infra* Part III.B.1 (discussing a narcotics enforcement case study).

Departmental decisions regarding enforcement priority are tightly braided with decisions about enforcement tactics. The former determines *what* misconduct to focus upon while the latter determines *how* to focus upon it. Making arrests is, in and of itself, a significant tactical choice. Police departments have a host of other tactics available, and maintaining a uniform police presence in a park may better deter homeless people from sleeping there than does arresting the occasional sleeper. A department might elect to increase arrest rates for particular kinds of conduct in different ways. For example, a department might incentivize patrol officers to make more arrests than they ordinarily would.[98] Patrol represents the largest portion of a department's sworn force.[99] Typically, patrol officers tend towards leniency and make fewer arrests than they have opportunities to make.[100] A departmental decision requiring patrol officers to make arrests can very quickly change that, as occurred in New York City when it adopted a version of "broken windows" policing in the 1990s.[101] Departments may also create (or enlarge) specialized, arrest-intensive units for particular categories of offenses. For example, undercover units that focus on street crimes will generate significantly more arrests per officer than does patrol.[102] Choices about whether to carry out one kind of operation or another will also have consequences for the volume and nature of arrests. For example, buy-bust operations targeting street-level narcotics transactions are likely to yield more arrests (but less contraband) over time than warrant-based operations targeting indoor transactions.[103]

The specific processes by which the three modes of departmental discretion operate are often opaque. Take a department's decision to generate more arrests through its patrol unit.[104] To the extent that patrol officers are directed to make more arrests, it is often unclear as to how that mandate is transmitted. Police departments are loath to admit that officers have "arrest quotas." But, it periodically emerges that a particular department has quotas (or the functional equivalent thereof).[105] Sometimes it is possible to ascertain how senior department personnel

---

[98] *See, e.g.*, Klement & Siggins, *supra* note 85, at 199. This may be why patrol officers are typically the subject of observational criminological studies. *See, e.g.*, Alpert et al., *supra* note 77, at 426; Douglas A. Smith et al., *Equity & Discretionary Justice: Race and Police Arrest Decisions*, 75 J. Crim. L. & Criminology 234, 239 (1984).

[99] *See* David E. Barlow & Melissa Hickman Barlow, Police in a Multicultural Society 14 (2000) (discussing a study that found patrol officers spend less than 15% of on-duty time fighting crime); *see also* Conlon, *supra* note 84, at 158 ("On patrol, [officers] dealt with the fluid whole of peoples' lives," not just "criminals."). Even calls for service tend not to be arrest-intensive. *See* David Weisburd & John E. Eck, *What Can Police Do to Reduce Crime, Disorder, and Fear?*, 593 Annals Am. Acad. Pol. & Soc. Sci. 42, 44, 49–51, 57 (2009).

[100] *See* Wilson, *supra* note 12, at 49.

[101] *See infra* Part III.B.2.i.

[102] *See, e.g.*, Conlon, *supra* note 84, at 158 (comparing the author's work on a street-crimes unit to that he did while on patrol).

[103] *See, e.g.*, Katherine Beckett et al., *Race, Drugs, and Policing: Understanding Disparities in Drug Delivery Arrests*, 44 Criminology 105, 122–23 (2006).

[104] *See infra* Part III.B.2.i (discussing quality-of-life policing).

[105] *See* Alice Gendar, *NYPD Captain Allegedly Caught in Arrest Quota Fixing*, N.Y. Daily News (Nov. 17, 2007, 4:00 AM), http://www.nydailynews.com/news/ny_crime/2007/11/14/2007-11-14_nypd_captain_allegedly_caught_in_arrest_-1.html; Jim Hoffer, *N.Y.P.D. Officers Under "Quota" Pressure*, WABC (March 3, 2010), http://abclocal.go.com/wabc/story?section=news/investigators&id=7307336; John Marzulli, *We Fabricated Drug Charges Against Innocent People to Meet Arrest Quotas, Former Detective Testifies*, N.Y. Daily News (Oct. 13, 2011), http://articles.nydailynews.com/2011-10-13/

make choices about officer deployment and enforcement priority,[106] but that is rare. A host of budget and personnel decisions might account for why one precinct has more undercover street-crimes officers than another.[107]

Neither politics nor law compels police departments to be transparent about how they exercise discretion. The history of modern policing suggests why this is true. Bureaucratization and political insulation are the modern police department's birth traits.[108] Rationalized by a new "crime control" ethos in the mid-twentieth century,[109] the institutional shifts that gave rise to the modern police department generated new capacity for the kinds of choices described above. Bureaucratization and political insulation also deepened departments' commitment to using arrests to achieve crime control while a steadily expanding criminal code increased the opportunities for doing so.

Bureaucratization and Political Insulation

Modern police departments are hierarchical, command-and-control institutions that rely heavily on arrests in order to demonstrate their effectiveness. Paradoxically, in the proactive policing context, arrests often serve as measures for both crime-control exigency and crime-control success.[110]

The modern, urban police department took form in the mid-twentieth century. Its birth history is well documented, so only a caption version is provided here.[111] Well into the twentieth century, urban police departments were cogs in urban machine politics.[112] Police departments were prime sources of patronage jobs.[113] The beat cop was as much a sub-local functionary for the political machine as he was a watchman ensuring some measure of order on his beat.[114] He enjoyed substantial discretion to enforce or not enforce the criminal code as necessary to maintain a level of order consistent with community mores. Depending on the neighborhood, this frequently

---

news/30291567_1_nypd-narcotics-detective-false-arrest-suit-henry-tavarez; Graham Rayman, *The NYPD Tapes: Inside Bed-Stuy's 81st Precinct*, VILLAGE VOICE, May 4, 2010, at 12; *see also* Michael Murray, *Why Arrest Quotas Are Wrong*, POLICEMAN'S BENEVOLENT ASSOC. MAG. (Spring 2005), *available at* http://www.nycpba.org/publications/mag-05-spring/murray.html.

[106] *See infra* Part III.B.2.ii.

[107] *See infra* Part III.B.2.i. Even those criminologists that study departments' organizational structure offer few clues as to how departmental decisions are made. *See generally* EDWARD R. MAGUIRE, ORGANIZATIONAL STRUCTURE IN AMERICAN POLICE AGENCIES 31, 76, 90, 99 (2003) (hypothesizing as to why different departments have different structures).

[108] *See* SKLANSKY, *supra* note 19, at 35–36; *but see* John P. Crank & Robert Langworthy, *An Institutional Perspective of Policing*, 83 J. CRIM. L. CRIMINOLOGY 338, 342 (1992) (explaining that "legitimacy" is best understood in terms of police departments' relationship with other powerful actors whose decisions affect the continued flow of resources to the department).

[109] "Crime control" here is intended as a narrative about police purpose that police departments project and in which there is widespread belief. John P. Crank, *Institutional Theory of the Police: A Review of the State of the Art*, 26 POLICING: INT'L J. POLICE STRATEGIES MGMT. 186, 189, 194 (2003) (referring to such narratives as mythologies).

[110] *See* Harcourt, *supra* note 55, at 18 (quoting the former New Jersey attorney general); TONRY, *supra* note 5, at 106.

[111] *See, e.g.*, BARLOW & BARLOW, *supra* note 99, at 19–46; SKLANSKY, *supra* note 19, at 31–36.

[112] *See* BARLOW & BARLOW, *supra* note 99, at 31.

[113] *See id.*

[114] *See* ELI B. SILVERMAN, NYPD BATTLES CRIME 27 (1999) (describing the NYPD in early twentieth century); WILSON, *supra* note 12, at 31–32; *see also* LAWRENCE M. FRIEDMAN, CRIME AND PUNISHMENT IN AMERICAN HISTORY 149–50 (1993) (describing policing in the nineteenth century).

entailed permitting a fair amount of criminal misconduct.[115] As political functionary, the beat cop was the political machine's agent, gathering and dispensing information for his own benefit and the machine's sustenance.[116] The beat cop had a granular knowledge of the landscape and those who populated it. And arrests were not the preferred, let alone mandated, technique for controlling crime.[117]

Corruption was an endemic feature of watchman-style policing and was among the most salient rallying cries for reformers in the twentieth century.[118] The structure of big-city politics in the nineteenth and early twentieth centuries encouraged police officers to disregard crime for a price.[119] This was in grave misstep with Americans' increasing anxieties about crime and cities during the post-war period.[120] It was in that vein that the first wave of discretion scholars focused on big-city beat cops.[121] Professor Sklansky has persuasively argued that police reform in the mid-twentieth century resonated with a new ethos of post-war, American democracy: "pluralism." Pluralist democracy checked the potential danger of populist fanaticism by insulating technocratic decisionmaking apparatuses from mass politics.[122]

The chief mandate for reformed police departments was "crime control." And Chief William Parker's Los Angeles Police Department (LAPD) in the 1950s was a progenitor of the new model for urban police departments: a crime-control technocracy.[123] Rigidly hierarchical, it relied on centralized command for its squad-car-bound force. The LAPD's leadership, as would be true of the "reformed" police departments in other big cities, enjoyed considerable autonomy from elected office holders.[124] This arrangement continues to define police departments in many big, American cities.[125] This is not to say that modern police departments operate without political

[115] See SILVERMAN, supra note 114, at 27. This dynamic still prevails in poor, urban communities. See VENKATESH, supra note 93, at 7–8, 200–04 (arguing that police do not enforce law to the hilt when community mores do not permit it); Natapoff, supra note 35, at 1747.

[116] See LUC SANTE, LOW LIFE 237–43 (1991) (describing NYPD in the nineteenth century).

[117] See WILSON, supra note 12, at 49.

[118] See SANTE, supra note 116, at 240 (describing bribery in the NYPD); see also GARLAND, supra note 81, at 114–15 (describing police "professionalization"); SKLANSKY, supra note 19, at 35–36 (discussing the Wickersham Commission and reform movement).

[119] See MIKE ROYKO, BOSS: RICHARD J. DALEY OF CHICAGO 107–13 (2d ed. 1988) (describing corruption in Chicago); SILVERMAN, supra note 114, at 27–28 (describing corruption in New York City).

[120] See GARLAND, supra note 81, 152–54; SIMON, supra note 79, at 90–93; Stuntz, supra note 33, at 2000–05 (discussing "white flight" from cities and fear of crime).

[121] See, e.g., DAVIS, supra note 11, at 41 (discussing the Chicago Police Department).

[122] SKLANSKY, supra note 19, at 34–38.

[123] See SKLANSKY, supra note 19, at 36; see also MIKE DAVIS, CITY OF QUARTZ 250–51 (2d ed. 2006).

[124] See id. at 36–37.

[125] Most police departments are controlled at the municipal level. See MATTHEW J. HICKMAN & BRIAN A. REAVES, BUREAU OF JUSTICE STATISTICS, LOCAL POLICE DEPARTMENT 1 (2003). And in the largest American cities, police chiefs are appointed, not elected. See Pelpia Trip, More Information on Dallas Police Chief David Kunkle, CW33 NEWS (Nov. 11, 2009), http://www. the33tv.com/news/kdaf-dallas-police-chief-david-kunkle-story,0,5569866.story; Letter from Frank Fairbanks, Phoenix City Manager, to Jack Harris, Chief of Phoenix Police Dep't (May 5, 2009), available at http://www.phoenix.gov/police/ public_safety_manager_duties.pdf; Press Release, City of Houston, Mayor Bill White Announces Police Chief Nominee (Feb. 27, 2004), available at http://www.houstontx.gov/mayor/press/20040227.html; Press Release, City of San Jose, National Search for Police Chief Ends in San Jose (Jan. 6, 2004), available at http://www.sanjoseca.gov/cityManager/

constraint.[126] In order for senior personnel to maintain their positions and for the department to maximize its funding stream, it must demonstrate that it is advancing crime control. The audiences for such demonstrations of legitimacy are typically other institutional actors,[127] although it might on occasion be the general public—especially when a heinous crime captures public attention or when there is a generalized sense that crime is "out of control." In the latter case, creating the impression that a department is controlling crime need not mean that it is actually doing so.[128] Similarly, making arrests need not mean that a police department is actually reducing crime.[129]

Arrest is not only a key instrument in the modern police department's crime-control arsenal, it is an emblem of whether a police department is satisfying its crime-control mandate. Influenced by Fordist theories of industrial efficiency and postwar anxiety about popular democracy,[130] the new policing ethos abstracted crime control from the life of any particular neighborhood. The new ethos engendered what has become a broadly shared sense that making arrests is, itself, tantamount to crime control.[131] That arrests have this symbolic significance flows from the premium modern policing places on both crime control and measurability. Arrests, like certain kinds of crime, are readily measurable.[132] Some crime is parsed, catalogued, and studied by severity and distribution.[133] The kinds of crimes that most readily lend to measurement, however, are the same

---

releases/2004-01-06_policechief.pdf; City of San Diego, Manager's Report, No. 03-164 (July 25, 2003), *available at* http://docs.sandiego.gov/reportstocouncil/2003/03-164.pdf; *Office of the Chief*, City of San Antonio Police, http://www.sanantonio.gov/sapd/office.asp#LEGAL (last visited Sept. 27, 2011); *Office of the Chief of Police*, LAPD, http://www.lapdonline.org/inside_the_lapd/content_basic_view/834 (last visited Sept. 27, 2011); *Profile of Charles Ramsey*, Phila. Police Dep't, www.phillypolice.com/about/leadership/charles-h-ramsey/ (last visited Sept. 27, 2011); *Profile of Raymond W. Kelly*, NYPD, http://www.nyc.gov/html/nypd/html/administration/headquarters_co.shtml (last visited Sept. 27, 2011); *Superintendent's Office*, Chi. Police Dep't, https://portal.chicagopolice.org/portal/page/portal/ClearPath/About%20CPD/Bureaus/Superintendent%27s%20Office (last visited Sept. 27, 2011).

[126] *See, e.g.*, Crank & Langworthy, *supra* note 108, at 342.

[127] *See id.* (describing these actors as "sovereigns").

[128] *See* Crank, *supra* note 109, at 194 (summarizing research on the creation of specialized gang units).

[129] Harcourt, *supra* note 54, at 122–25 (explaining that whether racial targeting decreases crime depends on the relative elasticity of different groups to policing).

[130] *See* Sklansky, *supra* note 19, at 26.

[131] *See* Harcourt, *supra* note 54, at 113, 139 (noting that academics have modeled police "success" in narcotics interdiction context by "hit rate," which is the identification of an arrestable offense). This view is not universal. At least some argue that the "community policing" movement expressly questions this view and centralization more generally. *See* Kelling & Coles, *supra* note 26, at 158, 165 (advocating for community policing that entails greater officer discretion vis-à-vis the police department). Community policing was supposed to deemphasize arrests in favor of community engagement and more holistic approaches to community problem solving. *See id.* In practice, though, many police departments have enacted "community policing" in a top-down fashion that is a hallmark of a centralized police bureaucracy. *See* Silverman, *supra* note 114, at 17.

[132] *See* Harcourt, *supra* note 54, at 124.

[133] Data is a hallmark of modern policing; the federal Uniform Crime Records came into existence after World War II. Compstat may represent the culmination of this process. *See* Garland, *supra* note 81, at 115 (discussing "computerization" and the use of the information technology in the 1980s and 1990s). Compstat is a data-driven application that allows police departments to track the geographic distribution of criminal incidents and complaints. *See* Silverman, *supra* note 114, at 103–04. The NYPD pioneered Compstat in the 1990s and it has subsequently spread to numerous other urban law enforcement agencies. *Id.* at 123–24. *But see* William K. Rashbaum, *Retired Officers Raise Questions on Crime Data*, N.Y. Times, Feb. 6, 2010, at A1 (reporting that precinct commanders and administrators manipulated

victim- or witness-reported crimes that reactive policing is organized around. The preeminent measure of unreported crime in the United States is the Department of Justice's Crime Victims' Survey.[134] As the title suggests, the DOJ conducts a telephonic survey designed to estimate how many victims there are of certain enumerated crimes. The survey does not include the vice or minor crimes that proactive policing is typically concerned with.[135] On the other hand, the Uniform Crime Reports, which tabulate arrests, do include data for vice or minor crimes.[136]

Arrests play a contradictory and circular role in proactive policing. They are often held out both as proof of the need for crime control and as evidence of police enforcement's efficacy.[137] This contradiction is apparent with narcotics enforcement, where a high minority-arrest rate is used to show that the minority-offense rate is high.[138] Even the Supreme Court has indulged in this circularity.[139] The self-reinforcing nature of arrest rates in the proactive policing context likely entrenches the institutional arrangements that reproduce racial disparity. For example, take specialization. Modern, urban police departments tend to have a range of specialized units for narcotics, gangs, street crimes, domestic violence, and drunk driving. Arrest and specialization dovetail in that specialized units are often arrest-intensive.[140] Once created, a specialized unit will tend to generate arrests and intelligence that reinforce its very existence. If specialized undercover narcotics units are concentrated in minority neighborhoods, those units will generate arrests and intelligence regarding minority narcotics activity. This may create the impression that minorities inordinately engage in narcotics activity, which, in turn, may impel even more minority arrests.[141]

It is in the proactive policing context that police departments have the greatest discretion in shaping demographic outcomes. This is not just because of modern police departments' institutional structure, but because legislatures have generated a vast range of opportunities for police departments to make such choices.

Compstat data to favorably impact crime rate statistics for their precinct); *but cf.* Justin Fenton, *Baltimore Police Idle Comstat Meetings*, BALT. SUN (Apr. 9, 2010), http://articles.baltimoresun.com/2010-04-09/news/bal-md.ci.comstat08a-pr09_1_comstat-police-department-s-operations-anthony-guglielmi (reporting on Baltimore Police Department's suspensions of Compstat use due to the "staff friction" it caused).

[134] *See* U.S. DEP'T OF JUSTICE, THE NATION'S TWO CRIME MEASURES (2004), *available at* http://bjs.ojp.usdoj.gov/content/pub/pdf/ntcm.pdf.

[135] *Id.*

[136] *Id.*

[137] Harcourt, *supra* note 55, at 18. It is not state officials that are the only ones responsible for engaging in such circularity. *See, e.g.*, Marc Lacey, *U.S. Cites 175 Arrests of Traffickers in Drug Ring*, N.Y. TIMES, Sept. 18, 2008, at A15.

[138] *See* TONRY, *supra* note 5, at 106.

[139] *See* United States v. Armstrong, 517 U.S. 456, 469–70 (1996).

[140] *See, e.g.*, CONLON, *supra* note 84, at 158 (contrasting drug details with patrols); HARRY G. LEVINE & DEBORAH PETERSON SMALL, MARIJUANA ARREST CRUSADE 20 (2008) (stating that one-half of marijuana arrests in New York are made by specialized units); Jennifer R. Wynn, *Can Zero Tolerance Last? Voices From Inside the Precinct, in* ZERO TOLERANCE 107, 112 (Andrea McArdle & Tanya Erzen eds., 2001) (noting that a small number of officers made the most arrests in NYPD). *But cf.* Fagan et. al., *supra* note 55, at 815–16, 820 (noting that stops tend not to produce arrests).

[141] *See* HARCOURT, *supra* note 54, at 149 (discussing "ratchet effect").

Expansive Enforcement Opportunity

Legislatures have created virtually bottomless pools of prospective offenders by creating ever-more *mala prohibita* offenses. Doing so has amplified departmental discretion.

Federal and state criminal codes achieved binding-busting girth in the twentieth century. In most jurisdictions, the number of crimes increased twofold, if not substantially more.[142] Some of the growth is attributable to the need (or perceived need) to regulate new, modern behaviors such as vehicular crimes and identity theft. But legislatures have also demonstrated remarkable capacity for proliferating redundant crimes.[143] Legal scholars have criticized the phenomenon, referring to it as "overcriminalization."[144] The term captures both the sheer number of crimes and the vast swaths of behavior those crimes encompass. And much of that behavior is not *malum in se*, as in paradigmatic crimes such as murder, robbery, and the like. For example, narcotics convictions account for most of the dramatic increase in incarceration rates in the United States since the 1970s.[145]

Overcriminalization increases opportunities for enforcement (and non-enforcement) of the criminal code. Overcriminalization adds an exclamation point to the long-acknowledged fact that complete enforcement of the criminal code is chimerical.[146] This is readily apparent with vice crimes. Take narcotics distribution: at any given moment there are far more individuals engaged in narcotics distribution than law enforcement can possibly apprehend. The facial homogeneity of "narcotics distribution" as codified[147] is belied by the diversity of behaviors to which it applies. It applies in equal measure to the suburbanite who sells cocaine out of his home for cash, the club-goer who gives ecstasy tabs to his friends in exchange for drinks, and the chronically homeless addict who sells crack on the street in kind. Each of these examples, technically, constitutes the same criminal offense: narcotics distribution. Legislatures, however, rarely provide any guidance to police departments on how to prioritize amongst different offenders.[148]

Bloated criminal codes create a set of opportunities to indirectly address social problems, which are not criminalized per se. These opportunities exist in three dimensions. The surfeit of criminal laws allows police departments to arrest individuals (1) whose behavior is perceived as troublesome, but is not directly criminalized, e.g., in the 1990s, the NYPD aggressively used

---

[142] *See* William J. Stuntz, *The Pathological Politics of Criminal Law*, 100 MICH. L. REV. 505, 514–15 (2001) (describing state and federal criminal codes).

[143] *See* Erik Luna, *Principled Enforcement of Penal Codes*, 4 BUFF. CRIM. L. REV. 515, 527–28 (2000) (describing the numerous incarnations of assault and larceny in California).

[144] *See, e.g.*, Erik Luna, *The Overcriminalization Phenomenon*, 54 AM. U. L. REV. 703, 713 & n.49 (2005) (citing numerous criticisms of the phenomenon).

[145] *See* GARLAND, *supra* note 81, at 132; *see also* TONRY, *supra* note 5, at 49 (discussing the racial disparities in arrest and incarceration rates, which are particularly pronounced for drug offenses).

[146] *See supra* notes 9–16 and accompanying text.

[147] *See, e.g.*, CAL. HEALTH & SAFETY CODE § 11352 (West 2000).

[148] *See* Stuntz, *supra* note 142, at 529–33 (describing incentives that lead legislators to define crimes broadly and leave it to police and prosecutors to exercise enforcement discretion). Mandatory arrest laws in the domestic violence context are the rare exception. Weisburd & Eck, *supra* note 99, at 51.

pedestrian and traffic obstruction laws against panhandlers, an activity that was not directly criminalized;[149] (2) who are likely to engage in more serious criminalized behaviors in the future, e.g., avoiding the collateral, violent crimes associated with narcotics is often proffered as justification for aggressively enforcing narcotics laws;[150] and (3) who have likely engaged in serious criminal activity that cannot be readily proved, e.g., charging Al Capone with tax evasion.[151]

Legislators have every incentive to leave it to prosecutors and police to liberally exercise their discretion *not to* enforce the criminal code.[152] And courts are almost completely agnostic as to how they go about it.[153] Professor Stuntz has persuasively argued that it is full enforcement's impossibility that enables relentless passage of new criminal laws.[154] Taking a hard-line stance on crime defines political orthodoxy for both the left and right in the United States.[155] Passing a criminal law is the most visible way for legislators to substantiate their commitment to protecting the public, and the impossibility of full enforcement insulates legislators from the risk that new criminal laws will be politically unpalatable to large swaths of middle-class voters.[156] According to Professor Stuntz, "criminal law" is no longer even law per se, but just a "veil" for the distribution of discretionary power to punish.[157]

It is ironic that overcriminalization has amplified law enforcement's discretionary authority because it is the public's distrust of discretion that has animated the increasing sweep and severity of legislatures' criminal enactments. However, the most demonized forms of discretion have

---

[149] Tanya Erzen, *Turnstile Jumpers and Broken Windows: Policing Disorder in New York City* app, *in* Zero Tolerance, *supra* note 140, at 19, 35–36 (quoting sections from the NYPD Quality of Life Enforcement Options Reference Guide); Harcourt, *supra* note 79, at 40, 102, 128 (2001) (recounting when New York City tried to criminalize panhandling, but the ordinance was deemed an unconstitutional violation of the First Amendment).

[150] *See* Klement & Siggins, *supra* note 85, at 211; *see also* Harcourt, *supra* note 79, at 40, 102, 128 (expounding an analogous rationale for arresting aggressive panhandlers in New York City); Jim Dwyer, *Whites Smoke Pot, but Blacks Are Arrested*, N.Y. Times, Dec. 23, 2009, at A24.

[151] *See* Stuntz, *supra* note 33, at 2019–20 (describing the Boston Police Department's use of narcotics laws to arrest gang members believed to have been responsible for substantial violent crime).

[152] *See* Stuntz, *supra* note 142, at 575–77.

[153] *See, e.g.*, Whren v. United States, 517 U.S. 806, 818 (1996) ("[W]e are aware of no principle that would allow us to decide at what point a code of law becomes so expansive and so commonly violated that infraction itself can no longer be the ordinary measure of the lawfulness of enforcement.").

[154] *See* Stuntz, *supra* note 142, at 575–77 (noting that strict federal sentencing guidelines emblematize hostility towards judicial discretion).

[155] *See, e.g.*, Simon, *supra* note 79, at 59, 75, 102 (describing America's increasing punitiveness as driving from the political left and right); Stuntz, *supra* note 33, at 2008–10 (same). Even liberal Democrats must declaim their commitment to aggressively expanding and enforcing criminal law. Simon, *supra* note 79, at 49–52, 58–59 (describing Presidents Kennedy's, Johnson's, and Clinton's uses of crime as a political issue).

[156] Stuntz, *supra* note 142, at 528, 532–33. Most legislators have no interest in compelling enforcement of those portions of the code criminalizing "marginal middle-class behavior." *Id.* at 509; *see also id.* at 516–17 (listing examples of statutes criminalizing trifling conduct).

[157] *Id.* at 599.

been those that the public imagines as introducing leniency into the system.[158] Departmental discretion is not imagined in such terms.[159]

Proactive Policing Case Studies

Police departments enjoy considerable, unchecked authority to make policy as to how criminal laws are enforced. Racial disparity in narcotics and quality-of-life enforcement illustrate how departmental discretion can generate inegalitarian consequences.

The racial disparity in proactive policing arrests cannot, prima facie, be defended in terms of "colorblindness." Scholars acknowledge that proactive policing has driven racial disparity.[160] Both proactive policing and reactive policing generate arrest disparity, but the latter is less troubling because victims play a substantial role in accounting for offenders' demographic profile.[161] In an ideal world, arrestee demographics would perfectly mirror offender demographics. A racial group's overrepresentation amongst offenders would perfectly account for its overrepresentation amongst arrestees.[162] To the extent that crimes of violence are often intraracial,[163] doing justice by minority victims should mean a higher arrest rate for minority suspects.[164] Unfortunately, white crime victims inspire greater sympathy from individual police officers and police departments.[165] All of this suggests that arrest disparity for victim-reported crimes might even be higher without inspiring serious equality concerns.[166] The same is not true in the proactive context.

Arrest disparity in proactive policing is not readily explicable in terms of minority offense rates.[167] The case studies that follow illustrate how deployment decisions, enforcement priorities, and enforcement tactics yield dramatic racial disparity.

---

[158] SIMON, *supra* note 79, at 165. Judicial discretion in sentencing is a prime example of this phenomenon. *See* GARLAND, *supra* note 81, at 59–61.

[159] *See* GARLAND, *supra* note 81, at 132 (describing increased punitiveness); LaFave, *supra* note 18, at 215 (describing the invisibility of police discretion).

[160] TONRY, *supra* note 5, at 4, 6, 67 (arguing that differential arrest rate drives differential incarceration rate); Beckett et al., *supra* note 103, at 109; William J. Stuntz, *The Political Constitution of Criminal Justice*, 119 HARV. L. REV. 781, 834–35 (2006).

[161] Colorblindness is a fair metaphor for describing the police's enforcement priorities in the reactive context if: (1) individuals across demographic categories consistently alert the police to victimization *and* (2) the police consistently and symmetrically responded to victim-reported crimes. Neither one of these is completely true. There is a gap between reported crime and actual crime. *See* U.S. DEP'T OF JUSTICE, *supra* note 134.

[162] This is a false ideal to the extent that entrenched patterns of economic and social marginalization engender violence and other criminal misconduct. *See, e.g.*, THE NAT'L ADVISORY COMM'N ON CIVIL DISORDERS, *supra* note 28, at 266–74.

[163] *See, e.g.*, ERIKA HARRELL, BUREAU OF JUSTICE STATISTICS, BLACK VICTIMS OF VIOLENT CRIME 5 (2007).

[164] *See* Terrance J. Taylor et al., *Racial Bias in Case Processing: Does Victim Race Affect Police Clearance of Violent Crime Incidents?*, 26 JUST. Q. 562, 583 (2009) (noting the modestly lower violent-crime-clearance rate for black-on-black crime).

[165] *See* Smith et al., *supra* note 77, at 248; *see also* RANDALL KENNEDY, RACE, CRIME, AND THE LAW 76–135 (1997) (detailing the history of unequal enforcement).

[166] *See* Lawrence Rosenthal, *Policing and Equal Protection*, 21 YALE L. & POL'Y REV. 53, 87 (2003) (arguing that equal protection should oblige police to provide equal security from law breakers).

[167] *See* Robert J. Sampson & Stephen Raudenbush, *Seeing Disorder: Neighborhood Stigma and the Social Construction of "Broken Windows,"* 67 SOC. PSYCHOL. Q. 319, 323 (2004); Stuntz, *supra* note 33, at 2022 (noting that it is politically easier to enforce laws against poor minority communities); *see also* Dorothy E. Roberts, *Foreword: Race, Vagueness, and the*

Narcotics Enforcement

Departmental decisions regarding geographic deployment, enforcement priority, and enforcement tactics have led the Seattle Police Department (SPD) to arrest an inordinately high number of black offenders. In particular, the SPD's use of arrest-intensive, buy-bust operations in downtown Seattle targeting crack cocaine transactions yielded a black-arrest rate that far exceeds black participation in unlawful narcotics transactions. I focus on Seattle because there is more information about the demographic profile of offenders and police department decisionmaking there than for other cities.[168]

Narcotics convictions in Seattle, like most other places in the United States, have accounted for a dramatic spike in the incarceration of poor people of color since the 1970s.[169] Professor Tonry has argued that the racial disparity engendered by the war on drugs is the direct consequence of differential arrest rates.[170] That is to say that police practices, not prosecutorial or judicial discrimination, tend to account for increases in minority incarceration.[171] Police, who make arrests, determine the pool of offenders that generate indictments and convictions. Typically, it is difficult to find quantitative proof for the claim that narcotics arrests yield unjustifiable racial disparity. This is for two reasons: (1) it is difficult to construct a demographic profile of the offender population, because narcotics offenders are not likely to offer themselves up for demographers to count, and (2) there is little information on how and why police organize their enforcement priorities and tactics.[172] African-Americans are dramatically overrepresented amongst those arrested for narcotics offenses in Seattle. From January 1999 until April 2001, 64.2% of those arrested for narcotics delivery in Seattle were African-American.[173] During that period, African-Americans constituted only 8.4% of Seattle's population and were also a minority amongst Seattle's drug users and sellers.[174] Public health data, in conjunction with ethnographic and survey data, tend to suggest that drug sellers are white in roughly the same proportion

---

Social Meaning of Order-Maintenance Policing, 89 J. CRIM. L. & CRIMINOLOGY 775, 812–14 (1999) (arguing that the social distinction between "law-abiding" and "lawless" is racialized).

[168] *See generally* Katherine Beckett et al., *Drug Use, Drug Possession Arrests, and the Question of Race: Lessons From Seattle*, 52 SOC. PROBS. 419 (2005); Beckett et al., *supra* note 103; Klement & Siggins, *supra* note 85. Information is available on narcotics enforcement practices in Seattle in part because of litigation challenging racial disparity and the SPD's narcotics enforcement practices. *See* State v. Johnson, No. 52123-3-I, 2005 WL 353314 (Wash. Ct. App. Feb. 14, 2005). I helped represent the defendants in that litigation for a brief period.

[169] *See* TONRY, *supra* note 5, at 4, 6, 112; Klement & Siggins, *supra* note 85, at 177–78, 191 (noting minority overrepresentation amongst narcotics arrestees in 1999 and a proportional increase in drug arrests in comparison to total arrests throughout 1990s).

[170] TONRY, *supra* note 5, at 112–13.

[171] *Id.* at 51, 74; *see also* WASH. STATE MINORITY & JUSTICE COMM'N, THE IMPACT OF RACE & ETHNICITY ON CHARGING AND SENTENCING PROCESSES FOR DRUG OFFENDERS IN THREE COUNTIES OF WASHINGTON STATE 43 (1999).

[172] *See* TONRY, *supra* note 5, at 107 (noting that evidence regarding policing practices tends to be anecdotal).

[173] Beckett et al., *supra* note 103, at 118 (reporting on data collected for methamphetamine, heroin, powder cocaine, crack cocaine, and ecstasy because these drugs are treated comparably for punishment purposes). African-Americans are comparably overrepresented amongst those arrested for drug possession. *See* Beckett et al., *supra* note 168, at 427.

[174] *Id.* at 426.

as drug users in Seattle.[175] Seattle's drug-using and drug-selling populations are significantly whiter than in most other American cities.[176] This is unsurprising given that Seattle's general population is more white than most other American cities.[177] Seattle also is reputed for its heroin problem, and the demographic profile of heroin users in Seattle is overwhelmingly white.[178] The same is, by and large, true for other narcotics.[179]

African-Americans are, however, overrepresented among crack users and sellers,[180] but whites still represent approximately half of all crack users in Seattle.[181] This is to say that the demographic profile of drug users in Seattle is largely white. The same holds true for drug sellers.[182] This is consistent with national trends and crack's appeal to poor people.[183] There is little to suggest that crack use represents a particularly serious public safety problem in Seattle in relation to other narcotics, particularly heroin.[184] Nonetheless, the Seattle Police Department focuses its enforcement energies on crack transactions, and that focus, in turn, drives the stark racial disparity in its arrest rates.

Institutional discretion substantially accounts for the arrest disparity described above. At least one trial-court judge found that the most relevant decisionmakers were at the institutional level.[185] Professor Beckett's work also suggests that institutional-level decisionmaking drives racial disparity in narcotics arrests in Seattle.

The SPD opted for an arrest-intensive narcotics enforcement strategy that relied upon specialized undercover units. As is true for many big-city police departments, patrol does not generate high numbers of arrests (for any sort of offense) per officer in Seattle.[186] Specialized narcotics units, on the other hand, generate high numbers of arrests per officer; this is particularly true of units that focus on street-level narcotics transactions. These units typically focus on "retail" transactions, where other specialized units, often called "Narcotics" or something similar, tend to focus on larger distributors further up the supply chain.[187]

---

[175] *Compare* Beckett et al., *supra* note 103, at 119, *with* Beckett et al., *supra* note 168, at 427.

[176] Beckett et al., *supra* note 168, at 424, 427.

[177] *Id.* (stating that 70.1% of Seattle residents are white).

[178] *Id.* at 424, 426.

[179] *Id.* at 427.

[180] *See* Beckett et al., *supra* note 103, at 119.

[181] Beckett et al., *supra* note 168, at 427.

[182] This is not to say that "drug sellers" and "drug buyers" are separate and discrete communities.

[183] On average, Seattle's blacks are significantly poorer than its whites. *See* Office of the Exec., *Per Capita Income in King County by Race/Ethnicity, As a Percent of County Average (2009)*, KING COUNTY (Oct. 16, 2011), http://www.kingcounty.gov/exec/PSB/BenchmarkProgram/Economy/EC02_Income/PerCapitaIncomeRaceChart.aspx (reporting that per capita income of the county's white residents is more than twice that of its black residents).

[184] Beckett et al., *supra* note 168, at 434.

[185] *See* State v. Johnson, No. 52123-3-I, 2005 WL 353314, at *7 (Wash. Ct. App. Feb. 14, 2005) (affirming the trial court's determination that relevant decisionmakers could be in central command).

[186] *See* Klement & Siggins, *supra* note 85, at 195. To the extent that patrol generates substantial numbers of arrests, it is typically because so many officers are dedicated to such units. Patrol typically generates traffic-related arrests (whether for traffic-related offenses, narcotics, or other contraband), but making arrests is a small fraction of what the unit (and individual officers in the unit) do. *See id.*

[187] *See id.* at 192–94.

For those officers assigned to work street-level details, making arrests is, quite literally, their daily work.[188] In the SPD, "Anti-Crime Teams" focus on street-level narcotics enforcement,[189] and "buy-bust" is among their staple tactics.[190] In a buy-bust, an undercover officer purchases a small quantity of narcotics using marked currency. Upon completing the transaction, the undercover officer alerts the "arrest team" with a prearranged signal. The arrest team then proceeds to arrest the seller and any individuals who might have helped facilitate the transaction. Although effective at generating arrests, buy-bust operations are labor-intensive. A buy-bust in Seattle often involves upwards of ten officers and generates six to ten arrests.[191] The capacity for any precinct to regularly carry out buy-busts depends on whether it has sufficient officer resources to do so and what the enforcement mandate for the particular precinct happens to be.[192]

Historically, the SPD has used undercover buy-bust operations most heavily in the downtown precinct where African-American narcotics sellers are concentrated.[193] The vast majority of narcotics arrests made in Seattle occur downtown.[194] The Anti-Crime Teams in the downtown precinct are afforded the resources and charged with doing narcotics enforcement.[195] Although there is considerable outdoor narcotics activity in downtown Seattle, there is also considerable outdoor activity in other parts of the city, not to mention indoor activity.[196] There are, however, significantly more African-American participants in outdoor drug transactions in downtown Seattle than in other parts of the city.[197] SPD's focus on making outdoor arrests downtown generates the stark racial disparity in narcotics arrests. But use of arrest-intensive specialization and geographic concentration do not entirely account for the disparity.

The SPD appears to target its enforcement effort on crack transactions as opposed to other comparable narcotics.[198] This is particularly surprising given the prevalence of heroin and Seattle's reputation for being a "heroin city."[199] The SPD's narcotics enforcement tactics directed at both

---

[188] See CONLON, *supra* note 84, at 157–58 (describing the NYPD).

[189] See Klement & Siggins, *supra* note 85, at 195.

[190] See Troy Duster, *Pattern, Purpose, and Race in the Drug War: The Crisis of Credibility in Criminal Justice, in* CRACK IN AMERICA 260, 265 (Craig Reinarman & Harry G. Levine eds., 1997) (noting prevalence of buy-bust operations in various American cities).

[191] See Klement & Siggins, *supra* note 85, at 198.

[192] See id.

[193] See Beckett et al., *supra* note 168, at 45 (noting that 65% of buy-busts were concentrated in three downtown census tracts); Klement & Siggins, *supra* note 85, at 196 (noting that fewer buy-bust operations occur in the southern suburban areas).

[194] See Klement & Siggins, *supra* note 85, at 197–98 (noting that 54% of all narcotics arrests were made in the West Precinct, which includes downtown).

[195] See id. at 198.

[196] See Beckett et al., *supra* note 103, at 122–23. Indoor enforcement, although more time-consuming in absolute terms because of the warrant requirement, tends to be more "productive" when measured in terms of arrests and contraband seized per officer hour. *Id.* at 121.

[197] Id.

[198] See id. at 123 (arguing that the focus on crack drives disparity); Beckett et al., *supra* note 168, at 435.

[199] See Vanessa Ho, *Drug Is Infiltrating All Walks of Seattle Life*, SEATTLE POST-INTELLIGENCER, Apr. 13, 2000, at A1.

indoor and outdoor narcotics transactions inordinately target crack.[200] In fact, Professor Beckett estimates that nearly 50% of all indoor enforcement operations in Seattle are for crack-related transactions.[201] And, this far exceeds estimates for the proportion of total narcotics transactions that crack accounts for.[202]

The SPD has offered some justifications for the racial disparity in narcotics arrest rates. Those justifications focus on the uniqueness of the downtown precinct, the heightened dangers created by outdoor narcotics transactions, and the administrative difficulties of carrying out indoor narcotics enforcement.[203] None of these justifications completely explains Professor Beckett's conclusions. Even if they did, it would only beg the question of whether the SPD was fairly balancing competing goals, by asking whether the department's choices to focus on crack, prioritize outdoor transactions downtown, and use arrests (as opposed to other deterrence-based tactics) sensibly promote security, public health, or some other community benefit. That sort of balancing is not for any particular officer to carry out. It is squarely within the department's discretionary ambit.

Quality-of-Life Policing

Quality-of-life policing sounds euphemistic when considered from the vantage of the countless minority arrestees against whom it has been directed. Such policing places a high premium on arresting individuals because of their contribution to "disorder" rather than violating any law per se.[204] Again, the three incidents of institutional discretion—geographic deployment, enforcement priority, and enforcement tactics—substantially account for arrest disparity.

Quality-of-life or "order-maintenance" policing has its theoretical mooring in James Wilson and George Kelling's now-iconic "broken windows" argument.[205] Numerous scholars have described it, so only a brief summary is needed here.[206] Wilson and Kelling argued that the dominant crime-control strategies of the late twentieth century failed, not only on their own terms, but more generally in making "citizens" feel more secure.[207] Instead of focusing on isolated instances of crime, the broken windows theory suggests that law enforcement should minimize "low-level disorder."[208] Panhandling, graffiti, vandalized buildings, street prostitution, low-level

---

[200] Beckett et al., *supra* note 103, at 123, 125. Beckett's analysis suggests that individual officer discretion also plays a role in targeting crack. Her study revealed that some individual officers tend to ask for crack when carrying out a buy-bust. *See* Beckett et al., *supra* note 168, at 429.

[201] Beckett et al., *supra* note 103, at 125.

[202] *Id.* (estimating that 25% of total drug transactions are for crack).

[203] *See* State v. Johnson, No. 52123-3-I, 2005 WL 353314, at *7 (Wash. Ct. App. Feb. 14, 2005).

[204] *See* Harcourt, *supra* note 79, at 128.

[205] James Q. Wilson & George L. Kelling, *Broken Windows*, Atlantic Monthly, Mar. 1982, at 29.

[206] *See, e.g.*, Harcourt, *supra* note 79, at 128.

[207] Kelling & Coles, *supra* note 26, at 70–71. The broken windows theory is not necessarily built upon an inclusive conceptualization of citizenship. For a discussion of how broken windows assumes and reproduces relations of class dominance, see Harcourt, *supra* note 79, at 215–16 (quoting Kelling & Coles, *supra* note 26). That an individual's feelings of "security" should be a priority for law enforcement represents a recent innovation in policing theory and one that also assumes and reproduces relations of class dominance. *See* Garland, *supra* note 81, at 152–54.

[208] Kelling & Coles, *supra* note 26, at 15.

narcotics transactions, squeegeeing, and the like engender public fear.[209] Disorder engenders fear, withdrawal from public space, and serious crime.[210] Urban anonymity fuels disorder and is, in turn, fueled by disorder: if left unchecked, the feedback loop yields an ever-accelerating descent into criminogenic pathology.[211] Normatively, the broken windows theory supports the diversion of police resources from 911 call-and-response and incident-driven crime solving to "order maintenance," i.e., the containment and elimination of "low-level disorder."[212] The broken windows theory counsels in favor of directing resources towards proactive policing, in which institutional discretion has the greatest sway in determining arrestee demographics.[213] In its theoretical formulation, however, the broken windows hypothesis does not necessarily counsel in favor of making more arrests.[214] Rather, it stresses the importance of deterring disorder by increasing the police's visible presence in a neighborhood through increased patrols, greater police–citizen contact, and remedying the signs of disorder.[215] Both Kelling and Wilson candidly acknowledge that the exercise of institutional discretion is the key in creating and shaping an order-maintenance policing strategy.[216]

The most notable implementation of order-maintenance policing was in New York City in the 1990s. Contrary to the theory, however, the NYPD opted for an arrest-intensive version of order-maintenance policing dubbed "zero tolerance."[217] During the 1990s, the NYPD dramatically increased the number of misdemeanor arrests in what was billed as an effort to "retake" New York City's public spaces for law-abiding citizens.[218] Although much-touted for reducing crime in New York City,[219] quantitative evidence suggests that factors other than quality-of-life policing account for the drop.[220] What is clear, however, is that the vast majority of arrestees were minorities.[221] The police assessment was, of course, that arrestee demographics mirror offender

---

[209] *Id.*

[210] *Id.* at 15–16, 20, 242.

[211] *Id.* at 20. The relationships between "disorder" and fear or insecurity were based exclusively on the authors' limited observations and informed conjecture. *See, e.g., id.* at 26–27, 236–37.

[212] *Id.* at 15.

[213] *See* Wilson, *supra* note 12, at 86, 100.

[214] Kelling & Coles, *supra* note 26, at 23, 84.

[215] *Id.* at 19.

[216] *Id.* at 170; *cf.* Wilson, *supra* note 12, at 100 (noting the extent to which institutional discretion shapes vice enforcement).

[217] *See* Harcourt, *supra* note 79, at 101; Wynn, *supra* note 140, at 107. The proponents of the broken windows theory hardly seemed upset with the arrest-intensive interpretation of their theory. *See* Kelling & Coles, *supra* note 26, at 158–70 (praising NYPD's order-maintenance policing strategy).

[218] *See* William Bratton with Peter Knobler, Turnaround 228 (1998); Harcourt, *supra* note 79, at 10 (noting misdemeanor arrests jumped 50% between 1993 and 1996 despite a constant complaint rate).

[219] *See, e.g.,* Bratton, *supra* note 218, at 259, 280, 289; Eli B. Silverman, *Crime in New York: A Success Story*, Pub. Persp., June-July 1997, at 3.

[220] *See, e.g.,* Bernard Harcourt & Jens Ludwig, *Broken Windows: New Evidence from New York City and a Five-City Social Experiment*, 73 U. Chi. L. Rev. 271, 277 (2006).

[221] Andrew Golub et al., Does Quality-of-Life Policing Widen the Net? 11 (Aug. 13, 2002) (unpublished manuscript), *available at* https://www.ncjrs.gov/pdffiles1/nij/grants/198996.pdf.

demographics.[222] Analyzing how institutional discretion operates in this context goes a long way in undermining that claim.

New York City

Upon taking office, Mayor Giuliani and Police Commissioner William Bratton consciously adopted the broken window theory's core premise: proactively enforcing against minor crimes decreases more serious crimes and makes communities feel more secure.[223] The NYPD has elected to enforce against minor crimes using arrest-intensive tactics.

The mayor and police commissioner used the expressions "quality-of life-policing," "zero tolerance," and "order maintenance" interchangeably.[224] Both also believed that aggressively and proactively enforcing against minor crimes would forestall more serious crimes later and create greater "order." New York City's criminal code, like most others, was replete with crimes that typically went unenforced. The Bratton NYPD sought to enforce many of these laws both to interdict the specific behavior criminalized and to contain "disorderly" persons not otherwise engaging in criminalized conduct.[225] The NYPD explicitly prioritized enforcement against low-level narcotics offenses in public prostitution, graffiti, public intoxication, public urination, and a host of pedestrian and traffic violations.[226] Aggressive enforcement against such minor crimes was explicitly premised upon the expectation of discovering crimes unrelated to the reason for arrest or, alternatively, preempting commission of more serious criminal acts later. For example, the man arrested for turnstile jumping sometimes turned out to have an outstanding warrant for failing to appear in court or the man arrested for drinking beer in public sometimes turned out to possess an unregistered firearm.[227]

Departmental decisionmakers in no uncertain terms communicated to line officers that they were to use their arrest power to effect the department's quality-of-life agenda. Many officers understood this mandate to mean arrest first, ask questions later.[228] Departmental decisionmakers, however, did more than just communicate the importance of enforcing against minor crimes. Rather, the NYPD's order-maintenance program embraced an incapacitation scheme that sought to take the "disorderly" off the streets altogether. As discussed below, the designation "disorderly" is far from objective, particularly given the extent to which race and class shape perceptions of disorder.[229] Towards that end, the department privileged high arrest rates as the rubric of success and tailored geographic deployment and used specialized units accordingly.

---

[222] *See* HARCOURT, *supra* note 79, at 174 (quoting Commissioner Safir).

[223] *See id.* 185–86 (quoting Giuliani); BRATTON, *supra* note 218, at 138, 152, 179.

[224] *See* HARCOURT, *supra* note 79, at 50.

[225] *See* Erzen, *supra* note 149, at 35–36; HARCOURT, *supra* note 79, at 101–02.

[226] BRATTON, *supra* note 218, at 227–29.

[227] *See id.* at 168, 214, 229.

[228] *See* Wynn, *supra* note 140, at 109–11.

[229] *See* Sampson & Raudenbush, *supra* note 167, at 323.

To execute its order-maintenance scheme, the NYPD relied upon arrest-intensive, specialized units and created new incentives for patrol officers to make more arrests.[230] Targeting low-level narcotics transactions in public spaces was a high priority for the NYPD under Bratton. The department increased its spending on arrest-intensive narcotics units.[231] The department also increased the number of officers and times of day that the specialized units engaged in under-cover operations such as buy-bust operations.[232] Later in the 1990s, under Commissioner Howard Safir, the department increased the number of officers in specialized street-crimes units with a principal mandate of weapons interdiction.[233] The street-crimes units made aggressive use of stop-and-frisk tactics in their efforts. The tactics were controversial because of the impact on innocent minority pedestrians.[234] The arrestee demographic deserves as much scrutiny. The focus on low-level marijuana arrests has continued to the present day.[235] The NYPD arrested a record 40,300 individuals in 2008 for misdemeanor marijuana offenses.[236] The vast majority of these arrestees were minorities, and specialized undercover narcotics units made nearly half of the arrests.[237] The NYPD's reliance on arrest-intensive specialized units was not simply limited to guns and narcotics.[238] Undercover street-crimes units were directed to arrest individuals for a host of quality-of-life crimes. Among the more notable examples was the apprehension of turnstile jumpers.[239] Under its zero-tolerance mandate, the NYPD converted patrol into a more arrest-intensive unit than is typically true.[240] The department accomplished this by requiring patrol officers to arrest where they had previously issued citations and by using officer's arrest figures as a measure of occupational success. Many of the misdemeanors that were at the heart of New York City's order-maintenance scheme had erstwhile been offenses for which officers, in their discretion, issued citations or simply ignored.[241] This was true for various "public nuisances" such as drinking, public urination, panhandling, prostitution, and smoking marijuana.[242] The ze-

---

[230] *See* Wynn, *supra* note 140, at 111 (citing George L. Kelling & William J. Bratton, *Declining Crime Rates: Insiders' Views of the New York City Story*, 88 J. Crim. L & Criminology 1217 (1998)).

[231] *See* Bratton, *supra* note 218, at 227–28.

[232] *Id.*; *see supra* notes 186–197 and accompanying text (discussing racial disparity generated by Seattle Police Department's reliance on buy-bust operations).

[233] *See* Harcourt, *supra* note 79, at 50.

[234] *See generally* Eliot Spitzer, The New York City Police Department's "Stop and Frisk" Practices (1999) (discussing disparate impact of the NYPD's stop and frisk practices on minorities).

[235] *See* Dwyer, *supra* note 150.

[236] *Id.*

[237] *Id.*

[238] Some have argued that the NYPD's aggressive stop-and-frisk policing played a significant role in reducing New York City's homicide rate in the mid-1990s. *See, e.g.,* Lawrence Rosenthal, *Pragmatism, Originalism, Race, and the Case Against* Terry v. Ohio, 43 Tex. Tech L. Rev. 299, 326–28 (2010) (extrapolating from studies of intensive patrol in specific, high-crime locations).

[239] *See* Silverman, *supra* note 114, at 3.

[240] Bratton, *supra* note 218, at 227; *see also* Wynn, *supra* note 140, at 111 (citing Kelling & Bratton, *supra* note 230); Judith A. Greene, *Zero Tolerance: A Case Study of Police Policies and Practices in New York City*, 45 Crime & Delinq. 171, 175 (1999) (citing Bratton, *supra* note 218, at 227).

[241] Bratton, *supra* note 218, at xv, 153, 155, 229.

[242] *Id.* at 228–29; Andrew Golub et al., *The Race/Ethnicity Disparity in Misdemeanor Marijuana Arrests in New York City*, 6 Criminology & Pub. Pol'y 131, 131 (2007).

ro-tolerance mandate for such disorderly persons was to take them off the street. Patrol officers were no longer to be lenient upon encountering such persons. Not only did the department instruct patrol officers to make more arrests,[243] but management was supposed to monitor arrest numbers generated by individual patrol officers.[244] At least some patrol officers understood this to mean that they should arrest whenever encountering a "disorderly" person.[245] Unsurprisingly, the effects of the new arrest-intensive approach were not evenly distributed across the city.

To understand why misdemeanor narcotics arrestees were inordinately minorities, the NYPD's enforcement priorities and use of arrests must be understood in conjunction with geographic deployment decisions.[246] There is mixed evidence on whether, given an opportunity, any particular individual NYPD officer would elect to arrest a minority offender over a white one.[247] But, as discussed, patterns of residential segregation make individual officer discretion less of a factor than institutional discretion in accounting for arrestee demographics. New York City is no exception. There have been multiple studies focusing on misdemeanor marijuana-possession arrests, a hallmark of zero-tolerance policing.[248] The studies conclude that, from the late 1990s onward, the NYPD has targeted poor minority communities for misdemeanor arrests.[249] Although no one has undertaken a comprehensive study of the geographic distribution of quality-of-life arrests in New York City, the number of minorities involved in marijuana arrests suggests that the NYPD directed arrest-intensive policing at minorities.

The spatial logic of zero-tolerance policing in New York City revolved around the twin axes of high crime and disorder. The two were often elided, but the former was identified through quantitative measures while the latter was not. Under Bratton, the NYPD began using Compstat, a computerized tool for tracking crime reports and arrests.[250] Because Compstat only accounts for reported crime, it did not necessarily create a portrait of low-level crimes that are at the core of the broken windows theory.[251] Nonetheless, because the broken window theory posits a direct relationship between quality-of-life crimes and more serious crimes, the department targeted

---

[243] See LEVINE & SMALL, *supra* note 140, at 18.

[244] See WYNN, *supra* note 140, at 112.

[245] See *id.* at 118–19.

[246] HARCOURT, *supra* note 79, at 10 (discussing misdemeanor arrests in New York City). Researchers have found that the demographic profile of those arrested for quality-of-life type offenses is similar to that of those arrested for more serious offenses. In both cases the profile is largely minority. Quality-of-life policing, thus, did not shift the demographic profile of arrestees. It increased the number of misdemeanors arrestees across the board. See Golub et al., *supra* note 221, at 15.

[247] See Fagan et al., *supra* note 55, at 820 (noting that officers are more likely to arrest a white individual than an individual of a minority once stop has been effected).

[248] See LEVINE & SMALL, *supra* note 140; Golub et. al., *supra* note 242; Andrew Golub et al., *Smoking Marijuana in Public: The Spatial and Policy Shift in New York City Arrests 1992–2003*, 3 HARM REDUCTION J. no. 22, Aug. 4, 2006, *available at* http://www.harmreductionjournal.com/content/pdf/1477-7517-3-22.pdf.

[249] See Golub et. al., *supra* note 248, at 23. The study notes, however, that in the early 1990s, the NYPD focused its enforcement efforts in lower Manhattan. The demographic profile of arrestees was nonetheless overwhelmingly minority, suggesting an inordinately minority offender population or racial bias (whether implicit or explicit) on the part of individual officers. See *id.* at 9, 23.

[250] See BRATTON, *supra* note 218, at 233–39.

[251] Compstat also creates incentives for police to underreport crimes. See Rayman, *supra* note 105.

"high crime" areas—low income, minority neighborhoods tend to have higher rates of reported crime than other neighborhoods—for zero-tolerance policing.[252] This targeting was based on the assumption that incapacitating low-level offenders would have ameliorative effects on serious crime, even if particular reported incidents of serious crime went unsolved.

Even more troubling is the extent to which generic notions of disorder animated zero-tolerance policing. The authors of the broken windows theory suggest a highly impressionistic understanding of disorder. Their conception is shot through with middle-class assumptions of what urban decay looks like.[253] While the theory of order maintenance assumes that "disorder" can be objectively distinguished from "order,"[254] both are deeply subjective.[255] Based on survey data, Sampson and Raudenbush have concluded that the racial and economic makeup of a neighborhood go much further in predicting observers' perceptions of disorder than does any objective standard of disorder.[256] One's ability to recognize disorder is a product of cultural cognition and, accordingly, structured by race and class affinities—affinities that one might not consciously espouse.[257] There is limited, anecdotal evidence to suggest that the NYPD, like other police departments, made deployment decisions based on just such perceptions of "disorder."[258]

Chicago's Anti-Gang Ordinance

Although Chicago did not embrace as comprehensive a zero-tolerance policing program as New York City did, it did target gangs with an anti-loitering ordinance that might be considered an example of order-maintenance policing.[259]

The ordinance, enacted in 1992, became the subject of the Supreme Court's opinion in *Chicago v. Morales*.[260] The ordinance empowered the police to order known gang members found "loitering in any public place with one or more other persons" to disperse.[261] The city council assumed that there was a causal relationship between loitering and more serious crimes.[262] It further empowered the police to arrest anyone failing to obey the dispersal command.[263] Before it was finally held unconstitutional, the police arrested 42,000 persons for violating the

---

[252] *See* LEVINE & SMALL, *supra* note 140, at 48 (noting and criticizing NYPD's claim that low-level marijuana enforcement reduces more serious crime).

[253] *See* HARCOURT, *supra* note 79, at 215–16 (quoting Wilson & Kelling, *supra* note 205).

[254] *See id.* at 132–34.

[255] *See generally* Sampson & Raudenbush, *supra* note 167 (discussing the connection between perception and disorder).

[256] *See id.* at 323.

[257] *See id.* at 320.

[258] *See id.*

[259] *See* HARCOURT, *supra* note 79, at 1–3.

[260] *See* City of Chicago v. Morales, 527 U.S. 41 (1999).

[261] *Id.* at 41.

[262] City of Chicago v. Morales, 687 N.E.2d 53, 58 (Ill. 1997) (quoting ordinance preamble). Before the Supreme Court, Chicago argued that the ordinance actually prevented a substantial number of more serious crimes. *See Morales*, 527 U.S. at 48. Subsequent research, however, calls this conclusion into question. *See* HARCOURT, *supra* note 79, 104–06 (citing Stephen J. Schulhofer & Albert W. Alschuler, *Getting the Facts Straight: Crime Trends, Community Support, and the Police Enforcement of 'Social Norms,'* LAW & SOC'Y REV. (2000)).

[263] *Morales*, 687 N.E.2d at 58.

ordinance.[264] The Supreme Court struck the ordinance down on due process grounds, explaining that the generic prohibition of "loitering" encompasses much "innocent conduct" and thus leaves "lawmaking to the moment-to-moment judgment of the policeman on his beat."[265]

The Chicago gang ordinance highlights institutional discretion's relationship with racial disparity in arrest rates. The department's role in making deployment decisions likely had significantly more to do with the demographic profile of arrestees than did any individual officer's exercise of discretion. A departmental general order directed district commanders to designate those areas, frequented by gang members, in which the ordinance would be enforced.[266] In *Morales*, the Court rejected Chicago's argument that the police department's general order sufficiently limited individual officer discretion.[267] The Court may have been right to reject the argument as a technical matter, but the notion that simply replacing the word "loitering" in the ordinance with more specific words would prevent arbitrary or racially skewed enforcement is implausible. Even without the ordinance, there were already numerous laws on the books that permitted similar kinds of order-maintenance policing.[268] Changing the statute's wording essentially solved the vagueness problem. Fine-grained lexical distinctions in law tend not to have significant impact on an individual officer's decisionmaking in the field.[269] However, personnel policies and orders from senior command do, particularly in the proactive policing context.[270] To the extent that the Chicago Police Department directs officers to go to particular areas and make arrests, individual officers will do so. And to the extent that the individuals loitering on the street are all young men of color, it is inevitable that the arrestees will be as well. The decisive moments of discretionary decisionmaking will have occurred before the arresting officers even leave the precinct station.

Morales, like criminal procedure generally, tells us virtually nothing about how to understand the relationship between departmental discretion and race, let alone how that relationship ought to be calibrated to serve democratic principles.

Policing Police Departments

Distributive justice theory suggests a much more active role for courts and prosecutors in regulating the three dimensions of departmental discretion identified in Part III. In proactive policing, police departments have considerable discretion to ration arrests as they see

---

[264] *Morales*, 527 U.S. at 49 (relying on the City of Chicago's brief).

[265] *Id.* at 60 (quoting Kolender v. Lawson, 461 U.S. 352, 360 (1983)).

[266] *Id.* at 48.

[267] *Id.* at 62.

[268] *Id.* at 52.

[269] *See, e.g.*, Stephen D. Mastrofski, *Organizational Determinants of Police Discretion: The Case of Drinking-Driving*, 15 J. Crim. Just. 387, 394 (1987) (arguing that the existence of criminal law is only one factor in explaining officer decisionmaking); Meghan Stroshine, *The Influence of "Working Rules" on Police Suspicion and Discretionary Decision Making*, 11 Police Q. 315, 320 (2008) (noting that police rely on "rules of thumb" rather than legal specifics).

[270] *See* Wilson, *supra* note 12, at 49.

fit. These departmental choices generate winners and losers, with significant distributive consequences. This Section argues that the law should treat proactive policing arrests as distributive goods. It follows that departmental discretion should be regulated to control for inegalitarian consequences.

Arrest as a Distributive Phenomenon

Distributive justice is concerned with how democratic institutions in a community of autonomous individuals should ensure equal distributions of rights, resources, and obligations.[271] This Subsection will show that arrest policy can implicate all three. Arrest policy can impinge upon the right to be free of discrimination, limit economic and social opportunities, and differentially enforce the obligation to abide by the law. Part III showed that arrest is not the inevitable consequence of law-breaking; this is most acutely true in the proactive policing context. There, enforcement opportunities far exceed enforcement resources and departments have substantial discretion to selectively apply those resources. Because this is true, evaluating whether a police department employs its arrest discretion justly is not reducible to the question of whether each individual arrest is carried out lawfully. In contrast to the dominant theories of criminal punishment, distributive justice focuses on whether institutional policies spread costs and benefits across a heterogeneous citizenry in an egalitarian manner. I argue that arrest distribution will be egalitarian when it is in keeping with what the relevant political community *would have* authorized had its members: (1) possessed accurate information regarding the prevalence and distribution of criminal misconduct, and (2) been willing to absorb the range of costs associated with arrests in proportion to actual lawbreaking in their immediate social orbit—members of the relevant community would make choices expecting enforcement intensity to impact their family members, neighbors, colleagues, etc., in strict proportion to the actual law-breaking that occurs amongst those individuals.

Dominant theories of the criminal sanction offer little guidance on whether or how egalitarian principles should structure criminal law enforcement. By "dominant," I mean utilitarian, retributive, and expressivist theories.[272] It is beyond this paper's scope to offer more than a cursory account of each. Expressivism and retribution justify criminal enforcement by reference to a community's moral norms, i.e., criminal sanction is the social expression of moral condemnation.[273] Retributive theories typically assume Kantian notions of moral agency and responsibility—the criminal sanction ought to be imposed in accordance with an individual's moral desert.[274] Expressivist

---

[271] *See, e.g.*, Bruce Ackerman, Social Justice in the Liberal State 3–4 (1980); John Rawls, A Theory of Justice 3–6 (Harvard Univ. Press rev. ed. 1999) (1971); *see also* Samuel Scheffler, *The Morality of Criminal Law*, 88 Cal. L. Rev. 965, 966 (2000) (noting that distributive justice is preoccupied with institutionally defined entitlements and presumes no desert preceding such). Rawls and Ackerman represent contemporary examples of the social-contract tradition, which presupposes that self-possessed individuals can make agreements. For a discussion of the implicit identity assumptions upon which such theory depends, see Nirej S. Sekhon, *Equality & Identity Hierarchy*, 3 N.Y.U. J. L. & Liberty 349, 364–70 (2008).

[272] *See, e.g.*, John Kaplan et. al., Criminal Law Cases & Materials 31–71 (6th ed. 2008).

[273] *See, e.g.*, Joel Feinberg, *The Expressive Function of Punishment, in* Doing & Deserving 95, 99–100 (1970) (citing Henry Hart, *The Aims of Criminal Law*, 23 L. & Contemp. Probs. 401, 408 (1958)).

[274] *See* John Rawls, *Two Concepts of Rules*, 64 Phil. R. 3, 5 (1955).

theories, on the other hand, view condemnation as a means for communities to reaffirm their own foundational, moral tenets.[275] Morally anchored conceptualizations of the criminal sanction suggest that the police ought to pursue offenders in order of moral depravity. Only at the highest level of generality is it true that police departments actually do this; for example, most police departments would prioritize homicide investigations over petty theft investigations. That said, *within* the context of proactive policing, there is little to suggest that police departments are able to rank priorities according to moral exigency. It is unsurprising that moral exigency is an unwieldy mechanism for allocating scarce resources. In a pluralistic society, moral questions are the source of contentious disagreement.[276] For petty narcotics, quality-of-life, and other minor crimes, offenders' moral depravity affords limited justification for imposition of the criminal sanction at all, let alone providing a guide for allocating scarce enforcement resources between different target groups.

At first glance, utilitarian theories seem more promising for regulating police discretion because they are explicitly concerned with costs and benefits. Utilitarianism, however, is largely concerned with maximizing the latter and minimizing the former without regard for how either is distributed across members of a community. Utilitarianism is not preoccupied with whether any particular distribution is, in and of itself, equitable. Even when concerned with policing's negative effects upon disadvantaged populations, utilitarian approaches instrumentalize those effects, casting them in terms of optimal deterrence. For example, some have argued that overly aggressive policing undermines the police's legitimacy in poor neighborhoods and, consequently, erodes residents' commitment to abiding by the law and cooperating with the police.[277] The most salient concern here is preventing law-breaking in poor communities.[278] Distributive concerns are not important in and of themselves, but only to the extent that they consolidate law enforcement's legitimacy and, correspondingly, poor communities' willingness to cooperate with law enforcement. Put more generally, a utilitarian approach to policing will counsel in favor of enforcing against those offenders where deterrence is obtained most efficiently. Such an approach need not target those offenses or offenders that impose the greatest costs upon the relevant community. Utilitarianism, however, does overlap with distributive justice to the extent that both direct institutions to take a broad and thorough account of policies' costs and benefits. Distributive justice, however, seeks to ensure an egalitarian distribution of both costs and benefits as an end, in and of itself.

---

[275] *See, e.g.,* FEINBERG, *supra* note 273, at 115 (arguing that punishment is a ritualized disavowal of the offending act).

[276] *See, e.g.,* Dan M. Kahan, *The Secret Ambition of Deterrence,* 113 HARV. L. REV. 413, 433, 477 (1999) (discussing how political dialogue around expressive values is contentious).

[277] *See, e.g.,* Tom R. Tyler, *Procedural Justice, Legitimacy, and the Effective Rule of Law,* 30 CRIME & JUST. 283, 286 (2003).

[278] *See, e.g.,* Meares, *supra* note 35, at 681–82 (arguing that a lack of well-entrenched norms in poor communities accounts for failure to comply with law).

While criminal procedure scholars have noted that policing has a redistributive dimension,[279] no one has systematically analyzed policing through the lens of distributive justice.[280] Professor Stuntz, for example, has noted that policing is redistributive because the most intensive policing does not occur in those neighborhoods that foot most of the tax bill.[281] Professor Sklansky has suggested that policing should promote egalitarianism.[282] Neither, however, specifically addresses what distributive justice theory might require of police departments.[283]

Both utilitarianism and distributive justice require identification of proactive policing's costs and benefits. As shorthand, one might think of security as policing's primary benefit.[284] On the other side of the scale, policing imposes obvious costs on taxpayers and the individuals who are arrested.[285] The analysis of costs, however, should not end there. Policing generates a host of additional, less-obvious costs that recent scholarship has identified. Those costs include arrests' long-term consequences upon arrestees' earning and productive capacities, the collateral consequences upon arrestees' families and communities, and the consequences upon crime control itself.[286] Scholars have persuasively argued that focusing law enforcement upon specific groups may actually increase crime rates.[287] That police departments consistently get the cost-benefit balance egregiously wrong, particularly *within* minority neighborhoods,[288] is likely because police overlook the less obvious, less easily quantified costs of what they do. Quantifying these costs

[279] *See, e.g.*, David Alan Sklansky, *Police and Democracy*, 103 Mich. L. Rev. 1699, 1821 (2005); Stuntz, *supra* note 160, at 823, 832.

[280] *See, e.g.*, Stuntz, *supra* note 160, at 832. By the same token, distributive justice theorists have not focused on criminal justice. For example, Bruce Ackerman devotes only a handful of pages to criminal law, *see* Ackerman, *supra* note 271, at 83–88, while John Rawls devotes none at all, *see* Rawls, *supra* note 271. One notable exception is Sharon Dolovich's extrapolation from Rawls. Sharon Dolovich, *Legitimate Punishment in Liberal Democracy*, 7 Buff. Crim. L. Rev. 307 (2004). Dolovich attempts to make up for Rawls's silence on criminal justice by identifying the foundational agreements that a modified Rawlsian "original position" would have generated regarding criminal justice. *Id.* at 326–28. Dolovich does not speak to arrest policy specifically, but does identify abstract principles governing punishment. *See id.* at 408–09.

[281] *See* William J. Stuntz, *Local Policing After the Terror*, 111 Yale L.J. 2137, 2149 (2002).

[282] *See* Sklansky, *supra* note 279, at 1821–22 (discussing how privatization of police functions threatens egalitarianism).

[283] *See id.*; *see also* Darryl K. Brown, *Cost-Benefit Analysis in Criminal Law*, 92 Cal. L. Rev. 323, 326 (2004) (arguing for greater use of cost-benefit analysis in criminal law); Stuntz, *supra* note 280, at 823 (noting that police undertake cost-benefit analysis when deciding where to devote proactive policing resources).

[284] By "security" I mean some objective measure of harm prevention, not simply the amelioration of individuals' subjective fear. The latter tends to be exaggerated and racialized in ways that drive some of the institutional dynamics described in this Article. *See, e.g.*, Simon, *supra* note 79, at 75–76.

[285] *See* Stuntz, *supra* note 281, at 2164–66.

[286] *See* Brown, *supra* note 283, at 345–48 (summarizing research on costs of criminal law enforcement).

[287] *See, e.g.*, Harcourt, *supra* note 54, at 122–25 (discussing the connection between racial targeting decreasing crime and the dependency on the relative elasticity of different groups to policing); Tom R. Tyler & Jeffrey Fagan, *Legitimacy and Cooperation: Why Do People Help the Police Fight Crime in Their Communities*, 6 Ohio St. J. Crim. L. 231, 233–36 (2008) (discussing how overenforcing criminal laws may erode community support for the police, which, in turn, leads to increased crime).

[288] *See, e.g.*, Tracey L. Meares & Dan M. Kahan, *When Rights Are Wrong: The Paradox of Unwanted Rights*, in Urgent Times 3, 20–21 (Tracey L. Meares & Dan M Kahan eds., 1999) (criticizing civil libertarians for focusing on minority crime suspects' rights at the expense of minority crime victims' rights); Meares, *supra* note 35, at 696–702 (arguing that police overenforce narcotics and minor crimes in minority communities, but generally underenforce serious crimes); Natapoff, *supra* note 35, at 1772 (arguing the same).

presents a challenge to any utilitarian approach, but particularly those that suggest technocratic regulation of the police, i.e., an approach which assumes that a bureaucratic regulator can weigh costs and benefits with some empirical certainty.[289] The problem is that many of the "costs" and "benefits" at play in policing require value judgments about competing priorities. Such costs and benefits, by definition, resist quantification, presenting themselves as incommensurate. That is to say that utilitarian approaches may call for the impossible task of balancing what are essentially expressivist commitments.[290] For example, consider how an administrative rulemaker would balance the costs and benefits of arresting juvenile taggers. What if some of the taggers produce murals that many residents actually think of as public art? How should enforcing against tagging be balanced against other crimes?

Distributive justice recognizes the inherently political nature of such judgments.[291] It is appropriate to leave such difficult, value-laden questions to the political process, so long as that process operates within specified constraints. Distributive justice imposes limitations upon the democratic process such that it cannot be used to advance majoritarian (or parochial) interests that undermine fundamental liberal principles, including egalitarianism.[292] The state may not distribute benefits or burdens on the basis of morally irrelevant social attributes, even if supported by a democratic majority.[293] Thus there must be constraints on the democratic process that forbid infringement on fundamental rights and equality.[294] As discussed in the next subsection, this notion resonates with a democratic-representation-reinforcing theory of judicial review. Before considering the courts' role in regulating police department discretion, however, one must understand what an equal distribution of arrests should entail.

Distributive justice does not require absolute equality. John Rawls's two principles of justice, for example, permit inequality within roughly defined limits.[295] The first principle requires the "most extensive scheme of equal basic liberties" that are consistent with organized coexistence.[296] The second principle requires that any social and economic inequality be organized such that it inures to everyone's benefit.[297] The first principle permits deprivations of liberty for those who have grievously impinged upon others' basic liberties, so that equal liberties are permitted only as far as is consistent with *everyone* having those liberties.[298] Punishing violent crimes or crimes against property, for example, would be consistent with the first principle.[299]

---

[289] *Cf.* Brown, *supra* note 283, at 352–57.

[290] *Cf.* Kahan, *supra* note 276, at 427–28.

[291] *See, e.g.*, JOHN RAWLS, POLITICAL LIBERALISM 3–4 (1993).

[292] *See id.* at xxiii–l, 41.

[293] *See* RAWLS, *supra* note 271, at 129.

[294] *See* RAWLS, *supra* note 291, at 41.

[295] These two principles anchor Rawls's entire conception of liberal justice. RAWLS, *supra* note 271, at 10–14.

[296] *Id.* at 53.

[297] *Id.*

[298] *Id.* Equal liberty for all, by definition, cannot include the freedom to restrict others' liberty.

[299] While Rawls himself is not explicit about this, Professor Dolovich has persuasively demonstrated that, with slight modifications, Rawls's model generates principles of punishment. Dolovich, *supra* note 280, at 328 (noting modification

The second principle permits inequality to the extent that those who are uniquely productive or talented may take a larger share of the economic pie if their activities expand the pie for all, particularly the disadvantaged.[300] Distributive justice will be served when democratic institutions solve problems within the bounds suggested by the two principles of justice. That process will generate winners and losers, but distributive justice limits the bases upon which distinctions may be made and the scope of any resulting inequalities.

Distributive justice suggests two basic points about when the political process will yield outcomes consistent with Rawls's two principles of justice: when participants are well-informed and imagine themselves as both the potential beneficiaries and cost-bearers of their political choices.[301] Put differently, popular politics will yield egalitarian outcomes when citizens are well-informed and "other regarding."[302] To imagine oneself as a potential beneficiary or cost-bearer requires citizens to have the capacity for imagining themselves in the shoes of their co-citizens, particularly those who are less advantaged.[303] This, of course, is a highly idealized vision of citizenship and political community—these ideals are intended to serve both as a model for our political institutions and for identifying the specific constraints that should be imposed upon such political institutions and processes.[304] Of course our *is* is a far cry from Rawls's *ought*. That is doubly true for the politics of criminal justice.

The actual politics of crime in the United States scarcely resembles these liberal ideals.[305] Professor Stuntz has described America's politics of crime as "pathological."[306] Jonathan Simon has convincingly argued that middle-class voters imagine their political agency in a language of "victimhood" that presupposes a racialized divide between criminals and victims.[307] Political discourse around crime has expressly cast "criminals" as poor minorities—Michelle Alexander has recently described how that has been an express tactic of political campaigns since the 1960s.[308] And it has been a successful tactic—at least, if one imagines "success" in terms of win-

---

for partial compliance).

[300] RAWLS, *supra* note 271, at 65–66.

[301] *Id.* at 314–15 (describing an idealized legislative process). The principles of justice are themselves generated by an idealized democratic deliberation. *Id.* at 15 (describing the "original position").

[302] *See* ACKERMAN, *supra* note 271, at 6–7, 11, 72–73 (explaining that idealized liberalism is one in which individuals work out distributive questions through dialogue without recourse to claims of superiority); RAWLS, *supra* note 271, at 118–19 ("They must choose principles the consequences of which they are prepared to live with whatever generation they turn out to belong to."). In his later work, Rawls described the relation that prevails between members of the political community as "civic friendship." RAWLS, *supra* note 291, at xlix.

[303] *See* RAWLS, *supra* note 271, at 453; *see also* JURGEN HABERMAS, THE INCLUSION OF THE OTHER 96 (1998) (noting that Rawls's "original position" actually describes a state of intersubjective connection between all members of the political community); Dolovich, *supra* note 280, at 332–34 (describing the "veil of ignorance").

[304] *See, e.g.*, RAWLS, *supra* note 291, at 25–26 (noting that the original position is an analytical device and should not be confused with the actual political world).

[305] *See* Dolovich, *supra* note 280, at 430–40.

[306] *See* Stuntz, *supra* note 142, at 505; *see also* Stuntz, *supra* note 33, at 2003 (arguing that the suburbanization-generated white voting block undermines egalitarianism).

[307] SIMON, *supra* note 79, at 76.

[308] MICHELLE ALEXANDER, THE NEW JIM CROW 43–45 (2010) (describing the Republican Party's use of criminal justice as a racial "wedge" issue in the 1960s).

ning office.[309] This politics plays a substantial role in producing the glaring disparities in arrest rates for non-violent crime.[310] Michael Tonry has suggested that the political expendability and rhetorical criminalization of poor, urban minorities made them the most obvious "enemy" in the war on drugs.[311] This has all played out in a broader context marked by increased hostility to welfarism. Middle-class voters' hostility to welfare has choked public services for the poor and impelled the withdrawal of such state agencies from the poorest neighborhoods. Loic Waquant has convincingly shown that American cities have left it almost exclusively to police to "manage" the poor.[312]

Some criminal justice scholars have posited that local communities approximate the liberal ideal because of the associations between victims, offenders, and other residents.[313] Many have criticized this view of localism.[314] First, it assumes that police departments are politically accountable, which is not necessarily true.[315] Second, "process failure" is not unique to large political communities—majorities and minorities can form in small communities, and the former can be very parochial.[316] And third, police authority is not delimited in sub-local terms, but rather in terms of the larger political unit; i.e., police departments are city or county agencies. Contests over departmental discretion will often implicate the interests of multiple sub-local communities.[317] For example, intensive concentration of police resources in one neighborhood may come at the expense of deploying resources in another or even result in crime being displaced to another neighborhood. There is little reason to think that voters in American cities will behave in a manner that is consistent with liberal principles of equality,[318] although a few might.[319]

---

[309] *Id.* at 44–47.

[310] *Id.* at 44–56.

[311] Tonry, *supra* note 5, at 112–13.

[312] Loïc Waquant, Urban Outcasts 12, 30–34 (2008).

[313] *See* Dan M. Kahan & Tracey L. Meares, *Foreword: The Coming Crisis Of Criminal Procedure*, 86 Geo. LJ. 1153, 1161, 1182 (1998); *see also* Stuntz, *supra* note 33, at 2031–32 (arguing for more local control over criminal justice system). *But see* Richard C. Schragger, *The Limits of Localism*, 100 Mich. L. Rev. 371, 385–86 (2001) (arguing that the social norms scholars do not adequately address how to define a "community"); Robert Weisberg, *Norms and Criminal Law, and the Norms of Criminal Law Scholarship*, 93 J. Crim. L. & Criminology 467, 508–14 (2003) (criticizing the "social norms" approach to policing the "inner city").

[314] *See, e.g.*, Alafair Burke, *Unpacking New Policing: Confessions of a Former Neighborhood District Attorney*, 78 Wash. L. Rev. 985, 1005, 1010 (2003); David Cole, *Foreword: Discretion and Discrimination Reconsidered: A Response to the New Criminal Justice Scholarhip*, 87 Geo. LJ. 1059, 1086 (1999) ("[O]nce one looks beyond romanticized invocations of 'the community,' it becomes apparent that no community is united on these issues."); Schragger, *supra* note 313, at 416–58; Weisberg, *supra* note 313, at 508–14.

[315] *See* Wilson, *supra* note 12, at 230–33; *supra* note 125 and accompanying text.

[316] *See* Venkatesh, *supra* note 93, at 72 (noting that community policing meetings favored those with "social clout" in the neighborhood); Schragger, *supra* note 313, at 445 ("[T]he disenfranchised and marginal are almost never considered members of any community.").

[317] *See* Schragger, *supra* note 313, at 470–71 ("[W]hat is called 'local' is always 'interlocal.'").

[318] *See* Stuntz, *supra* note 33, at 2003.

[319] A number of jurisdictions have passed laws directing law enforcement to de-prioritize enforcement against marijuana possession. *See* Phillip Smith, *Lowest Law Enforcement Priority Marijuana Initiatives Face the Voters in Five Cities*, Drug War Chron. (Oct. 26, 2006, 5:51 PM), http://stopthedrugwar.org/chronicle/459/marijuana_lowest_enforcement_priority_initiatives.

All of this is to say that popular politics are not likely to act as a meaningful constraint on police departments. It should be up to legal institutions to make up for that.

"Political Failure" and Departmental Discretion

Distributive justice principles suggest that law ought to guarantee an egalitarian distribution of proactive policing's costs and benefits when majoritarian politics cannot. Building on the discussion above, this Subsection shows that courts should ensure that members of the relevant political community (1) bear a fair share of proactive policing's costs, including those associated with arrest, and (2) have full information as to crime's occurrence and the demographic profile generated by proactive policing arrests.

Rawls himself suggested that it may be up to the "judicial virtues [of] impartiality and considerateness" to effect liberal justice in the real world.[320] His ambition was to formulate an "objective" measure of liberal justice that could be held up to our own political institutions.[321] Where they fail to live up to those standards, we might reasonably expect that the judicial virtues would save us. This hope resonates with other liberal conceptions of judicial review,[322] including John Ely's.[323] In his famous formulation, Ely argues that constitutional courts ought to constrain political majorities' ability to systematically impose costs upon a disfavored minority.[324] Because minorities cannot use the political process to challenge such an imposition, Ely argues that constitutional courts should disallow it. This is tantamount to empowering courts to compel the outcome that *would have* resulted had the majority behaved in a manner consistent with idealized democratic fairness—i.e., a manner in which individual citizens, given full information, impose only those costs that they themselves would be willing to bear.[325] The obligation to distribute policing costs equitably ought to require police departments to make arrests in proportion to the rate of specific criminal misconduct in specific areas. Police departments should not arrest offenders in one community while allowing those in another community to engage in similar conduct with impunity.[326] That is to say, law should regulate police departments' geographic deployment, enforcement priority, and tactical policies in order to minimize disparate impact on minority offenders. For example, where drug crimes regularly occur in both wealthy and poor sections of a city, law enforcement should be required to make arrests in both parts of town. The same would hold true for all minor crimes that are the subject of proactive policing. If arrest-intensive units are to be deployed against

---

[320] RAWLS, *supra* note 271, at 453.

[321] *Id.*

[322] ACKERMAN, *supra* note 271, at 311.

[323] JOHN HART ELY, DEMOCRACY AND DISTRUST 136 (1980) (establishing that a distributive scheme that is just requires judicial analysis of the process that produced it). *But see* Kahan & Meares, *supra* note 313, at 1161, 1172 (arguing that police departments are accountable to minorities as evidenced by the number of black political leaders and police officers).

[324] ELY, *supra* note 323, at 151.

[325] *See id.* at 170 (arguing there is no danger of constitutional infirmity where a majority has elected to impose a cost upon itself).

[326] *Cf.* Stuntz, *supra* note 160, at 826 (suggesting that law ought to pay attention to criminal law outcomes, not just processes).

low-income minorities for narcotics possession offenses,[327] then so should they be against middle-class offenders who engage in comparable conduct. Not only will this outcome, in and of itself, be consistent with egalitarianism, it will also enhance popular democracy's capacity for producing egalitarian results. If the costs of proactive policing are evenly distributed, one would expect the political process to be a greater source of equality-enhancing pressure upon police departments—i.e., if politically empowered citizens dislike the effects of proactive policing in their communities, they are likely to bring their political power to bear on police departments and, perhaps more importantly, on legislatures to criminalize in a more restrained and circumspect way.[328]

An egalitarian mandate also counsels against making geographic deployment and enforcement priority choices based on highly subjective, impressionistic criteria such as the "disorderliness" of a neighborhood. As discussed above, social science research suggests that race and class stereotypes tend to animate such judgments. Because of its emphasis on disorderliness, policymaking regarding quality-of-life policing is particularly vulnerable to bias.[329] An egalitarian mandate would require police departments to make proactive policing arrests in proportion to the actual rates of offense-specific misconduct in particular places. Requiring police departments to distribute proactive policing arrests in this manner generates operational questions for which I can only give schematic answers at this point.

Courts and prosecutors should guarantee the equitable distribution of proactive policing arrests. Because they have substantial charging discretion, prosecutors exert indirect control over police departments' arrest choices.[330] If prosecutors refused to charge cases that contribute to an unjustifiably non-white conviction rate, for example, that might induce police departments to calibrate their enforcement choices to produce a balanced arrestee demographic. Prosecutorial regulation, however, is an imperfect solution to the police discretion problem. Whether prosecutors are able to use charging decisions to regulate police discretion will turn on the relationships between the police department, prosecutor's office, and the electorate. Because they are typically elected, prosecutors are likely more influenced by popular politics (and, thus, vulnerable to political failure) than police departments. It may be politically unpalatable for a prosecutor to refuse prosecuting substantial numbers of arrests. Therefore, it is unlikely that many prosecutors would, *sua sponte*, regulate departmental discretion in the manner distributive justice suggests.[331]

Courts should play the central role in preventing police discretion from undermining egalitarianism. Although criminal courts are equipped to interrogate exercises of individual officer

---

[327] *See* Dwyer, *supra* note 150.

[328] *Cf.* Illinois v. Lidster, 540 U.S. 419, 426 (2004) (noting police practice that has broad impact is the type that can be challenged through the political process).

[329] *See* Sampson & Raudenbush, *supra* note 167, at 323 (arguing that perceptions of "social disorder" are more a function of race and class assumptions than of actual disorder).

[330] *See* Daniel Richman, *Prosecutors and Their Agents, Agents and Their Prosecutors*, 103 Colum. L. Rev. 749, 778 (2003) (describing the relationship between federal prosecutors and enforcement agents).

[331] *See* Stuntz, *supra* note 160, at 836 (suggesting that prosecutors be made to demonstrate equality in charging decisions).

discretion, interrogating exercises of institutional discretion will entail a host of evidentiary and other practical challenges. Judging whether a police department distributes arrests equally will require delving into police departments' decisionmaking processes. As with any challenge of institutional practice, such litigation could be time-consuming and complex. Criminal defendants would often have an incentive to litigate such claims in cases generated by proactive policing. It may be that permitting such in the context of ordinary criminal prosecutions would impose a substantial burden on criminal courts; however, this would be most true early on. Over time, one would expect that police departments would begin distributing proactive policing arrests equally or develop the capacity for demonstrating how differential arrest rates were tied to differential offense rates.

Another, less compelling, alternative might be to vest the authority to bring such suits in a federal agency. The Department of Justice currently has the power to bring challenges against police departments that engage in systematic and egregious misconduct.[332] An analogous mechanism to regulate arrest disparity might allow for challenging those police departments that have the worst records for arrest disparity.[333] The federal government is much better equipped than individual defense attorneys or defender agencies to gather the data and develop the metrics that will be necessary to evaluate departmental discretion. However, given the Department of Justice's limited use of § 14141 to date, it is hard to imagine the Department using it aggressively to check arrest disparity, even if empowered to do so.

Critics will charge that courts are ill-equipped to balance competing crime-control priorities and therefore should not second-guess police department policymaking. Judicial review of arrest distribution, however, need not amount to wholesale second-guessing of police department policymaking. Equal enforcement is potentially consistent with a wide array of enforcement (and non-enforcement) decisions. Police departments should be free to constructively use their expertise to make those decisions in the manner that best responds to local conditions, provided that the decisionmaking protocol reflects equality concerns. Courts should ensure the legal adequacy of any given protocol and that any given police department is actually adhering to it. There is a rough precedent for such in the Court's checkpoint cases under the Fourth Amendment. Police are free to carry out stops without individualized suspicion at a fixed checkpoint, provided that it is deployed for a permissible purpose and there is a protocol regulating officer conduct at the checkpoint so as to minimize its intrusiveness for motorists.[334] The Court has not specifically enumerated what kinds of purposes are acceptable or, specifically, how officer discretion is to be circumscribed.[335]

---

[332] See 42 U.S.C. § 14141 (2006); see also Stuntz, supra note 160, at 828–30 (arguing that § 14141 creates an important tool for regulating police departments).

[333] See Rachel A. Harmon, *Promoting Civil Rights Through Proactive Policing Reform*, 62 STAN. L. REV. 1 (2009) (arguing that DOJ ought to enforce § 14141 against the worst offenders first).

[334] See Indianapolis v. Edmond, 531 U.S. 32, 47–48 (2000); Mich. Dept. State Police v. Sitz, 496 U.S. 444, 453 (1990) (holding a DUI checkpoint permissible in part because stops were conducted pursuant to department-issued guidelines).

[335] See *Edmond*, 531 U.S. at 44 (leaving it to police departments to use checkpoints for an unspecified range of purposes provided that they are not used for "ordinary crime control"); see also Mills v. District of Columbia, 571 F.3d 1304, 1312

Police departments retain discretion to craft such policy as required by circumstances, provided that it is exercised within the general parameters specified by the Court.[336] An equality mandate would function similarly. Courts would not require that police enforce any specific law in any specific way, but only that whatever proactive policing they elect to do generally comply with an egalitarian arrest mandate.

There are significant informational challenges for regulating arrest disparity. In particular, effective regulation will require developing the capacity for generating three kinds of data: (1) offense rates for particular crimes in particular places, (2) the demographic profile of arrestees by crime and location, and (3) detailed accounts of decisionmaking processes in police departments.[337]

The first category of information presents a challenge in that individuals engaged in criminal activity do not typically offer themselves up for counting. That said, with proper investment, it is possible to develop techniques for estimating offense rates for particular crimes amongst different groups in a city.[338] More than just that, however, it will be important to develop metrics for comparing crime-control exigencies across criminal-law categories. There will be rare instances where police departments enforce against particular crimes while permitting precisely identical conduct in another part of the city. Police departments must often distinguish between offenses that are comparable, but not identical, e.g., crack sales in a park versus ecstasy sales in a club. More difficult yet will be comparisons between different offenses.[339] It may very well be that comparisons between finely distinguished offense definitions is not possible, leaving arrest distribution to be measured in terms of broader categories. Such an approach would recognize that specific manifestations of misconduct might be quite different in one part of a city than from another. However, the categories should not be as broad and impressionistic as "disorderliness."[340] Nor should defining these categories be left entirely to the intuitive judgments of police department policymakers. As discussed above, these judgments should be subject to judicial review.

Departmental discretion receives little attention, in part, because there is little empirical information as to its dimensions and consequences. Pointing to a high minority-arrest rate to substantiate a high offense rate is circular.[341] The vast majority of America's police departments do not systematically assemble data for arrests by race, offense, arresting unit, geography, contraband seized, number of individuals arrested in the course of an operation, and number

---

(D.C. Cir. 2009) (upholding preliminary injunction of a police checkpoint that restricted entry to a Washington, D.C., neighborhood in which numerous assaults and homicides had occurred).

[336] *But see* Jason Fiebig, Comment, *Police Checkpoints: Lack of Guidance from the Supreme Court Contributes to Disregard of Civil Liberties in the District of Columbia*, 100 J. Crim. L. & Criminology 599, 600, 628 (2010) (criticizing the vagueness of Supreme Court cases and arguing that it should review police checkpoints with strict scrutiny).

[337] *See, e.g.,* Stuntz, *supra* note 160, at 834–35 (noting the importance of information collection in the regulation of police).

[338] *See, e.g.,* Beckett et al., *supra* note 168, at 426 (estimating demographic profiles of those engaged in drug selling).

[339] *But see* Wilson, *supra* note 12, at 36 (contending that there is no such thing as like cases in policing).

[340] *See supra* notes 253–258 and accompanying text.

[341] *See supra* notes 137–140 and accompanying text.

of officer hours required for the operation.[342] Such data would not only help illuminate the re-lationship between departmental discretion and the demographic profile of arrestees, but also cast light on proactive policing's efficiency. Without such information, it is impossible to address the discretion problem as a matter of equality or efficiency.

Courts can help with the information gap. Among the great triumphs of the racial profiling litigation in the 1990s and early 2000s has been the number of record-keeping agreements that the settlements have engendered.[343] The information has, in turn, spawned considerable research demonstrating the expense and futility of profiling in the traffic context.[344] As dis-cussed above, DWB is not the best analogy for the problem of institutional discretion. It is, however, a study in the cascading political and social effects of increased information flow. DWB litigation generated settlement agreements that bound police departments to collect and disseminate demographic information for traffic stops. That information has, in turn, helped generate greater public scrutiny of police practices.[345] It is only through litigation, whether over Freedom of Information Act requests or substantive challenges to policy or practice,[346] that academics and advocates will secure access to the kinds of data that might prompt greater transparency and information sharing. Increased information sharing by itself is unlikely to guarantee police departments' democratic accountability, but it would be a good start.

If generating the kind of information described above is impracticable or unduly expensive, it may be that randomization offers a second-best approach to achieving equitable arrest dis-tribution. Bernard Harcourt has persuasively advanced randomization as an antidote to racial profiling and, more generally, to the harmful distributive consequences of actuarial, predictive technique in criminal justice.[347] Randomization entails using a randomized procedure for select-ing targets of criminal enforcement, and Harcourt's examples include random numerical order-ing of highway vehicle stops or random selection of Social Security numbers for tax audits.[348] Randomization is primarily directed at ameliorating prediction's harmful consequences, such as disproportionate stops of minority motorists.[349] It is not explicitly concerned with policing's benefits. Notwithstanding, randomization could be a step in the direction of managing proactive policing's negative distributive consequences.

---

[342] Even when they do, police departments are not eager to divulge such data. *See, e.g.*, State v. Johnson, No. 52123-3-I, 2005 WL 353314, at *1 (Wash. Ct. App. Feb. 14, 2005).

[343] *See supra* note 52 and accompanying text.

[344] *See* HARCOURT, *supra* note 54, at 118–22 (describing various economic model studies of racial profiling).

[345] *See, e.g.*, Dwyer, *supra* note 150; Sam Skolnik, *Drug Arrests Target Blacks Most Often*, SEATTLE POST-INTELLIGENCER, May 15, 2001, at B1.

[346] *See Johnson*, 2005 WL 353314 at *1. *Cf.* Mark Mazzetti & Scott Shane, *Memos Spell Out Brutal C.I.A. Mode of Interrogation*, N.Y. TIMES, April 17, 2009, at A1 (describing the role of ACLU litigation in compelling disclosure of information).

[347] *See* HARCOURT, *supra* note 54, at 238–39 (noting that any person committing a given crime should have the same probability of getting caught).

[348] *Id.* at 238.

[349] *See id.*

The proposal here, of course, breaks dramatically with existing constitutional criminal procedure and equal protection jurisprudence.[350] The Supreme Court has rejected disparate impact as a basis for equal protection claims in most instances,[351] and more generally, it has rejected Ely's vision of the Fourteenth Amendment as a device for correcting political process failure.[352] The Court is also unsympathetic to civil rights claims in which the guilty challenge their convictions.[353] In that vein, the Court is particularly reluctant to entertain selective enforcement claims that question law enforcement discretion.[354] The Court's jurisprudence is symptomatic of guilt's exaggerated moral import in legal and political discussion. That jurisprudence pays no heed to departmental discretion's severe distributive consequences.

Conclusion

This Article has sought to reconceptualize policing in two ways. First, courts and scholars ought to consider police departments as discretion-wielding agents separate and apart from individual officers. Departmental discretion determines how arrests are distributed across a jurisdiction. Geographic deployment, enforcement priority, and enforcement tactics are the key dimensions of departmental discretion in the proactive policing context. Conceptualizing policing in terms of these choices brings the relationship between departmental discretion and egalitarianism into stark relief. That proactive policing generates a dramatically high minority-arrest rate suggests that police departments are not making these choices with sensitivity to equality. Neither courts nor legislatures give departments direction on how to distribute proactive policing arrests. That should change.

Second, distributive justice principles ought to guide the regulation of departmental discretion in the proactive policing context. Distributive justice suggests that police departments should distribute the benefits and burdens associated with proactive policing in a manner that promotes egalitarianism. John Ely's theory of judicial review and courts' already central role in regulating criminal justice counsel in favor of courts guaranteeing the egalitarian distribution of police departments' punitive power.

Over the last forty years, the United States has relied upon criminal law enforcement as opposed to social welfare policies to address the complicated problems that beset America's poorest urban communities.[355] That political and legal fact makes it all the more pressing that

---

[350] *See supra* Part II.B.

[351] *See* Washington v. Davis, 426 U.S. 229, 240 (1976).

[352] *Compare* ELY, *supra* note 323, at 170 (arguing there is no process failure if a majority elects to impose a cost upon itself for the benefit of a minority group), *with* Adarand v. Pena, 515 U.S. 200, 227 (1995) (holding affirmative action programs are to be subjected to strict scrutiny even if the program represents the majority's decision to impose a cost on itself).

[353] *See* Heck v. Humphrey, 512 U.S. 477, 487 (1994) (refusing to permit 42 U.S.C. § 1983 claims that "necessarily imply the invalidity of [a] conviction").

[354] *See, e.g.*, United States v. Armstrong, 517 U.S. 456, 465 (1996); Whren v. United States, 517 U.S. 806, 813 (1996).

[355] *See* WAQUANT, *supra* note 312, at 12, 30–34.

police departments advance crime control in a manner that is equality-enhancing. Distributive justice also lays the groundwork for questioning whether police departments are well-suited for addressing the range of social problems they currently face.[356]

Critical Thinking Questions

1 How do the three dimensions of departmental discretion explain inequality in policing?

2 What is the Supreme Court's current approach to determining whether the Fourth Amendment was violated? How does this approach differ from a distributive justice model?

3 Describe the three dominant theories of criminal punishment and discuss why none of them are appropriate for ensuring that egalitarian principles will guide criminal enforcement decisions.

4 What should the courts' role be in ensuring that police are following a distributive justice model?

Part III Key Points

• Arrests have become a primary measure of effectiveness in policing.
• Policing should consider other variables such as legitimacy perceptions and disparity when measuring effectiveness.
• Law makers and researchers should evaluate departmental policies in addition to individual officer discretion when investigating disparity.
• Implementing procedural and distributive justice models can ensure more equitable treatment and outcomes, which can improve perceptions of police legitimacy.

---

[356] For an interesting approach to the question of policing minor crime in poor neighborhoods, see Eric J. Miller, *Role-Based Policing: Restraining Police Conduct "Outside the Legitimate Investigative Sphere,"* 94 CAL. L. REV. 617, 665 (2006) (arguing for a "role-based" solution to the problem of police legitimacy in minority communities that involves reserving "muscular" policing for responding to calls, while relying on other municipal officials to respond to less serious conduct).

PART IV

POLICE IN A DIVERSE AND DIVIDED SOCIETY

Editors' Introduction

A division between the police and their community is not a new phenomenon. In the 1800s, Sir Robert Peel recognized the importance of the police and community relationship in order for police to serve their mission and for a community to feel safe. In the United States, the 1960s represented turmoil between the police and African American citizens. Today, the relationship between police officers and their communities embodies an uncertain time of trust between both police officers and the citizens they are to protect.

Modern policing requires more from police officers with limited support and resources. Technological advancements can help officers perform their jobs, as well as provide evidence-based policing tactics to work "smarter." Antiterrorism is a necessary element in departments large and small. The human component of these advancements has come at a slower and more complex pace. Body cameras can show a police-citizen interaction that people may not support, even if the officer was within legal limits. New laws create a cultural lag as there is time needed for values and behaviors to change, for both citizens and police officers. Strife between groups, such as police and citizens, may be an artifact of cultural change, causing distrust and conflict among groups.

Trust as a key factor between police and citizens, addressed in part II with young people, continues in part IV. Confidence in a respectful and appropriate interaction between police officers and their community members is of concern today. Possibly influenced by the question of trust in online interactions among all Internet users, and even those who do not use the Internet, can add to the concern and question of trust among all people. Understanding how to create a balanced relationship of respect and professionalism is complex and one that plagues policing today.

Haug and Stockton's brief overview of factors influencing the tension between police and citizens is followed by their suggestions on how to begin rebuilding this needed relationship. Hasisi's article reviews the strains between police and citizens as a worldwide issue influenced by cultural dynamics and politics. Police officers and minority group members have a relationship that can be significantly stressed by cultural variables that are not simply solved with multicultural understandings. Using Ghana as a case study, Boateng discusses where the lines of police-citizen trust have been broken and how a multidimensional approach is the tactic to build and maintain that trust again.

Editors' Introduction: Reading 4.1

The policing principles of Sir Robert Peel from the early 1800s are still relevant today. The police must balance their work with community needs that foster a collaborative relationship. The community plays an intricate role in the success of policing, then and now. Haug and Stockton provide a brief outline of effective strategies police departments could use to foster positive interactions with the community. Tactics must be goal oriented, for the community, and beyond the excuse of limited funds. Police departments must recognize the need to build partnerships with their community while also maintaining the integrity of their work. This is not a simple task to do, but one that is needed today.

Reducing Tensions Between Police and Citizens

Scot Haug and Dale Stockton

Recently, a three-day symposium was held in Las Vegas that explored the challenges faced by law enforcement when implementing camera-based technology in our agencies. A large part of the discussion among the 250 attendees dealt with the situations faced across the country as police and sheriff's departments struggle to effectively engage their communities. Agencies everywhere are scrambling to deal with ever-increasing demand for transparency. There was general consensus that our profession has never had to deal with the widespread level of tension we are seeing today.

Communities rely on the police to provide protection and the police rely on community relationships to solve crimes. Without solid relationships and the cooperation of the community, law enforcement cannot be effective. Check the national news on virtually any evening and you'll usually see the outcome of failed or struggling community-police relationships.

Building and maintaining a positive relationship with the community should be a priority of every police department. The great work the vast majority of police officers do on a daily basis is too often clouded by the unethical conduct of just a few. This is causing a significant divide, resulting in distrust, hatred and, in many cases, outright violence directed at the police.

After 9/11, there was a huge outpouring of support for law enforcement, even in areas far removed from the locations hit by terrorists. There was clearly a sense of respect from the citizens across the nation for those wearing a badge. The actions of a few courageous police officers on that fateful day caused the entire country to view law enforcement in an honorable and positive light. Police officers were recognized for their service and often afforded hero status by their communities.

Fast forward to the present and you can't help but be struck by the dramatic change. Once again, the actions of a few officers have had a huge impact on the way the public views us. Sadly, the sentiment is now often negative and the flames of distrust and uncertainty are being fanned by societal forces outside the control of the police.

In spite of officers often being cleared of wrongdoing, we are left with a public perception that law enforcement should be doing a better job of policing. Accusations of heavy handedness by the police, use of military-like equipment to address protestors, inadequate or delayed dissemination of information, and a seemingly endless stream of alleged police misconduct have left some communities polarized. In many cases, citizens who formerly supported the police now feel that law enforcement can't be trusted and must be continually "watched." That's a large part of the ever-increasing demand for body-worn cameras.

The Foundation

The police cannot be successful if they are not supported by the community. Go back to Sir Robert Peel who outlined the essentials of successful policing. "Police, at all times, should maintain a relationship with the public that gives reality to the historic tradition that the police are the public and the public are the police; the police being only members of the public who are paid to give full-time attention to duties, which are incumbent on every citizen in the interests of community welfare and existence."

While we can agree that technology such as body-worn cameras may soon be commonplace on uniformed officers, no level of technology by itself will fix the underlying problems. There is much more work to be done and additional steps that law enforcement agencies must undertake to restore public confidence.

The good news is that much can be accomplished without a huge commitment of funding or resources, just a genuine commitment to change the traditional policing paradigm. Some of these include improved community outreach efforts, relevant training for police officers, improved internal affairs procedures, mediation with those who file complaints and, most important of all, proactive building of relationships.

Building Relationships

It really is all about relationships. There are countless ways to build relationships, but one of the most effective is by hosting community events. Believe it or not, many community members actually want to interact with the police in a positive way, not just when they are in crisis. And doing this when there is not a crisis can build goodwill that can help carry you through a time when there is a crisis.

Coffee with a Cop programs have proven effective in many communities. Sharing ideas over a cup of coffee (provided by the agency) is a great way to open lines of communication. Businesses like the increased exposure.

Public relations events, particularly law enforcement events, do take a significant amount of careful planning. Any time tax-payer money is involved, a greater amount of scrutiny takes place, and rightfully so. We are entrusted with the best use of those dollars toward public safety.

With funding always a challenge, many agencies have experienced significantly reduced budgets. But that doesn't mean you should give up. There are ways to make it happen and, if you do it right, you'll see a meaningful and tangible return on the investment of your time and effort. Being inventive and creative is key. The following are some ideas that have proven to be effective.

Events don't have to be expensive to be effective. Simply providing a department tour and providing kids with badge stickers can open doors to other efforts.

Holding an open house at a police or fire department is not a new idea, but it's still a great way to start breaking down barriers. These events take on a variety of forms and mostly involve the department's staff opening the doors and allowing the general public the opportunity to look at the facilities, sit in the patrol or specialty vehicles, examine the technologies, and participate in programs like child safety seat checks, bike rodeos, and question and answer forums. These are generally a good time for the public to talk to department personnel and do some of the hands-on and interactive things they like to do.

Adding additional components to the open house can broaden the appeal, so make it a point to be creative and pull out all the stops to truly open your doors. Yes, it can be a challenge when there is an existing disconnect with the community, but it is incumbent on the police to take the high road and to affirmatively take action to open lines of communication.

Finding community volunteers who are willing to serve as police ambassadors can be of great assistance in building this relationship. If you have an existing volunteer or senior patrol effort, this is a great place to start. If you don't, reach out to community leaders who have already shown an interest in police operations and seek their assistance in putting together an event. It's important to include the entire community and this means people of all ages and backgrounds, not just those who are always going to support you.

The key to success is to actively involve the community by having interested participants join in the planned event, such as hosting a car show or an arts-and-crafts display. This type of approach often provides a degree of common ground and fosters two-way communication. Ultimately, you have police and citizens interacting face to face and this is where relationships are established.

The goal is to make it a community event, not just a police department event. This means an opportunity for citizens to actually interact with police staff while enjoying a community function that also includes a variety of police demonstrations or displays. This could be combined with inviting other public safety agencies (like fire or paramedic service) or an adjoining police or sheriff's department if appropriate for the jurisdiction.

Kids are an incredibly important part of building community relationships. After all, if the children are happy, the parents most often are as well. It's important to make a sincere effort to solidify the relationship between children and the police department. Children need to understand that police are not bad; they need to understand that police provide safety and security and provide help when needed. Ideally, police officers should be looked at as people children feel comfortable approaching.

An increasingly popular effort is often referred to as 'Coffee with a Cop.' These events promote community involvement through face-to-face discussions at a local coffee house. The police agency pays for the first cup of coffee, maybe even a doughnut or a bagel. Generally, there is not a specific agenda, just an opportunity to show up and visit with local law enforcement personnel. What better way to build a relationship than over a cup of free coffee! An often realized side benefit is the good will built with small business owners who truly appreciate the additional foot traffic and positive exposure to potential customers.

The success with community events comes at many levels. It's important to have specific goals, a target audience, effective marketing, and little to no tax dollars involved in its production. Above all, it needs to be an event that is clearly for the community yet reflects the philosophy of the police department.

Partnering with a business entity to help kids during the holiday season is always a winner. Programs like Shop with a Cop often result in long-lasting friendships and help kids to see officers in a positive light.

The community should feel comfortable approaching police personnel at any time to help answer questions or resolve problems they may have. The program needs to have full buy-in from the city leaders as well as police staff. Although it takes planning to make it happen, it doesn't have to be a burden. This should be a time everyone looks forward to.

The Role of Social Media

Another great and cost-effective way to build relationships in a community is through the use of social media. Large segments of every community use social media as a way to stay engaged and informed. This is often the most effective way to begin building relationships and for many people, social media is just 'where it's at.' Social media makes it easy to reach out to people, and there is no more effective way to engage thousands of people nearly instantaneously and for very little cost.

More and more law enforcement agencies are turning to social media to bridge the communication gap and provide a communication method that effectively engages the community in its policing efforts. In addition to keeping the public informed about major events, seeking tips and solving criminal cases, there are other unanticipated results of social media use for police. Social media can also provide enhanced transparency and many agencies find that some of their citizens are more comfortable sharing information in this manner.

It's important that citizens feel they have voices. Special events like an open house should provide plenty of time for department staff to be available and listen.

Using social media, police agencies can post information about daily activities they are performing in the community. Social media provides the ability for community members to ask questions and receive timely answers. Social media gives citizens insight to the agency and allows them to see that police are just regular, hardworking people who strive to ensure community safety.

Perhaps one of the most beneficial aspects of using social media is that an agency can control its message. That's in stark contrast to a biased reporter who may have his/her own agenda. It's important to remember that social media needs two-way interaction to be effective. It is a mistake to simply push messages and not actively encourage and engage the responses.

Community outreach efforts need to have a purpose and mission beyond holding an open house. That mission should be to host a community event and interact with the community in a positive and informative manner that actually builds relationships. The police and the community have common goals such as safe neighborhoods, targeting suspicious activities, and apprehending those who would seek to do harm.

Any community event should become an open channel for positive two-way communication between the police department and the community. And make no mistake, these events should not be 'one and done'—they should be part of an ongoing strategy designed to continually build, strengthen, and renew partnerships. It is these partnerships that can carry you through tough times.

Scot Haug is the chief of police in Post Falls, Idaho. Dale Stockton is a retired police captain from Carlsbad, Calif. Both are graduates of the FBI National Academy and have served as advisors and presenters for multiple NIJ and IACP committees. They recently founded Public Safety Insight, LLC, a consulting think tank for public safety. They can be reached at scothaug@gmail.com and dalestockton@gmail.com.

*All Photos Courtesy of Post Falls, Idaho Police Department Photographer Jon Dekeles

Critical Thinking Questions

1   How did Sir Robert Peel define successful policing?

2   Which strategy described in the article do you believe would be most effective for building community-police relationships? Why?

3   Discuss the role of social media in cases where police officers are cleared of wrongdoings, though citizen perceptions differ from the outcome.

4   What do you consider to be successful strategies for community involvement in police outreach events?

Editors' Introduction: Reading 4.2

Exploring the nature of police relations with various minority groups is complex and integrated within the social fabric of the community. Research in this area use numerous variables to study the correlations, interactions, and significant effects of police-minority relations. Hasisi adds to this literature by finding that a missing component in minority groups' perceptions of the police happens when minority groups are assumed to be homogeneous. The Arab group in this study varied in perceptions depending on their political and cultural differences. The need for power in statistical techniques is used to justify categorizing minority groups together, in most police-minority studies. This article suggests missing links may be present that have yet to be uncovered in understanding this relationship by assuming homogeneous groups.

Police, Politics, and Culture in a Deeply Divided Society

Badi Hasisi

Introduction

A review of the academic literature in the field of police-minority relations in deeply divided societies reveals that tense relations between the minority and the police are a frequent phenomenon. One of the sources of this tension is the political and social marginality of the minority, which is most often accompanied by unbalanced and unfair policing.[1] Researchers emphasize the centrality of the political variable in understanding police-minority interactions in deeply divided societies. In fact, often hovering above deeply divided democratic societies is the question of the legitimacy of the political regime in the eyes of the minority group.

The tense relations between the Arab minority in Israel and the police are common knowledge. Throughout the history of Arab-Jewish relations in Israel, this tension was sharply brought into relief in several mass political events, with the most violent example in October 2000. Prime Minister Ariel Sharon paid a visit to the Temple Mount in Jerusalem, an act perceived by the Arab minority as violating the sanctity of the Al-Aksa Mosque. The visit incited eight days of violent riots that ended with twelve Arab citizens dead, all of them by police gunfire. This event emphasized the influence of political variables on minority relations with the police in Israel, and yet this is not the sole variable on which we should focus.

---

[1] *See* JOHN D. BREWER, BLACK AND BLUE: POLICING IN SOUTH AFRICA (1994) [hereinafter BREWER, BLACK AND BLUE]; RONALD WEITZER, POLICING UNDER FIRE: ETHNIC CONFLICT AND POLICE-COMMUNITY RELATIONS IN NORTHERN IRELAND (1995) [hereinafter WEITZER, POLICING UNDER FIRE]; RONALD WEITZER, TRANSFORMING SETTLER STATES: COMMUNAL CONFLICT AND INTERNAL SECURITY IN NORTHERN IRELAND AND ZIMBABWE (1990) [hereinafter WEITZER, TRANSFORMING SETTLER STATES]; John D. Brewer, *Policing in Divided Societies: Theorizing a Type of Policing,* 1 POLICING & SOC'Y 179 (1991).

Badi Hasisi, "Police, Politics, and Culture in a Deeply Divided Society," *Journal of Criminal Law & Criminology*, vol. 98, no. 3, pp. 1120–1145. Copyright © 2008 by Northwestern University School of Law. Reprinted with permission. Provided by ProQuest LLC. All rights reserved.

In deeply divided societies where divisions are also based on different ethnicities, emphasis is put on the cultural distinction between the majority and the minority. This distinction is liable to find its expression in the cultural perception of governmental institutions, including the police. The impact of cultural pluralism on police-minority relations is reinforced due to the under-representation of members of the minority in the police force. The combination of these factors exacerbates the cultural disparity between the service-providers—police officers who belong to the majority group—and service-users—members of the minority group. We can assume that where there is greater cultural disparity between the majority and minority, there will be greater tension in minority-police relations. The Israeli-Arab minority is a native, traditional minority that differs significantly in culture from the Jewish majority, who are culturally Western-oriented. This cultural distinction, and not just political variables, will be reflected in minority attitudes toward the police.

This Article aims to evaluate the impact of political and cultural variables on minority perceptions of the police in deeply divided societies. First, I will try to illustrate the distinction between political and cultural variables and explain how making this distinction facilitates a better understanding of police-minority relations in deeply divided societies. Then I will compare the attitudes of Israeli Arabs and Jews toward the police and turn to the core of this Article: an in-depth analysis of the attitudes of different Arab sub-groups (Muslims, Christians, and Druze) toward the Israeli police. In so doing, I wish to elaborate upon the cultural explanations for the existing tension, along with the more obvious political reasons.

Politics versus Culture

When analyzing police-minority relations, the line between political and cultural variables can become quite vague. Nevertheless, I will try to argue that there is an analytical distinction between the two variables that has significant ramifications on police-minority relations. The political aspect in police-minority relations becomes manifest when we ask the following questions: How do minority groups perceive the role of the police in the construction of the (controversial) socio-political order? What is the image of the police in society? What do the police represent among minority groups? Are the police there "to protect and to serve" or "to chase after and repress"? What styles of policing are practiced toward minority groups? Is it "high" or "low" policing?

Criminological and sociological scholars have tried to answer these questions by addressing the socio-political variables that characterize several minority groups. Many studies have pointed to the tense relations that often exist between police and minorities in various societies. There is evidence of high rates of minority arrest and incarceration, high rates of police violence toward minorities, and negative attitudes among minorities toward the police.[2] Furthermore,

---

[2] *See, e.g.,* David H. Bayley & Harold Mendelsohn, Minorities and the Police: Confrontation in America (1969); Robert Blauner, Racial Oppression in America (1972); Randall Kennedy, Race, Crime, and the Law (1997); Austin T. Turk, Criminality and Legal Order

stereotypical images of minorities are prevalent among police officers. Most commonly, police view minority members as a potential criminal threat.[3]

Research also shows high rates of crime among minorities. These crime rates are influenced by various social factors associated with minority status.[4] For example, evidence shows overrepresentation of broken families, high rates of divorce, high residential density, low economic status, high levels of unemployment, and high adolescent drop-out rates. These variables increase social disorganization and affect crime rates. In addition, minority populations tend to be younger and more likely to be visible in the streets.[5] All of these factors create a supportive environment for the development of criminal behavior and, in turn, increase the contact between minorities and the police. Police officers face many obstacles in policing underclass minority neighborhoods because criminals and innocent citizens may share the same socio-economic characteristics.[6] This, in turn, increases complaints from minority groups regarding racial profiling by the police.[7]

Research shows that a tense and alienated relationship between police and the minority community strongly discourages police officers from enforcing criminal laws while also dissuading minorities from collaborating with police to prevent and report crime.[8] The primary complaint of minority groups is that they are simultaneously over-policed as suspects and under-policed as victims, which has reduced their confidence in and willingness to collaborate with the police.[9]

(1969); SAMUEL WALKER, THE POLICE IN AMERICA: AN INTRODUCTION (3d ed. 1999); Scott H. Decker, *Citizen Attitudes Toward the Police: A Review of Past Findings and Suggestions for Future Policy,* 9 J. POLICE SCI. & ADMIN. 80 (1981); Joe R. Feagin, *The Continuing Significance of Race: Antiblack Discrimination in Public Places,* 56 AM. SOC. REV. 101 (1991); Simon Holdaway, *Police Race Relations in England and Wales: Theory, Policy, and Practice,* 7 POLICE & SOC'Y 49 (2003); David Jacobs & Ronald Helms, *Collective Outbursts, Politics, and Punitive Resources: Toward a Political Sociology of Spending on Social Control,* 77 SOC. FORCES 1497 (1999); Michael D. Reisig & Roger B. Parks, *Experience, Quality of Life, and Neighborhood Context: A Hierarchical Analysis of Satisfaction with Police,* 17 JUST. Q. 607 (2000); Tom R. Tyler, *Policing in Black and White: Ethnic Group Differences in Trust and Confidence in the Police,* 8 POLICE Q. 322 (2005); Ronald Weitzer & Steven A. Tuch, *Race and Perceptions of Police Misconduct,* 51 SOC. PROBS. 305 (2004).

[3] *E.g.,* HUBERT M. BLALOCK, JR., TOWARD A THEORY OF MINORITY-GROUP RELATIONS (1967); PAMELA IRVING JACKSON, MINORITY GROUP THREAT, CRIME, AND POLICING: SOCIAL CONTEXT AND SOCIAL CONTROL (1989); Lawrence Bobo & Vincent L. Hutchings, *Perceptions of Racial Group Competition: Extending Blumers Theory of Group Position to a Multiracial Social Context,* 61 AM. SOC. REV. 951 (1996); Feagin, *supra* note 2; Malcolm D. Holmes, *Minority Threat and Police Brutality: Determinants of Civil Rights Criminal Complaints in U.S. Municipalities,* 38 CRIMINOLOGY 343 (2000); Karen F. Parker et ah, *Racial Threat, Concentrated Disadvantage and Social Control: Considering the Macro-Level Sources of Variation in Arrests,* 43 CRIMINOLOGY 1111 (2005); Lincoln Quillian & Devah Pager, *Black Neighbors, Higher Crime? The Role of Racial Stereotypes in Evaluations of Neighborhood Crime,* 107 AM. J. SOC. 717 (2001).

[4] *See, e.g.,* CLIFFORD R. SHAW & HENRY D. MCKAY, JUVENILE DELINQUENCY AND URBAN AREAS: A STUDY OF RATES OF DELINQUENTS IN RELATION TO DIFFERENTIAL CHARACTERISTICS OF LOCAL COMMUNITIES IN AMERICAN CITIES (1942).

[5] *E.g.,* Richard Block, *Community, Environment, and Violent Crime,* 17 CRIMINOLOGY 46 (1979); Robert J. Sampson & W. Byron Groves, *Community Structure and Crime: Testing Social-Disorganization Theory,* 94 AM. J. SOC. 774 (1989).

[6] *See* Rodney Stark, *Deviant Places: A Theory of the Ecology of Crime,* 25 CRIMINOLOGY 893 (1987).

[7] RONALD WEITZER & STEVEN A. TUCH, RACE AND POLICING IN AMERICA: CONFLICT AND REFORM (2006); BRIAN L. WITHROW, RACIAL PROFILING: FROM RHETORIC TO REASON (2006).

[8] *E.g.,* HUNG-EN SUNG, THE FRAGMENTATION OF POLICING IN AMERICAN CITIES: TOWARD AN ECOLOGICAL THEORY OF POLICE-CITIZEN RELATIONS (2002).

[9] *See* BENJAMIN BOWLING, VIOLENT RACISM: VICTIMIZATION, POLICING AND SOCIAL CONTEXT (1998); Harry Blagg & Giulietta Valuri, *Aboriginal Community Patrols in Australia: Self-Policing, Self-Determination and Security,* 14 POLICING & SOC'Y 313 (2004).

The political explanation of police-minority relations is quite common in many researches; nevertheless, it lacks any reference to the impact of societal-cultural diversity on minority interactions and perceptions of the police. The cultural explanation of police-minority relations focuses on the impact of police organizational culture and how it affects interactions with minority groups. The pertinent questions are: How does the cultural context of police activity interact with the cultural pluralism of some minority groups? How do the cultural characteristics of the minority groups affect their perceptions of police organizational knowledge? To what extent are police officers aware of the various cultural characteristics of the different communities in society?

The cultural approach focuses on the interaction between the formal rules of the police and the sub-cultural values of minority groups. Some of the disparities between the majority and the minority are not merely political, but can also be attributed to cultural differences, such as language, religion, customs, family structure, informal social control, moral perceptions, and gender relations. Some cultural minorities act according to their own cultural norms and consequently may be accused of committing crimes because the legal culture of the state reflects the views of the dominant group. Examples of such cases include bigamy, family honor, murder, spousal and child abuse, parent-child suicide, acts of blood revenge, and celebratory shooting. It is reasonable to expect that the interactions of the minority with the police will reflect these cultural differences.

Some studies have claimed that the police generally represent and act in accordance with the culture of the dominant group, and this is further emphasized by the under-representation of minority members in the police force.[10] As a result, some actions taken by the police might be viewed as culturally inappropriate by traditional communities. Standard police procedure among the majority group may create unpredictable reactions in the minority community due to cultural differences.

Police-Minority Relations in a Deeply Divided Society

There is no better case that draws attention to the dominance of the political explanation in police-minority relations than the example of deeply divided societies.[11] These are societies

---

[10] Edna Erez et al., Introduction: Policing a Multicultural Society, 7 Police & Soc'y (Special Issue) 5 (2003); Lorraine Mazerolle et al., Policing the Plight of Indigenous Australians: Past Conflicts and Present Challenges, 7 Police & Soc'y (Special Issue) 77 (2003).

[11] See, e.g., Mike Brogden & Clifford Shearing, Policing for a New South Africa (1993); Donatella Della Porta, Social Movements, Political Violence, and the State: A Comparative Analysis of Italy and Germany (1995); John McGarry & Brendan O'Leary, Policing Northern Ireland: Proposals for a New Start (1999); Richard Mapstone, Policing in a Divided Society: A Study of Part Time Policing in Northern Ireland (1994); Weitzer, Policing Under Fire, supra note 1; John Whyte, Interpreting Northern Ireland (1990); Graham Ellison & Greg Martin, Policing, Collective Action and Social Movement Theory: The Case of Northern Ireland Civil Rights Campaign, 51 Brit. J. Soc. 681 (2000).

divided along ethnic lines where the state traditionally is affiliated with the dominant group.[12] Examples of these societies include Northern Ireland until 1969, Israel, Georgia, Estonia, and Latvia.[13] The minority perceives the state as non-neutral, and this view, as a result, decreases the legitimacy of the government and police in the eyes of the minority. The minority's perception of the police is not only influenced by police actions, but also by what the police represent to the people.[14] Such perceived illegitimacy produces a threat to internal security, and the bulk of the state's policing resources are therefore consigned to the management of political offenses.[15] This pattern affects the nature of police activities in deeply divided societies so that when policing public events, for example, the police generally practice a "zero tolerance" policy toward minority group protesters and regard their actions as political subversion against the state.[16]

At the same time, the policing of non-political crimes among the minority is typically less effective. This is due to police neglect of incidents that occur in the minority community, particularly when the crime bears no threat to the dominant group.[17] Weak police performance in the minority community is also attributable to the minority group's lack of cooperation with the police. The literature shows that the main reason that minority groups in deeply divided societies tend to avoid cooperation with the police is due to political disagreements between majority and minority communities.[18]

Ronald Weitzer, a sociologist at George Washington University, has developed a comprehensive model of the policing of deeply divided societies based on his research in Northern Ireland and Zimbabwe.[19] Weitzer's model describes police policies or practices as institutionally biased against members of the subordinate minority group. There is chronic over-representation of the dominant ethnic group in the police force, especially in the top ranks. The police tend to repress the regime's opponents, holding dual responsibility for ordinary crime control and homeland

---

[12] For more research on deeply divided societies, see AREND LIJPHART, PATTERNS OF DEMOCRACY: GOVERNMENT FORMS AND PERFORMANCE IN THIRTY-SIX COUNTRIES (1999); Sammy Smooha & Theodor Hanf, *The Diverse Modes of Conflict-Regulation in Deeply Divided Societies*, 33 INT'L J. COMP. SOC. 26 (1992); Pierre L. Van Den Bereghe, *Multicultural Democracy: Can It Work?*, 8 NATIONS & NATIONALISM 433 (2002).

[13] For further elaboration, see THE FATE OF ETHNIC DEMOCRACY IN POST-COMMUNIST EUROPE (Sammy Smooha & Priit Järve eds., 2005) (discussing "ethnic democracy").

[14] WEITZER, POLICING UNDER FIRE, *supra* note 1.

[15] GRAHAM ELLISON & JIM SMYTH, THE CROWNED HARP: POLICING NORTHERN IRELAND (2000); AOGAN MULCAHY, POLICING NORTHERN IRELAND: CONFLICT, LEGITIMACY AND REFORM (2006); WEITZER, POLICING UNDER FIRE, *supra* note 1; Andrew Goldsmith, *Policing Weak States: Citizen Safety and State Responsibility*, 13 POLICING & SOC'Y 3 (2003).

[16] DELLA PORTA, *supra* note 11; MERCEDES S. HINTON, THE STATE ON THE STREETS: POLICE AND POLITICS IN ARGENTINA AND BRAZIL (2006); P. A. J. WADDINGTON, LIBERTY AND ORDER: PUBLIC ORDER POLICING IN A CAPITAL CITY (1994); Vince Boudreau, *Precarious Regimes and Matchup Problems in the Explanation of Repressive Policy, in* REPRESSION AND MOBILIZATION 33 (Christian Davenport et al. eds., 2005); Ellison & Martin, *supra* note 11.

[17] *See* BLALOCK, *supra* note 3; BOWLING, *supra* note 9; JACKSON, *supra* note 3; Feagin, *supra* note 2; Holmes, *supra* note 3; Stephanie L. Kent & David Jacobs, *Minority Threat and Police Strength from 1980 to 2000: A Fixed-Effects Analysis of Nonlinear and Interactive Effects in Large U.S. Cities*, 43 CRIMINOLOGY 731 (2005); Gustavo S. Mesch & Ilan Talmud, *The Influence of Community Characteristics on Police Performance in a Deeply Divided Society: The Case of Israel*, 31 SOC. FOCUS 233 (1998).

[18] *See* MCGARRY & O'LEARY, *supra* note 11; MULCAHY, *supra* note 15; WEITZER, POLICING UNDER FIRE, *supra* note 1; WEITZER, TRANSFORMING SETTLER STATES, *supra* note 1.

[19] WEITZER, POLICING UNDER FIRE, *supra* note 1.

security. In the absence of effective mechanisms of accountability, the police in these countries also enjoy legal systems that provide them with great latitude in their ability to control the minority population, including with respect to the use of force.[20]

The Weitzer model addresses very important political dimensions in police-minority relations in deeply divided societies, but lacks any reference to the cultural explanation. The reason might be that when Weitzer developed the model, he focused his analysis on Northern Ireland. There are few cultural dissimilarities between the Protestant majority and the Catholic minority in this country that might influence the relationship with the police. In contrast, in Israel there are marked cultural distinctions between the Arab native minority and the Jewish majority that might affect relations with the police. Arabs are part of a Mediterranean, Islamic-Arabic culture, while Jewish culture is often more Western-oriented. These differences are manifested in various cultural expressions, including languages (Hebrew versus Arabic), religion (Jewish versus Muslim, Christian, and Druze), family structure (nuclear family versus extended family), residential patterns (urban versus rural or patrilocal),[21] interrelations among the extended family (weak versus strong), the role of the clan as an informal social control institution (among Arabs), gender relations and segregation, and leisure patterns.

Arab society is still largely governed by traditional social structures and has not undergone radical urbanization, with a significant percentage of Arabs living in rural villages.[22] Communities have preserved informal mechanisms of social control.[23] The Arab society in Israel exhibits some of the characteristics of a stateless society, especially with regard to the culture of lawlessness (toward some Israeli laws) and community self-policing.[24] The stateless characteristics of the Arab minority intensify as a result of the social and geographical segregation of Arabs and Jews in Israel.[25] These cultural characteristics are prevalent enough to influence the relations between the minority and the police.

The cultural variable in police-minority relations is not applicable solely to deeply divided societies. It is relevant also to several Western immigrant societies — including the United States, Canada, New Zealand, and Australia — where native minorities still live in segregated communities and hold different cultural codes from the white majority, especially in terms of traditionally informal social control.[26] This makes police work a very complex task in these communities.

---

[20] BREWER, BLACK AND BLUE, *supra* note 1; WEITZER, POLICING UNDER FIRE, *supra* note 1.

[21] A patrilocal residence is one in which the family unit lives near the male relations. The concept of location may extend to a larger area such as a village, town, or clan area.

[22] Majid al-Haj, *Ethnic Relations in an Arab Town in Israel, in* STUDIES IN ISRAELI ETHNICITY: AFTER THE INGATHERING (Alex Weingrod ed., 1985).

[23] JOSEPH GINAT, BLOOD REVENGE: FAMILY HONOR, MEDIATION AND OUTCASTING (1997); BRYNJAR LIA, A POLICE FORCE WITHOUT A STATE: A HISTORY OF THE PALESTINIAN SECURITY FORCES IN THE WEST BANK AND GAZA (2006); Manar Hasan, *The Politics of Honor: Patriarchy, the State and the Murder of Women in the Name of Family Honor,* 21 J. ISRAELI HIST. 1 (2002).

[24] *See* STANLEY COHEN, INT'L CENTRE FOR PEACE IN THE MIDDLE EAST, CRIME, LAW, AND SOCIAL CONTROL AMONG THE ARABS IN ISRAEL (1990); LIA, *supra* note 23; Ginat, *supra* note 23.

[25] *See* Smooha & Hanf, *supra* note 12; Ghazi Falah, *Living Together Apart: Residential Segregation in Mixed Arab-Jewish Cities in Israel,* 33 URB. STUD. 23 (1996).

[26] *See* DENNIS P. FORCESE, POLICING CANADIAN SOCIETY (1992); Jhama Chatteijee & Liz Elliott, *Restorative Policing in Canada: The Royal Canadian Mounted Police, Community Justice Forums, and the Youth Criminal Justice Act,* 4 POLICE PRAC. & RES. 347

Furthermore, several Western countries host immigrants from non-Western cultures, and some of these immigrant groups have maintained cultural codes from their homelands, even creating a Diaspora in their host countries.[27] The immigrants are generally unfamiliar with the culture of the host country, and their vulnerability may make them targets for abuse by criminals in the community.[28] These immigrants may in fact hesitate to contact the police since many come from countries or cultures that had poor relationships with the police.[29] To sum up, in the case of native and immigrant minorities, the political variable is quite important when analyzing police-minority relations. However, we miss a significant part of the picture by ignoring the impact of cultural differences on the majority and the minority and how these differences may affect the minority's perceptions of the police.

Arabs in Israel: Between Political Threat and Cultural Estrangement

Arabs inside Israel's "Green Line" constitute about 17% of Israel's population, or 1.1 million people.[30] They are a native minority and part of the Palestinian nation. For more than 100 years, the Palestinian people have been engaged in a violent and ongoing national conflict with the Jewish national movement and, at a later stage, with the State of Israel. Immediately upon its establishment following the war in 1948, the State of Israel endorsed full, formal citizenship for members of the Arab minority who continued to reside in Israel. The national Palestinian identity of the Arab minority transformed them, in the eyes of the Jewish majority, into a group that was affiliated with the enemy and which possessed "dual loyalty." The solution to this threat

---

(2003); Mazerolle et at, *supra* note 10.

[27] Wing Hong Chui & Lai-Kwan Regin Ip, *Policing in a Multicultural Society: A Queensland Case Study,* 6 POLICE PRAC. & RES. 279 (2005); Eric D. Poole & Mark R. Pogrebin, *Crime and Law Enforcement in the Korean American Community,* 13 POLICE STUD. INT'L REV. POLICE DEV. 57 (1990).

[28] IMMIGRATION AND CRIME: RACE, ETHNICITY, AND VIOLENCE (Ramiro Martinez, Jr., & Abel Valenzuela, Jr., eds., 2006); Stephen Egharevba, *African Immigrants' Perception of Police in Finland: Is It Based on the Discourse of Race or Culture?,* 34 INT'L J. SOC. L. 42 (2006); Lars Holmberg & Britta Kyvsgaard, *Are Immigrants and Their Descendants Discriminated Against in the Danish Criminal Justice System?,* 4 J. SCANDINAVIAN STUD. CRIMINOLOGY & CRIME PREVENTION 125 (2003); David J. Smith, *Ethnic Origins, Crime, and Criminal Justice in England and Wales, in* ETHNICITY, CRIME, AND IMMIGRATION: COMPARATIVE AND CROSS-NATIONAL PERSPECTIVES 101 (Michael H. Tonryed., 1997).

[29] Robert C. Davis et al., *Immigrants and the Criminal Justice System: An Exploratory Study,* 13 VIOLENCE & VICTIMS 21 (1998); Robert C. Davis & Nicole J. Henderson, *Willingness to Report Crimes: The Role of Ethnic Group Membership and Community Efficacy,* 49 CRIME & DELINQ. 564 (2003); Cecilia Menjivar & Cynthia L. Bejarano, *Latino Immigrants' Perceptions of Crime and Police Authorities in the United States: A Case Study from the Phoenix Metropolitan Area,* 27 ETHNIC & RACIAL STUD. 120 (2004).

[30] The so-called Green Line is the 1949 Armistice line established following the war of 1948; later it became known as the pre-1967 border in order to demarcate the Arab territories occupied following the 1967 War (the West Bank, Gaza strip, East Jerusalem, and the Golan Heights), My use of the term the "Arabs in Israel" excludes the Palestinians in East Jerusalem and the Druze in the Golan Heights. If we chose to include these groups, then the Arabs in Israel would constitute about 19.9% (1.43 million) of the State of Israel's population. CENT. BUREAU OF STATISTICS, ANNUAL POPULATION REPORT, 2003 (2006).

was to enforce military rule on the minority community from 1948 to 1966. Though military rule has ended, it has not reduced the high threat perception currently held by the Jewish majority toward the Arab minority. A recent survey has shown that a majority of Israeli Jews (67%) believe that the Arab community's high birthrate endangers the state; that Arabs are intent on changing the state's Jewish character (72%); that Arabs might assist enemies of the state (78%); and that Arabs might launch a popular revolt (72%). It also showed that a majority of Israeli Jews (84%) fear Arabs because of their support of the Palestinian people and believe that most Israeli Arabs would be more loyal to a Palestinian state than to Israel (66%).[31]

The majority of the Israeli-Arab population lives in three geographic areas: the Galilee, the Triangle, and the Negev—areas at the periphery (and frontier) of Israeli society. Although there is an urban middle-class sector, a large number of Arabs live in rural towns and villages and continue to abide by traditional forms of social organization. In fact, 90% of Israeli Arabs live in small towns populated by Arabs exclusively. Only eight cities are ethnically mixed, and these are extremely segregated residentially.[32] Such segregation is accepted by many Israelis; only a minority of Jews or Arabs express willingness to live in a mixed neighborhood.[33]

The Arab minority is not a single homogenous group, but rather is characterized by an inner diversity that affects its relationship with the police. One of the features of this diversity is the religious-ethnic divide among Muslims, Christians, Druze, and Bedouins.[34] Ethnic distinctions among Arabs in Israel are institutionalized; for example, the State of Israel recognizes religious-ethnic divides and finances separate institutions for each of the Arab religious-ethnic groups. The sub-ethnic distinctions of the Arab minority are not limited solely to the religious aspect, but are also manifested in the political attitudes and behaviors of the various Arab groups.

Druze have a basic difference from Muslims and Christians in their relations with the State of Israel.[35] The Druze are an Arab ethnic group culturally. However, the Druze peoples' political identification with Palestinian national motifs is very weak, and thus they are perceived as less threatening by the Israeli state.[36] Members of the Druze group share similar political orientations with the Jewish majority and are in fact drafted into the Israeli armed forces and the police.[37]

---

[31] Sammy Smooha, Index of Arab-Jewish Relations in Israel (2004).

[32] Falah, *supra* note 25.

[33] Sammy Smooha, *The Arab Minority in Israel: Radicalization or Politicization?*, in Israel: State and Society, 1948–1988: Studies in Contemporary Jewry (Peter Y. Medding ed., 1989); *see also* Smooha & Hanf, *supra* note 12.

[34] According to the Israeli Central Bureau of Statistics, the ethnic distribution of the Arab population is as follows: a majority (65%) are non-Bedouin Muslims, 9% are Christians, 9% are Druze, and 17% are Bedouins. The majority of the Bedouins reside in the southern police district, while the majority of Druze and Christians reside in the Northern District. Central Bureau of Statistics, *supra* note 30.

[35] The Druze are a religious community, considered to be an offshoot of the Ismaili Islam, found primarily in Lebanon, Israel, and Syria. In Israel, the Druze are the only Arabs who are allowed to fight for the Israel Defense Forces, and many of them serve in the Israeli police.

[36] Sammy Smooha, *Part of the Problem and Part of the Solution: National Security and the Arab Minority*, in National Security and Democracy in Israel 81 (Y. Avner ed., 1993).

[37] Hillel Frisch, *The Druze Minority in the Israeli Military: Traditionalizing an Ethnic Policing Role*, 20 Armed Forces & Soc. 53 (1993).

In light of this, we may expect that compared to other Arab sub-groups, the Druze will express relatively more positive attitudes toward the police.

Although the Druze share similar political orientations with the Jewish majority, they still preserve the traditional ways of life in their segregated communities, customs that are very similar to those of the Muslim Arabs. This is quite salient in their patterns of patrilocal residence, the centrality of the extended family as an informal social control mechanism, and their maintenance of social separation between the genders. These characteristics indicate that the Druze politically identify with the Jews, but culturally identify with the Muslim Arabs. In recent years, few clashes between the police and the Druze have erupted, and these mostly have stemmed from the difference between the modern and traditional cultures. In October 2007, a violent clash took place between the police and the Druze citizens of a small northern village called Pki'in. Several Druze vigilantes from the community burned some new cellular antennas that were installed in the village. The people of the village believed that the cellular antennas were responsible for the increase in cancer rates in their community. More than 200 police officers sent to arrest the vigilantes were met with harsh community resistance. The police used live ammunition and many citizens and police officers were wounded. Some of the wounded police officers were Druze. This incident emphasizes the traditional structure of Druze society in Israel and its potential conflict with law enforcement.

When addressing the population of the Christian Arabs, we face the same complexity. Because they identify strongly with the Palestinian national identity and share the Muslim Arabs' political orientation, one might assume the Christian Arabs' attitudes toward the police to be more negative. However, the lifestyle of most Christian Arabs is more Western-oriented, similar to that of the Jewish population. In addition, this community is largely urban, better situated economically, and in consequence highly represented in the Israeli-Arab elite class.[38] The birthrate is significantly low among Christian Arabs; it is even lower than the rate among Jews and significantly differs from that of Muslims and Druze. The practice of naming children to reflect a European-Christian heritage and the use of foreign languages in daily speech are culturally Western characteristics of the Christian Arabs. Furthermore, Christian Arabs occupy a higher class position compared to the rest of the Arab subgroups, especially in terms of educational attainment and income.[39] Accordingly, we may conclude that the Christian Arabs are politically very close to the Muslim Arabs but culturally different from them, and from the Druze. Consequently, they still view themselves as a distinct cultural-religious minority among Arabs in Israel.[40]

I have several research hypotheses for this study. I expect that the political and cultural differences within the Arab minority will create a complex picture of their perceptions toward the police. For example, I expect that the Druze will express positive attitudes toward the

---

[38] Amalia Sa'ar, *Carefully on the Margins: Christian Palestinians in Haifa Between Nation and State,* 25 Am. Ethnologist 215, 215–16 (1998).

[39] V. Kraus & Y. Yonay, *The Power and Limits of Ethnonationalism: Palestinians and Eastern Jews in Israel, 1974–1991,* 51 Brit. J. Soc'y 550 (2000). The Christian schools in Israel have a reputation as elite schools and of offering a better quality of education than public Arab schools. Sa'ar, *supra* note 38, at 217–18.

[40] Sa'ar, *supra* note 38, at 231.

police in the political context. At the same time, I suspect that they will share similar (negative) attitudes to those of Muslim Arabs when community cultural codes are threatened by police practices. I also expect that Christian Arabs, similarly to Muslim Arabs, will express negative attitudes toward the police in the political context, but at the same time, they will be more likely than Muslim and Druze to contact the police for assistance due to their class position and Westernized cultural orientation.

Arab-Police Relations in Israel

The Or Commission—formed to investigate the violent clashes between the police (and the Border Police)[41] and the Israeli Arab minority in October of 2000—has noted that many Arabs do not believe that the police serve the Arab population, but are instead the "long arm" of a regime designed to control and suppress Arab political activities. At the same time, many police officers view Arabs as disloyal citizens. The police are inconsistent in enforcing ordinary criminal laws in Arab communities, a practice that leads to a degree of unchecked crime within minority communities.[42]

There is minimal research on police-minority relations in Israel, most of which emphasizes the negative attitudes of Israeli Arabs toward the police.[43] In one poll, only 53% of Israeli Arabs felt that they should obey the police, compared to 85% of Jews.[44] Surveys conducted between 2000 and 2002 show that Arab respondents express negative attitudes toward the police.[45] In the 2001 poll, approximately 70% of Arabs thought that the police force was not egalitarian in its attitude toward all citizens of Israel, while only 35% of Jews agreed. The violent clashes between the police and Arab citizens in the October 2000 mass events significantly influenced this disparity in views. Still, even by the time of the 2002 poll, a significant majority of Arab respondents (62%) maintained their belief that the police are not egalitarian toward all citizens of Israel.

Taking into consideration the political and cultural diversity among Israeli Arabs (Muslim, Christian, and Druze), it is surprising that we could not find even one researcher who addressed

---

[41] The Border Police was established in 1953 with the main function of preventing terrorist sabotage activities and the infiltration of Palestinians from neighboring Arab countries. COHEN, *supra* note 24. Over the years, this unit has become semi-militaristic and has come to deal mostly with public order policing. Arab protest in Israel has a traumatic and violent history of encounters with the Border Police. Furthermore, the Border Police is very active in the Palestinian territories, especially in policing terrorism, patrolling, and public order policing. These activities have given it a very negative reputation among Arabs in Israel. *See* Badi Hasisi & Ronald Weitzer, *Police Relations with Arabs and Jews in Israel*, 47 BRIT. J. CRIMINOLOGY 728 (2007).

[42] OR COMM'N, REPORT OF THE STATE COMMISSION OF INQUIRY TO INVESTIGATE THE CLASHES BETWEEN THE SECURITY FORCES AND ISRAELI CITIZENS IN OCTOBER 2000 (2003).

[43] Hasisi & Weitzer, *supra* note 41, at 740–42 (2007); Arye Rattner, *The Margins of Justice: Attitudes Towards the Law and the Legal System Among Jews and Arabs in Israel*, 4 INT'L J. PUB. OPINION RES. 358 (1994); David Weisburd et al., *Community Policing in Israel: Resistance and Change*, 25 POLICING 80 (2002).

[44] IRA CAHANMAN & TAMAR TZEMACH, ISRAELI POLICE IN THE EYE OF THE PUBLIC: ATTITUDES ON SELECTED ISSUES (1991).

[45] ARYE RATTNER & DANA YAGIL, THE CULTURE OF LAW: THE CRIMINAL JUSTICE SYSTEM IN THE EYE OF THE ISRAELI SOCIETY (2002).

the impact of this diversity on the attitudes of Arab minority sub-groups toward the police. The current research is therefore quite original.

Data and Methodology

Data for this study come from a telephone survey which was conducted over a period of two weeks in March 2003 among adult Arabs and Jews over the age of eighteen residing in the Israeli police force's Northern District. The Northern District ranges from the Hadera Valley (Wadi Ara) to the Lebanese border. The majority (70%) of the Israeli-Arab population lives in the Northern District, typically in communities that are highly segregated from the Jewish population.

Data were collected from a representative telephone sample drawn from locales in the Northern District with more than 1,000 residents. The sample included 255 Jewish and 471 Arab respondents. The 471 Arab respondents included 328 Muslim, 77 Christian, and 66 Druze Arabs.[46] Cluster sampling was used to ensure that each group was adequately represented in the sample, and the response rate was 40% both for Arab and Jewish respondents. Interviews were conducted both in Arabic and Hebrew by Arab or Jewish interviewers matched to the respondent's background.

Dependent Variable

In this study, two themes in citizens' attitudes toward the police were examined: trust in the police and community receptivity to contacting the police. The trust variable includes five measures in a five-point Likert scale ranging from "strongly disagree" to "strongly agree" in regard to the following statements: "I have trust in the police;" "I have trust in the Border Police" (also known as the Border Patrol); "The police do their job fairly;" "The police work to prevent crime near my residence;" and "I would permit a member of my family to become a police officer" (Cronbach's alpha = .77).[47] The receptivity variable includes four measures in a five-point Likert scale ranging from "strongly disagree" to "strongly agree" in regard to the following statements: "Reporting criminals to the police in my view is informing on them;" "I feel that police officers are not welcome in my community;" "In the event that I become a victim of property crime, I will report the crime to the police;" and "In the event that I become a victim of violent crime, I will report the crime to the police."[48] The receptivity variable eventually combined two items: willingness to report property crimes and willingness to report a violent crime to the police (Cronbach's alpha = .66).

---

[46] Bedouin Arabs were excluded from the sample due to their small number in the Northern District.

[47] *See* Table 4.2.1.

[48] *See* Table 4.2.3.

Independent Variables

The independent variables in this study include the standard demographic factors of age, gender, and social class, with the latter measured by educational attainment. Most studies of police-citizen relations find that age is a significant predictor of attitudes toward the police, with young people more likely than older age groups to hold negative views of the police.[49] Gender and class, however, are less consistent predictors.

I suspect that the fear of crime may affect the public perception of the police.[50] Some studies have found that people who are fearful of crime may blame the police for the crime they fear.[51] Fear of crime is measured in the present study by the following question: "To what extent are you afraid of becoming a victim of violent crime?" Responses were rated on a scale of 1 (not afraid at all) to 5 (very afraid).

A significant part of the Israeli-Arab minority holds dissident political attitudes toward the regime and rejects the Jewish identity of the state. I expect that those Arabs who express moderate attitudes toward the Israeli state will be more favorable in their perceptions of the police and more receptive to contacting the police. This variable was measured by asking Arab respondents if Israel, as a Jewish and democratic state, can guarantee equal rights to its Israeli-Arab citizens.[52]

We know that highly controversial incidents involving the police may have an immediate and powerful effect on citizens' opinions, particularly when the incident involves members of one's own ethnic group. In Israel, it is possible that Arab communities that experienced a violent conflict with the police in October 2000 would evaluate the police negatively. Arab respondents were asked whether their community had experienced such an incident.[53] Approximately half of our Arab respondents reported that such a clash had occurred in their community (scored 1) and the other half reported no such incident (scored 0). This variable was measured for Arab respondents only.

In a society as politicized as Israel, a person's ethnicity might be expected to influence his or her evaluations of the police. The variable of ethnicity distinguishes between Arabs and Jewish respondents, and also among Arab sub-groups (Muslims, Christians, and Druze).

---

[49] B. Brown & W. Benedict, *Perceptions of the Police: Past Findings, Methodological Issues, Conceptual Issues, and Policy Implications*, 25 POLICING 543, 554 (2002).

[50] Allen E. Liska et al., *Fears of Crime as a Social Fact*, 60 SOC. FORCES 760 (1982).

[51] *See* Brown & Benedict, *supra* note 49; Mary Holland Baker et al., *The Impact of a Crime Wave: Perceptions, Fear, and Confidence in the Police*, 17 LAW & SOC'Y REV. 319 (1983).

[52] This variable was measured for Arab respondents only.

[53] This variable is labeled police-community clash.

Analysis

I compared the attitudes and preferences of Arabs, Jews, and Arab subgroups (Muslims, Christians, and Druze) regarding the two key dimensions of police-citizen relations—trust and receptivity. Both bivariate and multivariate analyses were conducted. In the multivariate models, a linear regression analysis was performed only for the Arab respondents on each of the two indices reflecting the main dependent variables. The trust index of the police combined five items: trust in the police, trust in the Border Police, the fair performance of the police, the perception of police crime prevention efforts near the respondent's residence, and the likelihood of permitting a member of one's family to become a police officer. The receptivity scale combined two items: willingness to report property crimes and willingness to report a violent crime to the police.

Trust in the Police

Table 4.2.1   Trust in Law Enforcement Institutions and Police Performance

	PERCENTAGE AGREEING MEAN (STANDARD DEVIATION)	
	JEWS (N = 255)	ARABS (N = 471)
[a] Trust the Israel Police***	59.6 3.72 (1.10)	44.8 3.35 (1.32)
[b] Trust the Border Police***	82.1 4.27 (0.97)	39.3 2.96 (1.60)
[c] The police do their job fairly***	54.1 3.54 (1.12)	32.1 2.84 (1.43)
[d] Police work to prevent crime near your residence***	42.1 3.21 (1.19)	32.3 2.93 (1.34)
[e] You would permit a member of your family to become a police officer***	60.4 3.65 (1.55)	47.3 3.06 (1.78)

Asterisks denote significance levels from analysis of variance. * <.05 ** <.01 *** <.001

[a] The respondents were asked if they agree with the statement, "I have trust in the police?" The response format was ordinal; the ranges from 1 to 5: 1 = strongly disagree; 5 = strongly agree.

[b] The respondents were asked if they agree with the statement, "I have trust in the Border Police?" The response format was ordinal; the ranges from 1 to 5: 1 = strongly disagree; 5 = strongly agree.

[c] The respondents were asked if they agree with the statement, "The police do their job fairly." The response format is ordinal; the ranges from 1 to 5: 1 = strongly disagree; 5 = strongly agree.

[d] The respondents were asked if they agree with the statement, "The police work to prevent crime near my residence." The response format is ordinal; the ranges from 1 to 5: 1 = strongly disagree; 5 = strongly agree.

[e] The respondents were asked if they agree with the statement, "I would permit a member of your family to become a police officer." The response format is ordinal; the ranges from 1 to 5: 1 = strongly disagree; 5 = strongly agree.

The findings in Table 4.2.1 show that the police are highly trusted among Jewish respondents in comparison to relatively low levels of trust among Arab respondents—59.6% and 44.8%, respectively. A significant disparity between Jews and Arabs was found in relation to trust in the Border Police—82% and 39.3%, respectively. Jewish respondents are more likely to evaluate the performance of the police as fair and are also more satisfied with police crime control than are Arab respondents. The data in Table 4.2.1 also show that Jewish respondents are more inclined than Arab respondents to permit a member of their family to join the police force.

Table 4.2.2   Means (Standard Deviation) of Trust in Law Enforcement Institutions and Police Performance, by Arab Sub-Ethnic Group

| | ARAB SUB-ETHNICITY PERCENTAGE AGREEING MEAN (STANDARD DEVIATION) | | |
	MUSLIMS N = 328	CHRISTIANS N = 77	DRUZE N = 66
Trust the Israel Police**	40.2 3.25 (1.33)	41.6 3.30 (1.34)	63.6 3.74 (1.25)
Trust the Border Police***	31.4 2.70 (1.58)	41.7 3.04 (1.60)	75.8 4.09 (1.28)
The police do their job fairly***	32.2 2.84 (1.45)	26 2.75 (1.38)	41 3.05 (1.43)
Police work to prevent crime near your residence	30 2.88 (1.33)	39 3.06 (1.35)	32.2 2.92 (1.38)
You would permit a member of your family to become a police officer***	35.7 2.65 (1.71)	55.8 3.35 (1.76)	84.8 4.35 (1.33)

Asterisks denote significance levels from analysis of variance. * <.05 ** <.01 *** <.001

Table 4.2.2 presents the attitudes of Arab sub-groups (Muslims, Christians, and Druze). Findings from the table show that Druze respondents hold more positive attitudes toward the police than do Muslim and Christian Arabs. The Druze's level of trust in the police and Border Police is very similar to that of Jewish respondents.[54] More than Muslim and Christian Arabs, the Druze tend to evaluate the performance of the police as fair. Furthermore, the Druze are even more enthusiastic than the Jews about a member of their family joining the police (84.8%), and they significantly differ in their views on this issue from Muslim and Christian Arabs.

Receptivity to the Police

A receptive relationship between the police and the community is crucial for effective police performance. Table 4.2.3 shows that Arab respondents are more cautious than Jewish respondents in their interaction with the police. In comparison with Jewish respondents, Arabs generally endorse the statement, "Reporting criminals to the police is like informing on them." Similar views are also shown by the response indicating that police officers are not welcome in the community.

[54] See Table 4.2.1.

Furthermore, this dynamic is observed in the case of reporting both property and violent crimes, as Arab respondents seem to feel restricted from either reporting crimes or complaining. This constrained relationship between the police and the Arab minority may be best explained by the political variable. Similar findings were documented among non-dominant groups in Northern Ireland and South Africa.[55]

Table 4.2.3   Receptivity to the Police

	PERCENTAGE AGREEING MEAN (STANDARD DEVIATION)	
	JEWS N = 255	ARABS N = 471
[a] Reporting criminals to the police in my view is informing on them***	15.7 1.87 (1.36)	31.0 2.55 (1.63)
[b] I feel that police officers are not welcome in my community***	15.8 1.82 (1.38)	34.7 2.73 (1.60)
[c] Willingness to report property crime to police***	85.8 4.49 (1.07)	68.4 4.01 (1.40)
[d] Willingness to report violent crime to police***	81.6 4.41 (1.07)	65.6 3.89 (1.45)

Asterisks denote significance levels from analysis of variance. * <.05 ** <.01 *** <.001

[a] The respondents were asked if they agree with the statement, "Reporting criminals to the police in my view is informing on them." The response format is ordinal; the ranges from 1 to 5: 1 = strongly disagree; 5 = strongly agree.

[b] The respondents were asked if they agree with the statement, "I feel that police officers are not welcome in my community." The response format is ordinal; the ranges from 1 to 5: 1 = strongly disagree; 5 = strongly agree.

[c] The respondents were asked if they agree with the statement, "In case you become a victim of property crime, you will report the crime to the police." The response format is ordinal; the ranges from 1 to 5: 1= strongly disagree; 5 = strongly agree.

[d] The respondents were asked if they agree with the statement, "In case you become a victim of violent crime, you will report the crime to the police." The response format is ordinal; the ranges from 1 to 5: 1 = strongly disagree; 5 = strongly agree.

As noted earlier, the Druze hold similar political attitudes to those of Jews, so if the explanation for police receptivity were solely political, then I would expect the Druze to express more receptivity to the police. Findings in Table 4.2.4 show that this is not the case. In reality, the Druze express similar attitudes to those of Muslims in all aspects of police receptivity. They even endorse, more than Muslims, the statement that reporting criminals to the police is like informing on them (40%). Thirty percent of Druze respondents think that police officers are not welcome in then-communities, and the Druze express an unwillingness, similar to that of Muslims, to report property and violent crimes to the police.

These findings suggest that the political explanation is not entirely adequate to explain the Arab minority's lack of receptivity to the police. However, that the Druze share a similar political orientation with Israeli Jews while maintaining cultural similarities with

[55] John Brewer, *Policing, in* THE ELUSIVE SEARCH FOR PEACE: SOUTH AFRICA, ISRAEL, AND NORTHERN IRELAND (H. Gilomee & J. Gagiano eds., 1990); *see* BREWER, BLACK AND BLUE, *supra* note 1 ; WEITZER, POLICING UNDER FIRE, *supra* note 1.

the Muslims, and this might be the explanation. The cultural explanation is also manifest when focusing on Christian Arabs' receptivity to the police. Table 4.2.4 shows that although Christian Arabs share a similar political orientation with Muslim Arabs (as expressed in their negative attitudes toward the police in Table 4.2.2), they still are significantly more willing to contact the police in the event of property and violent crimes, and in this they are more similar to Israeli Jews.

Table 4.2.4 Receptivity to the Police, by Arab Sub-Ethnic Group

	ARAB SUB-ETHNICITY PERCENTAGE AGREEING MEAN (STANDARD DEVIATION)		
	MUSLIMS N = 328	CHRISTIANS N = 77	DRUZE N = 66
Reporting criminals to the police in my view is informing on them	30.4 2.53 (1.64)	23.4 2.35 (1.53)	40.0 2.78 (1.74)
I feel that police officers are not welcome in my community	36.8 2.83 (1.61)	32.5 2.68 (1.52)	30.8 2.42 (1.60)
Willingness to report property crime to police***	67.7 3.97 (1.43)	83.1 4.44 (1.09)	60.6 3.73 (1.51)
Willingness to report violent crime to police*	63.7 3.81 (1.50)	75.0 4.28 (1.18)	66.7 3.92 (1.38)

Asterisks denote significance levels from analysis of variance. * <.05 ** <.01 *** <.001

The data presented above point to differences among Arab sub-groups. The Druze express positive perceptions of the police in the political context, but like Muslim Arabs, they are more restricted in their willingness to contact the police. Conversely, Christian Arabs express negative perceptions of the police in the political context, but also express positive perceptions in regard to making contact with the police. At this stage, I will first try to determine if these differences persist, independent of the influence of other variables. The survey included questions regarding respondents' demographic attributes and other potentially relevant predictors. Second, I will try to determine what other factors, in addition to ethnic background, predict the Arab minority's perceptions of the police in Israel.

I conducted a multivariate analysis to estimate the effect of several predictors on the public's perceptions of the police. This was done in two stages. First, I used the complete survey sample including Israeli Jews as the reference category. By conditioning out this variable, I could estimate the impact of the independent variables and focus on the differences between each Arab minority group relative to Israeli Jews. Second, I estimated the model solely for the Israeli Arab minority sub-groups, excluding Jewish respondents since some of the independent variables were measured only for Arab respondents—e.g., endorsing the Jewish-democratic state in Israel and experiencing violent clashes with the police during the October 2000 events.[56]

---

[56] See Table 4.2.6.

In general, the police trust model in Table 4.2.5 is more powerful than the community receptivity model, as indicated by the adjusted R^2 figures in the models.[57] We can see in the police trust model that education has a strong effect on predicting the public's trust in the police: the higher the education of the respondents, the lower their support of the police. This finding can be explained by the effect of education on the politicization of public awareness of police performance.

Table 4.2.5   Regression Estimates for Effects of Predictors on Public Perceptions of the Police

	TRUST MODEL B(β)	RECEPTIVITY MODEL B(β)
Education	−.34 (−.25)***	.02 (.03)
Gender (1 = male)	−.60 (−.07)*	−.69 (−.15)**
Fear of Crime	.31 (.11)**	.21 (.14)***
Ethnicity		
Jewish (ref.)	———	———
Muslim	−4.25 (−.48)***	−1.15 (−.25)***
Christian	−2.68 (−.19)***	−.21 (−.03)
Druze	−.77 (−.05)	−1.33 (−.17)***
R^2 (Adjusted R^2)	.22 (.21)	.10 (.09)
N	654	712

Asterisks denote significance levels from analysis of variance. * <.05 ** <.01 *** <.001

Gender has significant impact both on the trust and the receptivity model. Women tend to express more trust and be more receptive in their interaction with the police than men. One reason that Israeli women hold positive views of the police may have to do with the fact that they are more concerned than men about becoming victims of crime.[58]

Fear of crime may affect one's perceptions of the police insofar as the police are evaluated for their performance in preventing or solving crimes.[59] The findings indicate that fear of violent victimization affects both the trust and the receptivity models; the greater the fear of crime, the higher the evaluation of the police and the greater the inclination to contact the police. As suggested above, this finding might be affected by the fact that the fear of crime is more prominent among women.

Finally, I examined the effect of Arab sub-ethnicity in both models using Israeli Jews as the reference group. The results show that ethnic differences persist. Net of the other factors, Muslim and Christian Arabs are more likely than Druze (and Jews) to hold negative perceptions of the police in the trust model. Reviewing the receptivity model, we can see that Druze are more

---

[57] Variance Inflation Factor (VIF) was conducted to verify if any independent variable in the model is a linear function of other independent variables. VIF values were less than two among all variables in the models.

[58] *See* Hasisi & Weitzer, *supra* note 41.

[59] See Brown & Benedict, *supra* note 49.

similar to Muslims in their restricted receptivity to the police, whereas Christian Arabs express receptive attitudes similar to those expressed by Jewish respondents in regard to contacting the police.

In the second stage, I estimated the trust and receptivity models solely for Arab respondents. In the police trust model we can see that education has a strong effect on predicting Arab trust of the police. The higher the education of an Arab individual, the lower their support of the police. One reason that highly educated Arabs might be critical of the police is that they typically live, not with middle-class Jews, but with poor and working-class Arabs, and therefore experience the same kind of treatment from the police.[60] Education had no significant effect on the receptivity model.

Table 4.2.6   Regression Estimates for Effects of Predictors on Israeli Arab Perceptions of the Police

	TRUST MODEL B(β)	RECEPTIVITY MODEL B(β)
Education	–.46 (–.27)***	–.05 (–.06)
Gender (1 = male)	–.71 (–.06)	–.64 (–.13)**
Fear of Crime	.40 (.12)**	.32 (.21)***
Community-Police Clash (Oct. 2000)	–1.00 (–.10)*	–.15 (–.03)
Israel as a Jewish-democratic state can guarantee equal rights to the Israeli Arabs	1.2 (.19)***	.13 (.09)*
Ethnicity		
Druze (ref.)	————	————
Muslim	–3.12 (.27)***	.21 (.04)
Christian	–1.80 (–.13)*	1.20 (.18)**
R^2 (Adjusted R^2) N	.25 (.24) 425	.11 (.10) 454

Asterisks denote significance levels from analysis of variance. * <.05 ** <.01 *** <.001

Fear of crime may affect one's perceptions of the police insofar as the police are evaluated for their performance in preventing or solving crimes.[61] The findings indicate that fear of violent victimization affects both the trust and the receptivity models; the greater the fear of crime, the higher the evaluation of the police and the greater the inclination to contact the police.

Gender had no significant impact on the trust model, but there was some impact on the receptivity model. Arab women tend to be more receptive in their interaction with the police than Arab men. One reason that Arab women might be more receptive to contacting the police may have to do with the fact that they are more concerned than Arab men about becoming victims of crime, especially when traditional social controls in the Arab community are gender-biased.[62]

---

[60] Noh Lewin-Epstein & Moshe Semyonov, The Arab Minority in Israel's Economy: Patterns of Ethnic Inequality (1993).

[61] See Brown & Benedict, supra note 49.

[62] See Women Against Violence, Attitudes Towards the Status and Rights of Palestinian Women in Israel (2006); Hasan, supra note 23; Nadera Shalhoub-Kevorkian, Law, Politics, and Violence Against Women: a Case Study of Palestinians in Israel, 21 Law

Another reason may have to do with the negative political image of the police among Arab men, who frequently—more than Arab women—experience violent clashes with police at political events.[63]

Police-community conflict during the riots of October 2000 had a significant effect on the trust model of policing. Arabs who report that their community had experienced a violent clash with police officers are more inclined to express negative attitudes toward the police. This finding is consistent with other studies that document the effects of highly controversial policing incidents on citizens' perceptions of the police.[64] This variable has no significant effect in the case of the receptivity model.

I expected that Arabs who agree that Israel, as a Jewish and democratic state, can guarantee equal rights to its Arab citizens would be more supportive of the police. This was confirmed in the two models: Arab respondents who agree with the statement express more positive attitudes toward the police and are more inclined to contact the police. The effect of this variable is, however, more salient in the (political) trust model.

Finally, I examined the effect of Arab sub-ethnicity in both models. The results show that ethnic differences persist; net of the other factors, Muslim and Christian Arabs were more likely than Druze to hold negative perceptions of the police in the trust model. When reviewing the receptivity model, we can see that Druze are more similar to Muslims in their restricted receptivity to the police, whereas Christian Arabs express more receptive attitudes than Muslim and Druze in regard to contacting the police.

Discussion

Most of the research on police-minority relations in deeply divided societies has emphasized the political explanation, yet very little research has addressed the influence of cultural pluralism on police-community relations. In this article I have tried to elaborate on the influence of the cultural diversity and resistance of the Arab native minority in Israel upon police performance, alongside political variables.

The major contribution of this Article is that it sheds light on the differences within minority groups and their ramifications on police-minority relations. We usually refer to minority groups as a coherent, homogeneous group. By doing so, we may miss important distinctions within the minority group that have an effect on their relations with the police. This Article shows that, depending upon political and cultural affiliations, the Arab minority has different perceptions toward the police. Arabs who hold similar political attitudes to the Jewish majority (i.e., the

---

& Pol'y 190, 196 (1999).

[63] *See* Hasisi & Weitzer, *supra* note 41.

[64] Robert J. Kaminski & Eric S. Jefferis, *The Effect of a Violent Televised Arrest on Public Perceptions of the Police,* 21 Policing 683 (1998); Ronald Weitzer & Steven A. Tuch, *Perceptions of Racial Profiling: Race, Class, and Personal Experience,* 40 Criminology 435 (2002).

Druze) expressed positive attitudes toward the police. By the same token, Arabs with a cultural similarity to the Jewish majority (i.e., the Christians) expressed a more open receptivity to the police. Both political and cultural variables contributed to a better understanding of police-minority relations in Israel.

This research can be extended to explore the relationship between police and minorities in other countries. Native-aboriginal populations reside in several Western countries, and recent studies have revealed the tense relationship between the police and the aboriginal population in these countries.[65] Furthermore, this research can also be extended to several Western countries who host immigrants from different cultures. Several studies have shown the tense relations between these immigrant groups and the police. This Article suggests that a deeper analysis of the relationships between minority groups and the police should be conducted, and that researchers should be more attentive in their analysis of the differences within minority groups.

This research can also be extended to explore the relationship between the police and other social groups in Israeli society. Indeed, the Jewish population is not a homogenous group in cultural terms. For instance, ultra-Orthodox Jews are culturally distinguishable from the secular Jewish majority. Consequently, they hold significant negative attitudes toward the police.[66] Further research should be directed toward analyzing police performance as perceived by ultra-Orthodox Jews, which might clarify the impact of cultural diversity on their criminal behavior and attitudes toward the police.

There are some limitations to this research that should be mentioned. Less than 25% of the statistical variance is explained in each model, and this raises the question of what factors are not taken into account and how they might affect the findings. The suggested models take into account many possible variables that have confounded other studies. Nonetheless, as in all multivariate analyses, we should be cautious in drawing conclusions.[67] Future studies should even more closely specify their models of minority attitudes toward the police.

Conclusion

This Article offers a framework for analyzing police-minority relations in deeply divided societies. In these kinds of societies, the regime has severe problems with its legitimacy among the minority group, which in turn affects the group's relationship with the police. Research shows that the political and cultural disparities between Arabs and Jews in Israel have reduced the trust and the willingness of Israeli Arabs to cooperate with the police. The political explanations

---

[65] Blagg & Valuri, *supra* note 9.

[66] MINISTRY OF PUB. SEC., STATE OF ISRAEL, PUBLIC ATTITUDES TOWARDS THE ISRAELI POLICE (2002); MINISTRY OF PUB. SEC., STATE OF ISRAEL, PUBLIC ATTITUDES TOWARDS THE ISRAELI POLICE (2001); RAFI SMITH, KEREN SHARVIT & SMITH CONSULTING & RESEARCH INC., PUBLIC ATTITUDES TOWARDS THE ISRAELI POLICE: EXECUTIVE SUMMARY (2000); MINISTRY OF PUB. SEC., STATE OF ISRAEL, PUBLIC ATTITUDES TOWARDS THE ISRAELI POLICE (1999).

[67] David Weisburd, *Magic and Science in Multivariate Sentencing Models: Reflecting on the Limits of Statistical Methods*, 35 ISRAEL L. REV. 225 (2001).

assume that the major source of the tension between the police and the minority group stem from political variables, and in order to improve this relationship, socio-political reforms regarding the minority group are necessary. The cultural explanations assume that the tensions between the police and the minority group are also influenced by cultural variables, and not just socio-political factors. Thus, in order to improve the relationship between the minority and the police, cultural reforms are required in order to change the police culture both in the making of management-level and street-level decisions with respect to minority groups.[68]

The cultural and political differences between Jews and Arabs in Israel pose a challenge for police performance in the minority community. While the police are focused on law enforcement, they must also be aware of and sensitive to the cultural distinctiveness of the minority community and suitably adjust themselves to it when providing services to Arab citizens. Increased distribution of community police stations in Arab communities would create better access to police and facilitate the procedure of filing complaints. In order to improve Arab-police relations, a multicultural approach is needed. This approach could be put into practice by recruiting more Arab policemen and policewomen, especially non-Bedouin Muslims[69] and, at the same time, by creating strong ties between the local political leadership and the chiefs of police stations, ties which have proven to be valuable in times of crisis.[70]

However, a multicultural approach is not without risk. A policy of cultural relativity that is too flexible in the policing of a minority group is liable to create a differential enforcement of laws and may even perpetuate criminal behaviors. I conclude that a balanced approach to police presence is necessary and that greater consideration and judgment should be exercised when enforcing the law. The complex task of policing the Arab minority in Israel must take into account the population's political and cultural composition, balancing its particular and diverse needs with the need to maintain the rule of the law.

Critical Thinking Questions

1   What are some reasons that explain why minority groups are distrustful of police or view the police as illegitimate?

2   How do cultural differences between majority and minority groups impact interactions between minority groups and the police?

3   What do the study findings suggest about treating minority groups as homogenous when examining issues between police and minorities?

4   What steps can police take to improve relations with minority groups?

---

[68] Janet Chan, *Changing Police Culture,* 36 Brit. J. Criminology 109 (1996).

[69] Although non-Bedouin Muslims compose about 12% of the Israeli population, their representation in the police force is less than 2%. *See* Hasisi & Weitzer, *supra* note 41.

[70] Indep. Comm'n on Policing for Northern Ireland, A New Beginning: Policing in Northern Ireland 81–90 (1999).

Editors' Introduction: Reading 4.3

Community trust in the police is a delicate, yet integral component in police legitimacy. Trust is necessary to the relationship that exists between the police and community members. As in any relationship, when trust is broken, it can be challenging to repair. Boateng discusses the issues of trust with a case study of the Ghana Police Service. Historical experiences, cultural artifacts, and excessive accounts of police corruption and brutality created a profound sense of mistrust of the police by the citizens of Ghana. A multidimensional approach was used in suggesting strategies to begin rebuilding trust of the Ghana police. These tactics are relevant to many police departments across the world when trust is broken and legitimacy is lost by citizens.

Restoring the Lost Hope

A Multidimensional Approach for Building Public Trust in the Police

Francis D. Boateng

S everal studies have documented the importance of public trust in policing, especially in democratic societies where policing by consent is paramount (Boateng, 2012; Hough & Roberts, 2004; Jackson & Bradford, 2010; Mazerolle Antrobus, Bennett, & Tyler, 2013; Murphy & Cherney, 2012; Rosenbaum et al., 2005; Tyler, 2005). These studies have collectively shown that trust in the police leads to citizens' voluntary cooperation with law enforcement, as well as voluntary compliance with the laws being enforced. Citizens who trust the police willingly cooperate with police officers by either reporting crimes they witness or providing vital information leading to the apprehension of individuals who have violated criminal law (Flexon & Greenleaf, 2009). Prior studies have found evidence suggesting that public trust influences police effectiveness and legitimacy (Goldsmith, 2005; Hough, Jackson, Bradford, & Myhill, 2010; Hough, 2012; Sunshine & Tyler, 2003), and have argued that public trust legitimizes police actions (Hough et al., 2010). A legitimate police force faces minimal to no challenge to its authority and enjoys citizen cooperation (Tankebe, 2013; Resig, Tankebe, & Mesko, 2012). It is therefore apparent that public trust in the police is a vital ingredient to police operation and police effectiveness. An absence of trust can make police institutions ineffective and incapable of performing their duties. A police force suffering from the lack of trust faces difficulties in securing public cooperation and compliance (Memmo, Sartor, & di Cardano, 2003). Moreover, researchers have argued that without citizens' approval and consent, law enforcement agencies cannot fulfill their mission to police and consequently, public safety suffers (Frazier, 2007).

Recognizing the need for the police to build and maintain public trust, this article discusses strategies to enhance public trust and confidence in the Police. It needs to be mentioned that, though the article uses Ghana as a case study, the recommendations offered can be applied to other contexts, especially developing nations. The Ghana Police Service has suffered from public distrust and a lack of legitimacy for several years. Citizen trust in the police is currently very low, with only about 35% trusting the police to a great extent (Boateng, 2012). The low trust can be partly explained by excessive police misconduct, abuse, and corruption (Tankebe, 2010). This paper adopts a multidimensional framework perspective towards restoring and maintaining Ghanaians' trust in the police. The framework is based on the assumption that there is no single most effective way of building citizens' trust in the police; instead, a constellation of strategies must work together to build trust.

This article is structured in the following way: It begins by discussing policing in Ghana from a historical perspective, followed by a discussion on the contemporary relationship between the police and the public. The article then presents an analysis of the levels of trust in the police and the factors that influence these levels. Based on this literature, the paper develops an integrated model for explaining trust in the police. Recommendations for building and maintaining public trust follow, and the article concludes by recapping salient points and suggesting directions in which police can move to enhance legitimacy.

Policing in Ghana: From Colonialism to Present

Professional policing in Ghana was first introduced by the British colonial authorities to the then Gold Coast in 1831; the police force was called Gold Coast Constabulary. Prior to that, social control was organized by traditional authorities led by local kings or chiefs. Policing during British colonial rule essentially had two goals. First, to enforce and maintain security for trade in European goods and to serve as a vanguard for colonial expansion into the hinterland for increased exploitation of agricultural and mineral resources (Ward, 1948, p. 184). The second aim of policing during the colonial era was to protect the ruling and propertied class. Thus, in 1896 George Maclean, who was the governor at the time, instructed that "no police should be stationed where there were no Europeans" (Gillespie, 1955, p. 36).

During the colonial era, concerns were raised by the public about the moral standing and efficacy of the police. Gillespie (1955) contended that successive governors and police commissioners variously described the police as worse than inefficient. This observation underscored the apparent ineffectiveness of the colonial police in maintaining colonial government machinery. When the country attained political independence, the nature and character of post-colonial policing did not change much from that of colonial policing. Tankebe (2008a) argued that the colonial militaristic orientation to policing with its quintessential lack of accountability and respect for the fundamental rights of citizens remains strong and visible.

Since Ghana's independence from colonial rule, the Ghana Police Service has remained a centralized organization structured into 12 administrative regions, 51 divisions, 179 districts, and 651 stations across the country. The strength of the police service increased progressively from the few years prior to independence until 1971. At that time, the police force numbered 19,410 personnel and served a population of about 8.5 million people (Aning, 2002). Currently, the police force numbers approximately 23,702 and serves a population of about 25 million.

Ghana police today perform both crime-related and service-related duties. The crime-related functions of the force are stipulated in Section 1 of the Police Force Act, 1970 (Act 350). The Act emphatically states "it shall be the duties of the Police Force to prevent and detect crime, to apprehend offenders and to maintain public order and safety of persons and properties" (Police Force Act, 1970, Art. 350). The service-related functions which are not stated by the Act include: performing motor traffic duties, vetting and issuing of police criminal record certificates, and helping women cope with traumatic and psychological problems as a result of sexual abuse (www.police.gov.gh). To strengthen the capacity of the police to perform these service duties, a five-year Strategic National Policing Plan was launched in 2010 with the following objectives:

1   To increase the level of protection of life and property, increase the ability to prevent and detect crime and speed up the apprehension and prosecution of offenders to enhance public confidence and satisfaction.

2   To enhance the capacity of the force by improving its human resources through training and development and by recruiting the best candidates.

3   To acquire relevant and modern information and communication technologies that would enable the force to perform its services.

4   To establish closer and mutually beneficial working relationships with external stakeholders to improve the partnership and public image of the Police Service.

Police administrators believe that this plan will positively impact crime reduction and improve the relationship between the police and Ghanaian citizens.

Police-Citizen Relationship in Ghana

Relationship between police and citizens in Ghana has been marked by suspicion, hatred, discontent, and mistrust. These negative feelings are largely due to the brutal character of the Ghana police force under British colonialism (Atuguba, 2003; Tankebe, 2008a). To understand the present nature of police-citizen relationship in Ghana, a brief discussion of the relationship that existed during the colonial period is necessary to provide historical context.

During the colonial era, the police, as noted above, were ineffective especially in protecting the indigenous Ghanaians. Ineffectiveness was not the only issue confronting the police, equally important was the extreme public distrust in the police as a result of massive police brutality. The brutal nature of the Gold Coast Constabulary was not a mistake, but rather a calculated attempt by the British colonial authorities who believed that the only means of developing a conducive atmosphere for successful trade was to have a police force that would brutalize indigenous citizens. The aim was achieved through the recruitment of the Hausas, mostly from Northern Nigeria, who were charged to enforce colonial laws through brutalization. Historians have long contended that this brutal and alien character of the force made the police unpopular among the citizenry (Killingray, 1991; Gillespie, 1955; Ward, 1948).

Today, though the Ghana Police Service is composed of only Ghanaians, the police remain excessively corrupt and brutal (Atuguba, 2003; Tankebe, 2008a), which mars the force's relationship with the public. Researchers have argued that police misconduct appears to even be worse than during the colonial period (Tankebe 2008a). A 2010 report on human rights practices in Ghana remarked that police brutality, corruption, negligence, and impunity were problems facing the police. The report added that the police extorted money by acting as private debt collectors, setting up illegal checkpoints, and arresting citizens in exchange for bribes from disgruntled business associates of those detained. These are all evidence of police misconduct, which has contributed to public mistrust of the police.

The most high profile act of police brutality, which threw the whole country into a state of mourning, and has since left an indelible mark in the minds of citizens, occurred on May 9, 2001. On this day, 126 soccer fans were crushed to death and several hundred spectators were injured when the police used tear gas in response to soccer hooliganism during a local match. The incident received worldwide attention and has been considered the worst stadium disaster in Africa, further undermining the level of trust between Ghanaians and police. Today, according to Aning (2006), though the public welcomes the new service orientation of the police, there remains an underlying sense of mistrust and discomfort. An analysis of the current levels of trust in the police is offered in the next section.

Current Levels of Trust in the Police

There is a deep sense of mistrust and discontent between the police and the citizenry of Ghana. Recent surveys conducted in Ghana have documented low citizen trust in the police. For instance, research shows that more than half (53%) of Ghanaians do not trust the police at all (Boateng, 2012). Similarly, surveys by the Afrobarometer, a regional public attitude survey organization, do not only indicate that Ghanaians have low trust in the police but also indicate that trust in the police continues to decline. For instance, in 2005, almost 38% of Ghanaians trusted the police "a lot." This declined to 28% in 2008, and 18% in 2012 (see Figure 4.3.1).

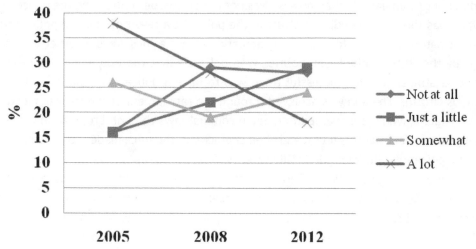

Figure 4.3.1   Trends in Ghanaians' Trust in the Police

Source of data: Afrobarometer Surveys—2005, 2008, 2012

Figure 4.3.2 compares trust in the police among Ghanaians to citizens of two other African countries with similar economic circumstances to further demonstrate the negative attitudes of Ghanaians toward the police. About half (50%) of Malawians and 45% of Burkinabes trusted the police "a lot" in 2012 compared to only 18% of Ghanaians.

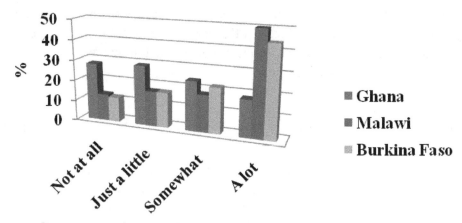

Figure 4.3.2   Comparison of trust in the police in three nations

Source of data: Afrobarometer Surveys—2012

To explain why Ghanaians have lower trust in the police, the answers lie in the extreme levels of police corruption and brutalities in Ghana. Police corruption is endemic and takes many forms (Tankebe, 2010). According to Tankebe (2010), corrupt police practices in Ghana include failures to arrest, investigate, or prosecute offenders because of family and friendship ties, and bribe-taking from suspects. To buttress Tankebe's assertion, observations made by the author suggest that some police officers mount road barricades to extort money from law-abiding commercial drivers. The magnitude of police corruption in Ghana has been evidenced in recent survey findings. For instance, the 2008 Afrobarometer survey found that about 78% of Ghanaians perceived the police to be corrupt. Pervasive police brutality also explains Ghanaians' low trust in the police. Police officers beating suspects during arrest and interrogation as well as manhandling innocent citizens during demonstrations are common practices among police personnel in Ghana (US Department of State Human Rights Report, 2010).

Since it has now been established that Ghanaians have low trust in the police and some plausible explanations have been offered, the next task is to elucidate, based on evidence, the factors that influence citizens' trust in the Ghanaian police. The following section discusses this issue. However, it needs to be mentioned that little empirical research exists in the literature that has examined factors influencing public trust in the Ghanaian police.

Determinants of Ghanaians' Trust in the Police

As noted, few studies have examined the factors that influence variation in levels of trust in the police among Ghanaians. These studies have collectively found several predictors of public trust in the Ghana police service. In two separate studies, Tankebe (2008b, 2010) found that perceptions of police effectiveness, procedural fairness, personal encounters, and vicarious experiences with police corruption affect trust in the Ghana police service.

In his 2008 study, Tankebe argued that public perceptions of police effectiveness exercise a direct impact on perceived police trustworthiness. A trustworthy police force is one adjudged by the public to have the interests of the public at hand rather than personal or political interests. Hence, citizens who perceive the police not only as effective in controlling crime but also as effective in meeting citizen expectations and interests will correspondingly consider the police to be trustworthy. Further, Tankebe (2008b) found that Ghanaians who considered the police to be procedurally fair in dealing with citizens would be more likely to trust the police than those who considered the police to be unfair. The effect of procedural fairness on trust has been widely studied and similar conclusions have been found in other societies (Mazerolle et al, 2012; Mazerolle et al., 2013; Murphy & Cherney, 2012).

Research on public trust in the police has also found that vicarious experiences of police corruption influence Ghanaians' levels of trust in the police (Tankebe, 2010). This study found that Ghanaians who have indirectly experienced police corruption by witnessing the police taking bribes from other persons or refusing to investigate, arrest, or prosecute because of friendship or family ties would be less likely to trust the police. However, Tankebe (2010) did not find any effect for personal experiences of police corruption. This was rather surprising considering the frequency of police corruption in Ghana, according to the 2010 human rights report. His inability to find an effect may be due to the nature of the questions asked or some inherent limitations with the data such as the study's failure to fragment personal experiences of police corruption into its two components, i.e. citizen-initiated and police-initiated, and test each effect independently since they may have opposing effects on trust in the police. For instance, citizen-initiated police corruption, which involves citizens voluntarily paying bribes to officers to overlook their criminal acts, may possibly result in positive attitudes toward the police or will have no effect at all. However, police-initiated corruption, which involves solicitation of bribes from citizens in order to render a service or perform a requested task is likely to result in negative ratings by citizens of the police. Therefore, combining these two variables to form a single variable of direct or personal experience of police corruption will obscure the true effect of corruption on citizens' ratings of the police.

Boateng (2012) conducted a study to examine factors that shape Ghanaians' trust in the police and found that fear of crime and satisfaction with police work have significant influence on trust in the Ghanaian police. Fear of crime had a negative relationship with trust, indicating that when fear of crime is high, trust in the police will be low. Ghanaians decide where to live, shop and socialize based on their perceptions of relative safety (Boateng, 2012). As a result, persons who fear attack or victimization anywhere in the city or neighborhood will consider the police ineffective, and consequently will demonstrate low levels of trust in the police. Furthermore, Boateng (2012) found that when citizens are satisfied with the work of the police in their respective neighborhoods, they tend to have higher trust in the police than when they are not satisfied, a finding that has also been observed in other social contexts (Reynolds, Semukhina, & Demidov, 2008; Wu & Sun, 2009).

Discussions of factors that influence Ghanaians' trust in the police would be incomplete without considering the effect of perception of corruption among other government institutions. This variable was found to have a negative effect on public trust in the Ghanaian police (Boateng, 2012). Ghanaians who considered other government officials, not necessarily the police to be corrupt, tend to have low trust in the police as well. The effect is possibly due to the fact that the police is viewed not as an organization operating in a vacuum but rather in an institutional setting which interacts with other institutions such as the courts, corrections, and the government on a continuous basis. Therefore, any act of misconduct that occurs in other institutions undoubtedly affect public ratings for the rest of the institutions. Political affiliation only influenced trust at the bivariate level. The influence was negative, suggesting that Ghanaians who have affiliations with political parties demonstrate lower trust in the police than those with no such affiliations. Still, this effect disappeared when accounting for multiple variables.

These latter findings demonstrate that there are some factors that exist outside the police organization but contribute significantly to variations in citizens' trust in the police. Based on this observation, scholars have argued that determinants of public trust in the police can be classified into two categories: organization specific, which include factors over which police have control, and non-organization specific, which include factors that the police have little control over but greatly influence public trust in the police (Boateng, 2012). It is based on this categorization that the current paper develops an integrated model for trust in the police (see Figure 4.3.3). This model takes into account the effects of both organization- and nonorganization-specific variables on trust in the police.

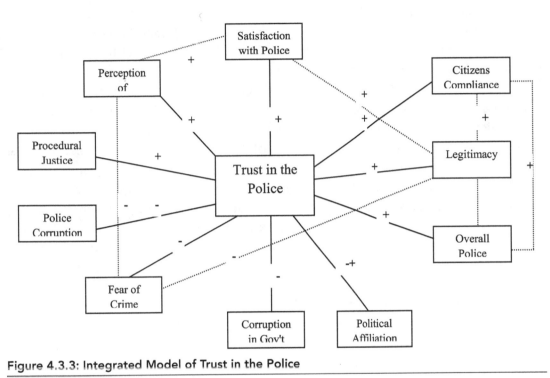

Figure 4.3.3: Integrated Model of Trust in the Police

Note: Lines (broken and unbroken) indicate relationship; Arrows indicate direction of influence; + sign indicates positive effect; −sign indicates negative effect.

Recommendations for Building Trust in the Police

It is clear that the Ghana Police Service, an institution charged with the protection of lives and property, suffers from massive public distrust. Trust literature suggests that public trust is a valuable asset to police organizations mainly because it is crucial for voluntary citizen compliance, legitimacy, and enhanced police performance. Due to this, it is necessary that the police and their stakeholders must develop strategies of building and maintaining public trust. It could be argued that citizens play a marginal role or no role in building this trust. To suggest ways of building and maintaining trust in the Ghanaian police that will have practical utility, based on the integrated model presented above, this paper adopts a multidimensional approach. This approach reflects the idea that there is no single most effective way of building citizen trust in the police. Instead, a constellation of approaches can collectively result in sustained public trust in the police. Further, the multidimensional approach requires other agencies to be involved in building public trust. Based on this perspective, the author recommends that the following strategies be adopted by Ghana police administrators.

Fear reduction Strategies

It has widely been documented that fear of crime is a major factor influencing citizen confidence and trust in the police (Reynolds et al., 2008). As a result, reducing fear of crime is an indispensable consideration for improving trust. High fear of victimization prevents citizens from leaving their homes as well as isolating them from community engagement. At present, the majority of the Ghanaian population is either directly afraid of crime in their neighborhoods or worried they may become victims of crime (Boateng, 2012). The burden of reducing fear among this cross-section of the population therefore rests on police administrators of the Ghana Police Service. To reduce fear, police administrators must consider fear reduction as their ultimate responsibility and explicit police priority. Police administrators must consider incorporating the following fear reduction strategies into the daily routines of the police service: increasing police presence in the neighborhoods; ensuring constant patrolling in the neighborhoods; reducing disorderly behavior; and ensuring rapid response to calls for service (Cordner, 2010). These strategies are aimed at reducing fear of victimization and insecurity and when properly adopted will restore a sense of security and safety and eventually lead to greater trust in the police.

Increasing Citizen Satisfaction

Citizen satisfaction with police work is a positive indicator of trust in the police (Reynolds et al., 2008; Wu & Sun, 2009). Therefore, dissatisfaction with the services provided by the police will have severe implications for police work. Dissatisfaction simply implies that the public is not satisfied with police services partly because of apparent ineffectiveness or nonperformance on the part of the police. A lack of police services in the neighborhood can also result in citizen dissatisfaction with the work of the police. Currently in Ghana this is a major issue because the majority are deprived of police services. Police stations in the urban areas are mostly located far from residences and accessing them for the purpose of reporting criminal conduct becomes a problem. This situation is even worse in the rural areas of Ghana, where police stations are hardly found. To enhance police performance and increase public satisfaction, police administrators must develop effective and reliable communication systems that will ensure increased public accessibility to the police. Quick response to citizens when called for help as well as fair treatment of citizens during encounters would be great steps in improving public satisfaction with police work.

Adherence to Professional Standards

Public trust must be built on the foundation of a strong police culture that values integrity and holds officers accountable for their behavior. Police misconduct e.g., bribe-taking and extortion of money, plays an important role in eroding public trust (Goldsmith, 2005; Sabet, 2012). Therefore, the Police Service must strive to maintain high ethical and accountability standards. Individual police officers, irrespective of rank, must be held accountable for what they do on the street or in the station/department. The Internal Affairs Unit of the Service will have to play an important role in this pursuit. The unit must institute stringent disciplinary and accountability measures, punish officers who behave unethically, and reward those who behave pro-socially or ethically. Punishments could include but are not limited to demotion, dismissal, unfavorable transfer, and prosecution whereas rewards could take the form of promotion, increase salary, bonuses, and open recognition at special police ceremonies or events.

Institutional Involvement

To reiterate, building and maintaining citizen trust in the police requires the involvement of other governmental agencies because factors that contribute to eroding trust in the police are not solely caused by the police. Inter-agency collaboration is necessary to ensure trust in the police. In Ghana, agencies like the Electricity Company of Ghana (ECG) can team up with the police to reduce fear of crime among the citizenry. Specifically, the police, as the agent of security in the country, can negotiate with the government for the provision of streetlights in unlighted areas where crime rates and fear of crime are considered to be high. Once this is done, quick response from the electricity company would be necessary to ensure that such areas are provided with streetlights. It is worth mentioning that the police cannot provide lights in these areas without the custodians of power in the country getting involved.

Similarly, external controls are needed to ensure proper behavior of police officers in Ghana. The courts can play a significant role in several ways, including facilitating the prosecution of officers charged with misconduct as well as restraining the police from engaging in unwarranted acts, especially during arrests and interrogations. Likewise, citizens review boards charged with hearing complaints about police misconduct and unlawful behavior, and endowed with the powers of subpoena, can significantly build citizens' trust in the police by ensuring professional standards of behavior among officers. Further, it is recommended that other government officials be subjected to similar ethical scrutiny, since their behavior indirectly affects citizens rating for the police.

Police-Community Partnership

To build and maintain citizen trust in the Ghana Police Service, the author recommends that the police foster positive relationships with the communities they serve. Apart from eschewing unethical behavior, which undoubtedly destroys their good relationship with the community, police administrators should also hold open meetings and seminars with the public to mutually discuss issues of relevance. These types of meetings will allow the public to express their griev-ances and feelings about the police and their activities, while the police attempt to address such complaints. In addition to organizing meetings and seminars, the police must also properly train their officers to equip them with skills necessary in ensuring positive interaction with citizens. Good communication skills are essential for ensuring positive encounters with citizens. Citizens can easily form negative views of the police based on the outcome of their interaction with a single officer. Therefore, police must do what they can to avoid negative encounters with the public.

Police-Researcher Collaboration

Researchers and academicians play an indispensable role in building and maintaining trust in the police. Their role is crucial because researchers can help the police gauge the extent of pub-lic satisfaction with police services. This will enable the police to boost their performance when public dissatisfaction is high. Similarly, through extensive surveying, researchers can provide the police with vital information about specific areas of the community where fear of crime is high, whether fear of crime is increasing or diminishing, and how to reduce fear of crime among com-munity members. Based on this, it is recommended that, to maintain citizen trust in the police, police administrators should foster a strong collaborative relationship with researchers. Such collaboration will be useful and vital to the police organization given the nature of information researchers can provide to enhance their performance and relationship with the public.

Conclusion

This paper has demonstrated that citizens' levels of trust in the Ghana Police Service are low and that there is a need to build and maintain trust in the police. It outlined a multidimensional approach to building and enhancing citizen trust in the police. The approach is based on the assumption that there is no single most effective way of building trust; instead, a constellation of strategies must be used together. The police, other governmental institutions, and researchers all have significant roles to play in the pursuit of sustaining citizens' trust in the police. However, police have the greatest responsibility in this pursuit. The police must reduce citizens' fear of being victimized as well as ensuring public satisfaction with the numerous services they now provide. Reducing fear of crime calls for putting more officers on the street and in the neighbor-hoods to patrol day and night by car, bicycle or foot.

Increasing the police presence in neighborhoods by putting more officers on the street may seem costly to implement. However, this is not entirely so, especially in Ghana. The implementa-tion of this strategy will only call for a change in the attitudes and practices of the police. Today, a large percentage of officers assigned to carry out police duties as stipulated by the Police Force Act of 1970 end up performing non-police duties during their entire shift. Most of these officers are assigned to work as "errand boys" or "gatemen" in senior officers' residences. As noted by Atuguba (2003), one senior officer (the rank of assistant superintendent or above) may have as many as two police personnel in his/her house at any given time.

The same can be said about those who hold political positions in Ghana. According to Atuguba (2003), most members of the political class today have one or two police officers (sometimes a whole platoon) at their service. Ministers of state and their deputies, the Speaker of Parliament, judges and other political appointees appropriate this disproportionate amount of public security at the expense of the citizenry (Atuguba, 2003:15). Therefore, if the police stop assigning personnel to senior officers' and other individuals' homes and assign more officers to the neighborhoods, it would be a positive step toward reducing the fear of crime among citizens and achieving a positive public-police relationship in the long term.

References

Afro barometer Survey (2012). Retrieved from http://www.afrobarometer.org

Aning, E. K. (2002). An Historical Overview of the Ghana Police Service' in K. Kariakri (Ed.) *The Face and Phases of the Ghana Police,* pp. 7–53. Accra: Media Foundation for West Africa.

Aning, E. K. (2006). An Overview of the Ghana Police Service. *Journal of Security Sector Management*, 4, 1–37.

Atuguba, R. A. (2003). Police Oversight in Ghana', Paper presented at a Workshop on Security Sector Governance in Africa, Organized by African Security Dialogue and Research (Unpublished).

Boateng, F. D. (2012). Public Trust in the Police: Identifying factors that shape trust in the Ghanaian Police. IPES Working Paper Series, No. 42. *www.ipes.info/WPS/WPS_No_42.pdf.*

Cordner, G. (2010). Reducing Fear of Crime: Strategies for Police. *U.S Department of Justice, Office of Community Oriented Policing Services (COPS).*

Flexon, J. L., Lurigio, A. J., & Greenleaf, R. G. (2009). Exploring the Dimensions of Trust in the Police among Chicago Juveniles. *Journal of Criminal Justice*, 37:180–189.

Frazier, L. S. (2007). The Loss of Public Trust in Law Enforcement. *Retrieved http://libcat.post.ca.gov/dbtw-wpd/ documents/cc/40-frazier.pdf.*

Gillespie, W. H. (1955). *The Gold Coast Police: 1844–1938.* Accra: The Government Printer.

Goldsmith, A. (2005). Police Reform and the Problem of Trus. *Theoretical Criminology* 9(4):443–470.

Hough, M. (2012). Researching Trust in the Police and Trust in Justice: A UK Perspective. *Policing and Society: An International Journal of Research and Policy* 22:3:332–345.

Hough, M., Jackson, J., Bradford, B., & Myhill, A. (2010). Procedural Justice, Trust, and Institutional Legitimacy. *Policing: A Journal of Policy and Practice,* Vol. 4, pp. 203–210.

Hough, M., & Roberts, J. V. (2004). Youth Crime and Youth Justice: Public Opinion in England and Wales. Criminal Policy Monograph. Bristol: Policy Press.

Jackson, J., & Bradford, B. (2010). What Is Trust and Confidence in the Police? *Policing: A Journal of Policy and Practice,* Vol. 4, pp. 241–248.

Mazerolle, L., Antrobus, E., Bennett, S., & Tyler, T. (2013). Shaping Citizen Perceptions of Police Legitimacy: A Randomized Field Trail of Procedural Justice. *Criminology* 51(1):33–63.

Mazerolle, L., Bennett, S., Antrobus, E., & Eggins, E. (2012). Procedural Justice, Routine Encounters and Citizen Perceptions of Police: Main Findings from the Queensland Community Engagement Trial (QCET). *Journal of Experimental Criminology*, 8, 343–367. doi: 10.1007/s11292-012-9160-1.

Memmo, D., Sartor, G., & di Cardano, G. Q. (2003). Trust, Reliance, Good Faith, and the Law. In Nixon, P., Terzis, S. (eds.). *Proceedings of the First International Conference on Trust Management*. LNCS 2692, 150–164. Heraklion, Crete, Grece.

Murphy, K., & Cherney, A. (2012). Fostering Cooperation with the Police: How do Ethnic Minorities in Australia Respond to Procedural Justice-Based Policing? *Australian & New Zealand Journal of Criminology*, 44:235–57.

Police Force Act, 1970 (Act 350). Functions. The Ghana Police Service. www.police.gov.gh.

Resig, M. D., Tankebe, J., & Mesko, G. (2012). Procedural Justice, Police Legitimacy, and Public Cooperation with the Police among Young Slovene Adults. *Journal of Criminology and Security* 14:147–64.

Reynolds, K. M., Semukhina, O. B., & Demidov, N. N. (2008). A Longitudinal Analysis of Public Satisfaction with the Police in the Volgograd Region of Russia, 1998–2005. *International Criminal Justice Review* 18:158–189.

Rosendaum, D. P., Schuck, A. M., Costello, S. K., Hawkins, D. F., & Ring, M. K. (2005). Attitudes toward the Police: The Effects of Direct and Vicarious Experience. *Police Quarterly 8(3):* 343–365.

Sabet, D. M. (2012). Corruption or Insecurity? Understanding Dissatisfaction with Mexico's Police. *Latin American Politics and Society*, 55(1): 1–45.

Sunshine, J., & Tyler, R. T. (2003). The role of Procedural Justice and Legitimacy in Shaping Public Support for Policing. *Law & Society Review* 37:513–48.

Tankebe, J. (2008a). Colonialism, Legitimation and Policing in Ghana. *International Journal of Law, Crime and Justice* 36(1): 67–84.

Tankebe, J. (2008b). Police effectiveness and Police Trustworthiness in Ghana: An empirical appraisal. *Criminology & Criminal Justice* 8:185–202.

Tankebe, J. (2010). Public Confidence in the Police: Testing the Effects of Public Experiences of Police Corruption in Ghana. *British Journal of Criminology*, 50, 296–319.

Tankebe, J. (2013). Viewing Things Differently: The Dimensions of Public Perceptions of Police Legitimacy. *Criminology* 51(1): 103–135.

Tyler, R. T. (2005). Policing in Black and White: Ethnic Group Differences in Trust and Confidence in the Police. *Police Quarterly* 8(3):322–342.

U.S Department of States (2010). Human Rights Report. Retrieved at http://www.state.gov/j/drl/rls/hrrpt/2010/af/154349.htm.

Ward, W.B.F. (1948). *A History of Ghana*. London: G. Allen & Unwin.

Wu, Y., & Sun, I. Y. (2009). Citizen Trust in Police: The Case of China. *Police Quarterly* 12:170–191.

Critical Thinking Questions

1   How do perceptions of government impact perceptions of police?

2   What are some organizational and nonorganizational determinants of police trust described in the reading?

3   How is the multidimensional approach recommended for improving citizens' trust in Ghanaian police similar to new professionalism?

4   Discuss the role of police ethics in building public trust of the police.

Part IV Key Points

- Accountability, transparency, and communication can help to enhance the relationship between police and the communities they serve.
- Increasing diversity in policing can help strengthen police-community relations.
- Research is a necessary tool to assess police effectiveness and community satisfaction.

Conclusion

Editors' Conclusion

The readings solidified the need for police departments to recognize the unique balance they must seek in maintaining positive relationships with their community. More demands have been placed on officers to increase the "hats" worn on a daily basis, as well as the parties they must answer to. Increased use of surveillance and social media, by police officers and citizens alike, adds another dimension to the already complex nature and role of police officers today.

The articles as a whole represent key issues in police practices. Adapting to new forms of communication within evolving technology and changing demographics influences the way police officers serve their communities and maintain legitimacy. Incorporating a new professionalism is one such adjustment brought forward in part I and extended into part II with understanding the need to build positive interactions with youth to build an environment of collaboration rather than conflict. Part III focused specifically on police legitimacy to bring forward new tactics police agencies should consider, while part IV addressed factors that affect legitimacy through the eyes of minority group members.

Incorporating application of theory and innovative practices to policing problems was also consistent across all four parts of this book. "Knowing it when you see it" is not the answer to police professionalism today, as more objective actions are needed and demanded by society. Specific tactics to interact with young people are important for the future of policing practices. Broaddus, Scott, Gonsalves, Parrish, Rhoades, Donovan, and Winch (part II) use Allport's contact theory to apply structured events for police officers and junior high school students to gauge new perceptions of police and youth by those who attended. Several articles in part III provided practical models to build police legitimacy beyond those tried in the past. The last section enhanced the need for police to interact with their communities, even in times of budget constraints. Social media outlets, as well as focused community events, are options to be considered. Adding practical experiences to existing research provides students with actions they can take when they are police officers, as well as envisioning new ideas for the future.

A subtle theme in these articles are thoughts and practices for future research. Concepts such as professionalism and legitimacy have been staple policing topics in past years. Reevaluating and possibly redefining these terms may guide future research that encompasses more objective actions for engaging police departments. Understanding the development of perceptions of the police is complex. More complexity arises when members of a single minority group have different historical, political, and cultural experiences with police agencies. This adds a greater need to use research methods that can tap into this understanding rather than the issue of power and sample size driving the data source.

Our hope is that students gained a modern understanding of policing issues that bridge academic scholarship with practical applications. Controversies from the past are still key issues for the present and future, though more attention and acknowledgment of these issues will help ensure they are discussed and solutions are sought. Challenging perceptions and existing practices can be uncomfortable but necessary to initiate creative and modern ideas to progress policing into the future.

CPSIA information can be obtained
at www.ICGtesting.com
Printed in the USA
FSHW021643051219
64760FS